THE SOCIOLOGY OF WORK

SAGE has been part of the global academic community since 1965, supporting high quality research and learning that transforms society and our understanding of individuals, groups, and cultures. SAGE is the independent, innovative, natural home for authors, editors and societies who share our commitment and passion for the social sciences.

Find out more at: **www.sagepublications.com**

2nd EDITION

STEPHEN EDGELL

THE SOCIOLOGY OF WORK

CONTINUITY AND CHANGE
IN PAID AND UNPAID WORK

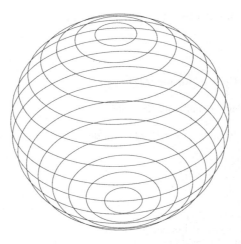

Los Angeles | London | New Delhi
Singapore | Washington DC

First edition published 2005; reprinted 2007, 2008, 2009, 2010
This edition reprinted 2013

SAGE Publications Ltd
1 Oliver's Yard
55 City Road
London EC1Y 1SP

SAGE Publications Inc.
2455 Teller Road
Thousand Oaks, California 91320

SAGE Publications India Pvt Ltd
B 1/I 1 Mohan Cooperative Industrial Area
Mathura Road
New Delhi 110 044

SAGE Publications Asia-Pacific Pte Ltd
3 Church Street
#10-04 Samsung Hub
Singapore 049483

Library of Congress Control Number: 2011929888

British Library Cataloguing in Publication data

A catalogue record for this book is available from the British Library

ISBN 978-1-84920-412-5
ISBN 978-1-84920-413-2 (pbk)

Typeset by C&M Digitals (P) Ltd, India, Chennai
Printed by MPG Books Group, Bodmin, Cornwall
Printed on paper from sustainable resources

To V, M and B

CONTENTS

LIST OF FIGURES AND TABLES

Figures

Tables

PREFACE AND ACKNOWLEDGEMENTS

I was pleased to be asked to revise and update the first edition of *The Sociology of Work: Continuity and Change in Paid and Unpaid Work* although it involved more work than I anticipated. This is mainly because I took the opportunity to restructure Chapters 5 and 6 by separating the discussions of industrial and service work, and to reverse the order of Chapters 7 and 8 to improve the flow of the analysis. Some new material has been included in various chapters, for example, technological and organizational change in the first chapter and call centres in the last chapter. To make room for all the changes, the sections on the Swedish car production system (Chapter 5) and voluntary work (Chapter 9) have been cut, the former because it is a minor alternative to Fordism and the latter because it is the least well-researched type of work. In the light of the constructive comments by the anonymous reviewers, there are over twice as many tables and at the suggestion of the publisher I have included some articles in the Further reading section at the end of each chapter where I have also listed some relevant websites. Hopefully these changes will be welcomed by readers.

I am also pleased to record my gratitude for the support, encouragement and suggestions of the following friends/colleagues: Chris Birkbeck, Edward Granter, Philip Hodgkiss, and Paul Kennedy. Jai Seaman and Chris Rojek of SAGE were similarly helpful, as too were the University of Salford librarians, especially Jennifer Earl. Needless to say, the usual disclaimers apply. Finally, I am pleased to acknowledge the permission granted by the following for the use of the material listed below:

John Eldridge for permission to draw upon his figures on Blauner's American Inter-Industry Comparison, in *Sociology and Industrial Life* (M. Joseph, 1971: 186–7).

Sage Publications Ltd for permission to reproduce an extract and an amended and abridged version of Table 1, 'Great Britain: relative and absolute changes in skilled employment in the private construction and engineering and related industries, 1965–1976' and extract from 'Skill, craft and class', by D. Lee, *Sociology*, 1: 57, 64 (© British Sociological Association, 1981).

Sage Publications Ltd for permission to reproduce an amended version of Table 10, 'Changes in skill and responsibility by sex', in Gallie, D. (1991) 'Patterns of skill change: upskilling, deskilling or the polarization of skills?', *Work, Employment and Society*, 5(3): 344.

Sage Publications Ltd for permission to reproduce an amended and abridged version of Table 3, 'Non-regular forms of employment, selected countries, 1973–93', in Standing, G. (1997) 'Globalization, labour flexibility and insecurity: the era of market regulation', *European Journal of Industrial Relations*, 3(1): 20.

Sage Publications Ltd for permission to reproduce an abridged version of Table 2, 'International comparisons of unemployment rates, May 2010', in Bell, D. and Blanchflower, D. (2010) 'UK unemployment in the great recession', *National Institute Economic Review*, 214(1): 5.

Sage Publications Ltd for permission to reproduce an amended version of Figure 1, 'Expert division of labour in "late modernity"', in Reed, M. (1996) 'Expert power and control in late modernity: an empirical review and theoretical synthesis', *Organization Studies*, 17(4): 586.

Sage Publications Ltd for permission to reproduce an abridged version of Table 1, 'Descriptive statistics of analysis variables', in Bernhardt, E., Noack, T. and Lyngstad, T. (2008) 'Shared housework in Norway and Sweden: advancing the gender revolution', *European Journal of Social Policy*, 18(3): 281.

Sage Publications Ltd for permission to reproduce an amended version of Table 2, 'Household allocative systems showing different forms of pooling', in Volger, C. and Pahl, J. (1993) 'Social and economic change and the organization of money within marriage', *Work, Employment and Society*, 7(1): 77.

Sage Publications Ltd for permission to reproduce an abridged version of Table 6, 'Percentage of couples in domestic division of labour categories by employment status of partners', in Sullivan, O. (2000) 'The division of domestic labour: twenty years of change?', *Sociology*, 34(3): 449.

Sage Publications Inc. for permission to reproduce an abridged version of Table 1, 'Percentage of bad job characteristics and mean number of bad characteristics by employment status', in McGovern, P., Smeaton, D. and Hill, S. (2004) 'Bad jobs in Britain: non-standard employment and job quality', *Work and Occupations*, 31(2): 236.

While every effort has been made to trace/contact all the copyright holders, in the event that any have been inadvertently overlooked, I am confident that the publishers will be pleased to make the necessary arrangements at the earliest opportunity.

ABOUT THE AUTHOR

I have been interested in the sociology of work all my academic career. At the beginning I taught undergraduate courses at the University of Salford on the Sociology of Industrial Capitalism and researched the work–family nexus with reference to professional workers and their wives (*Middle-Class Couples: A Study of Segregation, Domination and Inequality in Marriage*, 1980). Although my research career moved in the direction of political sociology (*A Measure of Thatcherism: A Sociology of Britain*, 1991), social class (*Class*, 1993), consumption (*Consumption Matters: The Production and Experience of Consumption*, 1996), and the social theories of Thorstein Veblen (*Veblen in Perspective: His Life and Thought*, 2001), throughout this period I maintained an interest in the Sociology of Work via teaching. This varied research career encompassed qualitative methods (case studies), quantitative methods (panel study), and historical methods (archival research). The tendency for sociology of work textbooks to focus on standard paid work to the relative exclusion of non-standard work and unpaid work prompted me to suggest to Chris Rojek at Sage that I write a sociology of work textbook that covers 'work' more comprehensively. With his encouragement the first edition of this book was published in 2006. I welcomed the opportunity to revise and update completely the first edition since it enabled me to address many of the issues that I had become aware of, many of which were noted in the constructive criticisms by reviewers enlisted by Sage.

Be sure to visit the companion website at http://www.sagepub.co.uk/edgell to find a range of learning materials for students, including the following:

- Student Exercises

Here you will find a range of exercises that will help you understand and engage with the theories discussed in the book.

- Useful Websites

The internet provides a bewildering range of material and resources. Here you can go straight to the most useful websites in this field to help you with your studies.

- Glossary

Sociology can often present new concepts and ideas that can be a little daunting to grasp at first. This resource provides a useful and accessible collection of those key concepts and terms.

- Journal Articles

Full access to selected SAGE journal articles related to each chapter, providing you with a deeper understanding of the topics presented.

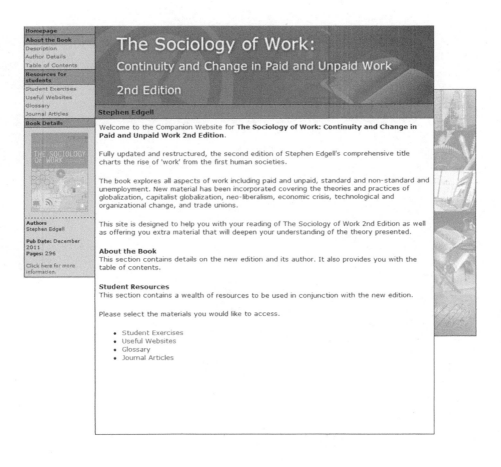

1

THE HISTORICAL TRANSFORMATION OF WORK

Before the advent of industrial capitalism approximately 200 years ago in England, work referred in a generalized way to activities directed at satisfying the human need for survival, for the vast majority, at a subsistence level. In terms of the 40,000 years plus history of human societies, it is only in the recent past that work has become synonymous with regular paid employment, a separate sphere of specialized economic activity for which one receives payment. Thus, the current conception of work is a modern social construction, the product of specific historical conditions that are typically denoted by the term 'industrial capitalism'. The first part of this term indicates that work is a productive activity involving machines powered by inanimate energy sources that is undertaken outside the home in a dedicated building that one has to travel to each work day. The second part indicates that work involves monetary payment, typically agreed in advance in relation to time and/or output, and is part of a market system in which productive property is privately owned with a view to making a profit and that everything has a price, including labour. The term 'modern society' refers to industrial society and although the process of modernization may start with industrialization, it is one that covers all aspects of social change, not just economic change. At the beginning of the twenty-first century, there is some controversy about the extent to which the most advanced industrial capitalist societies have changed and how best to conceptualize it.

Work in pre-industrial societies

In order to appreciate the revolutionary character of the modern conception of work, it is useful to consider briefly the main features of work in pre-modern societies before comparing them with work in modern societies. However, such an exercise is not without its difficulties, notably that it implies, wrongly, that change is unilinear, and it understates the heterogeneity of work activities and beliefs in pre-modern societies, particularly with reference to the meaning of work and the division of labour. Since the objective here is to contextualize historically in a succinct way the contrast between work in pre-modern and modern societies, Table 1.1 summarizes the great variety of pre-modern societies by excluding hybrid societies and by collapsing the Nolan and Lenski (1999) classification based on the predominant method of subsistence into four types of society: (a) *hunting and gathering*; (b) *horticultural*; (c) *agrarian*; and (d) *industrial*.

Table 1.1 Types of society and main types of work in different historical periods

Type of society	Approximate dates	Main kinds of work	Historical period
Hunting and gathering (i.e., 'Stone Age')	40,000 BP + to 10,000 BP (or 8,000 BP)	Hunting and gathering	
Horticultural	10,000 BP to 5,000 BP (or 3,000 BP)	Gardening	Pre-modern period
Agrarian	5,000 BP to late 18th century	Farming	
Industrial capitalist	19th and 20th centuries	Manufacturing	Early modern period
Post-industrial/ Informational/Global capitalism	Late 20th century and early 21st century	Services (and information processing)	Late modern period

Note: BP: Before the present.

Source: Pre-modern and early modern based on Nolan and Lenski (1999).

Unless otherwise indicated, in the following discussion of pre-industrial societies I have drawn heavily upon the vast amount of comparative material collated by Nolan and Lenski (1999). In the case of the most recent type of society, the industrial, two caveats are in order. First, the label 'industrial capitalism' is preferred since an essential element of the earliest and subsequently the most economically successful industrial societies which dominate the world economy is that they are capitalist as well as industrial. Second, the development of human societies is ongoing, hence the debate about whether, and in what ways, advanced industrial capitalist societies have become post-industrial is indicated by the use of a broken line after the industrial type in Table 1.1, which summarizes the main types of human society.

Hunting and gathering societies

The earliest known human societies were based on hunting and gathering and lasted longer than any other type of society, namely from the beginnings of human society, estimated to be at least 40,000 years ago, to around 10,000 years ago. Somewhat surprisingly given the globalization of industrial capitalism, a small number of these 'Stone Age' cultures have survived into the modern era, for example, Aborigines in Australia and Pygmies in Africa. In these essentially nomadic and small-scale societies, their exceedingly limited technology, involving the widespread use of stone for tools and weapons, typically did not produce a regular economic surplus or lead to marked inequalities. Consequently, everyone in such societies participated, to a greater or lesser extent, in productive work; the young and old, men and women, even political and religious leaders undertook their roles on a part-time basis. Biological differences between the sexes and age groups led to adult males specializing in hunting and fishing and adult females in gathering and food preparation, with everyone often contributing to the building of shelters. Preparation for the sex-based adult work roles in such a limited division of labour was informal, although formal ceremonies (initiation rites) typically marked the transition to manhood and womanhood. Sharing work and the products of work typified this era since the survival of the group put a premium on co-operative rather than competitive behaviour. In Veblen's (1964 [1914]) terminology, they were more peaceable than predatory societies.

Horticultural societies

The emergence of semi-nomadic and later settled horticultural societies based on the cultivation of plants and the domestication of animals about 10,000 years ago, combined with the use of metals instead of stone for tools and weapons, led to the creation of a more reliable economic surplus, an increase in the size of the population, and the differentiation of economic activities. Essentially, such societies are dominated by gardening work using a digging stick and hoe, and are characterized by an increase in socio-economic specialization, for example, workers and warriors, and a corresponding growth of inequality associated with the beginnings of a stratification system dominated by male warriors. The increase in trade and the conquest of people were not only made possible with technological innovations such as metal working, but were found to be a viable economic alternative to the 'conquest of nature' (Nolan and Lenski, 1999: 138). The production of a 'margin worth fighting for, above the subsistence of those engaged in getting a living', led Veblen to call this stage the first predatory era (1970 [1899]: 32). Thus, in addition to the by

3

now established pattern of women doing most of the productive work, in the more advanced horticultural societies, the creation of a stable economic surplus by the majority allowed a minority to form an hereditary aristocracy of males who specialized in politics, religion and warfare.

Agrarian societies

The next major stimulus to production occurred sometime around 5,000 years ago, it involved the widespread use of the plough and the harnessing of animal power for agriculture and transport, and heralded the development of agrarian societies. The farming of fields using animals to pull a plough rather than gardening based on human energy to operate the hoe became the predominant method of cultivation. Following these technological innovations, production expanded markedly, the population grew, and social differentiation increased, especially along class lines, with dominant groups specializing in the ownership of land and people, and subordinate groups specializing in a range of economic activities, including the production, transportation and distribution of everything from food and spices, to tools and weapons. Economic growth led to a greater diversity of occupations and the emergence of urban centres in which the use of money became the preferred medium of exchange, which in turn further stimulated trade and therefore production and community specialization. For the vast majority, home and work were still not separated, with the household being the unit of production as well as consumption for its members, not all of whom would have been related, for example, apprentices and servants. The expansion of those engaged in the increasing variety of occupations encouraged the establishment of craft guilds to promote their interests – the pre-modern equivalent of trade unions. Contrary to Sennett (2008), guild membership was open to both men and women via apprenticeship (Applebaum, 1992; Oakley, 1976), although from the fifteenth century onwards, there was a trend in Europe to restrict women to lower status guilds or even exclude them altogether (Farr, 2000).

It was at this historical juncture that the important distinction between a productive class of people who worked for a living and a non-productive, parasitical leisure class reached its fullest development. In Europe, this class prevailed during the feudal era when its members were 'not only exempt, but by prescriptive custom' they were 'debarred, from all industrial occupations' (Veblen, 1970 [1899]: 22). This degree of social differentiation involved the emergence of work and leisure as separate spheres of activity for the dominant class, whereas formerly such activities were embedded in a range of other institutions, notably kinship and religion. In Veblen's terms, there are upper-class and male-dominated leisure class occupations, such as government, warfare and religious observances, that are concerned with predatory, non-industrial activities and are accorded the highest status, and there are lower-class and female-dominated productive activities, such as farming and craft work, which are considered ignoble according to the standards of the leisure class. In order to further enhance their status, the leisure class demonstrated their superior wealth and power by engaging in a variety of other non-work activities, the defining features of which were that, in addition to the conspicuous abstention from useful work, they involved conspicuous expense and the conspicuous waste of materials. In short, the conspicuous consumption of time, money and resources, namely the consumption of the most elaborate food, drink, clothes, and sports.

Discussion: pre-industrial societies

Thus, prior to the growth of industrial capitalism, the main kinds of work were all non-industrial and varied from everyone working co-operatively on a minimally differentiated basis, to a degree of gender and class specialization culminating in some social groups being exempt from productive work. Above all, in pre-industrial societies: 'Work was not a special subject, it was part of the general social and spiritual framework' (Anthony, 1977; 37). However, variation in terms of gender was marked, ranging from women taken as trophies and enslaved following conflict between horticultural societies (Veblen, 1970 [1899]), to women owning land and managing the production of linen and beer in agrarian England (Applebaum, 1992). Notwithstanding such variations, the development of industrial society tends to enhance the liberation of women (Boserup, 1970), although this generalization is not without its complexities and critics (Walby, 1990), as will become apparent below.

Occupational specialization was minimal in the earliest known societies whereas in horticultural and agrarian societies 'occupational specialties numbered in the hundreds, and there was a complex division of labour that often involved specialization by communities and even regions' (Nolan and Lenski, 1999: 206). Yet, compared with today, rural pre-modern societies were characterized by a rudimentary and essentially ascriptive division of labour, such is the unparalleled degree of economic specialization intrinsic to industrial capitalism. The increase in the division of labour was accompanied by a move from learning work roles informally via watching adults work and practical experience, to acquiring specialist knowledge and skills formally in dedicated organizations such as schools and universities. Even in the most advanced agrarian societies, education was not universally available but restricted to the dominant classes in order to prepare its members for political, religious and military roles, rather than for economically productive ones.

Variations between the different types of pre-modern society also relate to beliefs about the meaning of work, although, as in the case of the division of labour, the multiplicity of meanings attached to work in such societies are revealed to be of minor social significance by the radically new and elevated meaning of work occasioned by the onset of industrial capitalism. In pre-industrial societies labour was typically unfree to a greater or lesser extent in the form of slavery, serfdom and bonded service, and persisted with the growth of industrial capitalism in Britain, America and elsewhere (Corrigan, 1977). For example, female bonded farm labour in south-east Scotland declined but did not end completely until the 1930s (Robertson, 1990). It is unsurprising therefore that useful work tended not to be highly valued as an economic activity, despite its indispensability for the survival of everyone. Hence, it has been shown that in pre-modern societies as different as ancient Greece and medieval Europe, work was regarded negatively, as a necessary evil or as an expiation of sins committed by others in the past (Applebaum, 1992; Tilgher, 1977 [1930]). Moreover, even such vital activities as farming and craft work received only limited approval from dominant political and religious leaders because, although they were conducive to an independent livelihood and produced goods and services for the parasitic ruling class, they detracted from the ability to engage in politics or spiritual contemplation. Consequently, physical labour, however essential or skilled, did not enjoy the wealth, power and therefore status of non-manual work, such as owning (land and people), governing or praying. It was also considered ceremonially unclean and therefore to be avoided at all costs (Veblen, 1970 [1899]).

The shame associated with certain kinds of work for particular social groups is not of course unique to pre-modern societies. The disrepute that attaches to the performance of certain kinds of work in industrial capitalist societies, particularly when it is conventionally undertaken by marginal groups, is due to a range of factors. Arguably, among the most important are the historical persistence of the moral indignity of manual work, namely cultural lag (Veblen, 1970 [1899]), a labour market in which the supply of unskilled manual workers exceeds the demand (Fevre, 1992), the gendering of jobs which discourages women from entering male work cultures and vice versa (Hakim, 1996), and the operation of a widely accepted social hierarchy, characteristic of modern occupational structures and most work organizations, that assigns zero prestige at best to jobs at the bottom of the pyramid (Rothman, 1998).

In the transition to industrial capitalism in Britain and elsewhere, before wage labour became the norm for the vast majority, wage work in agriculture was common but it was typically irregular, and was merely one of a number of economic activities upon which people depended for their survival. For example, in addition to seasonal wage labour, workers could obtain a supply of food via the cultivation of a small parcel of land, make and sell clothes, plus hunting and gathering (Malcomson, 1988). Whatever the combination of different forms of work, the family remained the basic productive unit in the sense that all members contributed to its economic survival. This was a pattern which persisted during the rise of industrial capitalism (Anderson, 1971). Thus, it was not until the full development of industrial capitalism that a marked contrast between work in this new type of society and work in all pre-modern societies became apparent.

Work in industrial capitalist societies

Consideration of the many models of evolutionary change shows that there is near universal consensus regarding the social significance of the rise of industrial capitalism, namely that it transformed the life and work of everyone. Hence the tendency to focus on the contrast between this new type of society and all types of traditional rural societies and the plethora of dichotomies to summarize the differences, for example, community and association (Tönnies). In the heyday of evolutionary theory around 100 years ago, an exception was Veblen, whose model emphasized the handicraft era by virtue of its importance in the establishment of a competitive market. Yet <u>Veblen</u> also acknowledged that capitalist industrialization involved a radical departure from the past, the productiveness of which impressed him but the social costs did not, and in this respect he has more in common with Marx than Weber (Edgell, 1975, 2001).

Veblen = respected industry → not, social impact

The term 'Industrial Revolution' is invariably used to convey the significance of this transformation, one that centres on the nature of work above all else. Such was the scale and intensity of this social change that it is widely thought to have prompted the rise of sociology as a distinct discipline (e.g., Giddens, 1971). Notwithstanding the ongoing and possibly never-to-be-resolved debate about whether it was economic factors which changed ideas about work (Marx's view) or ideas about work which changed economic life (Weber's view), or a mixture of both (Veblen's view), what is certain is that work was transformed by the rise of industrial capitalism. What is also agreed is that the process of capitalist industrialization started in England towards the end of the eighteenth century, developed soon after in America, France and Germany, and subsequently the rest of the world to the point where it is now a global phenomenon in the sense that goods and services are made from materials sourced from many parts of the world, and sold around the world.

The first part of the term 'industrial capitalism' refers to the use of inanimate energy sources such as electricity, gas or nuclear power, and the consequent reorganization of production involving machine technology, which results in the establishment of large-scale <u>specialized workplaces</u> such as factories and the increased time synchronization of labour and technology in an economy based primarily on manufacturing rather than agriculture. 'Capitalism' refers to a <u>profit-oriented system</u> based on the private ownership of production, on an individual/family or corporate basis, that operates in a competitive market system in which the owners of capital employ free wage labour on a monetary basis. The apparent clarity of these definitions does not imply, in the case of the word 'industrial', any suggestion of technological determinism and, in the case of the word 'capitalist', any suggestion of admiration or antagonism. However, the use of the two words in combination does imply that industrialism and capitalism are inextricably linked without giving theoretical priority to either.

An illustration of the interconnectedness of the industrial and capitalist dimensions of modern societies is afforded by consideration of the experience of workers. The spatial separation of home from work, initiated by the creation of specialist work sites following the introduction of inanimate energy sources to power machine technology, represents the first major change from what had been the norm in all pre-industrial societies, the unity of home and work. In a capitalist system in which making a profit is the priority, workers are recruited on the basis of potential productiveness rather than parentage. Hence the move from working and living at home in a rural community to working away from home in an urban area meant being treated as a cost of production in a large-scale organization and interacting with people to whom one was not related or even knew personally prior to working in the same workplace. In other words, the industrial (factory work) and capitalist (labour treated as a commodity) aspects of work reinforce each other, thereby accentuating the impersonality of the new work situation and the contrast between this and family relationships.

The characterization of work in industrial capitalism presented below applies to a greater or lesser extent to both the early organizational structure in which individuals, often members of the same family, owned and managed one or a relatively small number of local productive units, and the more recent bureaucratic form in which numerous shareholders, individually or institutionally, own but tend to employ others to manage a large number of productive units in many countries. Table 1.2 presents in summary form the ten main contrasts between work in pre-industrial and industrial societies. It is not intended to be exhaustive or to imply that some features are more significant

Table 1.2 Work in pre-industrial society compared with work in industrial capitalist societies

Key features	Work in pre-industrial society	Work in industrial capitalist society
1 Production system	Hand tools/water/human/animal energy	Machine tools/inanimate energy (coal, gas, oil, etc.)
2 Unit of production	Family/household	Individual adults/large-scale organizations
3 Division of labour	Rudimentary/low degree of differentiation	Complex/high degree of differentiation
4 Time	Irregular/seasonal	Regular/permanent
5 Education and recruitment	Minimal/generalized Particularistic/family	Extensive/specialized Universalistic/individual adults
6 Economic system	Traditional/non-market	Rational/market
7 Meaning of work	Necessary evil	Work as a virtue
8 Purpose of work	Livelihood/subsistence/short-term profit	Maximum reward/income/long-term profit
9 Payment	In kind/cash	Wages/salaries/profits
10 Embeddedness of work	Embedded in non-economic institutions	Separate from other institutions

than others. It is, however, intended to clarify the issues, albeit at the risk of exaggerating the discontinuities which are often less marked in practice than in theory. For example, it is problematic how 'free' labour is under industrial capitalism, hence the use of the term 'wages-slavery' by Marx and Engels (1962 [1845]: 467, 513), and the persistence of physical and economic coercion in global capitalism today (Bales, 2000).

Main features of work in industrial capitalist societies

(1) Production system

The re-organization of work started with the introduction of new sources of inanimate energy to drive machinery, replacing water or wind power and human or animal muscle power. The key innovation was arguably the invention of the condensing steam engine to power cotton machinery in 1785 (Smelser, 1972 [1959]). The steam engine not only revolutionized industry, but also transportation and mining, and led to a huge increase in production. For example, output increased by over 300 per cent when power looms replaced handlooms in the British textile industry during the early nineteenth century (Berg, 1994). The increased scale of the power sources and the complexity of the machines meant that a large amount of capital was required to finance production and work was moved out of the home and into factories, which in turn had profound implications for workers. In contrast to pre-industrial production, in which 'the workman makes use of a tool', in the new factory-based system of production under the control of the capitalist, 'the machine makes use of him ... we have a life- *Contrast to feudal* less mechanism independent of the workman, who becomes its mere living appendage' (Marx, 1970 [1887]: 422). Also, the unrelenting uniformity of machinery that requires limited skills 'deprives the work of all interest' (ibid.: 423). Marx used the term 'alienation' to describe the increasing estrangement and powerlessness of wage labour when confronted by the power of capital (Marx, 1970 [1959]: 108), an issue that will be considered in the next chapter.

The deleterious impact of the introduction of the factory system on workers led them to contest the introduction of machinery, which threatened their livelihood and relatively independent way of life. Opposition often took the form of attacking in vain the machines (Luddism), which from the standpoint of displaced workers 'symbolized the encroachment of the factory system' (Thompson, 1970: 599). The Luddites were depicted as being irrational, whereas the new technology was considered the epitome of rationality (Grint and Woolgar, 1997). Wherever industrial capitalism developed, workers organized themselves into trade unions and political parties in an attempt to temper the most harmful effects of the new system of production or even to overthrow it.

(2) Unit of production

The change from the household as the productive unit in which family and non-family members lived and worked together, pooling resources, and producing food and goods for their own consumption, to the factory and other large-scale specialist units of production, such as offices, in which individuals worked for wages, was gradual. Initially whole families were recruited to work in the factories, with parents effectively subcontracting work to their children. This system had many advantages; it maintained parental authority, facilitated occupational training, and enhanced the family income. Also, in the absence of state welfare, the family was the only resource available to individuals when faced with a crisis, such as sickness or lack of work (Anderson, 1971). So long as these circumstances pertained, families 'continued to work and live as a unit' (Kumar, 1988b: 157). Most importantly from the standpoint of capital, the move from household to factory production removed control over the work process and the product from the worker and enabled capitalists and their managers to supervise and discipline workers more easily, thereby reducing the costs of production (Marglin, 1980).

The increased control of workers by employers, facilitated by the introduction of the factory, was reinforced as alternative sources of income disappeared and non-family sources of labour and non-family relationships became more significant. Consequently, individuals became more independent of their family of origin and more dependent on the labour market and hence an employer. Thus over time, '[f]amily members, male and female, increasingly come to think of their wages as their own, to be disposed of as they individually see fit' (Kumar, 1988a: 190). By this stage, the process of individualization was virtually complete in the sense that a person's identity was no longer tied to family and place, as it was in the pre-industrial situation, but to 'one's occupation in the formal economy' of the industrial capitalist society (ibid.: 190). In effect, the loss of its productive function reduced the role of the family to that of consumption and reproduction; meanwhile, work, in the form of employment in the market economy, increased in importance as it became the sole or major source of income.

(3) Division of labour

The advent of capitalist industrialization caused a decline in a range of premodern types of work, especially those connected to agriculture, such as blacksmiths and basket-makers, a large proportion of whom were self-employed, and created a vast number of new types of industrial work. Machines were designed, built, installed, supplied with energy and raw material, operated, maintained, and supervised by different types of worker who, following the separation of conception and execution, were divided by education (e.g., professional and elementary) and skill categories (e.g., skilled, semi-skilled, and unskilled). New professional specializations were created, notably those based on the application of scientific and technical knowledge such as mechanical engineering, and a mass of factory workers, consisting of 'individuals of both sexes and of all ages', were organized with 'barrack discipline' and divided hierarchically 'into operatives and overlookers, into private soldiers and sergeants of an industrial army' (Marx, 1970 [1887]: 423–4). Weber concurred with Marx that 'military discipline is the ideal model for the modern capitalist factory', but unlike Marx, he seemed to admire its rationality and approved of 'the American system of "scientific management"', or Taylorism as it is also known (Weber, 1964 [1947]: 261). This aspect of work in industrial capitalism will be considered more fully in Chapter 3.

The expansion of the factory system and the related increase in production led to an improvement in the means of transportation and communication, and an increase in the number of people employed in new industries such as canals, railways, gas, post and telegraphy. The consequent change in the occupational structure can be illustrated with reference to the shift in employment from primary sector work which dominated pre-industrial societies (e.g., farming and fishing) to secondary sector work (e.g., mills and factories) and tertiary sector work (e.g., education and communication) which together dominate industrial capitalist societies. For example, in 1840, nearly 70 per cent of the American labour force worked in the primary sector and just over 30 per cent in the secondary and tertiary sectors; by 1900, employment in the primary sector had declined to 40 per cent and employment in the other two sectors had risen to 60 per cent (Nolan and Lenski, 1999).

(4) Time

Prior to the rise of industrial capitalism, the working year was interspersed with a generous number of religious and secular holidays, the working day varied from long days in the summer to short ones in the winter, and the pace of work ranged from periods of intensity during harvest time to a more relaxed tempo once a specific activity had been completed (Kumar, 1988b; Schor, 1993; Thompson, 1967). This was because work tended to be task-oriented and influenced by the seasons. At the risk of romanticizing the past, before industrial capitalism, work was intermittent and irregular, and involved a semblance of time freedom in that a person could decide when to start and stop work, and how hard to work. Work discipline, such as it was, tended to be minimal other than that imposed by the workers' definition of their needs and the weather (Thompson, 1970).

The rise of the factory with its ubiquitous clock was a revolutionary event that came to dominate the lives of wage workers. Industrial work involved fewer holidays, much longer hours, and timed labour, with the factory bell demarcating the relatively unstructured non-work time from the highly structured and supervised work time in which a higher tempo than previously experienced was set by the technology owned by the employers on whom employees were dependent for work. Schor (1993) has estimated that hours worked nearly doubled between 1600 and 1850 in Britain, from under 40 hours a week to over 70; it took around 100 years of trade union and political pressure to reduce the working week back to 40 hours.

Thus, work and life ceased to be task-oriented and characterized by irregularity and independence, and became the epitome of regularity and dependence, measured with increasing precision in hours, minutes and eventually even seconds. The stricter division between life and work and the increased synchronization of labour within the factory raised time-consciousness, provoked resistance, including the attempt to retain the tradition of the non-working 'Saint Monday' that was widespread in many pre-industrial work cultures in Europe and America (Reid, 1976; Thompson, 1967).

The centrality of time to work in industrial capitalism has led some to argue that the time piece rather than the steam engine symbolizes this era. For example, Mumford (1934) has argued that the increased scale of industrial production put a premium on the synchronization of people and technical processes and that this was achieved via the clock. Similarly, Thompson (1967) has claimed that what was different about work in industrial capitalism was its focus on time rather than tasks and a clearer distinction between work and non-work. Conversely, it has been argued that the distinction between pre-industrial task time and industrial clock time has been exaggerated (Ingold 1995) and that Thompson underestimated the contested and variegated nature of time and work during the transition (Whipp 1987). The advantage of time is that it provides management with a standardized unit with which to co-ordinate the human and non-human elements of production and to measure the contribution of labour, with or without reference to output. Hence the tendency for pay to be based on the amount of time spent at work and the requirement to 'clock on and off' accompanied by a schedule of fines or dismissal for repeated lateness. Thus, in industrial capitalism time took on a new and exacting meaning; it was money.

(5) Education and recruitment

The increase in the division of labour with its new work–time discipline occasioned by the development of industrial capitalism, necessitated a marked expansion of compulsory education, which prioritized punctuality and regularity, and specialized training in vocational subjects. The tendency for educational institutions to parallel the expected workplace experiences of their pupils has been called correspondence theory (Bowles and Gintis, 1976). The introduction and expansion of formal education in all industrial societies also led to the growth of examinations and the award of credentials to certify competence for impersonal recruitment to different types of work (Collins, 1979). Weber referred to this as the '"rationalization" of education and training' and noted that the process of bureaucratization 'enhances the importance of the specialist examination' (1961 [1948]: 240, 241).

During the transition to industrialization, whole families, including young children, were recruited to work in the new urban factories, but over time the introduction of legal restrictions on the employment of children (and women) in factories, combined with state provision of education for all, undermined the kinship basis of factory labour. In Britain, the first Act of Parliament to limit the employment of young children to a 12-hour working day was in 1802 but was restricted to cotton and woollen mills. Later Acts covered other work-places and raised the age at which children could work, thereby reducing the number of child workers. Public funding of education was provided for the first time in 1833, but a national system of free elementary education up to the age of 10 was not established in England until 1891, and 1902 in the case of secondary education, well after similar reforms in other industrializing countries, such as Germany and France (Hill, 1971). Thus, gradually the recruitment of workers as individuals on the basis of their formal education and qualifications, replaced informal family recruitment and training.

(6) Economic system

The rise of industrial capitalism involved the development of a market econ-omy in which capital, labour, goods and services are exchanged for money free of traditional social obligations and constraints such as restrictions on who could engage in certain economic activities. In other words, the idea and prac-tice of free trade or *laissez-faire*. Most importantly, in industrial capitalism economic relations become separated, formally at least, from non-economic relations, and distinguished by the primacy accorded to the freedom to maxi-mize economic gains by employing free wage labour. In contrast to pre-modern paternalism, employers had no obligations beyond paying the lowest wages possible in the new competitive market system, since to do otherwise risked economic failure, although industrial paternalism limited the more extreme operation of the free (labour) market culture (Joyce, 1982).

From Marx's perspective, the fundamental capitalist feature is production for sale, and therefore profit, not use, involving the buying and selling of labour power in a market in which money wages are paid on the basis of the time worked and/or the output achieved. Hence, for Marx, industrial capitalism is distinguished by its class dynamic which is rooted in the inevitable conflict of economic interests between the owners of capital and those they employ, namely exploited and oppressed propertyless free wage labourers. Separated from direct access to the means of subsistence, wage labour is compelled in a competitive market system to sell their labour power in exchange for wages, which in turn are exchanged for the goods and services essential to maintain life. Thus, social relations under capitalism are reduced to market values expressed in monetary terms and, as a consequence of this commodity status, workers are 'exposed to all the vicissitudes of competition, to all fluctuations of the market' (Marx and Engels, n.d. [1848]: 60).

Weber agreed with Marx that industrial capitalism involved the development of a class system in which both capital and labour are freed from all restrictions, but emphasized the rationality of modern capitalism: 'capitalism is identical with the pursuit of profit, and forever *renewed* profit, by means of continuous, rational, capitalistic enterprise' (Weber, 1976 [1930]: 17). In practical terms, this meant making a calculation about the most efficient means to achieve certain goals, rather than selecting means with reference to historical tradition, namely on the basis of how things were undertaken in the past. This wholly new approach to work was exemplified by the rational principles of bureaucratic organization and book-keeping adopted by capitalist enterprises.

Although Marx focused on exploitation and Weber on rationality, both agreed that in industrial capitalism, waged work (i.e., employment) is both separate and different from non-work, especially family life. Where previously the two spheres had been united in the form of the household economy, under industrial capitalism, the commodified and rational character of work is the opposite of the non-commodified and non-rational character of relationships beyond employment.

(7) Meaning of work

According to Weber, the rationality of economic action in industrial capitalist society required dispensing with the traditional attitude that work was at best something to be avoided and at worst a necessary evil, and replacing it with a positive evaluation as an activity that was considered virtuous. One of the main sources of this new rational attitude to work, which revolutionized economic and social life, was to be found in Protestantism, or more precisely in the symmetry between certain Calvinist beliefs, notably the calling of working hard to make money and the economic spirit of modern capitalism. Suitably imbued with the ethics of Protestantism, individuals work to please God and to demonstrate their worth to themselves and members of their group. Meanwhile, the asceticism of their religious beliefs discouraged people from spending their earnings wastefully. The unintended consequence of these religious prescriptions was accumulation rather than dissipation: 'When the limitation of consumption is combined with this release of acquisitive activity, the inevitable practical result is obvious: accumulation of capital through ascetic compulsion to save' (Weber, 1976 [1930]: 172).

Work as a religious duty was exported to America by the Puritan settlers and a range of homilies emerged to sum up the modern spirit of capitalism and to inspire entrepreneurs and workers alike, for instance, 'time is money', and others that praised 'frugality' and 'punctuality', and deprecated 'idleness' (ibid.; 48, 49). Ascetic Protestantism involved a major change in the meaning of work; it meant a reversal of the traditional attitude of doing no more than is necessary, to one in which the creation of wealth via unrelenting hard work became the main object in life. What had started as a peculiarly Protestant attitude to work became secularized over time largely because this new conception of work was so 'well suited' to the emergent capitalist system in terms of encouraging workers to be diligent and employers to be profit-oriented, and over time 'it no longer needs the support of any religious forces' (ibid.: 72). Thus the Protestant work ethic became simply *the* work ethic, promulgated by non-religious institutions such as governments, business corporations and schools, although in the process the ascetic dimension has arguably declined as consumption has increased (Beder, 2000).

An alternative perspective on the change in the meaning of work in industrial capitalism is provided by Marx, who argued that when workers are separated from the means of production and constrained to enter into a subordinate relationship to capital, they forfeit the ability to act creatively through work and instead become alienated since the competitive necessity to maximize profit requires that 'the labourer exists for the process of production, and not the process of production for the labourer' (1970 [1887]: 490). Thus, the meaning of work for Marx cannot be understood without reference to the antagonistic and unequal class relationship that lies at the centre of the labour process of industrial capitalism.

(8) Purpose of work

In pre-modern societies, the main purpose of economic activities that we call work was to provide the essential goods and services necessary for the survival of the group or household. For the vast majority, therefore, work was a matter of making a living. This changed dramatically with the rise of the capitalistic organization of work, the main purpose of which became 'the pursuit of profit and forever renewed profit, by means of continuous, rational, capitalistic enterprise', for to do otherwise was to risk economic failure (Weber 1976 [1930]: 17). In other words, making things became subordinated to making a profit. If there was no profit to be obtained, things would not be made, however much people needed them.

On an individual level, the new idea of the relentless pursuit of profit by all work organizations, although sanctified by religion in the early years, was not embraced by everyone caught up in the rise of industrial capitalism. The privileged few who owned and controlled the business enterprises clearly had an interest in the accumulation of profit and therefore supported and promulgated the idea that hard work was not only a necessity that resulted in economic success, but morally worthwhile. However, for those recruited to work in the more routine and boring jobs for far smaller economic rewards, work remained more of a necessary evil than a virtuous activity in its own right. This kind of instrumental orientation to work, one that puts a premium on pay and security rather than on intrinsic interest and satisfaction, can still be found among manual workers (Goldthorpe et al., 1969). Finally, there is the case of professional workers who are considered to be motivated primarily by a commitment to provide a public service on the basis of their specialist knowledge, such as vocationally inspired health or education professionals. However, it has also been argued that the relatively high prestige and autonomy of certain professions, for example law, enable their members to act as much for their own benefit as they do for others. In other words, professional work can involve both a selfish orientation as well as a selfless one (MacDonald, 1995).

(9) Payment

In pre-modern societies, economic activities such as farming and handicraft work were organized on a small scale and were concerned primarily with 'earning a livelihood rather than with a view to profits on investment' (Veblen, 1975 [1904]: 24). For the vast majority, this meant subsistence, involving a mixture of payments in kind and in cash. However, once workers had been separated from the means of production, their only option was to seek work for wages as an employee.

In the early phase of industrialization in England, the payment of wages in kind rather than cash, known as the truck system, persisted until an efficient monetary system had been established. It was outlawed effectively following a series of Truck Acts in the nineteenth century (Hilton, 1960). It had been virtually universal in pre-modern England and took many forms; sometimes the workers were paid in the goods they had produced, in coupons that were exchangeable only in shops owned by the employer, or a mixture of the two. Whatever form it took, the truck system was highly exploitative since it tended to lower wages via either the falsification of weights and measures, and/or high charges for materials and goods. Consequently, it was resented by workers, and even some employers, who regarded it as inflexible since it tied some workers to their employers through debt (ibid.). The truck system was a kind of transitional payment system between a predominantly payment in kind subsistence system, characteristic of pre-industrial capitalism, and a money payment system in which wages are the sole or main source of income and therefore sustenance.

As the diversity of life-maintaining forms of work shrank, viable alternatives to wage labour declined markedly, although they did not disappear totally (Pahl, 1984). By the late nineteenth century, the transformation from a complex mixture of different forms of task work, common rights and self-provisioning, typical of pre-modern England (Malcomson, 1988), to a system characterized by regular, full-time employment in one job was well advanced (Kumar, 1988b). However, this change 'was a protracted one in that pre-modern forms of work persisted throughout the nineteenth century in Britain, especially in London where the seasonality of production, for example in high-value consumption goods, dock work and the building trade, favoured irregular casual employment (Stedman Jones, 1984).

The gradual erosion of a culture characterized by multiple sources of income and sustenance to one way of making a living meant that to be without employment meant to be out of work, and by the 1880s in Britain the now familiar terms 'unemployed' and 'unemployment' had entered public discourse (Burnett, 1994). The equation work equals employment is therefore only meaningful in a society, namely an industrial capitalist one, in which a wage via formal paid employment is effectively the only way of securing the means to obtain the goods and services necessary to sustain life.

(10) Embeddedness of work

The cumulative effect of all these radical changes to the nature and organization of work associated with capitalist industrialization was that work ceased to be embedded in non-economic social institutions, such as the family and became a separate, distinct institution in terms of space, time and culture. Thus it has been noted that the spatial separation of work from family also involved the differentiation of work time from non-work time, and a set of impersonal work relations which contrasted with the affective bonds of family life, although the extent to which work was embedded in social relations in pre-modern society and the extent to which this pattern has been reversed since is a matter of some debate (Granovetter, 1985).

To use more technical language, behaviour within the two realms of home and work in industrial capitalist societies are guided by particularism and universalism respectively. In other words, participation in the modern world of work is no longer linked directly to family life in the sense that workers are typically trained, recruited, employed and dismissed by rational organizations in which they are not given preferential treatment. Hence neither gaining qualifications, nor obtaining, retaining or progressing at work on the basis of a family connection or close friendship are regarded as fair or appropriate since it would compromise the rationality of the work system and risk the charge of cronyism. In theory, the equal treatment of all is the rule in a modern economy and is backed up by the force of law. However, universalistic norms are so well established (i.e., institutionalized) and accepted (i.e., internalized) that individuals do not expect to be treated in a preferential way in any non-family structure, for instance, promoted on the basis of kinship or friendship ties.

This model of the contrast between the particularism of family life and the universalism of work organizations associated with the rise of industrial capitalism is often referred to as structural differentiation and in many respects it is an idealized version of the two spheres (Smelser, 1972 [1959]). In practice, the autonomy of work and family is relative rather than absolute. This is mainly because although the direct influence of family membership on the attainment of an occupational position has been disconnected, except where the inheritance of capital is concerned as in family businesses, family background continues to have an indirect influence via the purchasing of educational privilege, the acquisition of cultural capital, and the operation of social networks (Scott, 1991). Even today therefore, getting a job and getting on at work may depend as much on personal ties at the club or pub than impersonal factors such as formal qualifications. Moreover, research on the multiplicity of ways in which home and work intersect in modern societies, particularly for those who work at and/or from home, suggests that work has not been separated totally from home (e.g., Allen and Wolkowitz, 1987; Edgell, 1980).

Thus although it is difficult to deny the dislocation caused by capitalist industrialization to family and work life, the thesis that it occasioned the separation of home from work tends to exaggerate the degree to which social life became segmented. This is especially the case for the early stages of the separation of the two spheres when recruitment to the new urban factories persisted on a kinship basis, either directly as in the case of the recruitment of family members, or indirectly as in the case of recommending relatives to prospective employers (Anderson, 1971). In due course, however, the increasing reliance on the wages from work as an employee contributed to the enhanced economic and social significance of paid work outside the home and the marginalization of all other kinds of work, especially unpaid work inside the home.

Capitalist industrialization and the primacy of work

The primacy of work over all other social activities in industrial capitalist societies is not difficult to fathom. Under industrial capitalism, paid work is effectively the only way to acquire sufficient income to be able to satisfy needs (e.g., food, shelter, warmth) and wants (e.g., consumer durables such as a car, television, etc). Work is the major influence on where you live, how you live, and how long you live. Consideration of the extent to which paid work shapes life led Beck to claim that: 'The importance that work has acquired in industrial society has no parallels in history' (1992: 139). Yet, the primacy of work goes beyond mere survival and how well one lives. For the vast majority of people in industrial capitalist societies, their whole lives are organized with reference to work; they spend their early years in education in order to be able to obtain work, the next 40 or so years in work, and their last years recovering from work: 'Even "old age" is defined by non-occupation. Old age begins where the world of work discharges people' (ibid.: 139). While in work, most waking hours are spent getting to and from work, doing work, and thinking about work. It is unsurprising therefore that paid work has such a fundamental impact on people's lives, that it plays a vital role in the formation of an identity (Jahoda, 1982). This is readily apparent from studies of people in work (Bain, 2005) and of those without work, especially the unemployed who typically report that they experience economic deprivation, disorientation, shame, and a 'loss of identity' (Marsden, 1982: 155). It is also clear from those who have won a large sum of money, yet continue to undertake paid work (Grandon,

2008). This suggests that paid work is not just about paying the bills (i.e., extrinsic rewards), it is also about a sense of satisfaction (i.e., intrinsic rewards). Thus the significance of paid work in industrial capitalism transcends the basic need for economic survival, it gives meaning to life and is therefore a crucial element in identity formation.

This view has not gone unchallenged. It has been argued that social changes such as deindustrialization and globalization have undermined the stability of work patterns associated with the development of capitalist industrialization, and that, as a consequence, paid work is no longer a key source of meaning and identity for most people (Offe, 1985). The idea of a fixed identity achieved through a life-long involvement in work is considered redundant, replaced by a fragmented and more flexible range of identities, rooted in rapidly changing patterns of consumption (Bauman, 1998). Research is beginning to address the decline in the significance of work thesis and this suggests that for both standard (permanent full-time) and non-standard (temporary part-time) workers, work has retained its life-shaping and identity-forming significance (Doherty, 2009). Thus, despite the alleged increase in job insecurity, work has arguably not become any less important as the primary means of satisfying economic and social needs for most people.

Crises and industrial capitalism

Although the terminology varies from 'contradictions' to 'irrationalities' and 'derangements', the analyses of industrial capitalism by classical social theorists such as Marx, Weber and Veblen, all identified sources of instability; respectively overproduction, overspeculation and overcapitalization, that led invariably to recurrent economic crises. However, their accounts of the development of industrial capitalism diverged when it came to assessing the consequences of frequent crises.

According to Marx, industrial capitalism is inherently unstable due to endemic fluctuations in the business cycle that cause overproduction from time to time, leading to lower prices, less profits and eventually reduced output and hence economic failure of some companies; 'The life of modern industry becomes a series of periods of moderate activity, prosperity, over-production, crisis and stagnation' (Marx, 1970 [1887]: 453). Crises for Marx were 'the most evident manifestation of the internal "contradictions" of the capitalist system' (Giddens, 1971: 54) in that they reflected the exploitation of workers and their consequent lack of purchasing power. The silver lining for Marx was the possibility that capitalist crises could foster revolutionary class consciousness and lead, hopefully, to its overthrow. For Weber, capitalist crises were also inevitable due to the tendency for 'overspeculation' (Weber, 2003 [1927]: 290), and reflected the increasing rationalization of the economic system. However, they would not necessarily result in total collapse, rather a series of adjustments before expansion could restart and he surmised that 'capitalism could endure indefinitely as an economic system' (Collins, 1992: 104). Veblen also argued that capitalist crises were unavoidable on the grounds that the incessant quest for profit in an expansionary phase encouraged 'overcapitalization' based on the extensive use of credit by businesses (1964 [1923]): 221; see also Veblen, 1975 [1904]). In Veblen's view, the intermittent crises of capitalist industrialization were symptomatic of the conflict between business oriented to maximizing profit and industry concerned with maximizing production, but Veblen, in marked contrast to Marx, hesitated to predict the end of capitalism (Edgell, 2001).

In all three cases, the root of the problem of the recurrent economic crises of capitalist industrialization seems to be the competitive imperative for ever increasing profit (institutionalized greed), which leads to overconfidence and eventually to a mild (recession) or severe (depression) decline in production, resulting in bankruptcy for businesses, and a wage freeze, wage cuts, and/or unemployment for workers. The first major industrial capitalist depression was in Britain in 1793, it extended to all branches of industry and trade, and its impact was felt in other societies that were either trading partners and/or also industrializing (Mitchell, 1970 [1913]), unlike later economic crises which tended to develop an increasingly global character as industrial capitalism spread around the world. The tendency for industrial capitalism to generate periodic economic crises of varying depth and length, often provokes contemporary governments to intervene along Keynesian lines to limit their severity and therefore impact, such as by expanding public expenditure to stimulate demand, and to restore confidence in the system, thereby forestalling the possibility of what Habermas (1973) has called 'a legitimation crisis'.

In addition to the main features of work in industrial capitalist societies discussed thus far, at the forefront of the transformation of work associated with capitalist industrialization were technological and organizational change, trade unions, and the role of women; these topics therefore warrant further elucidation.

Technological and organizational change

The dominant image of work in industrial capitalist society is of a large number of people working together using machinery driven by inanimate sources of power; in short, organizations and technology. There is some controversy regarding which came first: the new organizational forms or the new technologies (Marglin, 1980), but this debate is of less importance than the tendency for these two features of modern work environments to be associated inextricably with the transformation of work during capitalist industrialization. The interconnectedness of technology and organization is indicated by consideration of what these terms refer to. At first sight, the concept of technology conjures up a picture of machines, but this is a very narrow understanding of the term since all technology has a social dimension. First, new technologies do not just appear, they are shaped by social forces, such as interests (MacKenzie and Wajcman, 1999), and, second, the technology has to be operated and deployed to fulfil its productive capacity, otherwise it is useless (Grint and Woolgar, 1997). It is difficult therefore to separate out the non-human from the human, the artefact from the social conditions out of which it emerged and was implemented.

Definitions of technology range from the narrow, as tools or machines, to the broad, as production systems including the organizational context of machinery (Clark et al., 1990). There are advantages and disadvantages of each definition. A narrow definition allows a researcher to explore the possible independent influence of technology on work but runs the risk of neglecting the social processes that gave rise to its introduction and implementation. Conversely, a broad definition acknowledges that technology involves more than just machinery, but makes it difficult to appraise the impact of technology on work separate from other possible independent variables such as organizational factors. In order to be able to consider the causal significance and interconnectedness of technology, a narrow rather than a broad definition is preferred.

From a historical perspective, it has been suggested by Coombs (1985) that, since the advent of the Industrial Revolution, three overlapping phases of technological change have occurred; primary, secondary and tertiary mechanization. Primary mechanization refers to the introduction of steam-powered machinery during the nineteenth century to transform raw materials into products. Secondary mechanization emerged at the end of the nineteenth century and involved the use of electricity to drive machinery, which enabled the transfer of materials between machines that was crucial for the development of continuous flow and assembly-line production. Tertiary mechanization in the form of electronics-based computing and information technologies dates from the second half of the twentieth century and facilitates the co-ordination and control of production. Coombs emphasizes that his discussion of these three technological phases in the evolution of production processes are 'at a very high level of abstraction and generality' (1985: 156), but he provides some empirical data from the UK and the USA to support his historical typology, particularly the second and third phases.

From a similar historical perspective, namely, since the advent of capitalist industrialization, organizational changes may be reduced to a comparable three-stage typology. Following Weber's famous distinction between pre-bureaucratic (traditional and charismatic authority) and rational bureaucratic authority (1964 [1947]), and by adding the category post-bureaucratic authority (Heckscher, 1994), a three-phase historical typology of organizational change may be constructed. Pre-bureaucratic organizations are characterized by the personal authority of the owner-manager by virtue of their

Table 1.3 Phases of technological and organizational change and the development of capitalist industrialization

Historical phases	Technological change	Organizational change
Phase I	Primary mechanization	Pre-bureaucratic
19th century	Steam power	Autocratic personal authority
Phase II	Secondary mechanization	Bureaucratic
Late 19th > 20th century	Electric power	Hierarchical rational authority
Phase III	Tertiary mechanization	Post-bureaucratic
Late 20th > early 21st century	Computing power	Democratic consensual authority

Sources: Based on the theories of Coombs (1985), Weber (1964 [1947]), and Heckscher (1994).

traditional and/or charismatic sources of legitimation; in a bureaucracy, authority is impersonal and based on rational criteria with actions governed by rules, and positions in the hierarchy are achieved on merit via qualifications and experience; and in a post-bureaucratic organization, authority is decentralized and democratized in a flattened hierarchy characterized by a culture of empowerment and consensual dialogue.

Table 1.3 shows that, considered together, these two historical typologies of technical and organizational change correspond in that primary mechanization tended to coincide with the pre-bureaucratic organizational form, secondary mechanization with bureaucratic, and tertiary mechanization with post-bureaucratic. This is a highly oversimplified model of overlapping phases but the parallels are indicative of the interconnectedness of technological and organizational change.

The rise of trade unions

Resistance by workers to exploitation and oppression was not unknown in pre-modern societies, but tended to be sporadic, such as the Peasant Revolt of 1381 in feudal England and the San Domingo slave revolution of 1797. It is only in industrial capitalist societies that workers have established permanent organizations to resist exploitation and improve their pay and conditions of work. Although there are parallels between pre-modern associations of workers, namely guilds, and their modern equivalent, trade unions, in terms of their concern for the wages and welfare of their members, and their sense of collectivism, there are also some contrasts in that guilds were composed of employers and employees, and limited to skilled crafts (Farr, 2000)

At the onset of capitalist industrialization, employers were all-powerful, economically, legally and politically, whereas individual workers were powerless. In order to redress this marked imbalance of power, workers combined together to form their own organizations to represent their interests and limit the power of employers to hire and fire, cut wages, lengthen working hours, and generally improve the dangerous physical conditions of work. Typically, employers responded to the emerging challenge to their power by refusing to recognize, and hence negotiate with, trade unions, and enlisted the support of the state in the form of the police, the courts, and sometimes the army, to repress workers and their attempts to organize opposition to the unlimited power of 'tyrannical' employers (Kirk, 1994: 63). During the first half of the nineteenth century in Britain and America, union activity was subject to the law of conspiracy, which along with a lack of financial support, hindered the effectiveness of unions. In the absence of legitimate means to express their grievances, conflict between employees and employers during the rise of capitalist industrialization tended to become violent, often resulting in the destruction of machinery, and even the death of workers, famously the machine-breaking Luddites in the new urban industrial centres in England between 1811 and 1812 and the Peterloo Massacre of 1819 in Manchester (Reid, 2005). Trade union activists in this formative period of unionization risked being blacklisted, imprisoned, deported, or executed.

It was not until the mid to late nineteenth century, following considerable collective agitation, that trade unions gained legality and national trade union confederations were founded in Britain in 1868 and in America in 1886 (van der Linden, 2003). Repression gave way gradually to recognition; the key turning points in Britain were a series of Acts in the 1870s which excluded unions from the threat of the conspiracy laws and strengthened their legal position, but much later in America where workers and their unions did not achieve full legal recognition until two Acts in the 1930s which, among other things, protected workers' rights to organize and bargain with employers (Booth, 1995). On the basis of their more secure legal position and in the context of full employment during the economic expansion of the 1950s, union membership increased and relatively peaceful collective bargaining ensued, in contrast to the more confrontational worker and employer relationship characteristic of the previous century. In short, conflict had been institutionalized in that the rules of the contest between capital and labour had been agreed.

However, union rights are never totally secure in a capitalist society. As unions grew in strength numerically and politically during the last century, employers and political parties representing their interests sought to limit their power. Anti-union legislation was enacted in America (e.g., The Taft–Hartley Act 1947) and Britain (e.g., The Employment Act 1980), which outlawed the sympathy strike and weakened the ability of trade unions to organize successfully during a dispute with employers (MacInnes, 1987; Sweet and Meiksins, 2008). During the second half of the twentieth century union membership declined in America, Britain, and many other societies, until stabilizing towards the end of the century (Fairbrother and Yates, 2003). Currently unions face the problem of global corporations who relocate production to countries where they can employ non-union workers at lower wages (Beynon, 2003). At the beginning of the twenty-first century, trade unions are following the example of corporations by seeking to act more globally to defend their members' interests.

Women and work in the development of industrial capitalism

The impact of capitalist industrialization on women, particularly the transfer of paid work out of the home, has been the subject of considerable debate. The majority view, or pessimistic perspective (e.g., Thomas, 1988), is that the rise of industrial capitalism had a negative impact on the work prospects of women (e.g., Oakley, 1976; Walby, 1986). The minority view, or optimistic perspective, argues the reverse (e.g., Goode, 1970; Shorter, 1976). The important study by Pinchbeck (1969 [1930]) has been credited with being the precursor of the optimistic viewpoint by virtue of her judgement that over the long term the Industrial Revolution benefited women because it increased their employment opportunities, which in turn contributed to their economic independence (Richards, 1974). However, it has also been noted that Pinchbeck's account was not wholly unambiguous (Bradley, 1989), and in this sense it is a forerunner of the suggestion that the impact of industrialization was mixed rather than simply beneficial or detrimental to women (Hudson and Lee, 1990). This debate affords many opportunities for disagreement, such as the issue of the time frame under consideration, hence the focus will be on Britain with reference to both the initial and longer-term impact of industrial capitalism on women. Although these phases overlap, this distinction offers a way out of the debate between the 'pessimists' and the 'optimists'.

Initial phase circa 1800–1840s

Historical research on the factors associated with female employment suggests that there are several grounds for arguing that work opportunities for women expanded during the rise of industrial capitalism:

- the continuity of female labour in the transition to factory work (Scott and Tilly, 1975);
- the female input in trade unions and the co-operative movement (Lewenhak, 1980);
- demographic forces which created a supply of female labour (Richards, 1974);
- economic expansion and the demand for women workers (Hobsbawm, 1969);
- physical strength ceased to be crucial to operate machinery (Hudson and Lee, 1990);
- the relative cheapness of female labour compared to male (Rendall, 1990);
- male reluctance to enter factories due to loss of independence (Thompson, 1970);
- the perception that female workers were compliant (Pinchbeck, 1969 [1930]);
- machines were designed with female workers in mind, namely their alleged greater manual dexterity (Berg, 1994).

Many of the factors that encouraged the employment of women during the initial phase of capitalist industrialization were mutually reinforcing, such as the tendency to employ female labour on the basis of their presumed docility, dexterity and, above all perhaps, cheapness. Similarly, the forces of supply and demand were complementary in that the greater availability of female labour coincided with increased opportunities for work in the expanding textile factories.

Studies of specific industries such as textiles and metals, confirm that the impact of this combination of factors was conducive to an increase in the employment of women during the early years of capitalist industrialization (Berg, 1988). In the silk industry, which was slower to mechanize than cotton and wool, this gender pattern was repeated and by the middle of the nineteenth century there were at least two women workers for every man, and in areas such as Essex they outnumbered men in the workforce by over four to one (Lown, 1990).

In addition to being in the vanguard of those occupations affected by the initial impact of capitalist industrialization, women continued to work on an irregular, pre-modern basis, at and from home, and such work, especially by married women, was recorded inconsistently in the early censuses (Davies, 1980), or not recorded even in 1851 (Anderson, 1971). There is therefore a strong case for the view that, during the initial phase of industrial capitalism, women not only worked as they had done before when work was organized in the household, but became a prominent part of the waged workforce recruited by the first factory owners. Thus, whatever the actual timing of the capitalist industrialization of production, the absence of any constraints on the employment of women encouraged the employment of the cheapest labour available, which in the short run meant women (and children) rather than men, albeit in the less skilled and lower status work.

Mature phase circa 1850s–1890s

The separation of work from home and the initial increase in the employment opportunities for women created a problem for men in the short term and employers in the long term. It threatened male authority in the home, the supply of healthy male labour, future supplies of labour, and raised the issue of who should care for vulnerable family members such as children. The solution was to exclude women from paid work outside the home and assign them primary responsibility for all things domestic. As a consequence, by the late nineteenth century the economic activity rate for women had declined to 32 per cent and the decline was even more marked for wives; in 1851, one in four married women was employed and by 1901 the proportion had shrunk to one in ten (Hakim, 1980), although the under-reporting of women workers was still an issue during this period. The exclusion of women from work outside the home was achieved by a combination of factors, including:

- male trade union restrictions on women workers (Hartmann, 1979; Walby, 1986);
- the campaign for a family wage by male workers (Creighton, 1996; Land, 1980);
- legislative restrictions by male parliamentarians (Bradley, 1989; Walby, 1986);
- the introduction of a marriage bar by male employers (Lewenhak, 1980);
- limits on child labour and the introduction of compulsory education (Rendall, 1990);
- the twin ideals of male breadwinner and female domesticity (Hudson and Lee, 1990);
- the large size of the Victorian family (Richards, 1974);
- the decline of the family production unit (Scott and Tilly, 1975);
- lower pay rates for women which discouraged them from working outside the home (Hudson and Lee, 1990);
- changes in business structure which limited the possibility of women inheriting businesses (Hudson and Lee, 1990).

The patriarchal dimension of these factors is unmistakable, less obvious is the class one. Out of economic necessity, working-class women were far more likely to work outside the home than their middle-class counterparts, and as a result were criticized heavily for neglecting their domestic respon-sibilities (Roberts, 1995). In contrast, there was no economic urgency for middle-class wives to go out to work. In fact they could afford to employ staff to undertake their domestic work, thereby creating employment for a large number of unmarried working-class women (Oakley, 1976). This left the middle-class wife free to engage in voluntary work, which, being unpaid yet time-consuming, demonstrated the economic status of the male head of the household (Veblen, 1970 [1899]). For working-class men this model was not merely a status aspiration, but one of practical necessity to ensure their ability to perform the family breadwinning role (MacRaild and Martin, 2000). Hence, the Victorian ideals of full-time female domesticity and full-time male breadwinner were more likely to be met by the middle class, whereas the majority of women who worked outside the home during the mature phase of capitalist industrialization were working class (Scott and Tilly, 1975) and unmarried (Hudson and Lee, 1990). Thus, the 'exclusion of women should be seen as a result of the intersection of patriarchal relations and capitalist rela-tions' although the 'articulation of these factors varied between industries' (Walby, 1986: 97).

Considered together, the two phases of capitalist industrialization suggest that in the case of paid work of women, 'the pattern was one of increase followed by decline' (Scott and Tilly, 1975: 37). The decline in the propor-tion of women, especially married women, who worked outside the home during the late nineteenth century, paralleled the rise of women's work inside the home, as unpaid housewives or managers of domestic servants. Hence, the attempt to exclude women from paid work does not mean that women ceased to work, rather, it indicates a major change in the meaning of work and the tendency for married women to become dependent economically on their husbands.

The dominant conception of work in industrial capitalism

The term 'dominant concept of work' has been used to refer to a distinctive model of work that emerged during the process of capitalist industrialization (Callender, 1985: 50; see also Hakim, 1980; Ransome, 1996). A systematic articulation of this model suggests that once industrial capitalism has become established, the defining features of the dominant conception of work are that it is work that is undertaken outside the home (i.e., industrial), for pay (i.e., capitalist), by adult males on a full-time and uninterrupted basis (i.e., patriarchal), and is allocated individually with reference to impersonal universalistic criteria (i.e., modern). This model is summarized in Table 1.4 along with the possible threats to its dominance.

With the maturation of industrial capitalism, this conception of work became dominant, although the historical process was uneven and as far as the male breadwinner–female homemaker dimension is concerned, it was arguably more dominant culturally than empirically (Janssens, 1997; Pfau-Effinger, 2004). Notwithstanding these caveats, the demise of the family-economy

Table 1.4 Dominant conception of work in industrial capitalism and threats to its hegemony

Dominant conception of work	Threats to its hegemony
Capitalist	**Non-capitalist**
Profit-oriented organizations	Non-profit-oriented organizations
Monetized market system	Socialist trade unions
Labour power exchanged for pay	Radical social movements
Industrial	**Global post-industrialism**
Outside the home: bureaucratic organizations	Working at/from home: post-bureaucratic organizations
Contractual regulation	Contractual deregulation
Fixed hours	Flexible hours
Modern	**Traditionalism**
Universalism	Particularism
Achievement	Ascription
Specialization	Non-specialization
Patriarchal	**Feminism**
Adult male worker	Adult female worker
Full-time	Full-time
Permanent	Permanent

system in which men and women worked together in the household, elevated paid work outside the home as the only kind of work that was considered 'real' work, and this was reflected in the official data collected on work (Hakim, 1980). Consequently, any work that did not conform to this dominant conception, such as unpaid housework, was not only excluded from the official statistics of work, but tended to be regarded differently, namely that it was a less important type of work. Since women were the largest social category who deviated from the dominant conception of work yet were over-represented in unpaid domestic work, their economic role was correspondingly under-reported and under-valued (Hakim, 1996). In effect, work became synonymous with employment which with the rise of Fordism became standardized in terms of contract, location and working time.

For those who worked as an employee, the majority of whom were men, a regulatory framework developed covering eventually all aspects of work, namely pay and conditions. If a member of the permanent labour force was out of work, from the late nineteenth century onwards, they were considered to be unemployed and deserving of support, initially by charitable organizations and later the state (Burnett, 1994). However, for those who worked unpaid in the home, the majority of whom were women, there was a complete lack of regulations covering their work; it was, and still is to a large extent, considered a private matter (Oakley, 1976). Moreover, since eligibility for state benefits for the unemployed was related to one's degree of involvement in work as a form of employment, women typically have found it more difficult than men to claim benefits when unemployed (Dex, 1985). Thus, capitalist industrialization created a gender division of labour; a predominantly male group of adults who worked outside the home for pay on a regular basis, and a predominantly female group of adults who worked inside the home for no pay on a regular basis. The social category the unemployed and the role of full-time housewife are therefore both recent social constructions that emerged in the late nineteenth century in Britain and elsewhere.

The dominance of this conception of work is not a static phenomenon, but is subject to change. Over the past two decades or so, each of the dimensions of the dominant conception of work has come under threat from a variety of trends. First, as far as the capitalist dimension is concerned, co-operatives and other not-for-profit organizations, socialist trade unions, radical social movements all indicate that capitalism remains a contested system. Moreover, not all 'work' has been commodified and non-monetized exchange remains significant (Williams, 2002). Second, it has been argued that towards the end of the twentieth century, the industrial dimension was being undermined by globalization associated with the increasing emphasis on all forms of organizational and work flexibility and the destandardization of work (Beck, 1992). Third, the patriarchal dimension has been challenged by feminism in the recent past (Castells, 1997). Fourth, the modern dimension of the dominant conception of work is threatened by the revival of family-based enterprises and the persistent influence of family background on class destination (Edgell, 1993). However, it remains to be seen to what extent these threats to the dominant conception of work have been effective, an issue that will be discussed at the end of the book.

Summary and conclusions

At the risk of over-simplifying the complex and varied history of human societies, it has been argued that in pre-industrial capitalist societies – Stone Age, horticultural and agrarian – work was viewed negatively and was embedded in wider social relations, notably those of kinship. The emergence of industrial capitalism, initially over a long period in Britain, and later over a shorter time span in the rest of the world, involved a clear break with all previous types of society and culminated in work being accorded an unprecedented primacy. The main features of this new type of society include the use of machinery powered by inanimate sources of energy, the separation of home and work, specialist work roles and places, a profit-oriented market system, free wage labour, a positive value associated with work, endemic economic instability, and a distinctive patterning of technology and organization. It is important to remember that these characteristics are neither uncontested, as the term 'wage slavery' indicates, nor universal, as the persistence of homeworking testifies.

During the early development of industrial capitalism in Britain, work opportunities for women increased, but thereafter declined, especially for married women, who were excluded from some kinds of work and restricted to certain other types of work, such as low-paid, unskilled paid work and unpaid housework. The distinct gender division of labour that emerged has been designated the male breadwinner and female homemaker model and found in most countries (Warren, 2007). When this patriarchal dimension of work was combined with other key features of the new type of society – industrial, capitalist and modern – it created a dominant conception of work in which real work was equated with full-time employment for pay outside the home by adult males recruited on the basis of impersonal norms, and led to the devaluation of other kinds of work. This conception of work became standardized and dominated the twentieth century but is now under threat.

Three main conclusions may be drawn from the historical overview of the changing nature of work. First, that the rise of industrial capitalism occasioned a major transformation of work which dislocated work to a greater or lesser extent from all other social institutions. Second, during the establishment of this revolutionary type of society, a dominant conception of work emerged that prioritized work that was capitalist, industrial, partiarchal and modern over other types of work, such as unpaid housework, which did not conform to this model. Third, uncertainty prevails over the extent to which contemporary social processes, notably deindustrialization, computerization, and globalization, are changing the character and patterning of paid and unpaid work in the direction of a more flexible and individualized experience. A key part of the rationale of this book is to consider whether or not this is the case, and by implication, the degree to which work is being transformed, thereby creating a distinctively new type of post-industrial society.

The aim of this book is to cover paid and unpaid work, not just those in paid work, since a truly sociological account of work in advanced industrial capitalism should not take its cue from the dominant conception of work, especially at a time when this model is arguably in decline.

Further reading

BOOKS The history of work from a socio-cultural evolutionary perspective is provided by Nolan and Lenski (1999) *Human Societies: An Introduction to Macrosociology*, and for information on the key contrast between work in pre-modern and modern societies, see Applebaum (1992) *The Concept of Work: Ancient, Medieval and Modern*. For an account of Veblen's relatively neglected contribution to our understanding of changes in the nature of work in different eras, see Edgell (2001) *Veblen in Perspective: His Life and Thought*. Two books by Beck – *Risk Society: Towards a New Modernity* (1992) and *The Brave New World of Work* (2000) – provide a summary of both past and current trends in the patterning and significance of work. As a corrective to the inevitable compression of the arguments and evidence concerning the gender dimension of work during the development of industrial capitalism, consult Walby (1986) *Patriarchy at Work*. A succinct account of the emergence of the specialist role of housewife as a consequence of industrialization can be found in Oakley (1976) *Housewife*.

ARTICLES Reed, M. (1996) 'Expert power and control in late modernity: an empirical review and theoretical synthesis', *Organization Studies*, 17(4): 573–97 covers a range of relevant issues including social change and the division of labour. For an interesting ethnographically based critique of the decline of task time and the rise of clock time with industrialization, consult Ingold (1995) 'Work, time and industry', *Time and Society*, 4(1): 5–28.

WEBSITES For a timeline of the development of industrial capitalism from the standpoint of labour, consult the *Working Class Movement Library*, www.wcml.org.uk. The UK *Economic and Social Research Council* programme on the 'Future of Work' covered a range of issues relevant to this and later chapters, for example, the centrality of work and changing forms of work, www.leeds.ac.uk/esrcfutureofwork/

--------------------- **Questions for discussion and assessment** ---------------

1 What are the major differences between work in pre-industrial and industrial capitalist societies?
2 Consider the impact of capitalist industrialization on the meaning of time.
3 Assess the claim that new technology was a crucial factor in the rise of industrial capitalism.
4 Discuss the pattern of technological and organizational change during the development of capitalist industrialization.
5 Evaluate the view that the initial development of industrial capitalism improved the work opportunities for women.
6 Account for the decline in the labour force participation of women in Britain during the late nineteenth century.
7 Which dimension(s) of the dominant conception of work do you consider to be under most threat and why?

2
WORK AND ALIENATION

Chapter contents

- Marx's theory of alienation
- Blauner's technology and alienation thesis
- Critique of Blauner's technology and alienation thesis
- Empirical research on the Blauner thesis
- Summary and conclusions
- Further reading
- Questions for discussion and assessment

One of the most pivotal, if not the central, idea in Marx's sociological critique of work in industrial capitalist societies is his thesis that alienation is built into the nature of work under a capitalist mode of production. For Marx, alienation was both inevitable and universal in capitalist societies, but it could be overcome. In fact, de-alienation could be considered Marx's life project. Marx introduced the concept of alienation in his early philosophical writings in the 1840s, but they were published only in the 1930s and were not translated into English until the 1950s. Over the following half-century the idea of alienation was operationalized and used extensively in empirical research in the sociology of work (Blauner, 1964) and political sociology (Finifter, 1972), and entered popular discourse typically with reference to alienated youth. Yet an account of the economic elements of alienation can be found in Volume I of *Capital*, which was first published in the 1860s and translated into English in the 1880s. Marx's lifelong use of the concept alienation suggests that it 'is a vitally important pillar of the Marxian system as a whole, and not just one brick of it' (Meszaros, 1970: 227).

This chapter will be concerned to evaluate the transformation of the concept of alienation from its nineteenth-century Marxian philosophical and political economic origins to its mid-to-late-twentieth-century use in empirical sociological research on waged work, the most renowned example of which is the study by Blauner (1964).

Marx's theory of alienation

For Marx, alienation is rooted in the structure of industrial capitalism, under which

> all means for the development of production transform themselves into means of domination over, and exploitation of, the producers; they mutilate the labourer into a fragment of man, degrade him to the level of an appendage of a machine, destroy every remnant of charm in his work and turn it into hated toil. (1970 [1887]: 645)

In other words, work in industrial capitalist society is the dehumanized opposite of a satisfying experience which develops the human capacity for creativity. In Marx's most systematic account of alienation, he argues that there are four distinct yet related manifestations of alienation under industrial capitalism:

1 *Product alienation*. A worker is alienated from the product of his/her labour, which is owned by the employer: 'the worker is related to the product of his labour as to an alien object' (Marx, 1970 [1959]: 108).
2 *Activity alienation*. The activity of work itself is alienating because it is involuntary and fails to develop a worker's creative potential: 'it is forced labour ... that as soon as no physical or other compulsion exists, labour is shunned like the plague' (ibid.: 111).
3 *Species alienation*. As a result of product and activity alienation, workers become alienated from their essential nature; what makes them human: 'In tearing away from man the object of his production, therefore, estranged labour tears from him his species life, his real objectivity as a member of the species and transforms his advantage over animals into the disadvantage that his inorganic body, nature, is taken from him' (ibid.: 114).
4 *Social alienation*. Following from the above, workers are also alienated from each other: 'An immediate consequence of the fact that man is estranged from the product of his labour, from his life activity, from his species being is the estrangement of man from man' (ibid.: 114).

Marx often used the word estrangement as well as alienation to describe the effect of being a wage worker under industrial capitalism. The literal meaning of this word, to become a disaffected stranger, implies that, ideally, work should be an enjoyable experience. Moreover, Marx wrote quite passionately about alienation, where he analysed the impact of capitalist manufacturing on workers: 'It converts the labourer into a crippled monstrosity, by forcing his detail dexterity at the expense of a world of productive capabilities and instincts' (1970 [1887]: 360).

It is not just the workers who suffer alienation. The employer is also implicated in the treatment of workers as commodities and as a consequence they are also dehumanized by their role in the capitalist labour process, albeit less severely than workers. Hence, according to Marx, 'the whole of human servitude is involved in the relation of the worker to production, and every relation of servitude is but a modification and consequence of this relation' (1970 [1959]: 118). Thus, industrial capitalism is characterized by: 'Immorality, deformity, and dulling of the workers and the capitalists' (ibid.: 121). The dehumanization of capitalists is emphasized by Marx but is often overlooked in contemporary discussions of alienation, although there are some notable exceptions (e.g., Ollman, 1971; Swingewood, 1975).

For Marx, the problem of alienation under industrial capitalism cannot be solved by tinkering with the capitalist system, for example, paying higher wages or varying the range of tasks to be executed, since such reforms would merely alter the conditions under which exploitation takes place and alienation occurs. The only solution acceptable to Marx was the abolition of the structure which creates alienation, thereby achieving the 'emancipation' of both the sellers and buyers of labour power (Marx, 1970 [1959]: 118). Following the abolition of private property and the end of the exploitation of workers by employers constrained by competition and the threat of economic failure to be concerned solely with production of goods and services for profit, a communist society, in which the 'complete return of man to himself as a social (i.e., human) being', namely de-alienation, can be established (ibid.: 135).

Alienation and work are inextricably associated with Marx, but he was not alone among the founders of sociology in discussing the idea of alienation since Weber and Durkheim also focused on this issue (Nisbet, 1970).

Blauner's technology and alienation thesis

The catalyst for the conversion of Marx's idea of alienation to a measurable concept was Seeman's article, entitled 'On the meaning of alienation' (1959), although Mills had already raised the sociological profile of this concept by arguing that: 'The alienating conditions of modern work now include the salaried employees as well as the wage workers' (1968 [1959]: 227). Whereas Marx's perspective was societal and in particular how the capitalist labour process gave rise to alienation on a universal scale, Seeman considered alienation from the standpoint of the individual. There is a second very important difference between the two approaches: for Marx, alienation was a political issue, a problem endemic to industrial capitalism that could only be overcome by revolutionary change and the creation of a communist society, but for Seeman, the purpose of his analysis of alienation was not to change the world but to make the idea empirically usable. In other words, operationalize it. Also, in addition to Marx, Seeman drew upon the contributions of Weber, Durkheim and Veblen, plus various contemporary sociologists, including Mills, to examine the different meanings of alienation in classical and contemporary sociology.

Seeman distinguished five different meanings of alienation: (1) powerlessness; (2) meaninglessness; (3) normlessness; (4) isolation; and (5) self-estrangement. In the process of operationalizing the dimensions of alienation, Seeman recast them in terms of a socio-psychological framework of individual expectations and rewards, which he considered not too far removed from the Marxian legacy, aside from purging the concept of its political thrust.

The challenge to research alienation empirically with reference to work in industrial capitalism was taken up by Blauner (1964). Although Blauner accepted the 'Marxian premise that there are powerful alienating tendencies in modern factory technology and industrial organization', he rejected the assumption that alienation was inevitable under industrial capitalism on the grounds that the alienating tendencies emphasized by Marx are unevenly distributed among the labour force (ibid.: 4). His aim, therefore, was to investigate empirically the diversity of work environments in 'an attempt to demonstrate and to explain the uneven distribution of alienation among factory workers in American industry' (ibid.: 6). Blauner's four types of technology and the industries they are associated with are summarized in Table 2.1.

Table 2.1 Blauner's four types of technology and characteristic industry

1   Craft technology – Printing industry
    Simple machines operated by hand.

2   Machine-tending technology – Textile industry
    Relatively complex machines minded by operatives.

3   Assembly-line technology – Car industry
    Conveyor-belt technology with limited tasks performed using small power tools.

4   Continuous-process technology – Chemical industry
    Automated technology monitored and maintained by operatives.

Source: Summarized from Blauner (1964: 6–8).

More specifically, he set out to research the conditions under which the different dimensions of alienation are heightened or lessened by comparing systematically four factory-based industries: printing, textiles, automobiles and chemicals. According to Blauner, the 'most important single factor which gives an industry a distinctive character is its *technology*', which he defined as 'the complex of physical objects and technical operations (both manual and machine) regularly employed in turning out the goods and services produced by an industry' (ibid.: 6, italics in the original). Blauner adopted a sociological conception of technology in that he refers to the mechanical hardware (tools and machines) and to the human activities associated with using the mechanical hardware (knowledge and techniques). The reasons Blauner advances for prioritizing technology above all other potential causal variables are that it is the most influential factor that 'determines the nature of the job tasks performed by blue-collar employees and has an important effect on a number of aspects of alienation' (ibid.: 8). For example, technology influences the kinds of work activity required of an employee and the amount of physical movement a worker experiences, both of which are thought to affect the degree of worker powerlessness.

In order to be able to achieve his stated aim of investigating variations in the patterning of alienation, Blauner distinguished between four types of technology (the independent or causal variable) and four dimensions of alienation (the dependent variable or phenomenon to be explained). The four types of technology and the industries selected to represent different historical phases of its development were: (1) craft – printing; (2) machine-tending – textiles; (3) assembly-line – cars; and (4) continuous-process – chemicals. These are summarized in Table 2.1. Blauner denies that his four types of technology conform to a unilinear model of industrial evolution, but admits that exceptions, such as instances of regression, 'are very rare' (ibid.: 8).

Blauner considered alienation to be a complex idea and therefore divided it into four dimensions: (1) powerlessness or lack of freedom and control at work; (2) meaninglessness or lack of understanding and sense of purpose; (3) social isolation or lack of a sense of belonging and an inability to identify with the organization; and (4) self-estrangement or lack of involvement and hence fulfilment at work. As can be seen in Table 2.2, these aspects of alienation are contrasted with their non-alienated opposites, namely (1) freedom and control; (2) understanding and purpose; (3) belonging and identity or social integration; and (4) involvement and self-expression or self-actualization. Blauner claims that, like Marx, he too is adopting a multidimensional approach to alienation and makes the further claim that 'the connection between some of Marx's dimensions and those employed in the present chapter is clear' (ibid.: 16).

In between the independent variable technology and the dependent variable alienation, Blauner lists what may be called three intervening variables, which mediate between the cause (type of technology) and effect (form of alienation).

Table 2.2 Blauner's four dimensions of alienation and their polar opposites

Alienation	Definition/Key measures	Non-alienation
1 Powerlessness	Lack of freedom and control/freedom to move physically and socially; control over quality and quantity of work	Freedom and control
2 Meaninglessness	Lack of understanding and purpose/subdivided and limited work tasks	Understanding and purpose
3 Social isolation	Lack of belonging and identification/formal and informal social interaction	Belonging and identity
4 Self-estrangement	Lack of involvement and fulfilment/instrumental attitude and boredom	Involvement and self-expression

Source: Summarized from Blauner (1964: 15–34).

Independent variable	>	Intervening variables	>	Dependent variable
Technology	>	1. Division of labour	>	Alienation
		2. Social organization		
		3. Economic structure		

Figure 2.1 Blauner's model of causality

Source: Summarized from Blauner (1964: 6–11).

First, variations in the division of labour or the extent of the subdivision of work tasks within a factory are thought to 'affect the meaning and purpose' experienced by workers (ibid.: 9). Second, whether an industry is organized on the basis of tradition (personal ties) or bureaucratic principles (impersonal ties) is considered by Blauner to be an important factor that can increase or decrease alienation. Moreover, Blauner suggests that the 'implications of bureaucratic organization for social alienation are somewhat mixed' in that the impersonal character of bureaucracy tends to create a gulf between workers and bosses, whereas universalism with its element of fairness can enhance normative integration (ibid.: 25). Third, the economic structure of an industry and in particular its economic success are also thought to influence social integration. Figure 2.1 shows the direction of causality theorized by Blauner in his attempt to explain variations in worker alienation.

Blauner drew upon several data sources and used a variety of research methods to investigate empirically the technological (and economic and social) conditions which induce and intensify the different dimensions of alienation. First, he undertook a secondary analysis of a job attitude survey by Roper dating from 1947 which covered the four industries associated with his typology of technologies, namely printing – craft technology (n = 118); textiles – machine-tending technology (n = 419); cars – assembly-line technology (n = 180); and chemicals – continuous process technology (n = 78). Second, he supplemented his relatively meagre number of chemical workers with his own re-analysis of a survey by Davis of another 230 blue-collar chemical workers conducted in 1959. Third, he utilized some case studies reported by others on automated plants and assembly-line workers that were published between 1950 and 1960. Fourth, he undertook some small-scale fieldwork of his own in 1961–62 of 21 manual chemical workers selected randomly and involving formal interviews, informal discussions and observations. Fifth, he visited a number of cotton mills in the southern USA in 1962 'in an attempt to supplement the observations of students of the industry' (ibid.: 13). Finally, due to the limitations of his data, notably the problematic comparability of such a diverse range of studies, he referred extensively to various tables of comparative industrial statistics, the majority of which were official US statistics covering the years

Table 2.3 Blauner's type of technology and degree of alienation thesis

Type of technology (independent variable)	Degree of alienation (dependent variable)			
	Powerlessness	Meaninglessness	Social isolation	Self-estrangement
Craft technology (e.g., printing)	low	low	low	low
Machine-tending (e.g., textiles)	high	high	low	high
Assembly-line (e.g., automobiles)	high	high	high	high
Process technology (e.g., chemicals)	low	low	low	low

Source: Summarized from Blauner (1964) and Eldridge (1971: 186–7).

1949 to 1960, on such topics as the proportion of female employees and the skill distribution of manual workers in different industries. Blauner's model of causality is summarized in Figure 2.1.

Blauner was well aware that his concern to gather empirical evidence from a variety of sources could not mask the limitations of his study: 'There was no over-all research design applied to the four industries which would have assured precisely equivalent materials for each', and noted modestly that his research findings were 'suggestive rather than conclusive' (ibid.: 13, 14).

As shown in Table 2.3, for Blauner, the extent of alienation among workers varies – some work environments maximize alienation while others minimize it. For *printers, craft technology*, combined with favourable economic circumstances and a history of strong work organizations, 'result in the highest level of freedom and control in the work process among all industrial workers today' (ibid.: 56). In addition, the long apprenticeship, relatively highly skilled, and small size of plants characteristic of the work of printers using craft technology lead to it being meaningful and involving, and engendering considerable identification with the occupation. Blauner concluded that the printer 'is almost the prototype of the non-alienated worker in modern industry', but wondered how long this situation would last given that the beginnings of automation were already apparent in the production of newspapers (ibid.: 57).

In the case of *textile workers*, the use of *machine-tending technology* requires little training and is associated with the subdivision of work into unskilled, uninteresting and unfulfilling jobs in a pre-bureaucratic organizational context, all of which tend to enhance the powerlessness, meaninglessness and self-estrangement dimensions of the work. Conversely, Blauner suggests that despite the limited opportunities for social interaction and promotion in textile mills, social isolation is minimized and the impact of the other alienating tendencies are reduced for textile workers based in the southern USA thanks to the socially integrating and involving nature of their non-work environment, namely their family, religious and community ties. Thus, for these workers, 'objective tendencies toward subjective alienation are overcome, not by fulfilling or creative work, but through the traditional integration of work and non-work concerns' (ibid.: 88). This was especially so for women workers, who, notwithstanding their concentration in the less skilled and less rewarding jobs, were found to be less alienated than their male counterparts because '[w]ork does not have the central importance and meaning in their lives that it does for men, since their most important roles are those of wives and mothers' (ibid.: 81).

The *automobile assembly-line worker* has long been regarded by sociologists as the archetypal, profoundly alienated modern worker, and Blauner reinforces this narrative. On every dimension of alienation, the car assembly-line worker scores extremely high: 'In fact, the result of assembly-line technology and work organization may be the highest level of dissatisfaction in all industry' (ibid.: 121). It is not difficult to see why this is since such work typically involves a series of highly synchronized simple tasks repeated at a pace determined by others. In short, assembly-line work tends to be physically demanding but intellectually unchallenging. Unsurprisingly, therefore, assembly-line work tends to maximize powerlessness, since workers have no control over the speed of the moving assembly line; maximize meaninglessness, since the work tasks have been fractionalized to an extreme degree; maximize isolation due to a lethal combination of bureaucratization, large-scale factory environment, homogenization of the workforce, limited opportunities for advancement, and the individualization of the work tasks; and maximize self-estrangement since the work is excessively monotonous, tiring, simple yet requiring attention to detail, resulting in a markedly instrumental attitude to work. In sum, alienation is maximized for the assembly-line workers because '[h]is work is unfree and unfulfilling and exemplifies the bureaucratic combination of the highly rational organization and the restricted specialist ... he is relatively powerless, atomized, depersonalized, and anonymous' (ibid.: 122).

Finally, *chemical workers* operating *continuous-process technology* regain a sense of control, meaning, social integration, and self-fulfilment due not only to the automated technology which places a premium on individual responsibility as part of a production team, but also to the favourable economic situation of the chemical industry which improves job security and welfare benefits, and to the small-scale and decentralized plants which enhance communication and social interaction, even between management and workers. According to Blauner, therefore, the historical trend of increasing alienation is reversed by 'the unique combination of technological, economic, and social forces which counteract alienation in the chemical industry' (ibid.: 164). However, Blauner did note that even among the chemical workers he interviewed in a plant characterized by a 'remarkably high degree of morale and social cohesion', a minority were 'clearly alienated' (ibid.: 164).

Blauner concluded that, looked at historically: 'Alienation has travelled a course that could be charted on a graph by means of an inverted U-curve' (ibid.: 182). This trend (shown in Figure 2.2) reveals that alienation is at its lowest in the early industrial period when craft technology was dominant,

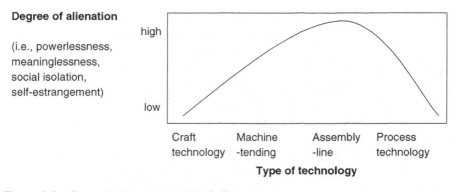

Degree of alienation

(i.e., powerlessness,
meaninglessness,
social isolation,
self-estrangement)

Figure 2.2   Blauner's historical trend of alienation

Source: Based on Blauner (1964: 182–3).

increases steeply with the introduction of machine-tending technology, and reaches its peak in the assembly-line technology industries during the mid-twentieth century. However, with the advent of continuous-process technology, a countertrend occurs and alienation declines from its previous high point 'as employees in automated industries gain a new dignity from responsibility and a sense of individual freedom' (Blauner, 1964: 182). In an important footnote, Blauner qualifies his optimistic conclusion by suggesting that in the future, automation will not necessarily lead to 'a continuation of the major trend toward less alienation' because of the diversity of automated technology and economic conditions (ibid.: 182). This theme is continued where he also notes that his study covers extreme situations, highly alienated textile and car workers, and non-alienated printing and chemical workers. Consequently, for most factory workers, the situation is 'probably' less clear-cut (ibid.: 182). Hence, in the final analysis, he concludes that 'alienation remains a widespread phenomenon in the factory today' (ibid.: 183).

Blauner's proposed solutions to the problem of worker alienation included an increase in the quantity and quality of leisure time, job enlargement and job rotation, research on industrial design and job analysis 'oriented to the goals of worker freedom and dignity as well as the traditional criteria of profit and efficiency', and, in the case of anti-union companies, government intervention to enable trade unions to contribute to the lessening of alienating working conditions (ibid.: 185). These policies and his reference to the legitimacy of private profit are indicative of reformism rather than radicalism.

Critique of Blauner's technology and alienation thesis

The criticisms of Blauner's technology and alienation thesis can be summarized under three headings: (1) methodological; (2) theoretical/conceptual; and (3) interpretative.

(1) Methodological limitations

Blauner's attempt to measure the extent of alienation among workers using different kinds of work technology is an example of verificational research. That is to say that he sought to test, using relevant empirical data, the Marxian hypothesis that alienation is universally high among workers in industrial capitalism. The bulk of Blauner's data was derived from a re-analysis of two attitude questionnaire surveys: one on job satisfaction conducted in 1947, which contributed 795 responses, and the other on attitudes to job redesign conducted in 1959, which contributed 230 respondents. An additional 21 chemical workers were interviewed by Blauner to compensate for the paucity of research on this relatively new industry. It has been noted that: 'Given his specific interests this data base was inherently unsuitable' (Gallie, 1978: 26). For example, 98 per cent of Blauner's empirical data was dated and collected not with alienation in mind but job satisfaction and attitudes to a programme of job redesign. In other words, Blauner's research was primarily a study of job satisfaction masquerading as one of alienation. Furthermore, levels of job satisfaction are known to be very context-sensitive (Gruneberg, 1979), hence attitudes to job satisfaction in the immediate post-war period in 1947 are likely to be different from those expressed after more than a decade of economic growth in 1959. Thus, the appropriateness of the data used to analyse alienation by Blauner is highly questionable.

Moreover, Blauner's survey data was collected and analysed in terms of four particular industries that he considered to have 'distinctive technological arrangements', yet he also admitted that 'no industry has a completely homogeneous technology' (1964: 7). Consequently, there is no way that Blauner could know how many of the workers in the studies he drew upon worked with the technologies characteristic of the industries selected. For example, as Blauner himself noted, in the American automobile industry in 1959, less than 20 per cent of manual workers in this industry 'actually worked on the line' (ibid.: 91). This led Eldridge to comment that since the 180 respondents from the automobile industry were not 'differentiated', 'it is difficult to get at the significance of assembly line work *per se* in assessing attitudes' (1971: 188). Similarly, in the case of the respondents selected from the chemical industry: 'Neither we, nor Blauner … can know precisely what proportion of workers in his sample were in fact working in a highly automated setting' (Gallie, 1978: 26). Even in the case of the chemical industry workers chosen at random and interviewed by Blauner, it is impossible to know how many were involved directly with the highly automated continuous-process technology because they were drawn from three different departments of the company – operations, maintenance and distribution. In his discussion of this point, Gallie noted that: 'If the departments had equal numbers he [Blauner] may have interviewed seven operators, hardly enough to provide a solid grounding for the argument [that technology determines alienation]' (ibid.: 329).

(2) Theoretical/conceptual limitations

Blauner's study was inspired by the Marxian theory of worker alienation and he claimed that 'the connection between some of Marx's dimensions of aliena-tion and those employed in the present chapter are clear' (1964: 16). However, in his discussion of his four dimensions of alienation, he draws upon Marx only with reference to powerlessness and self-estrangement, and even here the con-gruence between his conception of these two dimensions differs markedly from Marx's. In the case of powerlessness, Blauner differentiated 'four modes of industrial powerlessness': '(1) the separation from ownership of the means of production and the finished products, (2) the inability to influence general managerial policies, (3) the lack of control over the conditions of employment, and (4) the lack of control over the immediate work process' (ibid.: 16). He contended that the first two forms of powerlessness are not important to work-ers since they are accepted widely as a 'constant in modern industry' and are a '"given" of industry' respectively (ibid.: 17, 18). Conversely, Blauner argued that employment conditions powerlessness 'is considerably more meaningful to American workers' and that immediate work process powerlessness is 'greatly' resented (ibid.: 18, 20). Consequently, Blauner focused on the last two modes of powerlessness, especially control over the immediate work process, rather than the first two modes. It has been argued that dismissing the socio-logical significance of ownership powerlessness and decision-making power-lessness, on the basis of minimal evidence, 'is implicitly to acknowledge the universality of alienation in that society' (Eldridge, 1971: 190).

Although the nature of alienation is not without ambiguity in Marx's origi-nal works, it is clear that as far as the fate of workers was concerned, capitalism was the main villain, albeit aided and abetted by industrialization (see Chapter 1). However, in Blauner's transformation of the concept of alienation into a meas-urable feature of work, the major source of alienation in general, and power-lessness in particular, is industrialization, specifically technology, whereas capitalism plays an occasional minor role. An example of this can be found in his discussion of the cost structure of textile companies where Blauner sug-gests that it 'furthers the tendency to use the workers as "means", as com-modities in the classic Marxist sense' (1964: 180). The same can be said in the case of car workers, who, due to the insecurity of their employment, are 'likely to feel' that management view them 'only as a number, an instrument of pro-duction, and not as a human being' (ibid.: 110). To the extent that Blauner prioritized industrial factors, such as technology, over capitalist ones, such as ownership, he reversed Marx's theoretical explanation of worker alienation, and in the process distorted the Marxian meaning of alienation.

It has also been argued that by focusing on the subjective experience of alienation, Blauner trivialized Marx's conception of alienation in the sense that he reduced it to a study of job satisfaction (Eldridge, 1971). Notwithstanding Mills' argument that 'whatever satisfaction alienated men gain from work occurs within the framework of alienation' (1968 [1951]: 235), to the extent that Blauner attempted to link job satisfaction to structural conditions, his analysis aspired to a more complete account by including both the objective and subjective features of work.

(3) Interpretative limitations

The interpretation of data is invariably problematic, especially so in a study that relies on several data sources. Blauner's interpretation of his data is open to criticism with reference to the causal significance of trade unions, the role of gender in his account of textile workers, his optimistic interpretation of working in the chemical industry, and the deterministic thrust of his analysis.

In his first chapter, Blauner outlined the factors that may influence alienation with top causal billing being given to technology and supporting roles to the division of labour, social organization and economic structure. In the case of the intervening variable, social organization, the importance of trade unions is hinted at where Blauner refers to the move from traditional to bureaucratic principles of organization and its impact on the 'situation of workers in economic organizations (including their relations with their employers)' (1964: 9). By subsuming the potential causal significance of organized labour in this way, Blauner effectively minimizes the importance of this non-technological factor while simultaneously introducing a highly contradictory element into his account (Gallie, 1978; Hill, 1981).

This can be seen most clearly when, in marked contrast to the minor role allocated to organized labour in the opening chapters, his analysis of three of the four selected technologies/industries – craft/printing, machine-tending/ textiles, and assembly-line/autos – Blauner provided evidence to show that trade unions, or labour unions as they are known in America, are a vital force whose presence/absence can lessen/heighten alienation. More specifically, the 'unusual power of the [printing] union' to influence the printers' control over the pace of their work and their freedom from supervision, which reduces the powerlessness dimension of alienation, is fully acknowledged (Blauner, 1964: 44). In the case of textile workers, only a minority are protected by union agreements because the majority of textile companies are anti-union, which suggests to Blauner that, among other things, a 'strong labour union' would 'reduce the powerlessness and improve the working conditions of textile employees (ibid.: 186). In the car workers union (United Automobile Workers), Blauner noted that 'it has reduced through the years the worker's individual and collective powerlessness against the forces of technology and management' (ibid.: 114–15). It is only in the chemical industry that trade unions are viewed by Blauner as virtually irrelevant since he considered that integration in this industry 'is an outcome of continuous-process technology, favourable economic conditions, and worker satisfaction with superior wages and employee benefits' (ibid.: 154).

Thus, on the basis of Blauner's own data, there would seem to be good grounds for arguing that the power of trade unions is a major, not a minor, factor that influences alienation, particularly powerlessness via their impact on the conditions of employment. That Blauner was aware of the importance of organized labour is unsurprising given his background as a unionized ex-factory worker who had received financial support from a trade union; that he underplayed the causal importance of trade unions and left himself open to the criticism of faulty interpretation on this point is somewhat more surprising.

Interpretative problems have also been identified in Blauner's analysis of textile workers. It has been argued that 'the sexual division of labour characteristic of the middle period of industrial capitalism' (see Chapter 1) led to the emergence of 'two sociologies of work' which corresponded to the separate spheres involving the male breadwinner role and the female domestic role, namely a job model for men and a gender model for women (Feldberg and Glenn, 1979). The different assumptions behind each of these models are that studies of male workers tend to assume that paid work outside the home is the key factor in the analysis of their relationship to work, whereas in the case of female workers, it is invariably assumed that family life is the main influence on their relationship to work.

Feldberg and Glenn examined Blauner's study to illustrate the way in which the use of these models can distort the interpretation of data. They found that Blauner operated with the job model in his analysis of male-dominated industries, namely printing, automobiles and chemicals, but in his interpretation of the textile industry, in which there are a large number of women workers, he 'switches to the gender model to analyse the women's response to employment' (ibid.: 528). Feldberg and Glenn note that Blauner's data confirms that women are concentrated in the least skilled jobs in the textile industry and therefore tend to experience the most alienating work conditions. Understandably, more women than men complained that their work was too fast and tiring, yet Blauner 'shifts, without warning or justification, to a gender model to interpret women's responses' (ibid.: 528). In other words, he attributes the women's higher degree of pressure and fatigue to their biology ('less physical stamina than men') and to their family responsibilities ('working women often double as housewives and mothers') (Blauner, 1964: 71).

Feldberg and Glenn suggest that there are two interpretative problems with Blauner's analysis of textile workers: it 'obscures the previously argued link between working conditions and workers' responses', and it 'ignores data which show that women's work conditions are more demanding' (1979: 528–9). Thus, in addition to contradicting his main thesis that technology determines alienation, Blauner compounds his problematic interpretation by relying on assumptions about the primary roles of men and women rather than evidence in his analysis of male and female textile workers. In other words, instead of considering variations in working conditions and family responsibilities for male and female textile workers and relating them to his dependent variable, alienation, Blauner's interpretation of textile workers is flawed because alienation is explained inconsistently in terms of both his overall thesis and his account of male and female textile workers. With regard to the latter, the alienation of male textile workers is analysed with reference to the assumption that work is a central life interest for employed men, which discounts the possibility that their family role may influence their work attitudes and behaviour, whereas the alienation of female textile workers is explicated in terms of the assumption that the family is a central life interest for employed women, which discounts the possibility that their work conditions may influence their work attitudes and behaviour. Thus, Blauner's interpretation of textile workers is distorted by his selective incorporation of different assumptions about men and women, which may be plausible but are introduced into the analysis without the support of any empirical evidence.

Blauner's interpretation of chemical workers has also been criticized on the grounds that he provides 'an exaggerated picture of the positive aspects of work life in a continuous-process factory' (Gallie, 1978: 85). Blauner argues that: 'Since work in continuous-process industries involves control, meaning and social integration, it tends to be self-actualizing instead of self-estranging', hence it is essentially non-alienating (1964: 154). At the same time, Blauner provides evidence which seems to contradict this rosy picture of work in a chemical plant. For example, he notes that the complexity of continuous-process technology threatens the meaningfulness of the work and that working with highly automated technology on an 'invisible product' is conducive to sensory deprivation (Blauner, 1964: 145). In addition, he notes that 'considerable dissatisfaction' arises where expectations of rapid promotion are thwarted and that the work can be quite monotonous, especially for shift workers 'when there are no bosses around and no maintenance workers to make repairs and pass the time with' (ibid.: 152, 156). It has also been pointed out that Blauner 'cites one oil refinery personnel executive who has placed a limit on the IQs of workers hired for operating jobs, and another who calls them "only watchmen"' (Braverman, 1974: 224). Thus, far from being non-alienating, work in a chemical factory could, on the basis of Blauner's own data, be considered acutely alienating, especially for workers of above average ability.

Blauner was aware therefore that work in a continuous-process technology chemical plant was alienating in certain respects for some workers, yet he chose to emphasize the non-alienating features and to generalize on the basis that they were applicable to the majority of workers. Hence the suspicion remains that his interpretation of this highly automated work is an accurate one for those workers at or near the top of the team hierarchy, but an inaccurate one for all those at the bottom of the hierarchy. Given that there are invariably more people at the bottom of a hierarchy than at the top, Blauner's conclusion that there are 'proportionally fewer' alienated workers in the chemical industry is questionable (1964: 164).

Finally, arguably the most common criticism of Blauner is that he advanced a technological determinist account to the extent that he explained variations in alienation largely in terms of variations in technology to the relative exclusion of other factors, most importantly the meanings workers create and attach to work (Goldthorpe, 1966; Silverman, 1970). A strong example of this line of criticism is provided by Hill who asserted that Blauner's support for technological determinism 'surpasses anything in previous industrial sociology' (1981: 95). Thompson affords a much weaker example where he notes that Blauner 'merely tended to add a touch of determinism' to research on the technological influences on work (1983: 21).

Blauner certainly supplied his critics with plenty of material with which to construct a case in that he placed disproportionate causal weight on technology. At the beginning of his study Blauner made two statements that appear contradictory. Initially he asserted that 'modern factories vary considerably in technology, in division of labour, in economic structure, and in organizational character. These differences produce sociotechnical systems in which the objective conditions and inner life of employees are strikingly variant' (1964: 5). On the next page, however, Blauner argued that of the four variables, technology was the 'most important single factor that gives an industry a distinctive character' (ibid.: 6). Throughout his subsequent analysis, Blauner focused on the role of technology more than any other influence, although he continued to proffer evidence to the contrary, notably in the case of his analysis of women workers in the textile industry and his references to the role of trade unions, as noted above. In his final chapter, although Blauner reiterated his technology plus other factors argument in the context of advancing his inverted U-curve thesis, he qualified his technological determinism in two ways in the space of one footnote: 'Automated technology will take many forms besides continuous-process production, and the diversified economic conditions of future automated industries will further complicate the situation' (ibid.: 182). As Eldridge has indicated, this point 'ought perhaps to be emphasised' (1971: 189). I would concur, since had Blauner done so, his vulnerability to the charge of technological determinism would have been reduced.

Blauner was clearly uncertain throughout his analysis about the significance of the causal status of technology and intervening variables. Arguably, this nagging uncertainty was reflected in interpretative inconsistencies, particularly with respect to the ability of trade unions and community ties to alleviate alienation. The root of Blauner's hesitant technological determinism can be traced to his empirical evidence and his interpretation of it, which from the standpoint of his explanation of alienation, could also be considered a theoretical/conceptual limitation.

Empirical research on the Blauner thesis

At the extremes of alienation, non-alienated print workers and alienated car workers, there is an unusual degree of unanimity among sociologists that Blauner's depiction, though not necessarily his theoretical understanding, of craft work and assembly-line work was accurate. Thus, studies of craft workers (e.g., Harrison and Zeitlin, 1985) and assembly-line workers (e.g., Beynon, 1975) have shown that the former tend to enjoy a considerable degree of power, control, and so on, at work, whereas the latter tend not to. However, it does not necessarily follow that assembly-line workers are invariably alienated or that technology is the major determinant of work attitudes and behaviour since non-work factors, such as consumption and family-centredness, may lead such workers to adopt an instrumental orientation to work (Goldthorpe et al., 1969).

As far as textile workers are concerned, one reassessment of alienation using 1980s data produced only mixed support for Blauner (Leiter, 1985), while others have suggested that they were an inappropriate choice since in certain respects machine-tending technology is hardly any more advanced than that used by printers (Hull et al., 1982). Interestingly, at the end of his study, Blauner conflated machine and assembly-line technologies on the grounds that they were both involved in 'routine low-skilled operations' (1964: 169). These points tend to reinforce the problematic nature of machine-tending technology and Blauner's questionable interpretation of this case study data.

More generally, in a re-examination of Blauner's data, an analysis of their own empirical research on over 100 industrial organizations and 245 printers whose work had been automated following the introduction of computer technology, plus a review of the research on Blauner's increasing technology and decreasing alienation thesis, Hull et al. concluded that, when the problematic textile workers are excluded, 'the inverted U-curve hypothesis is supported' (1982: 33). Although the Hull et al. empirical research has been criticized strongly on conceptual, theoretical and methodological grounds (Vallas and Yarrow, 1987), their review of the research literature involving continuous-process technology is also problematic because it is highly selective in two ways. First, their review excludes consideration of one case study which contradicts the Blauner thesis, namely the research on chemical workers by Nichols and Beynon (1977). Second, their summary of the apparently supportive literature tends to overlook the limited nature of that evidence. For example, the research by Cotgrove (1972), cited by Hull et al. (1982), focused on only one of Blauner's dimensions of alienation, self-estrangement, and although the findings confirmed that process work is relatively non-alienating, Cotgrove's data on job interest and monotony revealed marked variations and is generally less convincing than the comparable data in Blauner.

Continuous-process technology is arguably the pivotal issue for Blauner's technology and alienation thesis since his predicted long-term trend that increasing automation leads to decreasing alienation is predicated on the adoption of this technology. Therefore, a more detailed review of the post-Blauner empirical research on continuous-process technology workers in chemical plants is crucial before one can conclude that Blauner's historical thesis is either correct or incorrect.

In Britain during the 1970s, there were three major studies of chemical workers which provided empirical evidence of direct relevance to Blauner's thesis that the introduction of continuous-process technology leads to decline in all the dimensions of alienation. First, Wedderburn and Crompton (1972) used similar indicators to Blauner and came to similar conclusions with respect to the powerlessness, meaningfulness and social isolation dimensions of alienation, namely that continuous-process workers were comparatively less alienated than workers using other types of technology. However, in terms of the self-estrangement dimension, Wedderburn and Crompton 'found little evidence of positive identification with the firm' and an instrumental orientation to work (1972: 149). This study conformed to Blauner's approach in that it accepted his theoretical point of departure that technology is an important variable for understanding work attitudes and behaviour. Thus, they not only confirmed his findings but also his main theoretical premise, albeit with the caveat that technology is a sound starting place but not the whole picture, since it fails to look beyond the factory gate.

Second, the research by Nichols and Beynon was based largely on conversations with chemical workers at one plant over a three-year period and contains no statistical tables but a description of what work is like in a chemical plant for the majority of employees (over 75 per cent) who do the unskilled 'donkey work' (1977: 10). Nichols and Beynon provide plenty of qualitative evidence to show that Blauner's thesis does not apply to the majority of chemical workers since they perform very similar work to that 'found on traditional assembly lines in technically less "progressive" sectors' (ibid.: 68). As far as the minority were concerned, namely the operators who monitored the process technology, the work was certainly less physically demanding but most of them worked alone rather than in a team, disliked the shift work, especially the double shift, and felt more trapped than secure. In marked contrast to Blauner, this study emphasized that complex technology was 'not designed to make chemicals, but to make chemicals for profit' (ibid.: 69). Thus, Nichols and Beynon not only repudiated Blauner's thesis, but rejected his assumption that the effect of technology can be understood without reference to the capitalist mode of production.

Third, the empirical research undertaken by Gallie (1978) involved a comparative study of chemical workers at two British and two French oil refineries. Gallie found that the French continuous-process workers were 'deeply alienated from the system of authority' and that consequently the 'predominant feeling was one of powerlessness', whereas the British workers 'felt that they had a fairly high level of control over decisions' that affected their immediate experience of work and regarded strategic financial decisions as a matter for management (ibid.: 145). As far as meaninglessness was concerned, Gallie reported that due to the complexity of the technology and the limited inter-unit flexibility, knowledge of the overall process was confined to a small number of multi-skilled workers. For the majority of French and British oil refinery operators, 'the job was probably less meaningful than many jobs in traditional industry' (ibid.: 80–1). Blauner's argument that a sense of belonging was enhanced by teamwork within a decentralized factory was also found wanting. Gallie reported that although the 'growth of a semi-team system among operators seems to have facilitated better relations in both countries', control had not been decentralized to the work team to the same extent in France as it had in Britain, and, as a consequence, French managers retained more power and French workers perceived a greater social distance between themselves and management (ibid.: 236). Gallie also noted that although work in a chemical plant is less boring and physically demanding, 'automation does not make work a deep source of satisfaction' sufficient to achieve self-actualization, and that '[t]he commonest attitude towards work in all our refineries was one of indifference' (ibid.: 87, 104). Gallie's findings show that French chemical workers were more alienated than their British counterparts in that they were highly alienated on every dimension of alienation whereas the British workers were highly alienated on only two dimensions: meaninglessness and self-estrangement. He concluded: 'It is extremely doubtful whether automation leads to the overcoming of alienation in work in any profound sense of the term' (ibid.: 296). Since the technology was similar in all the plants in both countries in this study, the explanation of the variations in alienation between the French and British workers must be attributed to non-technological factors such as managerial and union policies. In contrast to Blauner, Gallie did not completely ignore the capitalist context of his analysis. For example, he considered the issue of capitalist ownership versus forms of non-capitalist ownership and found a small majority in favour of the status quo in both France and Britain (54 per cent and 63 per cent, respectively). Yet other capitalist features, such as exploitation and profitability, were ignored by Gallie, which is surprising since his conclusions are more in line with those of Nichols and Beynon (1977), who are not cited, than with those of Wedderburn and Crompton (1972), who are cited.

Empirical research on the Blauner thesis was taken one step further by Shepard (1971), whose large-scale study included both factory workers and white-collar workers. He replicated Blauner's dimensions of alienation almost exactly with respect to powerlessness and meaninglessness, but defined and operationalized social isolation and self-estrangement differently and referred to them as normlessness and instrumentalism, respectively, and added a fifth dimension of alienation that he called self-evaluative involvement. He adopted a quota sampling method to ensure that 'only workers performing tasks corresponding to the different stages of technological development were selected', and distinguished between three types of worker–technology relationship: non-mechanized (i.e., industrial craft workers and traditional clerical workers), mechanized (i.e., industrial assembly-line workers and office machine operators), and automated (i.e., industrial continuous-process workers and computer operators and other types of computer worker) (ibid.: 17). In the case of the factory workers, he found that, with the exception of powerlessness, 'alienation was lower among craftsmen, reached a peak among assemblers, and declined again among monitors to a level below that of either assemblers or craftsmen' (ibid.: 40). With regard to white-collar workers Shepard revealed some inconsistent patterns, such as the tendency for female computer workers to be more alienated in certain respects than female clerks and machine operators, although in certain other respects his office worker data broadly supported Blauner's thesis, but not Mills' more general claim about the alienating conditions of white-collar work. Shepard concluded that while Blauner's thesis that 'automation reverses the historical trend toward increased alienation from work among factory workers appears to be supported', the impact of automation on alienation among white-collar workers is more variable (ibid.: 117). In the light of these findings, Shepard did not place as much weight on technology as an independent variable as Blauner: 'Factors affecting attitudes towards work are too many, and their interrelationships too complex, to assume that the technologically determined attributes of the job alone constitute an explanatory variable' (ibid.: 126). Thus, despite designing his research within Blauner's non-capitalist, industrial society framework, and operationalizing the independent and dependent variables in a broadly similar way, Shepard's evidence on blue- and white-collar workers using different types of technology provides mixed support for his thesis and he fails to endorse unequivocally Blauner's (alleged) technologically determinist theoretical position.

Fractional support for Blauner's U-shaped curve of declining, then increasing alienation under historically progressive forms of production is provided by Hodson (1996) who combined three of Blauner's technology-based models with two from Edwards' (1979) labour control model, and constructed five types of workplace organization: craft (e.g., printers), direct supervision (e.g., textile workers), assembly line (e.g., auto workers), bureaucratic (e.g., clerical workers), and worker participation (e.g., auto workers in Japanese factories). On the basis of a secondary analysis of over 100 English language workplace ethnographic cases, Hodson confirmed that the lowest level of alienation was among craft workers, but he also found that workers under direct supervision and those in bureaucratic organizations were more alienated than mass production assembly line workers, whereas those in participative organizations were less alienated though not to the same degree as craft workers. Hodson concluded that: 'Rather than a U-shaped pattern of falling then rising freedom and self-actualization, the pattern is better described as a reverse J-shape in which declining freedom and self-actualization are followed by an incomplete recovery' (1996: 734). This study effectively updates Blauner's by including post-bureaucratic workplaces that use the latest micro-chip technology, and revises rather than rejects his analysis and conclusions.

The possible influence of non-technological factors on alienation has been explored by Hochschild (2003 [1983]), Rogers (1995), Sarros et al. (2002),

DiPietro and Pizam (2008), and Korczynski (2009). Hochschild's analysis of the alienation caused by the commercialization of emotions in service work draws directly on Marx, particularly the product and labour process dimensions of alienation, rather than Blauner. She found that service workers are alienated from their emotional labour in the sense that they are expected to express feelings considered appropriate by management in the course of their work. Korczynski contested Hochschild's argument that all interactive service workers who perform emotional labour are alienated by suggesting that not all worker–customer relationships are marketized, unequal and fleeting. As an alternative to Hochschild, he contrasted the high alienation in worker–customer relations experienced by market-driven, instrumental interactive service workers employed in profit-oriented organizations, to the low alienation in worker–customer relations experienced by non-market-driven, caring interactive service workers employed in public or voluntary organizations. Rogers, on the basis of an in-depth study of a small number of temporary clerical workers in the USA, found that one of the main social costs of this type of flexible work, much lauded by employers, is alienation from work, from other workers, and from oneself. In another US piece of research by Sarros et al., staff in a highly bureaucratic fire department were less alienated in terms of powerlessness, meaninglessness and estrangement, the more they were consulted by their superiors; conversely, the more dictatorial the leadership style, the more alienated the personnel. The exploratory study of quick service restaurant staff by DiPietro and Pizam is supportive of the Sarros et al. research since they found that alienation was unevenly distributed, therefore it was not caused by the type of technology used but by the style of management in different restaurants. These studies suggest that contemporary work situations retain several possible sources of alienation, sufficient to temper any overly optimistic generalization about the historical decline of alienation.

Summary and conclusions

The concept of alienation was a major theme in European social theory in the nineteenth century, especially in the early writings of Marx. In the mid-twentieth century, American sociologists, notably Mills and Seaman, were instrumental in reviving interest in this idea, but it was Blauner who set about researching it in a theoretically informed empirical study.

The key points of Blauner's study are that: (1) it was a test of Marx's theory that all workers are alienated under industrial capitalism; (2) the data sources included a secondary analysis of attitudinal survey data, some purposefully collected interview data, and comparative industrial statistics; (3) four types of technology/industries were examined – craft technology/printing industry, machine-tending technology/textiles, assembly-line technology/cars, and continuous-process technology/chemicals; (4) four dimensions of alienation were distinguished – powerlessness, meaningfulness, social isolation, and self-estrangement; (5) it hypothesized that not all workers were equally alienated and that differences in technology were primarily responsible for the variation; (6) alienation was found to be relatively low for the least automated print workers, that it was higher for textile workers, highest for the mass-production assembly-line workers, but lower again for the most technologically advanced chemical workers; (7) when this pattern of variations in alienation was placed in historical context, it was described as an inverted U-curve; and (8) it concluded that increasing alienation was not inevitable due to the liberating influence of advancing technology.

The main criticisms of Blauner's technology and alienation thesis were reviewed under three headings and these suggested that, methodologically, his data sources were not ideal, his conceptualization of alienation vulgarized Marx's original idea, and that his interpretation was sufficiently problematic, especially with regard to the textile workers and his tendency to idealize continuous-process work, to cast doubts on the consistency of his theory, analysis and his conclusions.

Subsequent research on the impact of different types of technology on worker alienation provided mixed support for Blauner's thesis. In the case of the non-alienated craft workers and highly alienated car workers, Blauner's assessment has received broad support, but his analysis of textile workers has not been confirmed unambiguously. More generally, the closer a study replicated Blauner's industrial society model and key variables, the more likely that the findings would support his thesis (e.g., Wedderburn and Crompton, 1972) and vice versa (e.g., Nichols and Beynon, 1977). However, a replication study by Shepard (1971) that sought to extend Blauner's analysis by including a sample of office workers as well as factory workers, failed to confirm unequivocally his historical thesis in the case of the former but did so in the case of the latter. In research that built upon the work of both Blauner and Edwards (1979), and took into account the most recent technological (microelectronic) and organizational (post-bureaucratic) workplace changes, Hodson (1996) provided partial support for the historical dimension of Blauner's thesis, yet DiPietro and Pizam (2008), Hochschild (2003 [1983]), Korczynski (2009), Rogers (1995), and Sarros et al. (2002) demonstrated that alienation is still a problem for many workers. The issue of participative organizations of production raised by Hodson will be discussed in more detail in the relevant chapters on industrial and service work (Chapters 5 and 6), and the increasing prevalence of emotional labour will be considered more fully in the chapter on service work (Chapter 6). Virtually all Blauner's critics and those who have followed in his footsteps have tended to distance themselves from what some regard as the main weakness of his account of technology and alienation, namely its alleged technological determinist thrust.

Although Blauner's study has been criticized extensively and replicated several times with mixed success as far as his thesis is concerned, many of his detractors have also praised his research as a 'classic study' (Feldberg and Glenn, 1979: 528), 'seminal work' (Hodson, 1996: 720), in part on the grounds that it has been 'highly influential' in the field of technology and work (Vallas and Yarrow, 1987: 127). Similarly, specialists in the sociology of work have noted that his project was an 'ambitious' one that 'has never been surpassed as a study of automation that is empirical and speculative in equal measure' (Rose, 1988: 223).

In the seeming welter of negative comments, one should not lose sight of the many strengths of his contribution to our understanding of some of the influences on the attitudes and behaviour of workers in industrial capitalism. Blauner was one of the first sociologists to undertake a theoretically informed empirical test of Marx's important theory of worker alienation. Given that the meaning of this concept is contested by Marxists and non-Marxists, it is unsurprising that his attempt to operationalize this complex idea would generate considerable criticism. Second, rather than simply assume that the structure of industrial capitalism would result in increased alienation for all workers, Blauner tried valiantly to analyse the main causal variables that could explain variations in alienation among the industrial labour force, and the links between the objective and subjective aspects of alienation. As a consequence, he was successful in demonstrating that the diversity of work situations and associated degrees of alienation are to some extent due to variations in the type of technology that prevails in different industries. Third, Blauner's account of alienation may be viewed as flawed, especially from a Marxian perspective, but it was historically sensitive and cautiously presented. For example, he contextualized his types of technology historically and qualified his thesis by noting, albeit in an easily overlooked footnote, that, in the future, despite advances in technology and other relevant factors, such as economic conditions, a further decline in alienation is not guaranteed. Fourth, in terms of the organizational context of work, Blauner was concerned primarily with the lessening of alienation as a result of the change from pre-bureaucratic (i.e., textiles) to bureaucratic (i.e., chemicals) authority structures, thanks to the sense of fairness inherent in a universalistic system, yet his account of a chemical plant exhibits clear parallels with what has since been termed a post-bureaucratic organization (Heckscher and Donnellon, 1994). This is readily apparent in his discussion of team work, consultation, feedback, and job rotation in the small, decentralized organizational setting of the chemical plant he studied, and, as such, Blauner's analysis anticipates later theoretical and empirical research. Finally, although Blauner's focus was how different types of technology, in combination with other variables, influence alienation, it was also concerned with what has since become known as the skill debate. Behind his inverted U-curve thesis was the evidence-based argument that whereas machine-tending and assembly-line technologies deskill workers, continuous-process technology both increases the demand for traditional craft skills, for example, on the part of maintenance workers, and changes the nature of skills required from manual dexterity to non-manual responsibility, although both types of work 'require considerable discretion and initiative' (Blauner, 1964: 168). Looked at from this perspective, therefore, Blauner's thesis was a pioneering study of the historical fate of skill levels or, more precisely, an early example of the upskilling thesis, with a hint of polarization where he noted that 'a considerable amount of routine work that negates the dignity of the worker will very likely persist in the foreseeable future' (ibid.: 169).

The overlap between the debates about declining alienation and upskilling is illustrated clearly by the inclusion of Blauner's study on the upskilling side of the debate (e.g., Vallas, 1988). The issue over whether or not workers have been deskilled or upskilled continues to divide sociologists, and will be considered in the next two chapters. The concept of emotional labour and Hochschild's argument that performing it is alienating will be discussed in more detail in Chapter 6.

Further reading

BOOKS Before embarking on a journey into the Blauner-related literature, it is of course imperative to read the original: Blauner (1964) *Alienation and Freedom: The Factory Worker and His Industry*. Consideration of the material critical of Blauner should start with the important review by Eldridge (1971) *Sociology and Industrial Life*, which covers both Marx's and Blauner's conceptualizations of alienation. The study by Gallie (1978) *In Search of the New Working Class: Automation and Social Integration within the Capitalist Enterprise* combines a critique of Blauner's study with an analysis of cross-national data of workers who operate continuous-process technology. For an alternative understanding of chemical workers, consult Nichols and Beynon (1977) *Living with Capitalism: Class Relations and the Modern Factory*.

ARTICLES Support for Blauner is provided by Hull et al. (1982) 'The effect of technology on alienation from work: testing Blauner's inverted U-curve hypothesis for 110 industrial organizations and 245 retrained printers', *Work and Occupations*, 9(1): 31–57. Vallas (1988) 'New technology, job content, and worker alienation: a test of two rival perspectives', *Work and Occupations*, 15(2): 148–78 is relevant to the Blauner thesis and is a good introduction to the issue of skill discussed in the next two chapters.

WEBSITE For a review of Braverman that argues that science and technology are not neutral but social forces under the control of capital that amounts to a critique of Blanuer see www.human-nature.com/rmyoung/papers/blmc1.html

Questions for discussion and assessment

1 How Marxian is Blauner's operationalization of alienation?
2 Aside from Blauner's alleged technological determinism, what do you consider to be the major weaknesses of his study?
3 To what extent does empirical research support Blauner's technology and alienation thesis?
4 Consider the claim that Blauner's study was theoretically informed but methodologically flawed.
5 Assess the view that the gender dimension is the main weakness of Blauner's study.
6 Discuss the view that Blauner's analysis was sound for printers and car workers, but not for textile and chemical workers.
7 Why is Blauner's study so highly regarded by sociologists of work?

3
WORK AND DESKILLING

It is widely thought that one of the major consequences of the rise of industrial capitalism was the destruction of skill following the introduction of machinery. From the start of capitalist industrialization therefore, the concept of skill has been at the forefront of debates about changes in the nature of work. Subsequent technological advances, particularly the use of computers to design, direct and control production, have ensured that the concept of skill has remained a focal point in the sociology of work.

Despite the centrality of the concept of skill in the sociological analysis of work and its widespread use in everyday discussions of occupations, there is little agreement about how best to define and measure this familiar idea (Vallas, 1990). This lack of agreement is reflected in the ongoing debate concerning the historical direction of skill change. Basically, there are the 'pessimists', who have tended to use a definition of skill which emphasizes the skill content of a job and the amount of task-specific training required to do it and who argue that work has been deskilled. On the other hand, there are the 'optimists', who have tended to use a definition of skill which focuses on the change from manual dexterity to the exercise of responsibility and the increased educational qualifications required to exercise this new skill and who argue that work has been upskilled. There is also a third perspective, which typically combines definitional elements of both the above and whose advocates argue that skill polarization is occurring. The aim of this chapter is to evaluate the first of these views. (The alternative views will be considered in Chapter 4.)

Braverman's deskilling thesis

Braverman's historical account of deskilling is the leading and most powerful version of the pessimistic position. His thesis draws upon Marx's theory of work in industrial capitalism in that he starts from the proposition that in such a society workers are constrained economically, by the absence of alternatives, to sell their labour power to employers who are similarly constrained to seek a profit or go out of business. This is the capitalist mode of production, at its core is the unequal relationship between employer and employee, and Braverman's aim is to examine 'the manner in which the labour force is dominated and shaped by the accumulation of capital' (1974: 53). While Marx's empirical reference point was Britain in the nineteenth century, Braverman's was America in the twentieth century – respectively the first industrial capitalist society and the most advanced.

Braverman's ambitious analysis of the development of the capitalist mode of production over the past hundred years or so was predicated on the Marxian assumption that human labour power is unique in that it is 'intelligent and purposive' (ibid.: 56). These distinctive characteristics make human labour exceedingly adaptable, with unlimited potential for production. From the standpoint of the capitalist, this is good news, but the downside is that, in the context of the inherently 'antagonistic relations of production', there is 'the problem of realizing the "full usefulness" of the labour power' that has been purchased (ibid.: 57). Thus, if all the capitalist really buys is potential, it is imperative to exert control over the labour process in order to maximize the productive potential of labour and therefore profits.

By the end of the nineteenth century and the beginning of the twentieth century, capitalist production in America had developed on a large scale, was increasingly based on scientific knowledge and was concentrated among a declining number of big corporations. Consequently, the control of labour issue had become more complex. In an attempt to solve this problem, capitalists turned to developments in management and machinery, which not only enhanced the control of labour but also progressively deskilled the worker.

In the quest for managerial control, scientific management, or Taylorism, after the world's first management consultant, who pioneered it, is of first importance to Braverman for its practical implications and, above all perhaps, because it is 'a theory which is nothing less than the explicit verbalization of the capitalist mode of production' (ibid.: 86). For Braverman, it is a capitalist approach to the question of control, notwithstanding its claims to the contrary via the language of scientific objectivity. Hence Taylor, and all those management experts who followed in his footsteps, were more interested in developing and prescribing ways to ameliorate the alienating conditions of work in industrial capitalism than in abolishing the forces that gave rise to them in the first place. It is as a capitalist ideology therefore that Taylorism came to dominate managerial ideas about 'how best to control alienated labour' (ibid.: 90).

Taylor exemplifies this point well in that he regarded workers as inherently lazy, and 'soldiering', namely the tendency to work consistently at less than maximum output, as universal. He was also less than impressed by managers since they allowed workers to shirk and restrict output because work was still planned and executed by workers and not management. In order to overcome what Taylor therefore regarded as the natural recalcitrance of workers and the ignorance and therefore incompetence of managers, he recommended that managers should approach the organization of work more scientifically and take total control of the labour process, including every aspect of production, however small. The primary new managerial responsibility under scientific management was the 'gathering together of all the traditional knowledge which in the past had been possessed by the workmen and then classifying, tabulating and reducing this knowledge to rules' (Taylor, 1947 [1911]: 36). All this knowledge was then centralized in a planning department, and managers, armed with the knowledge of the best way of performing a task, could specify how it was to be done and how long it should take. Braverman summed up Taylor's systematic or scientific approach to management with reference to three related principles: 'the first principle is the gathering and development of knowledge of the labour processes', 'the second is the concentration of this knowledge as the exclusive province of management – together with its essential converse, the absence of such knowledge among the workers', and 'the third is the use of this monopoly over knowledge to control each step of the labour process and its mode of execution' (1974: 119). Implicit in these principles is the separation of conception from execution, namely the transfer of all mental labour from workers to managers while simultaneously simplifying and standardizing the tools and tasks that the worker is instructed to use in order to undertake a deskilled task within a designated time frame. Taylor's prescription that managers should appropriate the expertise and experience of skilled workers has been expressed memorably by Big Bill Haywood, founding member and leader of the radical union The International Workers of the World (known as the Wobblies), as 'the manager's brains' are under the 'workman's cap' (cited by Montgomery, 1987: 45).

Braverman considered this separation to be of major importance and that it was only feasible when the scale of production plus associated resources had advanced to the point where a class of managers could assume total responsibility for designing, planning and supervising the subdivided tasks of manual workers. The main effects of the insitutionalization of the separation of conception from execution, mental from manual work, are that, for the capitalist, 'the cost of production is lowered', but it has a 'degrading effect upon the technical capacity of the worker' (Braverman, 1974: 127). While Taylor agreed that 'the cost of production is lowered by separating the work of planning and the brain work as much as possible from the manual labour', he also claimed that the increased output that resulted from the application of scientific management would lead to higher wages, shorter hours, lower costs, and cheaper products (1947 [1911]: 121). According to Taylor, under scientific management workers would 'grow happier and more prosperous', with a corresponding diminution of 'friction and discontent' (ibid.: 39, 143).

Braverman's historical benchmark was the craft worker, who epitomized the unity of hand and brain work, and he noted that the initial opposition to Taylorism was not directed at the time study feature of his system, but at its attempt to denude the craft workers of their knowledge and autonomy. However, the effects of scientific management were felt far beyond the nineteenth-century (predominantly) male craftsman when it was introduced into office work during the first decades of the twentieth century. As in the case of Taylorized factory work, office and retail work were reorganized on the basis of the same principles with the same results, namely increased output to the benefit of capital and reduced skill to the detriment of labour. The class implications of Braverman's deskilling thesis are therefore inextricably linked to the work dimension; in a word, proletarianization. Although Braverman acknowledged that in expanding industries there are increased opportunities for a few workers to move into planning and supervisory positions, thereby hinting at polarization, he also noted that such a short-term trend does not contradict the longer-term one of progressive deskilling.

According to Braverman, the control of blue-collar and white-collar work, and as a consequence deskilling, were aided considerably by mechanization. For capitalists, the great advantage of machinery is that it not only increases the productivity of labour, but that it also enables the managers of capital to control workers impersonally and unobtrusively by mechanical means in addition to organizational means. More specifically, so long as it is maintained in good working order, machinery, or dead labour, has three major advantages over workers, or living labour: it is invariably more persistent, consistent and acquiescent. Thus, the use of machinery ensures that the same precise actions are performed repeatedly and without question. By comparison, a worker, however assiduous and conscientious, will tire, become distracted, perform variably, and protest about the conditions and rewards of work if necessary. In addition to these productivity advantages, capital also benefits from savings by reducing the number of workers required, plus the training time and pay of those retained. In short, mechanization cheapens labour while simultaneously deskilling it, both in the interests of capital. Little wonder that capitalists are keen to design machines that incorporate the knowledge and skill of the worker, ideally to the point where the majority of industrial and the service workers are reduced to monitoring the automatic production process.

Interestingly, in support of this part of his analysis, Braverman cites the research on automation and skill by Bright (1958), as did Blauner before him, but interprets his research findings quite differently. Blauner picked out one of only two dimensions of Bright's research which showed a mixture of an increase/decrease in skill with the most advanced mechanization, namely responsibility, and relegated to a footnote Bright's point that 'automation does not necessarily raise skill requirements. In some cases it actually reduces skill levels' (Blauner, 1964: 134). However, Braverman noted that all the other skill indicators used by Bright, such as dexterity, general skill, experience, decision-making, and so on, showed that the skill requirements of advanced automation were either decreased or nil, and quoted his conclusion that 'there was more evidence that automation had reduced the skill requirements of the operating work force, and occasionally of the entire factory force, including the maintenance organization' (Braverman, 1974: 220). As an alternative to Blauner's inverted, U-shaped declining alienation curve (see Chapter 2, Figure 2.2), Braverman cited Bright's inverted, U-shaped curve of declining skill and, in marked contrast to Blauner, argues that even in the most technologically advanced industries using continuous-process technology, such as the chemical industry, the automation of production places it 'under the control of management engineers and destroys the need for knowledge or training' (ibid.: 225).

Consideration of Bright's analysis of automation and skill shows that Braverman's interpretation is more in tune with his conclusions than was Blauner's. For example, in an article summarizing his research, Bright claims that the conventional wisdom that automation results in higher workforce skills is a myth since it 'often tends to reduce the skill and training required of the work force' (1958: 97). In the pivotal case of the potentially counteracting trend in which automation leads to increased responsibility, Bright concluded that 'those who appreciate the evolutionary nature of mechanization will anticipate that, at some future time, automatic controls will be introduced to provide for this "responsibility" function, too. Eventually even this operator contribution will be reduced or eliminated' (ibid.: 98).

While Bright and Blauner focused on the skill implications of the mechanization of factory work, Braverman analysed factory work, the deskilling of office work, and somewhat more briefly service work, in relation to both scientific management and mechanization. Braverman noted that one of Taylor's followers, Leffingwell, showed how the principles of scientific management were applicable to office work, especially in the larger offices increasingly to be found in the service sector, such as mail order companies. The Taylorization of office work was followed by its mechanization and achieved the 'conversion of the office routine into a factory-like process' and the 'great mass of office workers into more or less helpless attendants of that process' (Braverman, 1974: 347). Braverman's analysis of the deskilling of clerical work echoed Mills (1968 [1951]) who had argued a generation earlier that when the twin forces of scientific management and mechanization are introduced into large offices, work becomes standardized and resembles a factory production line. They also both noted that the combination of deskilled office work which required minimal training, and the feminization of the clerical labour force during the twentieth century in America, 'made it possible to lower wage rates' (Braverman, 1974: 353). Thus, the deskilling of skilled factory work is paralleled by the deskilling of office and service sector work, a process that is moving inexorably up the occupational hierarchy. In terms of the class structure, according to Braverman, manual workers and the expanded clerical and service sector workers are now part of an increasingly homogenized working class.

In his final chapter, Braverman turned his attention to the 'impressionistic' and 'self-evident' theory that the increased mechanization of work requires an increasingly better educated and trained workforce, namely the upgrading of work thesis (ibid.: 424). Braverman noted that the terms used in this debate, such as skill, training and education, are problematic in their vagueness and that those who advocate the upgrading thesis tend to rely on two alleged trends: first, that there has been a shift of workers from lower to higher occupational categories and, second, that the average amount of time spent in education has increased. Braverman argued that the retrospective introduction of the category operatives who are deemed to be semi-skilled achieved, 'with a mere stroke of the pen, a massive "upgrading" of the skills of the working population' (ibid.: 429). Hence, the upgrading of large numbers of manual workers is a statistical illusion that is compounded by the growth of non-manual work and the 'prejudice' which assumes all such work to be more skilled than manual work (ibid.: 435). Regarding the second reason commonly advanced in support of the upgrading thesis, Braverman agreed that the length of time spent in education prior to entering the workforce has lengthened, but argued that the 'connection between education and job content is, for the mass of jobs, a false one', since, for the majority, their educational achievements exceed those required by most jobs (ibid.: 440). Thus the raising of the school-leaving age and the growth of educational certification have more to do with reducing unemployment and screening, 'even when job content is not necessarily becoming more complex or requiring higher levels of skills', than it does with the alleged need for a better educated workforce (ibid.: 438). The issue of raising the school leaving age in the UK to 18 was high on the political agenda during a period of rapidly expanding unemployment, especially among the young (Seager, 2009), thereby confirming Braverman's argument. Figure 3.1 summarizes Braverman's deskilling thesis.

Braverman was not the first deskilling theorist (arguably Marx was), but he is the best-known contemporary one by virtue of the commitment and comprehensiveness of his account. Notwithstanding the important non-Marxist contributions by Mills (1968 [1951]), Friedmann (1955), and Bright (1958), all of whom were cited by Braverman, the case for deskilling remains dominated by Braverman's thesis.

Blue-/white-collar craft work > Taylorism + mechanization

= Increased managerial control and decreased work skills

Figure 3.1 Braverman's deskilling thesis

Critique of Braverman's deskilling thesis

Braverman's deskilling thesis has been the subject of a veritable plethora of critical comment as befits a study that sparked a prolonged bout of 'Bravermania' (Salaman, 1986: 17). After more than three decades of extensive criticism and research on the capitalist labour process, Braverman's account of deskilling has been accorded the status of a classic book on the grounds that it transformed both the sociology of work and the sociology of class (Burawoy, 1996). The many criticisms of his deskilling thesis can be summarized with reference to four main interrelated ones concerning his limited craft definition of skill, powerful managers and powerless workers, gender-blindness, and that he understated the possibility of upskilling.

(1) Braverman conceptualized skill from a craft perspective since he claimed that '[f]rom the earliest times to the Industrial Revolution the craft or skilled trade was the basic unit, the elementary cell of the labour process', and proceeded to depict factory work and clerical work in the nineteenth century as crafts (1974: 109). His craft perspective is also clear from his concluding chapter on skill, where he noted that, '[f]or the worker, the concept of skill is traditionally bound up with craft mastery – that is to say, the combination of knowledge of materials and processes with the practiced manual dexterities required to carry on a specific branch of production' (ibid.: 443). Thus, for Braverman, the decline of skill is the equivalent of the decline of craft work.

The main problem with this key aspect of Braverman's deskilling thesis is that of romanticizing the pre-modern skilled manual worker (Cutler, 1978; Littler, 1982). This line of criticism is more than a matter of idealizing the past; it concerns the empirical question of the representativeness of the craft worker prior to the rise of scientific management and mechanization in America from about 1900 onwards. On this crucial issue, Braverman implied that craft workers were central to all production processes in the nineteenth century, which 'distorts their numerical importance since skilled workers did not constitute even a majority of the labour force' (Stark, 1980: 94). It has been noted that the majority of the pre-industrial capitalist labour force were not craft workers, but 'farm-labourers and domestic servants' (Rose, 1988: 317). Consequently, assuming Braverman was correct in his claim that manual and non-manual craft-based workers were deskilled by the twin forces of Taylorism and mechanization, this process was not the experience of the majority of workers. Even among craft workers, there were clear variations in the extent to which they yielded to managerial power and were therefore able to resist deskilling, as point *(2)* below shows.

Braverman's tendency to idealize atypical craft work applies not just to manual workers but also to non-manual workers. Braverman likened clerical work to a craft and contrasted the 'small and privileged clerical stratum of the past' with the enlarged Taylorized and mechanized and hence deskilled clerical class of today (1974: 304). Research covering clerical workers in Britain and America has shown that Braverman's highly skilled clerical workers 'were a small minority (5 to 10 per cent) of [Victorian] clerks' (Attewell, 1989: 369). There was an office hierarchy in the nineteenth century and the majority of clerks undertook work of a routine and repetitive kind. It is difficult to avoid the conclusion that such 'false nostalgia' is an inadequate basis upon which to advance a theory of universal deskilling (ibid.: 384).

In the case of the development of data-processing work during the middle of the twentieth century, Braverman also argued that for a short time it 'displayed the characteristics of a craft' (1974: 329). However, 'along with the computer a new division of labour was introduced and the destruction of the craft greatly hastened' (ibid.: 329). At the upper echelons of the computer hierarchy a small number of technical specialists are retained but below this minority a mass of operators undertake work that has been 'simplified, routinized, and measured', ensuring the increasing similarity between work in an electronic office and a factory (ibid.: 335). Evidence on the degradation of computer work in support of Braverman is mixed. First, it has been argued that while Braverman's thesis with respect to the computerization of office work applies well to the USA, where Taylorism was implemented more extensively than elsewhere, it applies less well to Europe, notably Germany, where secretarial work skills 'are regarded as professional' (Webster, 1996: 121). Second, it has been shown that the computerization of office work involves a 'shift in personnel requirements', with an increased emphasis on social skills such as communication and the ability to learn new technical skills as the pace of technological change increases (Woodfield, 2000: 35). Either way, and notwithstanding the problem of getting social skills acknowledged and valued as highly as technical skills, the gender aspect of which is discussed below (point 3), at the very least this suggests that the degradation of computer work is far from assured. In fact, the use of advanced technology such as computers has been found to be 'strongly associated with having experienced an increase in skill requirements' (Gallie et al., 1998: 48).

(2) Braverman's picture of powerful managers and powerless workers has led to the claim that this aspect of his account of deskilling is 'seriously deficient' (Brown, 1992: 206). The claim is that 'Braverman portrays the capitalist class as veritably omniscient and the working class as infinitely malleable', hence he overestimates the extent to which capitalists were able and willing to implement Taylorism and underestimates the degree to which workers, especially craft workers, resisted individually and collectively the deskilling impact of Taylorization and mechanization (Stark, 1980: 92).

Three main reasons have been advanced for the reluctance of managers to embrace Taylorism. First, Thompson has suggested that they were unconvinced about the 'value' of Taylorism (1983: 14), in part, because it has been shown that implementing scientific management in a thorough manner could take between two and four years (Layton, 1971), and in part because Taylorized piece-rate schemes did not eradicate the problem of workers deceiving managers and continuing to restrict output (Edwards, 1979). Second, managers were concerned that the introduction of scientific management might provoke conflict in the form of strikes in the short run and jeopardize worker co-operation in the longer term (Friedman, 1977). Third, managers considered that their authority and hence their position were threatened by the new efficiency engineers who might be more interested in productivity than profits (Stabile, 1984). Taylor was aware of the reluctance of managers to implement scientific management since in his Testimony to the House of Representatives he stated that; 'nine-tenths of our trouble has been to "bring" those on the management's side to do their fair share of the work and only one-tenth of the trouble has come from the workman's side' (Taylor, 1947 [1912]: 43). This has been confirmed by several historians of American business, who have concluded that during his lifetime Taylorism encountered far more opposition from managers than from workers (Stark, 1980).

Worker opposition to scientific management was particularly widespread during the early attempts to implement it in America, such that in 1914 the government commissioned an investigation into the relationship between scientific management and labour, known as the Hoxie Report (Stark, 1980). In terms of Braverman's pivotal craft workers, historical research in America and Britain has shown that they were often successful in defending their control of the labour process, and hence their status as skilled workers, via a combination of local and national collective action (Montgomery, 1979; Zeitlin, 1985). Thus, while some craft workers conformed to Braverman's theory in the sense that they were unsuccessful in their efforts to resist the deskilling impact of Taylorism, notably engineers in Britain between 1890 and 1914, other craft workers, such as compositors, were able to defend and even enhance their position in the division of labour during the same period. According to Zeitlin: 'A crucial determinant of the balance of forces between skilled workers and employers in each case lay in the relative cohesion and capacity for collective action on each side' (1985: 238).

The combination of managerial and worker resistance to Taylorism meant that the ideas of scientific management, advocated by, among others, Henry Ford and Lenin, met with more approval than its practices (Friedman, 1977). Although Taylorism was implemented widely in America, but not always in a pure form and not without opposition, in Europe and Japan, it was adopted later, unevenly, and also in a diluted form when it was resisted by managers and workers (Littler, 1982).

Braverman was not unaware that in America Taylorism 'antagonized workers and sometimes management as well' but his 'self-imposed limitation' to consider only 'the shape given to the working population by the capital accumulation process', ruled out an analysis of the practical (class) consequences of the attempt to introduce scientific management (1974: 27, 87). This restriction not only left Braverman vulnerable to the criticism that he exaggerated the power of managers to implement Taylorism and underestimated the power of workers to resist it, but it also exposed him to further criticisms; that his account of deskilling was 'one-sided' and hence deterministic since he considered deskilling to be the inevitable outcome of the spread of Taylorism and increased mechanization without analysing the relationship between the managers and the managed (Mackenzie, 1977: 249). Such an analysis would have shown that, among other things, in the process of using their union-based bargaining strength to successfully defend their status and pay as skilled workers, some groups of male workers sought to exclude women from the same relatively privileged position (Rubery, 1980; Walby, 1986). The pattern of resistance to Taylorism indicates that the working class is not as homogeneous as Braverman claimed, it is divided by skill and gender.

(3) Braverman's gender-blindness is apparent from his failure to examine how patriarchy contaminates definitions of skill. Braverman defined skill in a gender-neutral way by reference to craft mastery, namely 'the combination of knowledge of materials and processes with the practiced manual dexterities required to carry on a specific branch of production' (1974: 443). This approach has been called 'technicist' because it defines 'skill as technique, a combination of manual and mental capacities for manipulating objects and tools' (Blackburn and Mann, 1979: 292). The alternative to Braverman's essentially technicist approach to skill is one that acknowledges that skill contains a social dimension in addition to a technical one, sometimes called the 'political' aspect of skill since it involves the element of power (ibid.: 292).

Patriarchal assumptions can influence the definition of skill in two main ways. First, irrespective of the content of a job, the 'work of women is often deemed to be inferior simply because it is women who do it' (Phillips and Taylor, 1980: 79). A good example of this is provided by Phillips and Taylor, who cite some empirical research in which the male workers who were undertaking less skilled work than women in a technical sense were classified as semi-skilled whereas the women were classified as unskilled. In another example of the same tendency, Phillips and Taylor quote the researcher's conclusion that for some women workers 'the only way to become skilled was to change sex' (ibid.: 83). Thus, upon entering work outside the home, women carry with them their subordinate status, namely that they are seen and treated by male managers and workers, and sometimes by women also, as being primarily responsible for the domestic sphere, the concomitant of which is that paid work is considered to be of lesser importance to women. Needless to say, the tendency to devalue women workers is to the advantage of employers in the form of lower wages and to male workers in the form of higher wages.

A second form of patriarchal bias is the tendency to undervalue female skills, notably emotional, social and caring skills, on the specious grounds that these kinds of skill are part of being a woman and as such are gained without formal training or via workplace experience (Davies and Rosser, 1986). Although there are clear parallels between these skills and those associated with being a wife and mother, they tend to be devalued by virtue of this association (Thornley, 1996). For example, historically, nursing has been a female-dominated type of work, and although it requires extensive knowledge and training, it has not been regarded as a 'technical job because it is women's work and therefore undervalued' (Wajcman, 1991: 36). Similarly, a study of life assurance sales work showed that a range of skills are required, some of which are associated with masculinity (e.g., ambition and competitiveness), while others are associated with femininity (e.g., caring and communication). It was found that masculine attributes were overvalued by management during recruitment and promotion, whereas feminine ones were not even included in job descriptions, to the advantage of men and to the detriment of women (Collinson and Knights, 1986). In non-traditional areas of female employment, such as insurance sales, the sexual harassment of women by their male colleagues was also used to exclude women from this type of work (Collinson and Collinson, 1996).

Braverman indicated his awareness of patriarchy and its implications for work when he noted: 'The sex barrier that assigns most office jobs to women, and that is enforced both by custom and hiring practice, has made it possible to lower wage rates in the clerical category' (1974: 353). To this extent his approach was not entirely technicist, but he failed to examine the extent to which the meaning of skill is influenced by ideas about gender as well as technical considerations. Ironically, social skills, which have been associated historically with femininity and hence undervalued, have become more important as a result of the growth of service work, especially in terms of the upskilling of women (Gallie et al., 1998). The possibility that upskilling exceeds deskilling is the subject of the fourth major criticism of Braverman's thesis.

(4) Braverman underestimated the extent of upskilling in a valiant attempt to counter the prevailing conventional wisdom that there has been a general upgrading of work, especially with regard to clerical workers. Braverman considered this to be a major myth promulgated by the 'practice of academic sociology and popular journalism' (1974: 293). Although he was aware of the unevenness of the deskilling process as a result of social changes in the organization and mechanization of production which created 'new crafts and skills and technical specialties', he considered such eventualities as temporary (ibid.: 170). According to Braverman, the best workers could hope for is to delay the 'historical process of devaluation of the worker's skill' when managers opt for 'patience' rather than 'a bitter battle with the union' (ibid.: 203).

In the case of the increased demand for maintenance workers and technical specialists, such as engineers, who are responsible for the conceptualization and planning of production, it is the same story. Braverman argued that there was a tendency for their work to be 'standardized in much the same fashion as that of the production worker', due in large part to the introduction of 'computers and numerical control instrumentation' (ibid.: 223, 244), although Braverman did concede that the computerization of clerical work creates the 'exception of a specialized minority whose technical and "systems" skills are expanded' (ibid.: 339). However, this exception to the deskilling imperative inherent in industrial capitalism is not thought by Braverman to be a threat to his thesis since the majority of new technical specialists are rationalized in due course, degraded via the familiar twin forces of Taylorism and mechanization.

Research on industrial workers, which focused mainly on the period between 1940 and 1980, concluded that 'skilled workers remain a central grouping within the division of labour in both America and Britain', and that while some skilled jobs have declined, such as compositing skills in printing, 'this has been compensated for by the rise of welding, sheetmetal working, car repairing and machine maintenance skills' (Penn, 1990: 166). A similar conclusion was reached in a study of skill and organizational and technical change, namely the introduction of teamwork and robots affecting car workers in America during the mid-1980s. It was found that already deskilled production workers remained deskilled or experienced further deskilling following these changes, whereas skilled workers experienced considerable upgrading, and that this was particularly marked for the 'high-tech maintenance workers' (Milkman and Pullman, 1991: 143).

Braverman's supporters

The force of these criticisms of Braverman's deskilling thesis could be interpreted as suggesting that little merit attaches to his analysis. This would be a mistake since there are many studies that are supportive of Braverman, notably the American research by Burawoy of a piecework machine-shop (1979), Gartman's historical account of the labour process in the American car industry (1987), and Garson's study of office automation (1988), plus several British studies (Cockburn, 1983; Cooley, 1987 [1980]; Cooper et al., 1998; Crompton and Jones, 1984; Lee, 1981), as well as reviews of deskilling research that are broadly favourable of Braverman's approach and conclusions (e.g., Thompson, 1983). Burawoy endorses Braverman's deskilling thesis but adds two important qualifications. First, he suggests that the destruction of craft skills was a more 'uneven' process than Braverman allows, and, second, he argues that capitalist control over workers is achieved not just by the coercive influence of Taylorism and mechanization, but by the active complicity of the workers themselves (Burawoy, 1979: 198). He focuses on the ways in which consent is generated as workers participate in work games, such as meeting output targets: 'Workers are sucked into the game as a way of reducing the level of deprivation' (ibid.: 199). Consent is therefore 'manufactured' via the managerial organization of work within the factory, which 'allows the degradation of work to pursue its course without continuing crisis' (ibid.: 94). This more subtle analysis of how capitalism achieves the co-operation of exploited and oppressed workers has been criticized for overestimating the degree of consent achieved by game playing, thereby underestimating the radical potential of workplace culture (Thompson, 1983).

Gartman's study is based on Braverman's thesis yet complements it by analysing the motives that informed managerial decisions about how to organize
and mechanize car production in America during the first half of the twentieth
century. Gartman distinguishes analytically between 'non-repressive control'
that arises from the need to co-ordinate production in large-scale organizations, and 'repressive control' that is 'made necessary by the antagonistic relations of production' (1987: 8). In practice, however, the Taylorization and
mechanization of car production work were motivated by a combination of
non-repressive advantages (e.g., increased efficiency) and repressive advantages (e.g., decreased discretion). Gartman suggests that while owners and
managers tended to emphasize, in public at least, their non-repressive motives,
documentary evidence shows that their main motivation was to repress the
resistance of workers to changes in production that increased their exploitation and degradation.

Garson traced the impact of computers on a variety of white-collar jobs,
selecting workplaces that were 'typical of the present and indicative of the
future', rather than extreme cases (1988: 12). Drawing upon the research by
Braverman, Garson updates his analysis with reference to expert systems to
argue that Taylorization and computerization have extended the deskilling
process to include all kinds of work that previously required expertise, such as
airline reservation agents, social workers and financial consultants. Expert systems are computer programmes developed by knowledge engineers after
interviewing a range of experts to replicate their professional knowledge, experience and judgement. The purpose of expert systems is Taylorist; 'to transfer
knowledge, skill and decision making from the employee to the employer'; the
result is deskilling; 'less skill, less autonomy and fewer good jobs' and standardized '"mass-produced" human services' (ibid.: 120, 159). From the standpoint
of the employer, expert systems enable them to recruit, train, monitor, control,
and replace workers with greater ease, and pay them less than they would have
to pay professional staff.

Cockburn's (1983) study of the deskilling of male print workers following
the introduction of computerized photo composition supported but modified
Braverman's analysis in two ways. First, it showed that initially the new technology 'did indeed bring the expected polarization of work into routine
unskilled occupations and enhanced technological occupations', but later produced 'a cluster of semi-skilled, semi-responsible linked occupations'; in other
words, deskilling (1983: 119). Second, the degradation experienced by the
male printers was made more acute by the perception that they were not only
'slipping perilously down the worker scale toward the general "hand" labourer',
but were also 'reduced to the level of women' (ibid.: 118). This was because
the new computer technology had made the work of a printer physically and
mentally easier, thereby undermining two of the historic arguments advanced
by men for excluding women from this work. The deskilled result was
regarded as transforming what was once a male job into one that a woman

could do; the equivalent of 'bloody typists' (ibid.: 118). Thus, for Cockburn, skill was a matter of gender power as much as class power.

On the basis of intensive case studies and questionnaire data involving local authority, insurance and bank clerks, Crompton and Jones' findings provide concrete evidence to support the '"Bravermanesque" thesis that clerical work *has* been "proletarianized"' (1984: 210; italics in the original). However, this support for Braverman was qualified in that office workers were not a 'mass', but stratified by age, qualifications and above all gender, with women predominating in the more numerous deskilled lower levels of the bureaucratic hierarchy and men in the fewer higher-level upskilled positions.

Cooley's analysis of the impact of computer-aided design (CAD) unambiguously supports Braverman: 'There is already evidence to show that CAD, when introduced on the basis of so-called efficiency, gives rise to deskilling of the design function and a loss of job security' (1987 [1980]: 72). This study lends powerful support to Braverman, especially the myth of the politically neutral technology and the non-manual dimensions of his thesis, although he diverges from Braverman's passive worker analysis by suggesting that class struggle offers the prospect of an alternative to the degradation of deskilling.

Lee's study using official labour statistics and other survey data is particularly pertinent because it focuses on industries where (male) craft employment is substantial and therefore deals with a central feature of Braverman's thesis. As Table 3.1 shows, though the percentage of skilled workers in engineering and shipbuilding was high, during the recession of the 1970s it declined in absolute and relative terms. Lee concluded that: 'There need be little doubt, therefore, about the deskilling effect of the recession' (1981: 67). Older workers are especially prone to cyclical deskilling as they are likely to experience greater difficulty than younger redundant craft workers in obtaining comparable skilled work. While this analysis supports the deskilling thesis, it does not do so by tracing it to forces internal to the labour process, but by looking at the external factor of the labour market for skilled workers during a slowdown in economic activity. Conversely, Lee points out that the development of new technologies and products during an expansionary economic era creates new skills and therefore opportunities for upskilling. Table 3.1 shows the absolute and relative changes in skilled employment in engineering and shipbuilding between 1965 and 1975.

Table 3.1 Absolute and relative changes in skilled employment in two industries, 1965–75

Year	Engineering		Shipbuilding	
	All skilled 000's	% of operatives	All skilled 000's	% of operatives
1965	961	37.4	84	56.4
1975	739	30.3	71	53.2

Source: Abridged version of Table 1 in Lee (1981: 64).

Finally, one of the most supportive studies of Braverman's deskilling of clerical work aspect of his thesis is the one by Cooper et al. (1998), who investigated newspaper advertisements in Glasgow between 1974–96 and found that the impact of Taylorization, computerization, and feminization on non-professionally qualified accountancy workers was to transform the nineteenth-century bookkeeping craft into a low-paid deskilled job with little prospect of promotion. This study validates Braverman's long-term perspective regarding the ongoing process of deskilling and corroborates all aspects of his thesis.

More generally, in a detailed review of research on contemporary vehicle and digital (call centres) assembly line production, it has been argued that,

every worker who has ever worked on an assembly line ... has to some degree been an object of scientific management ... This remains as true today as it was eighty-five years ago, and looks set to remain true well into the twenty-first century. (Head, 2005: 24)

Similarly, the continued relevance of Braverman's labour process approach rather than his deskilling thesis, is evident from empirical research on service work conducted since the 1980s (Warhurst et al., 2009). The contemporary manifestation of Taylorism in both industrial and service work, and hence to deskilling, shows that Braverman's view of the historical significance of scientific management was not misplaced.

Summary and conclusions

The idea that deskilling was an inevitable and universal tendency endemic to the historical development of industrial capitalism characterized by the unstinting search for profit and the control of labour derives from Marx's writings on nineteenth-century England. Braverman updated this account with reference to America and in doing so exemplifies this approach so clearly and thoroughly that the publication of his book *Labour and Monopoly Capitalism: The Degradation of Work in the Twentieth Century* (1974) had a profound impact on sociology. It redirected and revived both the sociology of work by refocusing research on the workplace and the labour process, and the sociology of class by refocusing research on the links between work and class (Littler and Salaman, 1982). Although in a reassessment of the debate that Braverman inspired, it has been argued that his radical agenda has been diluted by subsequent research (Spencer, 2000).

Braverman starts with a nineteenth-century craft model of skill, which emphasizes task-specific training, and goes on to argue that the combination of scientific management (Taylorism) and machinery (technology) under the direction of the owners of capital and their representatives, have a deleterious impact on the work skills of both manual and non-manual workers. Fundamental to Taylorism is that: 'All possible brain work should be removed from the [work] shop and centred in the planning or layout department' (Taylor, 1947 [1911]: 98–9). According to Braverman, this increased the power of managers to control the simplified task performance of workers. Similarly, the introduction of machinery involved the unobtrusive control over the pace of work, hence it too furthered the interests of capital rather than labour. Thus Taylorism transfers a worker's knowledge and control of work processes to managers, and technology transfers a worker's skill and control to the machinery owned by capital. For Braverman, deskilling and dehumanization were therefore built in to the structure of work of industrial capitalism, and culminate in the homogenization and proletarianization of an expanded working class. The growth of clerical and service sector jobs, noted by Braverman, is part of this ongoing historical process.

Although Braverman's contribution to the debate about deskilling is widely considered to be seminal, it has not escaped extensive criticism. He has been accused of idealizing craft work, portraying managers as all-powerful and workers as impotent, having a patriarchal bias, and underestimating the possibility of upskilling associated with new technology. Considered together, these criticisms suggest that Braverman's ambitious claim of one general deskilling trend was at best an exaggeration and at worst deterministic since subsequent empirical research has shown that deskilling is an uneven process which varies over time and space depending on a number of factors, such as technological and organizational changes in the workplace and the scale of resistance to Taylorism by workers and managers. The important implications of this conclusion are the possibility that deskilling has been exported via the transfer of low-skill jobs to industrializing countries and that deskilling was more prevalent in mass production and during the initial phase of computerization, whereas upskilling tends to be more common in advanced economies characterized by the increasing use of microcomputers in both manufacturing and service work (Castells, 2001; Coombs, 1985; Thompson, 1983). These possibilities will be explored in detail in the next and subsequent chapters.

However, Braverman's deskilling thesis is not without support, especially from those who share his Marxist approach, such as Burawoy (1979), Cockburn (1983), Cooper et al. (1998), plus others who have sought to put some contemporary empirical flesh on the nineteenth-century Marxian bones of his theory. Gartman (1987) in particular complements Braverman's account by placing the class struggle at the centre of his historical analysis of the motives of organizational and technical changes to car production in America that impacted negatively on manual workers. These Braverman-inspired studies show that when the issue of skill is seen in the context of class and gender struggles, it is a more complex matter than Braverman's theory of the capitalist labour process allows, while confirming that the overall direction of change is one of deskilling of both factory and office work.

There is evidence from Britain and America of both blue- and white-collar deskilling, which along with the criticisms, has led to an increased understanding of the capitalist labour process and some important modifications to Braverman's thesis. Consequently, it is impossible to ignore Braverman's deskilling thesis since it has been shown by many studies, including those by Garson, Head, and Warhurst et al., to be of continuing relevance to both industrial and service work.

The issues raised by Braverman's deskilling thesis remain the subject of research and debate in the sociology of work (e.g., Aronowitz and DiFazio, 1994), especially with reference to service and part-time work, topics that will be discussed further in Chapters 6 and 7. The key question prompted by Braverman's thesis is whether or not deskilling is a major or minor trend. In order to address this point, upskilling needs to be considered. This is the subject of Chapter 4.

Further reading

BOOKS In addition to reading Braverman's famous study, Wood (ed.) (1982) *The Degradation of Work? Skill, Deskilling and the Labour Process* covers the range of criticisms directed at Braverman's thesis as well as providing some supportive evidence. The significance of Taylorism historically and comparatively with reference to Britain, the USA, and Japan, is discussed by Littler (1982) *The Development of the Labour Process in Capitalist Societies*. The gender dimension of deskilling is demonstrated by Cockburn (1983) *Brothers: Male Dominance and Technological Change*, and the importance of antagonistic class relations is documented by Gartman (1987) *Auto Slavery: The Labour Process in the American Automobile Industry, 1897–1950*. In view of the centrality of scientific management to Braverman's analysis of deskilling and its relevance to later chapters, Taylor's writings on the subject should be consulted; *Scientific Management* (1947) contains his three major works, namely *Shop Management* (1903), *Principles of Scientific Management* (1911), and his *Testimony Before the Special House Committee* (1912). The specialist textbook by Thompson (1983) *The Nature of Work: An Introduction to Debates on the Labour Process* provides an in-depth analysis of Braverman's thesis. For accounts of the continuing relevance of Taylorism and deskilling, consult the very readable and provocative Garson (1988) *Electronic Sweatshop: How Computers are Transforming the Office of the Future into the Factory of the Past* and Head (2005) *The New Ruthless Economy: Work and Power in the Digital Age*.

ARTICLES Lee (1981) 'Skill, craft and class: a theoretical critique and a critical case', *Sociology*, 15(1): 56–78 provides an empirically informed evaluation of Braverman's thesis. Spencer (2000) 'Braverman and the contribution of labour process analysis to the critique of capitalist production – twenty-five years on', *Work, Employment and Society*, 14(2): 223–43 considers the debate inspired by Braverman's thesis with reference to his radical agenda.

WEBSITES
For a brief contextualization of the contribution of Braverman plus a useful annotated bibliography consult the material by Smith that can be found at www.ilpc.org.uk/Portals/56/ilpc-docs/ILPC- Background.pdf

Questions for discussion and assessment

1 On what grounds did Braverman advance his deskilling thesis?
2 Assess critically Braverman's deskilling thesis.
3 Evaluate the strengths of Braverman's deskilling thesis.
4 Examine the view that the gender dimension is the main weakness of Braverman's study.
5 Do you agree that Braverman overestimated the influence of Taylorism on the organization of work?
6 How has post-Braverman research advanced our understanding of deskilling?
7 Consider the impact of Braverman on the sociology of work.

4

WORK, UPSKILLING AND POLARIZATION

In order to assess fully the debate about deskilling, the issues of upskilling and polarization also need to be considered. In the same way that deskilling theories can be traced back to Marx, upskilling theories have their origins in the writings of Weber on the increased demand for educational qualifications by the expanding number of bureaucratic organizations (Edgell, 1993). This is apparent in Bell's version of upskilling, with its emphasis on the centrality of knowledge and the growth of technical specialists (1976 [1973]). Bell's version of post-industrial upskilling is not especially original but it is arguably the 'most frequently quoted' and 'most systematic' (Kumar, 1978: 196, 197). There are hints of skill polarization in Blauner's study of alienation, although this view gained momentum in the post-Braverman era of social research on work.

Bell's upskilling thesis

Private Prop vs knowledge

Like Braverman, Bell's empirical reference point is America, but in marked contrast to Braverman, Bell argues that in the post-industrial society, the possession of private property as a source of power will be relatively less important compared to the possession of knowledge: 'while property remains an important base [of power], technical skill becomes another, sometimes rival, base with education the means of access to the attainment of technical skill' (1976 [1973]: 115). He also claims that in the post-industrial society the 'non-profit sector' would expand, particularly health, education and research (ibid.: 147). Thus at the core of Bell's post-industrial society upskilling thesis is the idea that

Table 4.1 Industrial and post-industrial societies: contrasting features

	Industrial	Post-industrial
Regions	Western Europe Soviet Union Japan	USA
Economic sector	Goods	Services
occupational slope	Semi-skilled worker Engineer	Professional and technical scientists
Technology	Energy	Information
Primary institution	Business enterprise	University
Design	Game against fabricated nature	Game between persons
Stratification: Base-	Property	Skill
Access-	Inheritance	Education
Axial principle	Economic growth: state or private control of investment decisions	Centrality and codification of theoretical knowledge

Source: Summarized from Bell (1976 [1973]: 117, 118).

theoretical knowledge is the key factor of production in the sense that it becomes the 'source of innovation and policy formulation for the society' (ibid.: 14). Although Bell notes that 'the concept post-industrial society is an analytical construct, not a picture of a specific or concrete society', he considers that the 'United States is no longer an industrial society', but the first post-industrial society, and in the 1970s it was the only one (ibid.: 133). The contrast between industrial and post-industrial societies is summarized in Table 4.1.

Bell's idea of a post-industrial society focuses on changes in the social structure with reference to the economy, the occupational system, and science and technology. From a sociology of work perspective, the main contrasts between an industrial society (IS) and a post-industrial society (PIS) are outlined in Table 4.1. This shows that:

- an IS produces goods whereas a PIS produces services, with a decline in blue-collar workers and a rise in white-collar workers;
- created energy is the transforming resource of an IS whereas in a PIS it is information in the form of computer and data-transmission systems;
- the strategic resource of an IS is financial capital but in a PIS it is knowledge;
- access to capital is via inheritance in an IS and via education in a PIS;
- the key technology of an IS is machine technology but in a PIS it is intellectual technology epitomized by the computer;
- the skill base changes from one dominated by the engineer and semi-skilled worker in an IS to one in which the scientist and technical and professional occupations predominate in a PIS;
- work involves a 'game against fabricated nature' in an IS and a 'game between persons' in a PIS (Bell, 1976 [1973]: 116); and finally,
- the axial principle of economic growth characteristic of an IS is superseded by the codification of theoretical knowledge in a PIS.

educated
= skilled.

In short, a post-industrial society is a white-collar society dominated by service work and the 'centrality of theoretical knowledge' in which the system of social stratification is transformed by the creation of a new 'division between the scientific and technical classes and those who will stand outside' (ibid.: 112). In this new type of society, the 'central person is the professional, for he is equipped by his education and training to provide the kinds of skill which are increasingly demanded in the post-industrial society' (ibid.:127). For Bell, the transformation of the occupational structure in which white-collar workers form the majority of the labour force, with professional and technical workers at the apex of the new class hierarchy, is nothing less than a 'revolution' (ibid.: 125). In support of this claim, Bell provides two main types of past and projected evidence for the USA which shows: (1) a marked decline in semi-skilled manual jobs and a corresponding expansion of professional and technical occupations; and (2) an increasing proportion of young people attaining university degrees, especially higher degrees, particularly in science and engineering. According to Bell, therefore, a post-industrial society is a 'knowledge society' (ibid.: 212).

more people going to uni

Somewhat surprisingly, given the thrust of his thesis, neither skill nor work appear in the index of Bell's book, although these inextricably related issues are discussed widely in the text, usually with reference to social stratification and education. For example, Bell argues that in the recent past, 'the historic base of power has been property, and the means of access through inheritance. Yet while property remains an important base, technical skill becomes another, sometimes rival, base with education the means of access to the attainment of technical skill' (ibid.: 115). In the same vein, Bell emphasizes that technical knowledge as a factor of production puts a premium on the acquisition of technical and professional skills, and this in turn 'makes education, and access to higher education, the condition of entry to the post-industrial society itself' (ibid.: 128, see also 426). In a post-industrial society the demand for more services combined with the 'inadequacy of the market in meeting people's needs for a decent environment as well as better health and education lead to a growth of government' (ibid.: 128). Bell asserts that; 'today, we in America are moving away from a society based on a private-enterprise market system', hence a post-industrial society is also a more communal society in that economic decisions are 'subordinated to, or will derive from, other forces in society' and that other major decisions 'are made by the government, rather than through the market' (ibid.: 297, 344, 364). In effect, Bell is suggesting that in the future, the evolving post-industrial society will be less capitalistic and more meritocratic, with a greater importance attached to the possession of knowledge than the ownership of capital.

In addition to the quantitative changes associated with the emergence of a post-industrial society, notably the decline of blue-collar workers and the increase in white-collar workers, especially the scientific and technical occupational categories, and the inexorable growth of higher education, Bell also outlines some of the concomitant qualitative changes in relation to work. For example, first and most importantly, he argues that in a white-collar society dominated by service work, 'the fact that individuals now talk to other individuals, rather than interact with a machine, is the fundamental fact about work in the post-industrial society' (ibid.: 163). Consequently, the 'rhythms of mechanization' which put a premium on physical strength are less 'pervasive', and have been replaced by a series of images in which information is all important since work relationships are characterized by 'encounter and communication' whether one is selling a product or teaching a student (ibid.: 162, 163). Second, hierarchical work structures will be modified 'by encouraging committees and participation' which, when combined with 'the inevitable end of the "fee-for-service" relationship' in medicine and other non-profit sectors, will lead to the 'emergence of new structural forms of non-bureaucratic organization' (ibid.: 153, 154, 324). Third, compared to the large bureaucratic corporation typical of industrial society,

> the distinctive character of the services sector is the small size of the unit enterprise. ... Even where unit size is larger, in hospitals and schools, what is different about these enterprises is the larger degree of autonomy of smaller units ... and the greater degree of professional control. (ibid.: 161)

The contrast to work in an industrial society is stark; brains have replaced brawn, democracy has replaced despotism, and small work groups have replaced large-scale organizations. Bell uses the term 'non-bureaucratic', rather than the currently more usual term 'post-bureaucratic', to describe the emergence of new organizational forms that encourage 'initiative' and are characterized by 'joint consultation' (ibid.: 324).

In sum, Bell's upskilling post-industrial society thesis is a mixture of quantitative changes, such as the dramatic increase in education and white-collar work, and qualitative changes, such as the tendency for service work to involve interacting with people rather than machines. For Bell, this all adds up to a new type of society, a post-industrial society that is totally different from its predecessor, the industrial society, especially in terms of the predominant kind of work and workers, namely post-industrial services.

In support of his upskilling thesis Bell presents a large number of statistical tables and other quantitative data that purport to show that America is already well on the way to being a post-industrial society and that on the basis of trends at the time Bell was writing, by the end of the twentieth century, it would be one of about a dozen post-industrial nation states, and arguably the most advanced, with New York as the economic capital of the world.

In a later exposition of his thesis, Bell preferred the label 'information society' to his earlier one, post-industrial society, although this concept had already been used (ibid.: 467). Unsurprisingly, the basic thrust of his thesis remained unchanged, namely the inexorable rise of 'information workers' who displace industrial workers as the 'largest single group in the workforce' (Bell, 1980: 523). Hence Bell still refers to the growth of post-industrial services, both 'human' ones, such as teaching and health, and 'professional' ones, such as the programming and processing of information (ibid.: 501). Thus the change from a goods-producing to a service or information society involves the proposition that the organization and processing of information influence the 'character of the occupations and work in which men engage' (ibid.: 500). In practical terms, the expansion of knowledge-based jobs in the emergent post-industrial society requires a highly qualified and skilled labour force, in short, an upskilled one.

Critique of Bell's upskilling thesis

Bell is credited with advancing an upskilling thesis in the context of his theory of post-industrial society (e.g., Gallie, 1991; Penn, 1990). The basic claim that modern societies are dominated by service workers, not industrial workers, is not disputed. What has been disputed is Bell's interpretation of this trend. He has been criticized extensively on four main interconnected grounds: (1) that he idealized service work; (2) that he understated the growth of routine white-collar work; (3) that he misjudged the sociological significance of the expansion of professional work; and (4) that he neglected the gender dimension of work in post-industrial society.

(1) Bell idealized service work in the post-industrial society in the sense that he tended to 'take as the general pattern of work the conditions in the most attractive and prestigious parts of the service sector' (Kumar, 1978: 206). Aside from the problem that the distinction between an industrial sector and a service sector does not 'illuminate effectively the type of work performed' since service workers can be found in both sectors (Webster, 2002: 47), most work in the expanded service sector of advanced industrial capitalist societies is of a routine nature, typically undertaken by women, minorities, and those without a university education, often on a part-time basis for low wages (duRivage, 1992; O'Reilly and Fagan, 1998). For example, work in telephone-based customer services or call centres, 'has become the fastest growing job market in the UK' and was expected to account for over 3 per cent of all employees by 2008 (Kilpern, 2001). In marked contrast to Bell's optimism regarding the upskilled character of service sector work, in this type of service work the 'typical call centre operator is young, female' and 'is increasingly likely to be a part-time permanent employee' (Taylor and Bain, 1999: 115). Moreover, 'irrespective of the quality of service workflow', the majority of call-centre workers experience work routinization and intensification in the form of highly scripted and therefore repetitive conversations that are monitored, involving minimal discretion or creative responsibility (Taylor et al., 2002: 148). This evidence is far more supportive of Braverman's deskilling thesis than Bell's alternative upskilling thesis.

Thus, the growth of the service sector is far from synonymous with upskilling, and although service work often involves a demand for new communication skills and the kinds of specialist knowledge highlighted by Bell, recent research suggests that this does not apply to the majority of call-centre or other types of service workers, such as fast-food restaurant staff (Macdonald and Sirianni, 1996), or low wage, limited on-the-job training, female-dominated care and health assistants who are expected to be two of the fastest growing occupations in the USA between 2006–16 (www.bls.gov/news.release/ecopro. t06.htm). In short, Bell can be criticized for generalizing from the work experience of a relatively small and unrepresentative group of scientific and professional workers. Most service sector work, as the following overlapping criticism makes clear, does not conform to Bell's model of the upskilled knowledge worker, working autonomously and interacting with others in a small, non-hierarchical, post-bureaucratic organization.

(2) Bell understated the growth of routine white-collar work when he argued that '[t]he expansion of the service economy, with its emphasis on office work, education, and government, has naturally brought about a shift to white-collar occupations' (1976 [1973]: 17). Aside from the deterministic thrust of this assertion (Penn, 1983), within the emerging white-collar majority, Bell emphasized the 'startling' growth rate, 'twice that of the average labour force', of professional and technical employment, and in particular noted that the 'growth rate of the scientists and engineers has been triple that of the working population' (1976 [1973]: 17). He concluded that this massive growth would lead to the 'dominance of the professional and technical class in the labour force' (ibid.: 125).

As with the first criticism, the claim that the post-industrial society is a white-collar society is incontestable on the basis of the available employment statistics. However, the suggestion that white-collar work is qualitatively different in that it requires a college education and involves working with people rather than machines, particularly in non-profit organizations, and helps to promote a sense of community, and that such work is more skilled and satisfying, is less than convincing given the 'tendency to glamorize white-collar work by drawing selectively on some of its more attractive but quite unrepresentative areas' (Kumar, 1978: 209).

Although many of the newer white-collar jobs do indeed involve interacting with people rather than machines, Bell underestimated the extent to which such work has been rationalized, mechanized and, as a consequence, routinized by the imperative to make a profit in a competitive market system, in the manner described by Braverman and discussed in Chapter 3 (Kumar, 1978). Post-Braverman research on white-collar work has shown that computerization aided the Taylorization of work, and hence extended deskilling to clerical work and even managerial and professional work (Kumar, 1995). For example, one British study of the impact of computerization on clerical work concluded:

The clerk now typically performs more exclusively the functions of (deskilled) labour, being increasingly peripheral to the performance of the computer and having little or no responsibility for the co-ordination and completion of the many separate work tasks in the process as a whole. (Crompton and Reid, 1982: 176)

Similarly, as noted in the previous chapter, professionals such as industrial designers have found their work standardized and hence deskilled by the introduction of computer-aided design (Cooley, 1987 [1980]). Given the higher pay of such specialists, there is a major economic incentive to Taylorize their work, and at least one researcher has suggested that it is professional workers who are most at risk of being deskilled (Baran, 1988).

Thus, Bell's focus on the expansion of white-collar work, and especially professional experts, combined with his neglect to consider the potential and extent of Taylorization among non-manual occupations following the widespread adoption of computers in the workplace, contributed to his underestimation of the persistence of routine white-collar work.

(3) Bell misjudged the sociological significance of the expansion of professional work in the sense that he overlooked a range of influences on such work which undermine his upskilling thesis. Apart from the tendency to re-label work that is essentially unskilled manual work in a way that implies a degree of technical expertise, for instance, referring to a garbage collector as a 'sanitary engineer' (Bell, 1976 [1973]: 153), as noted above, professional workers are far from immune to the logic of the capitalist market system. Hence the growth of public sector professional workers, emphasized by Bell, has been accompanied by changes in the political and economic context in which they operate (Crompton, 1990). For example, government policy during the 1980s and 1990s in Britain and America exposed public sector professional workers to market forces via different forms of privatization of state services and the introduction of quasi-markets in the provision of state services, notably health (Edgell and Duke, 1991; Gabe et al., 1990; Schiller, 1996), which suggests that Bell's optimism regarding the decline of the capitalist market system and the 'inevitable end of the "fee-for-service" [doctor–patient] relationship' is misplaced (1976 [1973]: 154). Thus professional work in the public sector in Britain has become more like work in the private sector due to what has been termed 'entrepreneurial government' (Osborne and Gaebler, 1992: 19) and associated tendencies such as the commodification of knowledge (Smart, 1992). These changes have led to an emphasis on accountability, targets, league tables, competition, and value for money, all of which have undermined rather than enhanced the status and autonomy of the professional. Bell is not unaware of what he calls the 'constraints' on the changes he envisages, such as the productivity and cost of professional services, but it does not seem to have tempered his optimism regarding the future of work in a post-industrial society (1976 [1973]: 154).

Furthermore, Bell's emphasis on the growth of research spending as an indicator of the increasing centrality of theoretical knowledge overlooks the extent to which such budgets, and the researchers employed to work on them, are subordinate to the interests of capital (Robins and Webster, 1989). Part of this process is the tendency for university research to be placed on a commercial footing (Schiller, 1996). As a consequence, the expansion of scientific work, like that of routine white-collar work, is subject increasingly to the influence of the capitalist market system, including Taylorization (Kumar, 1995). This is in contrast to the claim that in a post-industrial society non-market forces would become stronger and that therefore it would be a more 'communal society' (Bell, 1976 [1973]: 159).

In advancing his case for the increased importance of professional and technical workers in post-industrial society, Bell placed great weight on the expansion of higher education and presented many tables to support his argument (ibid.: especially Tables 3.1 to 3.21). Yet again the bare statistical 'facts' are impressive and are interpreted to show a direct and simple relationship between more education and an upskilled workforce, which encouraged Bell to proclaim that a post-industrial society is a 'knowledge society' (ibid.: 212). In an early critique of this line of reasoning, Braverman argued that the lengthening of the period spent in education prior to entry to the labour force has 'many causes, most of them bearing no direct relationship to the educational requirements of the job structure' (1974: 437). He suggests that the expansion of education limits the rise of unemployment and expands the employment opportunities of 'teachers, administrators, construction and service workers' (ibid.: 439). He concluded that the 'commonly made connection between education and job content is, for the mass of jobs, a false one' (ibid.: 440; see also Kumar, 1978). In support of his alternative interpretation of the expansion of education, Braverman cited Berg, who had concluded that 'educational "achievements" have already "exceeded requirements in most job categories"', thereby undermining the argument that technical change requires a better educated workforce (ibid.: 441). Thus, far from improving productivity, this suggests that a better educated workforce may be disadvantageous to employers since it is associated with job dissatisfaction. Moreover, recent research which shows that the expansion of higher education has led to 'significant levels of overqualification in employment' is not good news for Bell's thesis that there has been an upskilling of the workforce in response to technological change (Brynin, 2002: 650). Consequently, using the historical expansion of educational qualifications as an indicator of the increased importance of knowledge and as evidence of upskilling is problematic.

(4) Bell's neglect of the gender dimension of work in post-industrial society is indicated by the small number of pages (less than ten in a book of over 500 pages) he devoted to the issue of women and work. Yet Bell noted that 'a service economy is very largely a female-centred economy' and that 'the proportion of women in the labour force is bound to rise – the efforts of women's lib apart – simply because of the expansion of service industries' (1976 [1973]: 146). For

Bell, the main problem raised by this trend is the difficulty faced by trade unions in recruiting women workers:

Fewer women have thought of their jobs as 'permanent' and have been less interested in unions; many female jobs are part-time or 'second jobs' for the family, and the turnover of the number of women at work has been much higher than that of men. (ibid.: 146)

Surprisingly, in view of his awareness of limitations of female service sector work (see also Bell, 1976 [1973]: 134), he neglected to examine the significance of the low skill content of such jobs for his upskilling theory. If he had, he might have modified his theory to take account of the tendency for many, if not most, of the new jobs created in post-industrial societies to be lower-level ones involving the delivery of basic services and routine information (Kumar, 1978; 1995).

Importantly, the whole thrust of Bell's account of women and work betrays a traditional view in that he stereotypes all women as workers for whom paid work outside the home is not as central as their family roles. This approach to women and work has been addressed by Feldberg and Glenn (discussed in Chapter 2 in relation to the work of Blauner), who argue that to adopt a gender model for female workers and a job model for male workers distorts the analysis of work behaviour and influences what is researched, for example, by defining 'job conditions as problematic for men and family responsibilities as problematic for women' (1979: 532). This is exactly what Bell does when he discusses the issue of corporations employing more women: 'A child-care centre is a necessary component of job satisfaction for young women, even though it may add costs to a company far beyond the "gains" in productivity from such women' (1976 [1973]: 290). For Bell, low skill and low pay are less of a problem for women workers than the lack of child-care facilities! Moreover, in the process of viewing all women as uncommitted workers, Bell neglects the tendency for women who work full-time to 'differ very little in their work commitment' from men who work full-time (Hakim, 1995: 433). Thus, Bell's upskilling theory fails to take women workers into account in any serious way and when this issue is considered, albeit briefly, the heterogeneity of the female labour force is overlooked in favour of an outdated stereotype that labels all women workers as primarily concerned with family life rather than paid work.

Bell's supporters

Bell's upskilling thesis has received widespread support from a variety of research undertaken in the UK (e.g., Felstead et al., 2002; Gallie, 1996; Penn et al., 1994) and the USA (e.g., Attewell, 1987; Hirschhorn, 1986; Womack et al., 1990). The UK studies were informed by the extensive restructuring of work from the 1980s onwards, involving among other things, the increasing use of computing technology. These studies were based on large-scale survey data and revealed a consistent upskilling trend during the 1980s and 1990s, albeit 'modest' in the Penn et al. study, and that this was linked to the continued growth of computers in the workplace (1994: 9). They also showed that it was male workers who benefited most from the upskilling process and women the least, especially those who worked part-time, although there was also evidence of a narrowing of the gender gap between the skills used in men's and women's jobs. Thus, according to these research findings, the overall pattern was clear: 'The data suggest, and they do so compellingly, that the direction of change was running against any *general* process of deskilling' (Penn et al., 1994: 7; italics in the original); 'The most striking feature of our data is the very extensive upskilling of the workforce' (Gallie, 1996: 156); 'There is a consistent pattern of generally increasing skills in recent years, according to most measures' (Felstead et al., 2002: 10).

The US research was also inspired by the transformation of work following the reorganization of production since the 1980s, again associated with the introduction of advanced computing technology. The US studies listed above focused on manufacturing and service workplaces; Attewell (1987) examined quantitative data on insurance jobs, Hirschhorn (1986) looked at a variety of US and European factories and offices, and Womack et al. (1990) concentrated on car production in advanced industrial economies. Despite their contrasting approaches to the issue of skill – UK survey data and US labour force data and production systems in different countries, the conclusions of the US research on skill trends were remarkably similar to those of the UK. First, Attewell analysed industry-wide data on insurance jobs between 1966–80 and discovered 'an aggregate *upgrading* of the insurance workforce' (1987: 338; italics in the original). Second, after studying 22 companies, the majority of which were factories using continuous-process technology, Hirschhorn concluded that: 'Postindustrial settings integrate work and learning. The new technology does not deskill workers: they must learn to manage technical transitions from one machine state to another, and from one product design to another' (1986: 163). Third, after a 14-country study comparing mass and lean car production systems, Womack et al. asserted that, 'by the end of the century we expect that lean-assembly plants will be populated almost entirely by highly skilled problem solvers whose task will be to think continually of ways to make the system run more smoothly and productively' (1990: 102). Thus, these three US studies of late twentieth-century industrial and service work claimed that new computer technology extends rather than restricts or replaces workers' skill; the worker is transformed from a deskilled passive supporting role in the labour process to an upskilled active lead role.

This mixture of criticism and support of Bell's post-industrial society upskilling thesis has led Webster to suggest that 'it is academically rich, boldly constructed, imaginative', yet 'the whole project is deeply flawed empirically, theoretically and methodologically' (Webster, 2002: 32–3). Rather than posit a single skill trend, it is possible that changes in the process of controlling and exploiting workers and/or in the technology used at work result in both deskilling and upskilling. This implies that social change is more complex than either Braverman or Bell suggest, hence the pursuit of overall trends, such as deskilling or upskilling, is 'likely to be both theoretically and practically in vain' (Wood, 1982: 18). The key question, therefore, is that if the pattern of skill change is uneven, is polarization the best explanation of skill trends?

The polarization of skill?

In the research literature on the sociology of work skills, there are hints of polarization as far back as Bright (1958: 93) and Blauner (1964: 169), both of whom noted counter-trends in their studies of automation and skill, notwithstanding their contrasting conclusions, namely deskilling and upskilling respectively. Similarly, there was evidence of both deskilling and upskilling in the studies which were supportive of Bell's upskilling thesis (e.g., Attewell, 1987; Penn et al., 1994). Recent research on work skills in advanced industrial capitalist countries favours a polarization of skills thesis.

An American study examined the impact of increased automation on workers at a single car assembly plant and found that the effect was to polarize the workforce within the factory: 'Skilled trades workers experienced skill upgrading and gained enhanced responsibilities, while production workers underwent deskilling and became increasingly subordinated to the new technology' (Milkman and Pullman, 1991: 123). More generally, in terms of occupational trends, further evidence from the USA has confirmed that polarization is occurring in the form of a highly educated and highly paid minority of information workers whose work is intrinsically satisfying (e.g., designers) and a poorly educated and poorly paid majority of production service workers whose work is not satisfying (Reich, 1991). Reich estimates that the highly skilled minority constitute about one-fifth of the workforce whereas the unfortunate 80 per cent undertake all the routine and mundane jobs.

A representative British survey (Gallie, 1991: 325) used five indicators of skill: educational qualifications, length of training after completing full-time education, time taken to acquire job proficiency, responsibility for supervising the work of others, and subjective assessment of whether or not their work was skilled. The main findings of this comprehensive national survey on the pattern of skill change in the 1980s were that the 'experience of deskilling was very rare and this was true for all occupational classes' and that the 'argument that is best supported [by the data] is that of a polarization of skill experiences between classes' (ibid.: 349; Gallie et al., 1998). The dominant upskilling trend was related to technological change, especially the use of computers at work, and the increased importance of social skills in work, particularly for women's

Table 4.2 Changes in skill and responsibility by sex

| | % increase in skill | | % increase in responsibility | |
	Men	Women	Men	Women
Professional/Managerial	68	64	75	67
Lower Non-Manual	56	55	66	58
Technical/Supervisory	61	38	79	59
Skilled Manual	52	42	63	28
Non-Skilled Manual	40	24	51	33
All Men/Women	56	45	66	50

Source: Amended version of Table 10 in Gallie (1991: 344).

work. However, there were several caveats, notably that there was a 'deep gender divide in skill experiences', with men gaining most from upskilling and women the least, and that this was mainly related to the tendency for women to be employed part-time (Gallie, 1991: 350). Table 4.2 shows that the upskilling trend is particularly pronounced for men.

Further research by Gallie et al. confirmed the 'growing polarization in skill experiences between lower manual workers and other employees', but also showed that 'the trend over time has been for gender differences in skill to diminish' (1998: 56). A comparable Dutch survey also showed that automation produced a net upskilling for white-collar and professional workers, but a 'pocket' of deskilling among blue-collar workers due to a process of internal differentiation among this group (DeWitte and Steijn, 2000: 260). These findings confirm the aforementioned British data since they show that polarization is occurring and that the white-collar majority are more likely to experience upskilling than manual workers.

Finally, in the context of advancing what amounts to an updated version of Bell's post-industrial society thesis, Castells' contribution to the upskilling debate builds directly upon Bell's thesis in two respects; conceptually, his analysis is within the post-industrial society paradigm that accords priority to knowledge and information, and theoretically he argues that the information technological revolution heralds a new type of society: the informational society. Within this framework Castells departs from Bell's model of a post-industrial society by noting that, among other things, concentrating on the de-industrialization of America and other advanced economies in isolation from industrializing societies is a mistake, since viewed 'overall, new manufacturing jobs elsewhere largely exceeded the losses in the developed world' (2001: 220). Second, Castells argues that along with the expansion of managerial, professional, and technical occupations, namely the upskilling of the occupational structure, 'there is also the growth of low-end, unskilled, service occupations' leading to 'an increasingly polarized social structure' (ibid.: 221). Castells concluded on the basis of a mass of cross-national statistical data, that 'there are simultaneous increases at both the top and the bottom of the social ladder, although the increase at the top is of greater magnitude' (ibid.: 241). However, for Castells, the pivotal point about the transformation of work is not deskilling or upskilling, but the pressure on all workers to be flexible – an issue that will be considered more fully in the next two chapters.

On balance, the empirical evidence regarding the polarization of skill tends to be more supportive of Bell's thesis in two respects. First, his focus on new technologies and social skills has been shown to be closely related to upskilling. Second, upskilling has been found to be far more prevalent than deskilling, although intensification often characterized upskilled work and deskilling was still apparent, particularly at the bottom of the occupational hierarchy, and especially for part-time female work.

The transformation of work can be considered from the standpoint of changes in the class structure in the manner advocated by Lee (1981). From this perspective, Lee has suggested that the debate about skill and the class structure may be summarized by noting that Braverman's thesis posits that exploitation leads inevitably to falling skill levels and eventually to proletarianization, and that, conversely, Bell's thesis posits that technical change leads inevitably to rising skill levels and eventually to professionalization, or the expansion of knowledge workers. This model is summarized in Figure 4.1.

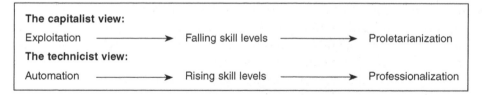

Figure 4.1   Changes in skill and the occupational class structure

Source: Adapted from Lee (1981: 57).

It is now necessary to compare the usefulness of approaching the debate about skill trends in terms of the contrast between Marxist (e.g., Braverman) and post-industrial (e.g., Bell) theories. Braverman was arguably correct for global capitalism but wrong in the case of the most advanced capitalist nation states. Bell's conceptions of social change has been acknowledged implicitly by Wright (1997). His study of changes in the class structure of America, the most advanced industrial capitalist society, shows that the post-industrial expectation of upskilling was confirmed, whereas the Marxist expectation of deskilling was not. This was especially marked during the 1980s and came as a major surprise and disappointment to the Marxist Wright. In mitigation, as it were, Wright pointed out that the Marxist theory of class proletarianization applies to capitalism in general and not 'national units of capitalism' (1997: 110).

In other words, upskilling may be occurring in the developed world, but the deskilled jobs have been transferred to developing countries.

Summary and conclusions

Upskilling theories tend to draw upon Weber and focus on technological imperatives, such as the need for a better educated and skilled workforce. The best-known version of this view is Bell's post-industrial theory of upskilling, which implies a new type of knowledge or information society rather than historical continuity. The importance Bell attached to theoretical knowledge, and hence people-centred, highly skilled, knowledge workers in the expanding service sector, positions him as one of the pioneers of the burgeoning field of research referred to as knowledge work – an issue that will be discussed in Chapter 6.

In contrast to deskilling theories which draw upon Marx, focus on capitalist imperatives, such as the need to make a profit, and tend to operate with a craft model of skill which emphasizes task-specific training (discussed in Chapter 3), Bell tends to operate with an educational model of skill which emphasizes knowledge and responsibility. Corresponding to their different conceptions of skill, upskilling theories have been criticized for idealizing white-collar work, whereas deskilling theories have been criticized for idealizing highly skilled manual work. Concomitantly, the class consequence of Bell's upskilling thesis is professionalization, but for Braverman it was the opposite, proletarianization. Both theories have also been censured for neglecting the gender dimension of work, and exaggerating certain trends among the labour force. Also in their desire to advance a general skill trend, Bell and Braverman both tend to be deterministic, to play down counter-trends, to focus on America rather than global trends, and to over-simplify the issue of skill. A critical review of the deskilling/upskilling debate concluded that the jury was still out on this key issue in the sociology of work (Vallas, 1990).

The search for a general tendency towards either deskilling or upskilling is thought by some to be a false trail since post-Braverman and Bell research has found evidence of both. This has led to the emergence of a polarization of skill thesis which has been largely confirmed empirically in that in advanced industrial capitalist societies the dominant tendency is upskilling rather than deskilling. Most tellingly, research by the avowed Marxist Wright (1997) found that changes in the American class structure between 1960 and 1990 supported Bell's post-industrial upskilling theory, not Braverman's Marx-inspired deskilling theory.

However, many workers, notably women and relatively less skilled manual workers, are more likely to experience deskilling than upskilling, even in highly developed societies. Moreover, the growth of low-skilled part-time work in such societies during the past couple of decades and the emergence of the deskillers being deskilled following the introduction of computer-aided design, suggest that the debate about deskilling is not yet over, especially if the global picture rather than any one nation state is considered (Aronowitz and DiFazio, 1994; Cooley, 1987 [1980]; O'Reilly and Fagan, 1998; Wright, 1997).

One way of looking at skill trends is to consider them in relation to how work is organized. Thus, deskilling is associated typically with Fordist mass production, which declined from the 1960s onwards in the most advanced industrial capitalist societies, and upskilling with post-Fordist alternatives to mass production (Wood, 1992). Hence among other things, the incidence of either deskilling or upskilling will depend on how work has been organized historically in different economic sectors in various societies. The alleged transformation of Fordism into neo-Fordist and post-Fordist production systems are the subject of the next two chapters with reference to industrial work (Chapter 5) and service work (Chapter 6).

Further reading

BOOKS In addition to reading the original works of Bell, the critiques of his upskilling thesis by Kumar (1978) *Prophecy and Progress: The Sociology of Industrial and Post-Industrial Society*, and Webster (2002) *Theories of the Information Society* (2nd edn) should also be read, although neither cover the gender dimension in depth. The most detailed and sophisticated review and revision of Bell's thesis, including the evidence for polarization, can be found in Castells (2001) *The Rise of the Network Society*. Recent research on the sociology of skill should be consulted, notably Crompton et al. (eds) (1996) *Changing Forms of Employment: Organizations, Skills and Gender*, and Gallie et al. (1998) *Restructuring the Employment Relationship*.

ARTICLES For an empirically based critical view of Bell, see Brynin (2002) 'Overqualification in employment', *Work, Employment and Society*, 16(4): 637–54, and for a supportive one, read Gallie (1991) 'Patterns of skill change: upskilling, deskilling or the polarization of skills?', *Work, Employment and Society*, 5(3): 319–51. An overview of the sociology of skill has been provided by Vallas (1990) 'The concept of skill: a critical review', *Work and Occupations*, 17(4): 379–98.

WEBSITES For an analysis that links alienation, skill, and employment security consult the Good Work Commission Provocation Paper 7 'The employment relationship and the quality of work' by S. Overell, T. Mills, S. Roberts, R Lekhi and R. Blaug published by the Work Foundation in 2010 at www.goodworkcommission.co.uk

Questions for discussion and assessment

1 Examine critically the grounds upon which Bell advanced his upskilling thesis.
2 Assess the strengths and weaknesses of Bell's upskilling thesis.
3 Consider the view that the gender dimension is the main weakness of Bell's study.
4 How convincing is the evidence for the polarization of skills thesis?
5 Has the upskilling trend in post-industrial societies been exaggerated?
6 Discuss the claim that the unevenness of skill trends precludes the possibility of an overall pattern.
7 Compare and contrast the contributions of Braverman and Bell to the issue of skill trends.

5

INDUSTRIAL WORK: FORDISM, NEO-FORDISM AND POST-FORDISM

Chapter contents

- The rise of Fordism
- The development of Fordism beyond the workplace
- The decline of Fordism
- Solutions to the crisis of Fordism: neo-Fordism and post-Fordism
- Summary and conclusions
- Further reading
- Questions for discussion and assessment

Implicit in much of the discussion of alienation (in Chapter 2) and skill (in Chapters 3 and 4) was the idea that the organization of the production of goods and services during the twentieth century had changed and that this has influenced the extent to which workers are alienated and skilled. This is readily apparent in Blauner's model of the evolution of manual work from highly skilled and non-alienating craft work, to relatively unskilled and alienating assembly-line work, and the move to '"non-manual" responsibility called forth by continuous-process technology' (1964: 169). Blauner's prescience was also discernible where he speculated that 'a more affluent and educated public, reacting against the standardization of values and products in a mass society, may increase its future demand for unique and individuated articles' (ibid.: 168).

In the sociological history of production systems a range of concepts have been developed in an attempt to comprehend the complexity of social change. Among the most widely used are Fordism, and the systems that replaced it, namely neo-Fordism and post-Fordism, although the precise meaning of these terms often varies. There are three inter-related meanings of the concept of Fordism (Lipietz, 1992). First and foremost, Fordism refers to a production system or labour process element characterized by mass production. Second, it refers to an economic system or regime of accumulation characterized by mass consumption. Third, it refers to a socio-political system or mode of regulation that is supportive of mass production and mass consumption, and which, among other things, ensures the supply of physically healthy workers and financially healthy consumers. Here the focus will be mainly, but not exclusively since all three dimensions are inter-related, on Fordism as an industrial production system and its successors. The aim of this chapter is to consider the rise, development and decline of Fordism, and the alternatives to Fordism, namely neo-Fordism and post-Fordism, primarily with reference to car production since this was the source and the main focus of research that utilizes these concepts.

The rise of Fordism

During the course of the nineteenth century, the factory became the dominant image of work in industrial capitalism in Britain, yet manufacturing often still involved a mixture of machine- and hand-made products by machine operators and craft workers producing a range of small batch and individual products (Samuel, 1977). The great variety and complexity of factory production systems in the nineteenth century make it difficult to generalize about pre-Fordism. However, those who have attempted such an exercise typically emphasize the role of highly skilled craft workers operating general purpose machines, the assembly of a whole product or large part of a product by one worker, and the use of non-standardized parts to produce a small number of high-quality products (e.g., Meyer, 1981). In the discussion of Blauner (in Chapter 1) and of Braverman (in Chapter 2), it was noted that craft workers typically controlled the technology and the work process. As a result of this way of organizing production, complex products, such as cars, were extremely expensive to build and buy.

At the beginning of the twentieth century, Henry Ford was aware that there existed a potentially vast untapped market for cars while he was just one of a number of small-scale car makers for the 5 per cent of the population who could afford one. In 1909, he announced: 'I will build a motor car for the great multitude … it will be so low in price that no man making a good salary will be unable to own one' (2008 [1922]: 52). On the plus side, there was a plentiful supply of unskilled rural migrants and immigrants, on the minus side, there was a shortage of skilled workers. In order to expand his output of cars he had to devise a production system that overcame the shortage of skilled workers and took advantage of the availability of unskilled workers (Babson, 1995). His solution was to combine the organizational innovations of Taylorism, namely the separation of conception from execution and associated task fragmentation and simplification (i.e., deskilled work), with the introduction of special or single-purpose machine tools which made standardized and therefore interchangeable parts and developed a sequential layout of the detailed tasks, and special machines culminating in progressive or continuous flow production in the form of a moving assembly line derived from meatpacking (Meyer, 1981). The effect of these innovations transformed production work; in 1910, the majority of Ford workers were classified as 'skilled', but by 1917 this group had declined to under 10 per cent, replaced by unskilled workers who now comprised the majority of workers (ibid.). Henry Ford acknowledged that the new production system involved the 'reduction of the necessity for thought on the part of the worker and the reduction of his movements to a minimum. He does as nearly as possible only one thing with only one movement', and added that: 'Dividing and subdividing operations, keeping the work in motion – these are the keynotes of production' (2008 [1922]: 58, 64). Ford also designed machines that were 'absolutely fool-proof' to improve quality and reduce accidents (ibid.: 80). Ford's innovations transformed productivity, profits and prices. The Ford Motor Company was founded in 1903 and in its first year of (craft) production 125 workers produced 1,700 cars and a company net income of $246,000, by 1921 the workforce had increased to over 32,000, output to over 900,000, and net income to just under $78,000,000 (Meyer, 1981). Production peaked in 1923 when 1.8 million Model T cars were mass produced (Hounshell, 1984). Meanwhile, the price of the Ford model T declined from $850 in the first year of production in 1908 to less than $300 by 1923 (Wells, 2007). Ford had revolutionized the way cars were made, extended the market down the class structure by producing a limited range of standardized cars, and in the process had become the 'world's first self-made billionaire' (Levinson, 2002: 49).

Ford achieved these unprecedented production figures and profits while reducing the working day from nine to eight hours and more than doubling wages to $5 a day in 1914, similar to Taylor's advocacy of 'high wages and low labour costs' (1947 [1903]: 22). This was an exercise in social engineering that involved an 'incentive to better living' in the form of a complex profit-sharing scheme divided into two components: a basic wage paid to all workers and a profit-sharing element that was only available to those who had worked for Ford for at least six months, married men 'living with and taking good care of their families', single men aged over 22 'who are of proved thrifty habits', and young men under 22 and women 'who are the sole support of their next of kin' (Ford, 2008 [1922]: 88). Ford's idea of an appropriate lifestyle was one that involved no drinking, no smoking and no gambling. Thus this was not an act of altruism but a policy for the social control of workers aimed at reducing the exceptionally high labour turnover, absenteeism, and the threat of unionism. For example, 60,000 workers had to be replaced in 1913, whereas only 2,000 had to be replaced in 1914; absenteeism also 'declined from 10 per cent to less than one half a per cent' (Beynon, 1975: 25). Ford also expected greater efficiency from his workers, sacking the less efficient more briskly (Meyer, 1981) and increasing pay dramatically had the extra advantage of generating extensive free publicity (Hounshell, 1984). More conventionally, Ford subscribed to the ideal of the male breadwinner since he did not employ married women if their husbands had a job; in other words, he operated a marriage bar.

These changes evolved following experimentation over a number of years. For example, the moving assembly line was the culmination of many mechanical conveyer and transfer devices introduced between 1910 and 1914 (Williams et al., 1992a). The first moving assembly line was introduced in the sub-assembly section concerned with the production of flywheel magnetos in 1913 and extended to other areas of production until an endless and highly synchronized chain conveyer for final assembly was achieved in 1914 (Hounshell, 1984). The flow production principle was basically an organizational innovation which necessitated changes to the layout of work processes and saved time by restricting workers to their position on the line. In the unending search for the most efficient production method, a stop-watch was often used to calculate how much time a worker spent walking to collect materials and tools, and how much working. For example, in the case of piston-rod assembly it was found that four hours out of nine were spent walking not working! Ford also automated processes such as riveting the crank-case arms to a crank-case, which once automated was operated by one worker instead of twelve (Ford, 2008 [1922]). These innovations increased production, productivity, and profits dramatically (Meyer, 1981).

The three main elements of the production system implemented by Ford after years of continuous refinement and which inspired the term 'Fordism' are:

- the fragmentation and simplification of work via Taylorized tasks;
- managerial control over the pace of work via the moving assembly line; and
- the standardization of parts and products via single-purpose machines.

Finally, the consent of workers was achieved via higher wages for those who complied with Ford's model of good behaviour, and in due course this was underpinned by state welfare policies which sought to provide an economic safety net for unemployed workers. This created a virtuous circle in which the gains in productivity meant that there were only winners. The employer achieved larger profits, the employee received higher wages, and the consumer was able to purchase cheaper products. The Fordist system of mass production democratized consumption by making what were previously luxury goods for the few, available in a standardized form to potentially everyone. The key features of Fordism and pre-Fordism are summarized in Table 5.1.

Table 5.1 Key features of industrial pre-Fordism and Fordism

Pre-Fordism: type of production system characterized by:
1 Craft skills
2 Non-linear and stationary assembly
3 Non-standardized parts and a low volume of high-quality products
Fordism: type of production system characterized by:
1 Fragmented and simplified (Taylorized) work tasks
2 Linear production and moving assembly line
3 Standardized parts and a high volume of low-quality products

The unparalleled success of Ford's new system of mass production was therefore based on changes to the division of labour and to the type of machines
workers operated, plus the switch from non-linear and stationary production to
progressive production and a moving assembly line. Ford had transferred craft
workers' skill to machines, removed control from workers to managers, and transformed productivity at the cost of heightening the monotony of repeating endlessly one simple task. The scale of Ford's achievement can be gauged by the
impressive increase in production and profits in a few years noted above, and also
by Ford's share of the total car market which increased from less than 10 per cent
in 1908 to nearly 50 per cent in 1914, and an amazing 96 per cent of all American
cars sold at under $600 (Meyer, 1981; Williams et al., 1992a). Ford had set out
to produce a car for the 95 per cent who were excluded previously from a market
that catered for the rich and he certainly accomplished his objective. Ford's success is also apparent from the extent to which the new methods of mass production were adopted not only by other car manufacturers in America and eventually
Europe, but also by makers of other products, notably household appliances such
as vacuum sweepers, consumer goods (e.g., radios), furniture, and even houses
(Hounshell, 1984). The steep decline in the price of Ford cars led to a major
growth in car consumption that was stimulated by advertising and financed
increasingly by instalment buying, with 75 per cent of cars purchased via loans
in 1924 (Rhode, 2002/03). Such was Ford's success that a prominent Boston
businessman of that time, Edward Filene, declared that competition 'will compel
us to Fordize American business and industry' (quoted in Hounshell, 1984: 305).

This straightforward account of the rise of Fordism is not without its complexities. First, Ford had accomplished his mission to provide a car for the
masses by 1923 when 74 per cent of American families owned a car compared
to less than half a per cent in 1910 (Gartman, 1987). However, market saturation required a new strategy, one that involved selling cars to those who already
owned one. Ford persisted with his limited range (i.e., different body styles) of
one low-priced, though not unchanging car, the Model T, whereas General
Motors (GM) introduced a far wider choice consisting of 'five basic price classes
by car makes and several subclasses of models' that covered the whole price
range, and evolved the idea of annual models, which showed that the 'mass
production of automobiles could be reconciled with product variation'; in short,
'a car for every purse and purpose' (Sloan, 1986 [1963]: 158, 438). In order to
achieve this degree of model diversification GM devised a more flexible mass
production system that facilitated frequent model changes with minimal delays
in production. This involved the development of a 'new middle-range machine
that used the unskilled labour of the Ford single-purpose machine and contained some of the flexibility of the general purpose ones' (Meyer, 2004: 6).
Importantly, semi-special machines did not alter the subordinate relationship of
the worker to machinery and the moving assembly line since the skill was still
built into the technology and the work still involved limited tasks and monotonous routines (Gartman, 1987). In other words, it was still based on the rules of

mass production founded by Ford. However, this technical development extended the advantages of Fordism from the lowest to the highest priced cars and by 1931 GM had overtaken Ford as the leading car maker in terms of sales, and had become the exemplar of corporate success (Williams et al., 1992a). Ford's achievement was to open up the car market to the masses, but it was GM who expanded the range of standardized cars and the frequency of new models.

Second, there is some debate about the exact relationship between Taylorism and Fordism. Hounshell (1984) has questioned the nature and extent of Taylorism in the early Ford factories on the grounds that Taylor was concerned primarily to improve efficiency using the existing technology whereas Ford tended to focus more on replacing labour by machinery and recruiting unskilled workers to attend to the machines. Yet Hounshell has also confirmed that Ford had a time study department by 1913 to establish work task standards and instituted a clear division of labour between management and workers in line with the Taylorist principle of separating conception from execution. More generally, Hounshell concurs with Meyer (1981) by arguing that: 'If by Taylorism we mean rationalization through the analysis of work (time and motion studies to eliminate wasteful motions) and the "scientific selection" of workmen for pre-scribed tasks, then … Ford engineers "Taylorized" the Highland Park factory' (1984: 249). Dassbach's more recent research supports this view by noting that studies were undertaken in the early Ford factories to calculate 'the total number of man-hours required to assemble various components, the number and type of operations performed, and the amount of time expended for each operation' (1991: 84). Dassbach concluded, like others before him, that Fordism was similar to Taylorism in that it was founded on the systematic study of work processes. This conclusion is in accord with Ford's claim that, 'by the aid of scientific study one man is now able to do somewhat more than four did a comparatively few years ago', and that a worker 'must have every second necessary but not a single unnecessary second' (2008 [1922]: 59). Thus there may be some differences between Taylorism and early Fordism, but Taylor and Ford were certainly 'reading from the same page', as can been gauged from their respective discussions of the limited abilities and ambitions of most work-ers, the imperative to eliminate wasted movements, the advantages of simplify-ing tasks by subdividing them, the marked division of responsibility between managers and workers, the ceaseless development of new and more efficient tools, and the cost-cutting benefits of paying higher wages for increased output. Moreover, the use of 'speed bosses' by Taylor (1947 [1903]: 100) and 'pace setters' by Ford (Gartman, 1987: 58), led them to be known by those who experienced the intensification of work as 'Frederick "Speedy" Taylor' (Beynon, 1975: 135) and the 'Speed-Up King' (Dassbach, 1991: 89) respectively.

Third, the extent of the diffusion of Fordism has been questioned, most nota-bly by Williams et al. who have argued that 'even in America there was only limited imitation' of Ford's production methods (1992a: 537). In Europe, the introduction of Fordism was constrained by weaker markets and stronger trade unions, especially craft workers who resisted the deskilling aspect of Fordism (Beynon, 1975). Conversely, it has been argued that Ford's pride in his achievements and his openness about his production methods encouraged technical journalists to write about them, and foreign car makers, such as William Morris from England and Kiichiro Toyado (Toyota) from Japan, to tour his factories. As a result of this positive publicity, Ford's methods of production spread to car makers world-wide. American engineers also travelled abroad, disseminating their knowledge of the new production techniques, including the Soviet Union where factory walls were adorned with pictures of 'the two men who had "revolutionized" the twentieth century', namely Lenin and Ford (Sussman, 1974: 450).

Fordism was exported more directly to Europe when Ford purchased a derelict factory in Manchester in 1911 and installed the first assembly-line method of production in Britain in 1914 (Lewchuk, 1989). Ford also exported Taylorism, anti-unionism, and an ultra strict approach to discipline, prompting one former employee to describe working for Ford in Manchester as 'worse than Alcatraz', but tolerated due to the relatively high wages and lack of alternative job options (McIntosh, 1995: 75). Later Ford established foreign subsidiary companies elsewhere (e.g., Japan) and GM followed suit when it took over the British car maker Vauxhall in 1925 (Littler and Salaman, 1984). Fordism became a global production system when mass production was established in developing countries to take advantage of lower wages and weaker trade unions. The term 'national Fordisms' and reference to different types such as 'state' (France) and 'peripheral' (Brazil) Fordism, indicate the global reach of Fordism and the context-specific nature of variations outside its 'classic' form in the USA (Peck and Tickell, 1994: 285–7). The diffusion of Fordism was greater if the car companies were American, for example, Ford in Britain, but less complete among British firms, such as Morris (Lewchuk, 1989). These multiple sources of variation suggest that the globalization of Fordism was not a smooth process, but an uneven one with different conditions resulting in diverse adaptations. Yet, thanks to the dissemination of technical knowledge and organizational practices nationally and internationally, plus the rise of the multinational corporation, Fordism spread around the world. Ford's success inspired the term 'Fordism', which became shorthand for standardization; a standardized product produced by standardized machinery using standardized methods and standardized human labour employed for a standard working day (Doray, 1988). Ford's achievement in creating a new way of organizing production was acknowledged at the time and since as epoch-making.

The development of Fordism beyond the workplace

So far, the discussion of Fordism has focused mainly on the production dimension but as indicated above, from the outset, Fordism was about more than how work was organized. Henry Ford was aware that workers carry cultural baggage into work and that some of their habits and values were not conducive to efficiency, hence he was concerned about the behaviour of his workers outside and inside the factory. To administer the momentous $5-a-day pay deal, Ford created a Sociological Department in 1914 (Beynon, 1975). Thirty investigators were recruited to ensure that Ford employees were not only punctual and performed their work well, but as noted above, also conformed to the non-work behaviour deemed appropriate by the company. In return for satisfying these work and non-work prescriptions, Ford offered the prospect of regular work for higher pay, initially only to men but extended to women who were heads of households in 1916 during the wartime shortage of male labour (Meyer, 1981; Gartman, 1987). In these and other ways, such as by encouraging adult male workers to buy houses, cars and life insurance, Ford promoted the idea of full-time male workers as 'responsible heads of households' (Lewchuk, 1995: 228). For the many immigrant workers among the Ford workforce, English language tuition was provided, but if an employee refused to learn English in the Ford school, they were sacked. Social provision also included a Ford hospital, trade school, band, athletic park, newspaper and shops (Meyer, 1981). The effect of the five dollar day and related welfare programmes introduced by Ford, and other car companies, was to reduce labour turnover and absenteeism, and increase output and the economic dependence and normative ties between the employee and the employer (Gartman, 1987). Thus higher pay was not the only inducement to change work and non-work attitudes and behaviour, the provision of welfare programmes also had a cultural as well as economic purpose, namely to encourage certain values and forms of behaviour, such as self-discipline and reliability that were considered vital to commercial success.

This kind of self-interested paternalism was typical of nineteenth-century capitalism, especially family-owned businesses, before the advent of state welfare (McIvor, 2001). For example, the Ford shops were an echo of the truck system discussed in Chapter 1, although unlike their nineteenth-century predecessors, the Ford shops were organized in the same way as Ford car production, namely a flow-system providing a limited range of standardized goods at low prices (Freathy and Sparks, 1992). However, Ford's paternalism developed in a less than benign direction. The Sociological Department was renamed the Service Department and expanded for an enhanced disciplinary role. Some 3,500 private policemen were employed to discourage union activity, spy on employees at work and at home, and punish and reward them accordingly. Ford was vehemently anti-union as well as anti-drinking and gambling, and his zeal for control over his workers inside and outside work led to him being referred to as an 'industrial fascist' (Beynon, 1975: 28). A more subtle version of his paternalist tradition was still in evidence at the beginning of the twenty-first century when Ford offered every employee a personal computer with internet access for $5 a month (Hammersley, 2000). This act of apparent generosity by Ford has several potential benefits for the employer: it opens up a new form of direct communication with employees when they are at home; it may increase loyalty to the company; and it could increase the computer skills of the work-force which in turn may enhance both production and sales (Coops, 2000).

Ford regarded an employee as a 'partner' and considered it 'utterly foolish for Capital and Labour to think of themselves as groups' (2008 [1922]: 81). This view of a capitalist work organization corresponds to a 'unitary' manage-rial ideology in that it admits to only one source of authority and loyalty, the company, and considers unions to be unnecessary (Fox, 1966: 3). However, Henry Ford eventually altered his view to a 'pluralistic' managerial ideology when he conceded the right of workers to join a union in the USA in 1941 and in the UK in 1944, thereby accepting that work organizations are made up of divergent as well as common interests (ibid.: 4). This was after many years of often bitter struggle and the backing of a 'reformist State apparatus' (Beynon, 1975: 45). It is significant that union recognition was achieved at Ford in the USA and the UK during the Second World War when their production facilities were redirected towards the war effort and the central state in both countries was concerned to ensure uninterrupted military production (Beynon, 1975; Gartman, 1987). The acceptance by unions and employers of the legitimacy of each other, including the understanding that productivity gains that accrue from the extreme rationalization of work will be shared, has been called the 'Fordist compromise' (Lipietz, 1992: 6). Mutual recognition, however, did not mean conflict-free factories. Two of the more famous instances of industrial conflict during the mature phase of Fordism were the equal pay strikes by women workers at Ford's UK Dagenham plant in 1968 – portrayed in the film *Made in Dagenham*, released in 2010 (Crocker, 2008) and the dispute at GM's Lordstown plant in the USA over work intensification in 1972 (Sallaz, 2004).

As noted above, the other main party to the Fordist compromise was the state, which provided a legal framework within which employers and employ-ees negotiated, notably the right to join a union and therefore enjoy represen-tation, and the provision of minimal income and welfare services. The term 'Fordist welfare state' has been used to describe the development of socio-political institutions and policies that are compatible with mass production and mass consumption (Lipietz, 1994: 351). For example, in addition to ensur-ing the supply of healthy workers, the state adopted interventionist Keynesian monetary policies in an attempt to smooth out the booms and slumps of the business cycle, and introduced welfare benefits to enable those who are not in full-time employment to avail themselves, albeit at a reduced level, of the products of mass production (Jessop, 1994). As a result of these compromises, workers became integrated to the extent that they accepted the legitimacy of the hierarchical structures that played such a large part of their lives – the private company, the trade union, and the capitalist state. The sum total of this arrangement as it developed during the middle of the twentieth century in Western industrial capitalist societies has been well expressed by Beck in the process of contrasting the Fordist model involving the standardization of work and life with the risk model involving the individualization of work and life:

> [T]he Fordist growth regime ... did not only mean fixed times for holidays and other activities that underpinned and standardized life together in family, neighbourhood and community. It was also shaped and reinforced by a 'mode of regulation', which supported the growth machine culturally, politically and legally. This involved a wide range of strategies, actors and conditions which tied company management, banks, trade unions and political parties, as well as governments, to a relatively uniform philosophy of growth and a corresponding set of measures that held out a promise of success. The cultural-political targets of these measures were citizens in full-time employment, who had expectations of rising living standards and job security, while the main recipes were workforce participation, free collective bargaining, strong trade unions, government intervention and Keynesian macro-politics. ... Thus, under the conditions of Fordism ... rising consumption, public affluence and social security constituted the 'social cement' of the regime. (Beck, 2000: 69)

Thus, Fordism culminated not only in standardized production, work and employment, but also in standardized consumption, and standardized lifestyles, even standardized politics, often referred to as the post-war consensus. According to this view, ultimately Fordism involved much more than a new way of working. It involved a new way of life, or to be more precise, an American way of life characterized by increasing prosperity for all via mass production and mass consumption.

The development of the Fordist compromise was the culmination of work trends discussed towards the end of Chapter 1, namely the emergence of a dominant conception of work epitomized by the employment of full-time, permanent male workers. This was especially the case in the car industry which was more male-dominated during the rise of Fordism than other assembly-line industries, such as food, clothing and electrical goods, in which the predominantly female workforce was not married (Glucksmann, 1990). From the beginning, therefore, in addition to a class dimension, the Fordist compromise involved a gender dimension which favoured male workers who were excused responsibility for domestic work whereas women were correspondingly restricted in the labour market on the grounds that they were primarily responsible for domestic work (Pfau-Effinger, 1993). Although a large minority of women have worked full-time since the beginning of industrial capitalism, the rate remained relatively stable at approximately one-third between the 1950s and 1980s in Britain, suggesting that the prevailing Fordist norm was that permanent full-time work was a male prerogative (Crompton and Harris, 1998; Hakim, 1996). In the same way that there were national variations in the adoption of Fordist production methods, there were differences in the gender contracts, which varied from a strong, male breadwinner and female carer pattern in Japan and Germany, to a weaker version in Sweden and the USA (Gottfried, 2000). The Fordist model of standardized mass production and the standardized male factory worker and female homemaker reached its peak in the West in the 1950s, since when it has declined and by the mid-1970s, the post-1945 era of prosperity and stability that was Fordism was in crisis.

The decline of Fordism

There are a number of theories about what happened to Fordism (Amin, 1994b). The two discussed here, the regulation approach and the flexible specialization approach, have been selected because they are among the most influential and connect to the topics discussed in the previous chapters, namely the historical development of industrial capitalism (Chapter 1), alienation (Chapter 2), and skill (Chapters 3 and 4). Both theories have been advanced in the context of increases in the cost of production during the 1970s, especially oil, plus growing competition from Japan and from lower wage production in industrializing countries.

Regulation theory was developed in France and argued that, as a capitalist production system, Fordism is inherently alienating and inevitably involves deskilling, which is likely to provoke a negative response from workers, no matter how well paid they are, and that discontented workers are not good news for productivity and hence profits. Regulationists claim that the negative features of work 'multiplied during the 1960s' and that this was reflected in an increase in accidents, absenteeism, defective products, and conflict at work (Aglietta, 1987 [1976]: 120). The increased scale of labour dissatisfaction contributed to declining productivity and higher costs of production, and therefore reduced profits, for example, by constraining employers to devote extra time and resources to quality control. Thus, according to this view, the demise of Fordism was due primarily to 'a crisis of the labour process, which, because it dehumanizes the worker, ends up by not being efficient, even from the employer's point of view' (Lipietz, 1992: 17). This crisis for labour and capital impacted on the ability of the state to fund the ensuing recession out of declining taxable income, thereby prompting cuts in welfare benefits, which compounded the problem as well as threatening the political dimension of the Fordist compromise.

The theory of flexible specialization originated in America and argued that as a production system, Fordism is intrinsically inflexible in that it is unable to respond to variable demand, especially once mass markets have been saturated and consumers' tastes have changed in the direction of more individualized and higher-quality products, as happened in the 1960s (Piore and Sabel, 1984). It is claimed that the success of Fordism created the demand for greater variety and the ability to pay for premium products which provoked manufacturers to 'radically modify, if not completely abandon' their Fordist principles and introduce more flexible technologies and workers (Sabel, 1984: 201). New computer technologies allowed companies, even small ones, to respond quickly to changes in fashion, thereby overcoming the crisis of declining consumer interest in standardized products.

Although these arguments have different points of departure, they end up in the same place, namely that Fordism had reached the limits of its shelf life as a profitable system of mass production and consumption. The first approach starts from the supply side and argues that Fordism is incapable of overcoming workers' dissatisfaction, whereas the second starts from the demand side and argues that Fordism is incapable of overcoming consumer dissatisfaction. Both approaches conclude that, by the 1970s, Fordism was in a profitability 'crisis' and that in this more competitive environment the search was on for new production methods that would increase productivity and therefore profits.

These complementary analyses of the decline of Fordism have been criticized extensively. As far as regulation theory is concerned, it has been pointed out that the rise in labour disputes in the 1960s may not have been due simply to the nature of the Fordist labour process, but to other factors, such as the wider political and economic conditions prevailing at that time, and that the alleged progressive degradation of labour may be overcome, partially at least, 'by further automation and labour displacement' (Sayer, 1989: 669). The theory of flexible specialization has been criticized on the grounds that replacement demand and new products compensate for market saturation, and that the argument about the break-up of mass markets 'does not rest on any sound empirical basis' (Williams et al., 1987: 427; see also Williams et al., 1992a). This suggests that neither theory provides an adequate explanation of the decline of Fordism and that it was probably a combination of worker militancy, consumer discontent, increased costs of production, and growing competition that turned a virtuous circle into a virtueless one of declining worker satisfaction, declining consumer satisfaction, and declining profits.

Notwithstanding these critical comments on the reasons for the decline of Fordism, there is broad agreement that in the main industrial capitalist societies there was an emerging crisis in the Fordist way of organizing production by the 1970s. By way of a summary of the rise and decline of Fordism as an industrial production system, Table 5.2 notes its main advantages and disadvantages from the standpoint of society as a whole, workers, employers, and consumers. The eventual decline of Fordism implies that over time and in the context of increased international competition, the disadvantages of Fordism as a production system outweighed its advantages.

Table 5.2 Advantages and disadvantages of industrial Fordism

	Society	Workers	Employers	Consumers
Advantages	Mass production > economies of scale > improved standard of living	Higher pay	Increased productivity and profits	Cheaper goods
Disadvantages	Standardization of work and life	Alienating low skilled work	Absenteeism, higher labour turnover and conflict	Low quality standard products and limited choice

Solutions to the crisis of Fordism: neo-Fordism and post-Fordism

Fordism and variants of it predominated for most of the twentieth century in industrial and industrializing capitalist societies. Since this system of organizing production entered a crisis of productivity and profitability in the 1970s, there have been various attempts to transcend the difficulties associated with it, including automating production, internationalizing production, and re-organizing production (Wood, 1992). The first typically involves the use of industrial robots, 50 per cent of which are in car factories (Williams et al., 1987). This solution tends to displace labour as living labour is replaced by dead labour, such as machinery which often reduces the amount of heavy and repetitive work for those retained. A second option is to relocate Fordist production to less developed countries where non-unionized, low-skilled, and cheaper labour is available. The third is the partial (i.e., neo-Fordist) or total (i.e., post-Fordist) re-organization of production. These strategies are not mutually exclusive as the unevenness of the growth of Fordism as a global production system testifies. The focus here will be on the third strategy with reference to the previous discussion of Fordism as a type of production system. More specifically, a neo-Fordist solution to the crisis of Fordism involves modifications to one or more of the key elements of Fordism, whereas a post-Fordist solution involves their transformation. It will be recalled that in Table 5.1 the key elements of a Fordist production system included: (a) the fragmentation and simplification of work via Taylorized tasks; (b) managerial control over the pace of work via the linear sequencing of production and the moving assembly line; and (c) the standardization of parts and low quality goods.

Four alternative production systems to Fordism emerged during the last quarter of the twentieth century: (1) Swedish socio-technical systems; (2) Italian flexible specialization; (3) German diversified quality production; and (4) Japanese lean production (Appelbaum and Batt, 1994). The Swedish and German production models both operate at the higher end of the car market and are dependent upon supporting social institutions such as government training policies, whereas Italian flexible specialization is best suited to small-scale production. These features inhibit their transferability and applicability to all segments of the global car market, consequently only Japanese lean production will be considered here.

Japanese lean production: a post-Fordist interpretation

Japanese car makers developed the most famous and widely emulated alternative solution to the Fordist production system and overtook American car companies as world leaders in terms of output, productivity, and profitability by the 1980s (Cusumano, 1985). Whereas Ford had pioneered mass production, hence the term Fordism, Toyota invented lean production which superseded Fordism as the exemplar of successful production methods (Babson, 1995), hence it is sometimes referred to as 'Toyotism' (Elger and Smith, 1994), but more usually simply as Japanese lean production (JLP) due to the extensive adoption of the Toyota production system by other Japanese car companies (Womack et al., 1990).

The success of the Japanese car companies prior to the 1980s was attributed to lower wages, government support, and/or automation, but continued success into the 1980s provoked international interest in their production methods and a reverse of the pattern earlier in the century when foreign car makers visited American car plants. Ford and GM executives went on fact-finding missions to Japan in 1981 and 1983 respectively and 'discovered the answer to Japanese success: lean production' (ibid.: 237). The same study noted that the diffusion of JLP was furthered during the 1980s by the establishment of Japanese transplant production facilities and joint ventures in the West. By the end of the 1980s, there were 14 transplants (typically non-unionized) and seven joint ventures (typically unionized) in North America and Europe. Books by US and UK management experts extolling the superiority and transferability of Japanese lean production (e.g., Schonberger, 1982; Wickens, 1987), academic studies of the development of Japanese car production (e.g., Cusumano, 1985), and an account of the historical evolution of the (lean) Toyota production system by its creator (Ohno, 1988), also played a part in disseminating detailed information about what lean production involves and how to implement it.

One book in particular, *The Machine that Changed the World* (Womack et al., 1990) which was a mixture of academic research and management style prescriptions was a hugely influential advocate of JLP and the source of the term 'lean production'. It claimed that the way Japanese companies organized production combined 'the advantages of craft and mass production, while avoiding the high cost of the former and the rigidity of the latter', and was born out of the necessity of a small market for a great variety of cars (ibid.: 13). In short, high quality, greater variety, plus low cost and flexible volume production. This system of production is called lean

> because it uses less of everything compared to mass production – half the human effort in the factory, half the manufacturing space, half the investment in tools, half the engineering hours to develop a new product in half the time …requires keeping far less than half the needed inventory on site, [and] results in many fewer defects. (ibid.: 13)

It also claimed that JLP involves upskilling rather than deskilling, and is fulfilling rather than alienating. The key questions are: how does JLP manage to accomplish all this? And does it represent a new, post-Fordist way of organizing production or is it a modified version of Fordism (i.e., neo-Fordist)?

The essence of JLP is captured by the concept *kaizen*, which means the continuous improvement (CI) of every phase of production in order to 'increase production efficiency by consistently and thoroughly eliminating waste' – the uneconomic use of labour, machinery, parts, raw materials, space, and so on (Ohno, 1988: xiii). Waste equals unnecessary expense hence the unending search to identify and abolish it is vital if costs are to be reduced progressively while the quantity and quality of the products are increased. To motivate workers to embrace CI, Japanese companies promised job security in the form of lifetime employment (Womack et al., 1990). Several interdependent practices were introduced to achieve the reductions in waste and improvements in the volume and quality of the output, the three most important were just-in-time production (JIT), total quality control (TQC), and teamwork (TW).

JIT refers to the supply of materials, parts and sub-assemblies for the final assembly exactly when they are needed, 'just-in-time', rather than in advance, 'just-in-case' they were needed as was the production method under Fordism (Cusumano, 1985: 264–5). Ohno recalled that the inspiration for JIT was the American supermarket in the 1950s which was organized so that 'a customer can get (1) what is needed, (2) at the time needed, (3) in the amount needed' (1988: 26). This way of organizing production reduces the size of buffer stocks to a bare minimum and requires the use of a *kaban* (or tag) to ensure that each part is available when and where it is needed, thereby facilitating the continuous flow of production. This approach epitomizes leanness since it saves on materials, space, labour, and stock inventories. For example, by predicating JIT on minimal buffer stocks, less space and fewer workers are needed to store and move parts. However, for JIT production to be effective, it is essential that components are produced and delivered defect-free 'in lots as small as possible' and that workers are trained to check that this is so and have the authority to stop the production line (Cusumano, 1985: 265). Thus the smooth operation of JIT necessitates the empowerment of workers in the process of quality control, which in turn cuts down the number of inspectors and the accumulation of defective parts. Moreover, to produce a variety of models economically meant that set-up times had to be reduced and workers had to change the machines, otherwise the assembly line and those who work on it would be idle during the changeover of models. Cusumano provides details of how parts were standardized, special-purpose machines were modified, and the tasks assigned to workers were increased, and, as a result, changeover times were reduced by Toyota from three hours to three minutes between the early 1950s and the early 1970s, whereas US and European car manufacturers were still taking between 4 to 6 hours to accomplish a changeover in 1977. In addition to checking, maintaining, and correcting machinery, plus taking responsibility for die changes when production was switched to a different model, multi-skilling was extended to the assembly line itself by the development of 'U-shaped' or 'parallel-configured lines' which enabled a worker to perform tasks on both sides of the line (Schonberger, 1982: 141). Ohno (1988) noted that the reconfiguration of the assembly line made it possible for workers to operate as many as three or four machines if necessary. JIT was not limited to the production process but applied backwards to the suppliers of parts and forward to the distributors of cars; parts are supplied when needed on a daily basis directly to the factory and production was geared to demand, both of which minimized stockpiling and saved on storage space. The JIT system took many years to perfect since it required the co-operation of suppliers, managers and workers, and resulted in significant cost reductions and improvements in quality while increasing the variety of models produced (product flexibility), the range of tasks workers performed (functional flexibility) and variations in the supply of workers to particular tasks (numerical flexibility).

It is clear from the above that a successful JIT system places a premium on total quality control (TQC). In fact, such is the symbiotic relationship between these two features of JLP that they are sometimes referred to as one, namely JIT/TQC (e.g., Schonberger, 1982). As with JIT, Ohno (1988) noted that TQC was imported from America. It was applied to all aspects of car production, from pre-production testing to eliminate design faults, to 'a given level of quality determined by what consumers desire and are willing to pay for' (Cusumano, 1985: 320). For example, keeping the factory clean and tidy, known as good housekeeping, is a TQC priority and the responsibility of every employee since it is conducive to the safety of labour and machinery – injury to either would disrupt production. Moreover, in addition to error-proof machines, workers check their machines before they start to operate them and undertake preventive maintenance. Thus, TQC is a company-wide exercise to improve quality at every stage of production; if a defect is detected, it is dealt with at source rather than at the end of the process by randomly selected inspections. This broad approach to quality is not only crucial for the successful operation of JIT, it also ensures 'higher quality finished goods' (Schonberger, 1982: 37). Like JIT, TQC saves on time (e.g., fewer rework hours), saves on labour (e.g., fewer inspectors), and saves on materials (e.g., fewer defective parts). The emphasis on quality and the transfer of responsibility for it from management to the shop-floor alters the role and therefore the training of production workers. JLP training programmes in Japanese companies are more comprehensive (Cusumano, 1985) and last much longer than those in US and European companies (Womack et al., 1990).

In order to achieve CI, training in quality issues does not stop at the recruitment stage, it is followed up with time set aside for workers to study production methods and make suggestions about how to enhance the production process as members of quality control circles (QCC). According to Cusumano (1985), formally structured QCC were developed as work groups because it was thought that workers would feel more comfortable studying in this structure than individually since working in groups was common in Japanese schools. He also noted that QCC are regarded by Toyota and Nissan executives as primarily concerned with increasing worker participation and morale.

The main purpose of QCC may be their human relations function, but they can also save money; for example, it has been claimed that between 1974 and 1984 quality circles saved Nissan '40 billion yen ($160,000,000)' which 'worked out to about $5,000 per circle, an amount typical of other firms in Japan' (Cusumano, 1985: 334). As a result of this holistic approach to quality, Cusumano noted that in the late 1970s the recall rate of Japanese cars sold in the USA was one-third that of American companies.

The third and final element in the triumvirate that constitutes the JLP system is teamwork (TW), yet another idea that Ohno imported from America. In the above discussion of JIT and TQC it was apparent that production TW was vital to the efficacy of both and hence integral to JLP. The team concept is also used as a metaphor for cordial co-operation as in a sports team, a perspective which favours the propagation of a unitary company culture, manifestations of which include single status uniforms and dining rooms. Both meanings of TW evoke egalitarianism and feature prominently in the rhetoric of managerial discourses that encourage all employees to identify with the company, thereby blurring divisions within the workforce. While both forms of TW will be discussed, the main focus will be on TW production since it is considered central to the success of JLP; 'it is the dynamic work team that emerges as the heart of the lean factory' (Womack et al., 1990: 99; see also Kenney and Florida, 1993: 102). Womack et al. note that there are three stages to the process developing efficient TW. Workers are trained in a variety of skills to facilitate job rotation; they are taught additional skills, such as simple machine repairs to ensure continuous production; and they are encouraged to think creatively to resolve problems before they become major ones. Team leaders coordinate the work of teams as well as undertake assembly tasks and responsibility is effectively transferred from management to work teams, not individual workers. As a result of TW, it is claimed that JLP increases productivity, work satisfaction, and that, like JIT and TQC, TW can be transplanted successfully.

For Womack et al. (1990), the contrast between Fordism and JLP is stark. Instead of the monotony of task fragmentation and extreme alienation, there is rotation of multi-skilled tasks and empowerment as part of creative work teams that produce a great variety of high quality products at lower costs. JLP is therefore the 'new best way' and such is their confidence in JLP, they assert that once implemented fully, companies will be able 'to automate most of the remaining repetitive tasks …[and] by the end of the century we expect that lean-assembly plants will be populated almost entirely by highly skilled problem solvers' (ibid.: 84, 102). Hence, they recommend that 'the whole world should adopt lean production and as quickly as possible', and expect JLP to replace mass production 'to become the standard global production system of the twenty-first century', by which time the 'world will be a very different, and much better place' (ibid.: 225, 278).

The Womack et al. study does not use the Fordism paradigm, though it is abundantly clear from their analysis and conclusions that they consider mass

Table 5.3 Key features of a post-Fordist interpretation of industrial JLP

JLP: post-Fordist production system characterized by:

1 Re-unification of mental and physical labour, job rotation and multi-skilling
2 Flexible assembly line operated by teams of empowered workers
3 Non-standardized parts and great variety of high quality products

production to be Fordist and JLP to be post-Fordist. For example, they characterize mass production as unskilled workers tending single-purpose machines to produce large volumes of standardized parts and low quality products, and lean production as multi-skilled workers operating flexible machines to produce small quantities of a great variety of high quality parts and products. Other advocates of JLP, notably Kenney and Florida, draw upon the concept Fordism and claim that; 'the social organization of production in Japan 'is postfordist' since 'Self-managing teams, just-in-time production complexes, and learning by doing have replaced the functional specialization, deskilling, and linear production lines of fordist mass manufacturing' (1988: 122, 145). Thus they too consider that JLP is a new and superior production system to Fordism. Table 5.3 summarizes the key features of a post-Fordist interpretation of JLP in terms of the three main characteristics of Fordism outlined in Table 5.1 earlier in the chapter.

A neo-Fordist critique and interpretation of JLP

Among those who extol the virtues of JLP there is a tendency to do less than justice to its negative features (Babson, 1995), and to exaggerate its discontinuities with Fordism (Williams et al., 1992b), the combination of which enables them to argue that it represents something different and better than Fordism, namely post-Fordism. Womack et al. admit that JLP workers 'may find their work more stressful' and that the 'pace of work was clearly harder', but claim that 'it also provides workers with the skills they need to control their work environment and the continuing challenge of making their work go more smoothly' (1990: 14, 80, 101). Furthermore, they speculate that 'lean production is unlikely to prove more oppressive than mass production', though they also note that 'it is vital to remove unneeded workers from the system so that the same intensity of work is maintained. Otherwise the challenge of continual improvement will be lost' (ibid.: 102–3, 259). Kenney and Florida (1993) are more critical of JLP in that they show that JLP has been transferred less successfully to consumer electronics transplants due to local opposition and traditions. Second, in addition to the lean deal of lifetime employment in exchange for total commitment to the company emphasized by Womack et al., they confirmed the point made by Cusumano (1985) and others (e.g., Wickens, 1987), that the recruitment of temporary workers, who are more easily hired and fired, is a feature of JLP. Third, they concede that

JLP involves 'long hours and high stress', and a higher incidence of injuries as a result of the 'fast work pace', consequently it is 'not a workers' paradise' (1993: 10, 25, 266). They surmise that these negative features arise from the incomplete implementation of JLP and will therefore disappear over time. In the meantime, they suggest that such problems are outweighed by the positive features of the JLP system, notably the creative potential unleashed by multi-skilled TW. In contrast to these celebratory accounts of JLP from a management perspective, data from those who work in JLP plants will be afforded greater consideration with reference to the three key features of Fordism outlined previously.

First, although the Taylorized fragmentation of tasks has been altered in JLP to the extent that workers are trained to perform a variety of direct (e.g., assembly line work) and indirect (e.g., preventive maintenance) functions, the essence of Taylorism is not only retained but applied more thoroughly. Cusumano noted that at Toyota, Ohno introduced time and motion studies to revise 'standard operation sheets to make it easier for unskilled workers to perform more efficiently' and sought 'to redistribute worker motions and cycle times to eliminate idle time for a series of workers, and then remove one or more of them or have the last person on the line take over the tasks of his neighbour, and so on down the line' (1985: 272). He also commented that while both these techniques for improving productivity had originated in America, Ohno 'applied them with much more rigour' in his determination 'to eliminate all unnecessary movements and allow no idle time for machines or workers' (ibid.: 272). Even advocates of JLP confess that, 'the Japanese out-Taylor us all' (Schonberger, 1982: 193). This is because JIT production requires workers to perform their tasks in a standard way/time, otherwise it will not work (Rinehart et al., 1997). Thus JIT is based on the same Taylorist principles as Fordism (Wood, 1992).

A survey of workers, team leaders, union representatives, and managers in a GM-Suzuki joint venture in Canada has shown that the rhetoric of CI, job enrichment, and job rotation, obscures the degree to which CI is operationalized narrowly in terms of cost reduction not safety or skills, and the rotated jobs are learned easily and quickly, highly standardized, repetitive, and involve very little discretion, hence the term 'multi-tasking' is considered as a more accurate description of work under JLP than 'multi-skilling' (Rinehart et al., 1994; Rinehart et al., 1997). Taylorism was also prominent in Nissan's UK factory where the standardization of work was company policy, rotation was rare except to cover for absentees, and job enlargement tended to be down rather than up, such as cleaning up the work space (Garrahan and Stewart, 1992). In a US transplant study based mainly on interviews with workers, Besser noted that: 'Toyota prides itself on standardized work', hence workers are not allowed to deviate from the detailed specifications of how to perform a particular job (1996: 63). In some Japanese transplants, management either discourages extensive job rotation or seeks to abolish it altogether since it can make it more difficult to locate the source of quality problems (Parker and Slaughter, 1990; 1995) and compromise efficiency (Elger and Smith, 2005). The claim that JLP plants place greater emphasis on training is undermined by research which found that although the total instructional time in one Japanese transplant was high (127.5 hours), less than half (56) were devoted to technical training while the majority (71.5) were concerned with socializing new recruits into the 'we' company culture (Graham, 1995). Absorbing a pro-company culture is clearly given a higher priority than acquiring multiple technical 'skills', which further reveals the vacuity of the designation 'multi-skilling'.

Reservations have also been expressed about the reunification of mental and manual labour, which, according to one of the Womack et al. study researchers, JLP 'stands Taylorism on its head' (MacDuffie, 1995: 56). Workers have always used their brains as well as their brawn, typically to make their work easier, much to the chagrin of Taylor who advised that managers gather their knowledge and use it to increase efficiency. What is different about JLP is the method used to collect workers' knowledge; in addition to employing specialists, workers share their knowledge with team members and in quality circles (Parker and Slaughter, 1995). JLP therefore involves a refinement of Taylorism not a rejection of it (Dohse et al., 1985). The prevalence of Taylorism in JLP is indicated by the use of the terms 'despotic Taylorism' and 'democratic Taylorism' by Adler (1995) to describe the different ways of harnessing workers' knowledge under Fordism and JLP respectively. The introduction of a participative form of Taylorism is more effective since it reduces costs by cutting down on specialists and lessens antagonism by encouraging workers to be actively complicit in their subordination to the JLP goal of CI (Rinehart et al., 1997). In this regard, JLP is just a 'more efficient form of Fordism' (Price, 1995: 101); in other words, it is neo-Fordist.

The second key feature of Fordist production concerns the assembly line, which post-Fordist interpreters of JLP admit involves a tougher pace of work than in a Fordist system, but still consider it more fulfilling. The alleged benefits of JLP assembly-line work are thought to derive from workers' ability to stop the line, the opportunity to perform multiple 'skilled' operations in teams, and the sense of pride in producing high quality goods. But even proponents of JLP have found that workers in US transplants are put under pressure by management not to stop the assembly line (Kenney and Florida, 1993). A study of a non-union JLP transplant by Graham reported that, contrary to what workers were told during orientation and training, 'unless there is a safety emergency, only team leaders or higher ranking company officials have the authority to pull the red cord and stop the line' and that when the line speed was increased, it resulted in more hand and wrist injuries to workers who were expected to continue working with splints on their wrists (1995: 79). Graham also found that a normal working day was nine hours but if production quotas were not met, overtime was compulsory and announced at short notice. Graham concurred with other critics of a post-Fordist interpretation of JLP that assembly-line work is monotonous under both Fordism and JLP, and the main difference between them is that 'speedup and work intensification' are greater in JLP (ibid.: 62). The tendency for the authority to stop the line to be limited to team leaders or supervisors and the pervasiveness of mandatory overtime were confirmed in a study of Toyota transplants in Europe (Pardi, 2007).

The intensification of work on a JLP assembly line has been corroborated by many studies including that of the GM plant in California in which workers were kept busy for 45 out of 60 seconds, but when it became a Toyota-GM joint venture they worked on average 57 out of 60 seconds (Adler, 1995). Similarly, the aforementioned study by Rinehart et al. found that the practice of line speedup without adding workers created an exceptionally heavy workload and concluded that: 'Lean production places greater demands on workers' time and effort than does mass production' (1997: 84). The main sources of intensification in a JLP plant, according to the Nissan UK study, were the requirement to help and/or cover for other team members and the extra responsibilities devolved to teams such as quality checks (Garrahan and Stewart, 1992; see also Stewart and Garrahan, 1995; Stewart et al., 2009). These accounts of the demanding nature of work in JLP plants are indicative of a 'management by stress' system (Parker and Slaughter, 1990). They also suggest that little has changed since Kamata's diary of working on a Toyota assembly line in Japan during the 1970s revealed an obsession to eliminate all sources of waste to achieve higher output at lower costs that resulted in increased work loads, hours, and fatigue, which in turn lead to more work accidents, injuries, and fatalities, which were called 'serious accidents' by management (1984: 107).

Working on an assembly line in teams is portrayed as a distinctive and positive dimension of JLP by those who consider it to be post-Fordist, but research on transplants reveals that there is a dark side to TW, namely peer pressure. This is recognized by some advocates of JLP, notably MacDuffie, who noted that when a team member is absent, work loads increase and that: 'The peer controls that emerge in such a situation can easily turn poisonous' (1995: 57; see also Kenney and Florida, 1993: 279–80). This point acknowledges that peer pressure is integral to a JLP system in which multiple responsibilities are devolved to teams. A study of JLP plants in the USA found that: 'When the team is made responsible for getting the assigned work done, a powerful peer pressure is set up; if one person is absent, the system forces other team members to take up the slack' (Parker and Slaughter (1995: 48; see also Garrahan and Stewart, 1992). In addition to covering for absent, injured or slower team members, pressure to work hard can result from the internalization of corporate goals (Besser, 1996), although there is often gap between the management TW rhetoric and the reality of infrequent and poorly attended team meetings at which only the team leader speaks (Stewart et al., 2009). However, even if workers are less than convinced by the company-as-one team discourse, teams operate as a powerful horizontal supplement to hierarchical supervision that can 'boast attendance, job performance, and kaizen activities' (Rinehart et al., 1995: 223). Peer pressure may be good for management, but for workers it is yet another source of social control. The requirement to meet output quotas via extra hours and extra effort by under-staffed teams means that the real buffers in a JLP system are the workers (Berggren, 1993; Rinehart et al., 1997). Thus, for workers, JLP tends to increase work intensification and is therefore clearly neo-Fordist.

The third key feature of Fordism, the standardization of parts and low quality products, was overcome in JLP by making every effort 'to put together a specialized, yet versatile production process through the use of machines and jigs that can handle minimal quantities of materials' to produce a variety of products without 'undermining the benefits of mass production' (Ohno, 1988: 40). Hence contrary to the claim that JLP is 'beyond mass production' (Kenney and Florida, 1988: 121), lean production is still mass production as Ohno has acknowledged, and many others have confirmed (e.g., Cusumano, 1985; Sayer and Walker, 1992). It would be more accurate therefore to describe JLP as a manufacturing system designed for a large number of small lots and Fordism as one for the production of a small number of large lots. Moreover, as noted above, product variation was developed by GM in the 1920s; it was only during the first decade of Fordism that consumer choice was limited to 'any colour ...so long as it is black' (Ford, 2008 [1922]: 52). The continued importance of economies of large-scale production to JLP is demonstrated by the tendency of such companies to reduce model variations in order to cut costs (Berggren, 1993). This trend has been documented by Coffey (2006) who showed that, in 2003, customers were offered a choice of 54 specifications of the Toyota Corolla and 130 for the Honda Accord, whereas there were over ten million specifications for the Ford Focus and twelve million for the Vauxhall (GM) Astra. Thus product variation was not only pioneered by GM during the rise of Fordism, but Western car companies still lead the founders of JLP in terms of consumer choice. This contradicts the assertion by Womack et al. that it was only under JLP that a 'true renaissance of consumer choice' was achieved (1990: 126). Hence, the association of product diversification and JLP is a 'myth' (Coffey, 2006: 40) and in this regard JLP does not represent a post-Fordist alternative to Fordism, but a neo-Fordist modification.

Finally, for advocates of JLP, the quality dimension of this new best way of manufacturing cars is a major improvement on Fordism and recent consumer surveys have confirmed this (www.consumerreports.org). However, the JLP reputation for high quality products was dealt a severe blow in 2009–10 when Toyota had to recall over 8.5 million cars for safety checks following numerous complaints and accidents, some of which were fatal, that were linked to problems with braking, accelerator pedals, and slipping floor mats (www.guardian. co.uk/news/datablog/2010/feb/09/toyota-recalls-full-list). Sales of Toyota in the USA were down nearly 10 per cent in February 2010 compared to the

Table 5.4 Key features of a neo-Fordist interpretation of industrial JLP

JLP: neo-Fordist production system characterized by:

1 Qualified Taylorized work tasks and limited job enlargement and rotation
2 Intensified work on a modified assembly line organized into teams with limited autonomy
3 Partial de-standardization of parts and an increasingly limited range of higher quality products

same month in 2009, whereas all the other main car makers reported increased sales, which suggests that Toyota's reputation for quality has been affected negatively by the massive scale of their recall problem (www.msnbc.msn.com/id/35662491/). Toyota's response was to embark upon an extensive advertising campaign to reassure current and future customers that quality is still their top priority. Until this global recall crisis, the view that JLP, pioneered by Toyota, resulted in high quality products was incontrovertible, but it is no longer so.

These criticisms of a post-Fordist interpretation of JLP suggest that it is essentially a neo-Fordist system of production. The key features of a neo-Fordist interpretation of JLP are summarized in Table 5.4, once again in terms of those outlined for Fordism in Table 5.1 earlier in the chapter.

The argument that JLP is more a development of, rather than a radical departure from, Fordism, is also discernible from evidence which shows that Henry Ford's approach to mass production was 'proto-Japanese' as he too operated with low stock levels, sought CI 'through labour intensification', and encouraged workers to make suggestions about how to improve the production process (Williams et al., 1992a: 519, 532). This analysis is supported by other researchers, notably Levinson (2002) and Wilson (1995) who have documented the parallels between Ford's version of Fordism and JLP, especially their mutual concern to eliminate waste, both of whom quote Ohno who when asked about the origins of his ideas about lean production, responded by saying that, 'he learned it all from Henry Ford's book' (Wilson, 1995: 59). When Japanese companies were not drawing upon Henry Ford for inspiration, they were borrowing other American innovations, such as Taylorism and quality control techniques (Cusumano, 1985).

Finally, it has been argued by critics of JLP that its successful transfer to the West has been based in part on four other factors related to the production process. First, Japanese companies show a clear preference for rural, non-union areas rather than urban union environments for locating transplants because this improves the prospect of recruiting a loyal and dedicated workforce (Rinehart et al., 1997). Second, such companies tend to adopt a lengthy and highly selective recruitment process to screen out those who do not express the required attitudinal and behavioural attributes (Graham, 1995). Third, those hired are often put on temporary contracts on a trial basis with the promise of a permanent contract if they conform and perform to company expectations (Jacobs, 1995). Temporary workers are also more disposable. For example, BMW, who won an award in 2003 for their successful implementation of a JLP system, sacked the entire weekend shift of temporary workers who did not qualify for redundancy payments at their Mini factory in Oxford when sales declined (Milner, 2009). Fourth, JLP plants favour a compliant workforce that lacks independent trade union representation and is therefore more likely to co-operate with management over a range of production rationalizations (Besser, 1996; Stewart et al., 2009). The anti-union tendency of Japanese car companies is a recurrent theme in the JLP literature in accounts of its rise in Japan (e.g., Cusumano, 1985), and even research by supporters of JLP who consider it to be post-Fordist (e.g., Kenney and Florida, 1993). In this respect, JLP is identical to the early decades of Fordism and its unitary managerial ideology and like its precursor has discovered that attempts to neutralize independent union activity does not guarantee conflict-free workplaces (Maguire, 2003; Rinehart et al., 1997) or solve the problems of labour recruitment and retention (Elger and Smith, 2005). These considerations have led some to conclude that JLP 'is simply the practice of the organizational principles of Fordism under conditions in which management prerogatives are largely unlimited' (Dohse et al., 1985: 141). The implementation of JLP is therefore not just a matter of an allegedly superior production system, the contribution of factors other than the production process need to be taken into account.

The continuities between JLP and Fordism are therefore extensive, particularly from the standpoint of workers who remain subjected to the imposition of Taylorized work standards with limited job rotation of multiple tasks and a fast-paced assembly line that they are discouraged from stopping, all predicated upon a divided workforce and a diminished role for independent unions. Hence, JLP tends to increase both work intensification and mandatory overtime, and is more accurately described as 'lean and mean' (Harrison, 1997). This suggests that JLP constitutes a neo-Fordist solution to the crisis of Fordism, notwithstanding the 'we' rhetoric, enhanced worker input, and higher quality products emphasized by advocates of JLP who regard it as post-Fordist.

The future of JLP seems far less assured than the confident assertions of Womack et al. (1990) since a neo-Fordist interpretation of JLP suggests that it has not solved many of the labour and consumer problems associated with Fordism. It is also apparent that there are several other limitations regarding the universality of the JLP model, notably opposition from local vested corporate interests who fear increased competition (Kenney and Florida, 1993), the perception that cost-cutting was a causal factor in the recent global safety recall crisis at Toyota, the originator and exemplar of JLP (Clark and McCurry, 2010), and the images of thousands of unsold cars parked at docks in the UK and the USA that appeared in the press during the 2009 recession (e.g., *Guardian* 7 April, 23 May 2009) which are indicative of Fordist just-in-case production and suggest that JIT has not been achieved fully. Finally, the JIT dimension of JLP has been criticized by unions in Japan for exacerbating road congestion and pollution (Berggren, 1993) and a US study has shown that

Table 5.5 Advantages and disadvantages of neo-Fordist industrial JLP

	Society	Workers	Employers	Consumers
Advantages	Abundance	Slightly more interesting work	Increased productivity and profits	Better quality products
Disadvantages	Pollution	Physical exhaustion and mental stress	Persistence of workplace discontent and conflict	Gridlocked roads

while JIT plants save on space, materials, and energy, the environmental impact of increased transportation in terms of toxic emissions has been transferred to suppliers and 'the general public (www.bren.ucsb.edu/academics/courses/289/Readings/Nathan- 2007.pdf). It is ironic that a production system celebrated for its focus on empowering workers and eliminating waste, and hence its social and ecological soundness, is a major contributor to both the degradation of workers and the environment.

Post-Fordist interpreters of JLP have been criticized for adopting a management perspective and emphasizing its positive features, but neo-Fordist interpreters are open to the reverse charge, namely that they view JLP from below and focus on its negative impact on workers. With this in mind, Table 5.5 notes the main advantages and disadvantages of JLP from the standpoint of society as a whole, workers, employers, and consumers. It is important to recognize that, just like the global spread of Fordism, JLP has been 'constructed and reconstructed' differently in specific countries and companies in response to local conditions, including product and labour markets, and management–worker relations (Elger and Smith, 2005: 358).

For example, it has been argued that statist neo-Fordism prevails in Japan as a result of an interventionist state and a weak labour movement, whereas corporate neo-Fordism exists in the USA where labour is also weak but state intervention on its behalf is minimal (Gottfried, 1995). It remains to be seen whether the disadvantages of JLP lead to a reassessment of the social and economic benefits of this way of organizing production, and if so, the nature and extent to which it is modified or transformed in the future. What is certain is that JLP is not the 'the end of history' (Berggren, 1993: 163).

Summary and conclusions

Fordism is primarily a type of industrial production system, typically referred to as mass production, one that was pioneered by Henry Ford during the first two decades of the twentieth century. During this period Fordism subscribed to a unitary managerial ideology which considered unions as unnecessary, but under pressure from workers and the state eventually acknowledged the legitimacy of union representation and accepted a pluralistic compromise. Fordism is also an economic system characterized by mass consumption thanks to the sharing of the benefits of the economies of large-scale production. The third inter-related dimension of Fordism concerns its political features, notably a supportive state welfare system that, among other things, ensures a supply of physically healthy workers and economically healthy consumers. Thus, the rise and development of Fordism involved mass production, mass consumption and political stability in the West. It marked a major departure from the craft-based, non-standardized, low-volume production and consumption characteristic of pre-Fordism.

As a new type of industrial production system, it was based in large part on Taylorism, although there is some debate about the exact relationship between Taylorism and Fordism. Taylor and Henry Ford advocated remarkably similar prescriptions for minimizing waste, maximizing output, lowering costs, the social control of workers inside and outside the factory, and neutralizing conflict. Fordism, by virtue of its defining features, namely fragmented and simplified work, assembly-line production, and standardized parts and products, became inextricably associated with deskilled work, conflict between labour and capital, and the mass production of low-quality goods. GM developed industrial Fordism in the direction of annual model changes and extended the mass production market to all income groups. The increase in productivity and decrease in costs achieved by Fordism resulted in it being adopted globally during the twentieth century, albeit variably in terms of place and time. In the process of stabilizing this problematic production system, it became synonymous with the standardization of work and workers' behaviour, cultural values that emphasized regular hard work for high pay, and contractual social benefits, underpinned initially by paternalistic company social programmes and later by state welfare systems, all of which culminated in the full-time male worker and the full-time female homemaker model. Fordism entailed economic, social, and political disadvantages, as well as the well-known advantages of mass production and consumption.

Various theories have been advanced as to why this successful yet flawed industrial production system experienced a crisis of productivity and profitability in the 1970s. Among the most influential are regulation theory, which attributed the crisis in Fordism to worker dissatisfaction, and flexible specialization theory, which attributed it to consumer dissatisfaction. Both theories have been criticized on empirical grounds which suggests that the decline of Fordism had a lot to do with higher costs of production and increased competition from new entrants to the global car market. Whatever the merits and demerits of these views, there is broad agreement that there was a crisis of profitability and that an alternative to Fordism was needed.

Several solutions to the crisis of Fordism emerged during the second half of the last century, including automating production, and/or internationalizing production, and/or re-organizing production. These solutions are not mutually exclusive. The main global solution to industrial Fordism was JLP, pioneered by Toyota and emulated by other manufacturers in Japan, especially car companies. The success of JLP in terms of productivity and profitability led to Western car companies adopting JLP, often via joint ventures. The key elements of JLP are *kaizen* or CI via JIT, TQC, and TW, the combination of which is thought by its advocates to improve productivity, quality, and profits while simultaneously enhancing worker satisfaction. A post-Fordist interpretation of JLP claims that this is a new way of organizing production as it involves the reunification of mental and physical labour, job rotation in multi-skilled teams of empowered workers who work harmoniously on modified assembly lines to produce non-standard parts for a variety of high quality products. According to this view, JLP is a major advance on Fordism that will become the dominant system globally during this century.

The post-Fordist interpretation of JLP has been criticized for its management bias, relative neglect of its negative impact on workers, and for exaggerating the discontinuities with Fordism. An increasing body of empirical research on workers' experience of JLP in the car industry and beyond suggests strongly that it involves Taylorized multi-tasking, limited job enlargement and rotation, heavier and more intense work by teams of workers with minimal discretion on modified assembly lines, producing standardized parts for an increasingly narrow range of quality products. According to this view, work in a JLP car factory, often lacking independent trade unions, is more oppressive and exploitative than under Fordism. This more critical interpretation of JLP suggests that the post-Fordist rhetoric of multi-skilled workers co-operating to improve continuously the quantity and quality of products is so far removed from the actual experience of work in a JLP system that it represents a neo-Fordist development of Fordism, rather than a post-Fordist transformation.

In terms of the organizational features of JLP that are thought to distinguish it radically from Fordism, namely CI via JIT, TQC, and TW, critical research on JLP plants shows that: (1) CI tends to be defined in terms of lower costs, not more humane work practices; (2) JIT depends on the rigorous implementation of Taylorism; and that (3) TQC, when combined with TW, institutionalizes the sharing of workers' knowledge. Thus these key features of JLP do not constitute a radical departure from Fordism. Moreover, the proto-Japanese character of Fordism confirms that post-Fordist interpreters of JLP have not only played down its negative features, but have exaggerated its discontinuities with Fordism. JLP has not replaced mass production, it has only modified it, has not transcended Taylorism, but revised and reinforced it, and it has not overcome worker alienation and unrest, it has merely contained it despite its attempts to ensure that a unitary managerial ideology prevails. Overall, therefore, it is difficult to escape the conclusion that since JLP is founded on Taylorism, the moving assembly line, and standardized parts, it 'may best be described as neo-rather than post-Fordist' (Rinehart et al., 1997: 202; see also Wood, 1992: 538). There are several obstacles to the global adoption of JLP in the car and other industries, including opposition from capital who fear competition, from labour who resist exploitation, from consumers who abhor gridlocked roads, and the general public who resent pollution. While post-Fordist interpreters of

JLP assert that it should and will become the standard way of organizing production in the future, a neo-Fordist exposition suggests that this possibility is problematic since it represents a partial solution to the crisis of Fordism.

The Fordist paradigm was used first and researched with reference to the evolution of industrial production, particularly car production. The next chapter explores the extent to which Taylorism and the Fordist conceptual framework are relevant to the sociological analysis of service sector work.

Further reading

BOOKS The historical accounts by Meyer (1981) *The Five Dollar Day: Labour Management and Control in the Ford Motor Company, 1908–21*, and Gartman (1987) *Auto Slavery: The Labour Process in the American Automobile Industry, 1897–1950*, are indispensable for an understanding of the rise of Fordism. There are some excellent articles on all aspects of the debate about Fordism (as well as neo-Fordism and post-Fordism) in Amin (ed.) (1994a) *Post-Fordism: A Reader*. For an analysis of the Fordist crisis, consult Lipietz (1992) *Towards a New Economic Order: Postfordism, Ecology and Democracy* and Piore and Sabel (1984) *The Second Industrial Divide*. The origins of JLP are covered by Ohno (1988) *Toyota Production System: Beyond Large-scale Production*, and Cusumano (1985) *The Japanese Automobile Industry: Technology and Management at Nissan and Toyota*. Post-Fordist interpretations of JLP include Womack et al. (1990) *The Machine that Changed the World*, and Kenney and Florida (1993) *Beyond Mass Production: The Japanese System and its Transfer to the US*. For a neo-Fordist interpretation of JLP, consult Babson (1995) *Lean Work: Empowerment and Exploitation in the Global Auto Industry* as it includes most of the important contributions to the debate. The best theoretically informed empirical analysis and critique of the post-Fordist view of JLP in the West is the one by Rinehart et al. (1997) *Just Another Factory: Lean Production and its Discontents*. The most up-to-date critical account of JLP from the perspective of workers is by Stewart et al. (2009) *We Sell Our Time No More: Workers' Struggles Against Lean Production in the British Car Industry*.

ARTICLES Williams et al. (1992a) 'Ford versus "Fordism": the beginning of mass production?', *Work, Employment and Society*, 6(4): 517–55 is instructive on the origins of Fordism, and Berggren (1993) 'Lean production – the end of history?', *Work, Employment and Society*, 7(2): 163–88 is suitably sceptical about lean production being the new one best way of organizing production.

WEBSITES The University of Michigan's *The Automobile in American Life and Society* website is an excellent resource – the webpages by Meyer are particularly relevant – www.autolife.umd.umich.edu/

For a useful but uncritical overview of the development of lean production with special reference to manufacturing, consult www.strategosinc.com/just_in_time.htm

---

Questions for discussion and assessment

1 What are the defining characteristics of Fordism and how do they differ from pre-Fordism?
2 Assess the advantages and disadvantages of Fordism.
3 Discuss the claim that Fordism involved more than just a new method of production.
4 Account for the decline of Fordism.
5 Consider the view that Japanese lean production constitutes a post-Fordist transformation of Fordism.
6 Examine critically the neo-Fordist interpretation of Japanese lean production.
7 Evaluate the advantages and disadvantages of Japanese lean production.

6

SERVICE WORK: FORDISM, NEO-FORDISM AND POST-FORDISM

Chapter contents

- Interactive service work
- The rise of Fordism and interactive service work
- Interactive service work: neo-Fordism and post-Fordism
- Knowledge work and the Fordist model of change
- Summary and conclusions
- Further reading
- Questions for discussion and assessment

In Chapter 1, it was noted that during the rise of industrial capitalism in the nineteenth century, the production of goods was transferred from the home to the factory. Once goods had been incorporated into the market system, it was the turn of services to succumb to what Braverman has called the 'universal market' and '[I]n time not only the material and service needs but even the emotional patterns of life are channelled through the market' (1974: 276). At the beginning of this century the growth of service work had reached the point where approximately three-quarters of all paid employment in advanced industrial capitalist countries was in the service sector (Warhurst et al., 2009). Work in the service sector is highest in the USA and the UK at nearly 80 per cent compared to less than 20 per cent in industry, yet it is only in the recent past that research on service sector work has become part of the 'empirical mainstream in the sociology of work' (Korczynski, 2009: 952).

The growth of service work during the twentieth century was discussed by Braverman (Chapter 3) in the context of his progressive deskilling of work in industrial capitalist societies thesis and Bell (Chapter 4) as an integral part of his upskilling in post-industrial societies thesis. While Braverman focused mainly on low-level service work and Bell on the increasing scale and importance of professional and technical work, others have emphasized the polarization of service work into a large number of relatively low-skilled and low paid routine workers and a small number of relatively high-skilled and highly paid non-routine workers (e.g., Castells, 2001; Kumar, 1978; Macdonald and Sirianni, 1996). To exemplify this occupational trend, interactive service workers who perform emotional labour and specialist service workers who perform knowledge labour, will be discussed in this chapter. The distinction between emotion workers and knowledge workers does not imply that knowledge is unimportant in interactive service work or that emotion is irrelevant in specialist service work; it is a matter of centrality rather than exclusivity.

Although the theoretical models of changes about how work is organized, including the Fordist paradigm, originated and developed primarily with reference to industrial work, they were intended to apply to all types of work organizations (Applebaum and Batt, 1994). For example, it was noted in Chapter 3, that manual work was Taylorized first and later non-manual work, and in Chapter 5 that some of the key features of JLP, notably JIT, were pioneered in the service sector. More recently, the Chairman of the Lean Enterprises Research Centre noted that lean management, defined as a 'customer focused approach to the delivery of outstanding products and services with the use of a minimum of resources', has spread rapidly to service industries (Hines, 2009: 2). However, despite this, the service sector 'rarely appears in debates over Fordism' (Beynon and Nichols, 2006: xvi). Some sociologists, notably Ritzer (1998) and his McDonaldization thesis, have forsaken industrial production-related models of work to advance alternative service work-specific theories (Warhurst et al., 2009). For others, such as Hochschild (2003 [1983]), the idea of alienation (discussed in Chapter 2) informed her analysis of emotional labour. The aim of this chapter is to consider changes in interactive and professional service sector work historically with reference to the Fordist paradigm, thereby building on the analysis of Beynon and Nichols (2006).

Interactive service work

Service work that involves communicating with service-recipients (clients, customers, patients, passengers, students, etc.) face-to-face or voice-to-voice is referred to by Leidner (1993) as interactive service work. The focus here will be on face-to-face interactive service work since voice-to-voice service work in call centres epitomizes the role of advanced information technologies in the globalization of service work and will therefore be considered in Chapter 10 on globalization. The performance of face-to-face interactive service work includes an emotional element since in addition to undertaking manual tasks and mental effort, the 'emotional style of offering the service is part of the service itself' (Hochschild, 2003 [1983]: 5). Hochschild defined emotional labour as 'the management of feeling to create a publicly observable facial and bodily display' and in her analysis of flight attendants showed that while they are performing manual tasks such as pushing a meal trolley and thinking how best to distribute refreshments, they are also expected to be friendly and reassuring (ibid.: 7). It is clear from Hochschild's definition of emotional labour and account of airline staff appearance codes that covered everything from hairstyles to shoe styles, that interactive service work also involves an aesthetic dimension, termed aesthetic labour, which has been defined as 'embodied capacities and attributes' including both visual and aural appearances (Warhurst et al., 2000: 4). What is distinctive therefore about interactive service work is the presence of the recipients of services, which in turn has major implications for the service work role in terms of its emotional and aesthetic style, and complicates the management–worker relationship by introducing a third party whose interests may or may not coincide with those of either workers or their managers (Leidner, 1993).

The rise of Fordism and interactive service work

Before the complete separation of home and work associated with the rise of industrial capitalism in the West, discussed in Chapter 1, the main type of interactive service work was that of domestic servants, who typically lived in the home of their employer. However, this female-dominated type of personal interactive service work had virtually disappeared by the 1920s in industrial capitalist countries (Castells, 2001). The main alternative employment opportunities were to be found in the growing number of shops and offices, though these kinds of service work were initially male-dominated.

Throughout the nineteenth century in Britain and other industrializing countries, sales work in fixed site producer-retail and retail shops expanded at the expense of itinerant and market traders that were more typical of the pre-industrial era. The growing number of non-family sales workers, mostly young men and boys, lived in the shop/household, performed a range of tasks involving specialist knowledge and the preparation of goods, and provided a highly personalized service under the direct supervision of the owner (Alexander, 1970; Benson and Shaw, 1992). The early fixed site shop was a living and working space that enabled the owner to control the work and non-work behaviour of both family and non-family workers. Craft skills concerned with the production and sales of all types of goods were important not only in producer-retail shops, but also in the 'more purely retail food trades, such as grocery and household stores' since the shopkeeper and assistants were responsible for preparing the items for sale (Alexander, 1970: 110). They also worked long hours as shops were open from 12–16 hours a day, six days a week, often aided on a part-time basis by the cheaper labour of domestic servants, and for both types of workers living conditions were a major issue, with some young apprentices sleeping under the counter (Alexander, 1970). The tradition of sales and other staff sleeping on the premises, which increased employers' control over workers, did not disappear even with the growth of large-scale retailing in the form of department stores and their shorter working hours in the late nineteenth century (Shaw, 1992). Most shop workers were isolated but the growth of large-scale retailing and living-out wage labour enhanced the prospects of collective resistance against the long hours, low pay, and living-in typical of the majority of retail sales clerks, and resulted in unions being established by shop workers during the 1890s in Britain (www.usdaw. org.uk) and the USA (Glazer, 1993).

Thus, aside from domestic work, the main interactive service sector job during the pre-Fordist era of nineteenth-century Britain and other industrializing countries was in retail sales, which involved working and living in small-scale organizations that were often indistinct from the household of the employer and resulted in highly personal work relationships characterized by emotional and aesthetic labour. The work itself was multiskilled and required the worker to be well informed about the services provided and/or the products sold, and attentive to the needs of individual customers. For the majority of workers who lived-in, employers' control over their work and non-work behaviour, attitudes, and appearance was virtually absolute since they could be dismissed for alleged misdemeanours committed outside of work as well as at work. Although retail sales clerks were expected to be knowledgeable and skilled in the whole service process, namely the preparation and sale of products, any satisfaction they derived from the accomplishment of their 'craft', as Mills called it (1968 [1951]: 181), was likely to be compromised by the highly unsatisfactory pay and working conditions they experienced. For shop workers, particularly for those who lived-in and were therefore doubly dependent, the intimacy of work relations in a small-scale enterprise and the absence of a trade union added to their relative powerlessness and were conducive to them deferring to and identifying with the interests of the owner-manager.

During the first decades of the twentieth century in the USA, Taylorism was applied to retailing, as noted in Chapter 5. More specifically, self-service was first used in restaurants in the USA in the 1890s and subsequently adopted in food shops by the Lutey Brothers in 1912 and by the Piggly Wiggly stores in 1916 (Glazer, 1993). Self-service shops were based on the production line principle that pivoted around the moving customer rather than the moving assembly line; standardized pre-packaged goods were delivered at one end of the shop, stacked on aisles ready to be selected by customers who transported them to the checkout counter and exited at the other end of the shop. In contrast to full-service shops where a knowledgeable shop worker could advise on prices and products, locate them, measure out the required amount, bag them, calculate the total cost, arrange payment, and delivery if required, self-service customers made their own judgements about their needs in terms of price, quantity, quality, and appropriateness of products, collected them, unloaded them at the checkout, bagged them, and carried them away. The organization of the shop ensured that customers had to pass all the products in every aisle in order to reach the cashier near the exit which had the unanticipated benefit of encouraging impulse buying. For doing most of the work of shopping without assistance, including acquiring knowledge about products prior to entering the shop, the customer saves both money in the form of lower-priced standard goods and time. In effect, the shop worker became deskilled while the customer became upskilled (du Gay, 1996). Employers gained from the unpaid skilled labour of customers and the lower wages of an increasingly feminized deskilled retail labour force, especially the checkout worker who no longer wastes time waiting for a customer, instead it is the customer who queues at the checkout. This assembly-line system of service provision which incorporates the customers' unpaid labour was very successful in terms of reducing costs and increasing profits and has since spread to most services, including department stores, petrol stations, and restaurants. The technology used in self-service shops was quite limited initially, such as one-way turnstiles and checkout counters, but in due course more complex machines were introduced including cash registers which obviated the need for workers to perform mental calculations. In sum, the specialized personal service retailing process was industrialized with the customer doing most of the work organized on assembly-line principles (Glazer, 1993).

In the process of eroding the craft-like knowledge and skills of the sales clerk, the expansion of self-service retailing was accompanied by a more detailed division of unskilled labour:

> the all-around grocery clerk, fruiterer and vegetable dealer, dairyman, butcher, and so forth, has long ago been replaced by a configuration in the supermarkets which calls for truck unloaders, shelf-stockers, checkout clerks, meat wrappers, and meatcutters; of these, only the last retain any semblance of skill, and none require any general knowledge of retail trade. (Braverman, 1974: 371)

Braverman also argued that recent technological advances, notably computerized checkout systems that involve bar code scanning, simultaneously decrease the skill of the checkout worker still further and increase centralized management control, whereupon 'the checkout counter then adopts as its own the assembly line or factory pace in its most complete form' (ibid.: 372). Scanning technology enables the checkout operator to process twice as many customers than before when items sold were recorded using a manual keyboard, a form of work intensification. Retail automation is associated with reduced staffing levels, especially full-time workers, instead deskilled workers, typically women and young people, are employed when needed on a part-time basis, such as at lunchtime and weekends. Further contrasts with pre-Fordist retail sales work include reduced training, pay, and job prospects, and just like the early years of Fordism, labour turnover increased markedly and an anti-union attitude by employers was widespread (Gardner and Sheppard, 1989; Glazer, 1993).

Fordist self-service retailing was pioneered in American grocery stores during the first half of the twentieth century and was exported to Britain, Japan and elsewhere from the 1950s onwards for the same reasons and with the same consequences for retail workers. The primary motivation for the introduction of an assembly line self-service system was to reduce costs via lower staffing levels, less skilled workers, and a higher proportion of part-time workers (Gardner and Sheppard, 1989; Matsunaga, 2000). Shelf-filler and checkout operator became the main jobs in self-service retailing, both of which require little skill and therefore training, are poorly paid, and monotonous; the contrast between a pre-Fordist skilled full-time and a Fordist deskilled part-time shop worker could not be greater in terms of intrinsic and extrinsic rewards. Moreover, the tendency to deskill supermarket jobs now extends to store managers who, in a recent study of four UK supermarkets, were found to have no control over products, pricing, store layout, special offers, and staffing, all of which were decided by experts at head office (Grugulis et al., 2010). This study found that there was a chasm between the managerial rhetoric of leadership and the managerial practice of obedience to prescriptions from higher up in the bureaucratic hierarchy. Thus, there was little difference between non-managerial and managerial supermarket employees in terms of their low knowledge and skill levels, their standardized and scripted work tasks, and the monitoring of their performance.

The commonalities of industrial and interactive service work highlighted in a critical way by Braverman were also noted in a less than critical way by Levitt (1972) who argued that the efficiency and quality of service provision could be improved by adopting the methods of mass production in the manner achieved by the McDonald's chain of fast-food restaurants. According to Levitt, the success of McDonald's was due mainly to the application of industrial mass production to a people-intensive service production system whose Fordist aim was to produce a high volume of low-priced standard goods speedily and cheaply. As with the mass production of cars, the mass production of burgers is characterized by fragmented and simplified work tasks, single purpose machines organized in the form of an assembly line, and the use of standardized parts and products. For example, the raw materials such as the meat is pre-measured, pre-packed, and cooked with the aid of lights and buzzers which indicate when to turn the burgers, thereby eliminating any discretion on the part of the worker. Levitt is full of praise for the McDonald's system that he likened to

[a] machine that produces, with the help of totally unskilled machine tenders, a highly polished product ... everything is built integrally into the machine itself, into the technology of the system. The only choice available to the attendant is to operate it exactly as the designers intended. (1972: 46)

Moreover, McDonald's aimed to convey the message that customers receive a large meal for a small price, for example, by ensuring that every bag of French fries was designed and filled to give the impression of generosity. Levitt concluded that until the provision of services is approached in the same way technologically and organizationally as the mass production factory, it will remain inefficient and hence expensive, and unreliable and hence variable in quality.

Levitt's analysis of McDonald's as an exemplar of a Fordist approach to interactive service provision was confirmed by Love (1995) whose historical account of McDonald's showed that in 1948 after several years of experimentation, the McDonald brothers closed their small but successful drive-in restaurant and recast their business model. The kitchen was redesigned to facilitate the speedy high production, disposable bags and cups replaced china, the menu was reduced dramatically to either a hamburger or cheeseburger, with a set range of condiments, and customers placed their order at a service window, all of which streamlined the service production process. The price was cut 'from a competitive 30 cents to an unheard-of 15 cents' (ibid.: 15). Their new type of fast-food restaurant was 'based on speed, lower prices, and volume', plus a strict adherence to detailed standardized work procedures (Dick McDonald, quoted in Love, 1995: 14). McDonald's was transformed into a national corporation in the USA in the 1950s and into an international one in the 1970s by Ray Kroc who ensured that every McDonald's restaurant followed the same technological and organizational specifications (ibid.). The McDonald's operations manual described in detail the correct way for workers to perform every task and the correct way for managers to organize a fast-food restaurant, which contributed to the 'operation of McDonald's like an assembly line' (ibid.: 141). Every McDonald's restaurant, including the franchised ones, were required to follow exactly the standardized operating procedures detailed in the manual. According to Love, in the same way that Henry Ford had revolutionized car production, the McDonald brothers and Ray Kroc revolutionized fast-food production.

Levitt's Fordist characterization of McDonald's was also confirmed and extended by Ritzer (1996) who argued that the principles of the fast-food restaurant pioneered by McDonald's, notably bureaucracy, scientific management, and the assembly line, were spreading to the whole of American society and indeed the world. Notwithstanding Ritzer's neo-Weberian theoretical perspective with its focus on the rationalization of work and society via his four basic dimensions of McDonalization, namely efficiency, calculability, predictability and control, he does discuss briefly the relationship between McDonaldism and Fordism. Ritzer concluded that McDonaldism 'has many things in common with Fordism', notably Taylorized work tasks, single purpose machines and conveyer belt assembly, standardized parts and the speedy delivery of a high volume of inexpensive low-quality products (1996: 152). Moreover, in addition to being monitored by managers, subject to extensive operating rules, and controlled by machines, fast-food workers are also put under pressure by the presence of customers who expect to be served quickly. In other words, the key features of Fordism noted by Levitt, Love, and Ritzer, and outlined in Chapter 5 with reference to industrial production (Table 5.1), apply equally well to the production of services pioneered by McDonald's in the USA. However, aside from mentioning the importance of front-line service workers being courteous, Levitt and Love's accounts of the Fordist character of fast-food service production neglected to discuss in depth the interactive dimension of service work. Ritzer, drawing heavily on the research by Leidner (1993), extended these analyses by noting that in fast-food restaurants it is not only the tasks that are standardized, but also what workers say and how they appear to customers are standardized via scripts and appearance codes: 'The scripting of interaction leads to new depths in the deskilling of workers' (1998: 64). Hence McDonaldism is a particularly severe form of Fordism.

The requirement to follow scripts, subscripts, wear uniforms, and smile, are not only indicative of standardization and deskilling, but also of the emotional and aesthetic labour intrinsic to interactive service work (Hochschild, 2003 [1983]; Warhurst et al., 2000). Hochschild's study of emotional labour built upon the pioneering analysis of the commodification of feelings and appearances by Mills (1968 [1951]), and as noted in Chapter 2, concluded that interactive service workers who are required by their employing organizations to express certain emotions, such as friendliness, and disguise their true feelings, experience alienation from both the service product and the labour process. Neither Leidner nor Ritzer consider in depth the possibility of alienation, yet they claim that interactive service work in fast-food restaurants is both satisfying and alienating. Leidner tends to emphasize that working at McDonald's is satisfying, though he cautions against overestimating it on the grounds that his 'sample probably excluded the most dissatisfied workers' (1993: 137). Ritzer cites Leidner's research extensively and although he supports her argument that employees and customers benefit from the 'routinization, even the scripting, of work', he also claims that 'the most notable irrationality of rationality in the fast-food industry is the creation of a dehumanized and dehumanizing setting in which to eat and work' and that this leads to job dissatisfaction and customer exploitation (1998: 67, 111). While Ritzer does not distance his analysis of interactive service work from Hochschild's account to the same degree as Leidner, they both fail to address fully the Marxist core of her alienation thesis and in this respect are part of the tendency to deradicalize her contribution (Brook, 2009).

As well as being subject to the control of managerial co-workers, bureaucratic rules, and machines, the presence of customers in the labour process of interactive service work transforms the basic worker–management dyad into a worker–management–customer triad which complicates considerably the 'struggle over control in this type of work' (Leidner, 1996: 39). In theory, the complex alignment of each interest group is unstable, but in practice: 'At McDonald's, the interests of managers and customers converged, diminishing workers' control and allowing customers to augment management's control strategies' (Leidner, 1993: 128). This was because customers not only shared the managerial concern for a quick and polite service outcome, but they supplemented the managerial supervision of interactive service workers via 'the power to direct, evaluate, and reward or punish workers' (ibid.: 133). The subordination of interactive service workers to customers as well as management is reinforced by the increasing popularity of consumer service reports, the results of which are then used to evaluate and discipline service workers (Fuller and Smith, 1991). The multiple sources of control that interactive service workers are exposed to suggests that they experience far less autonomy than even Fordist car workers who at least are not observed continuously by customers every minute of their time at work.

A dissenting view on the commonalities of industrial and service work has been advanced by Allen and Du Gay who have argued that since interactive service work includes both economic and cultural dimensions, it cannot be understood 'within the discourse of manufacturing, even when many of its constituent elements have been subject to standardization and routinization' (1994: 267). They contend that the inclusion of social skills, such as communication and presentation, renders interactive service work a 'hybrid' occupation (ibid.: 266). A similar view has been advanced by Gatta et al. who claim that the industrial model of skill that focuses on levels of education and training time, 'masks skill demands in service occupations' (2009: 973). Their analysis of the job content of service work shows that complex interactive skills, such as active listening, communicating, co-ordinating, and emotional management skills, rather than cognitive and manual skills, are crucial to successful job performance in the service sector, but that they are difficult to measure and undervalued in terms of status and pay. These interpretations of interactive service work imply that, notwithstanding the excessive standardization of such work, it involves a degree of multi-skilling and upskilling and therefore it does not fit neatly into the industrial model of Fordism. However, this line of argument is arguably outweighed by the above evidence that interactive service work is an extreme form of Fordism

The Fordist approach to the mass production of food cheaply and quickly pioneered by McDonald's was emulated by many other food and non-food service organizations, for example, Pizza Hut and Disney World. This contributed to the mass consumption of a wide range of services and resulted in the growth of low-skilled, low-paid, repetitive, dead-end jobs that are widely referred to as 'McJobs' (Ritzer, 1998: 59). Thus, in the same way that Fordism deskilled and dehumanized factory work and democratized car ownership, it has also deskilled and dehumanized interactive service work and democratized eating out in restaurants. Thus, the key features of pre-Fordism and Fordism noted in Chapter 5 (Table 5.1) are identical for industrial and service work except for the distinctive interactive dimension of the latter that has also been Taylorized and standardized, as Table 6.1 shows.

The parallels between the early Fordism of car production and that of fast-food production extend to labour relations in that both systems are characterized by patriarchy, high labour turnover, and overtly anti-union employers, especially in the USA and Canada (Love, 1995; Schlosser, 2002). In the same

Table 6.1   Key features of interactive service pre-Fordism and Fordism

Pre-Fordism: type of service system characterized by:
1 Craft skills and full-service
2 Stationary assembly
3 Non-standardized parts, high quality products, and personal service

Fordism: type of service system characterized by:
1 Fragmented and simplified (Taylorized) work tasks and partial service
2 Assembly line process
3 Standardized parts, low quality products, and impersonal service

way that female workers were a small minority in the mass production car factories and only increased during times of severe labour shortages, notably during the two world wars (Gartman, 1987), hiring women to work in fast-food restaurants such as McDonald's occurred in the 1960s when full employment made it difficult to recruit male workers (Love, 1995). However, unlike the car industry which eventually succumbed to the pressure for unionization, McDonald's and other fast-food service organizations have maintained successfully their anti-union policy for reasons that will be discussed below. Also, in contrast to the car industry, Fordist fast-food service organizations such as McDonald's offer employees the prospect of promotion from deskilled entry-level positions to middle-level ones that allow for more discretion (Ritzer, 1998; Leidner, 2002). However, Ritzer and Leidner have noted that most employees are young part-timers who do not qualify for advancement since this requires that they are full-time and that the managerial positions on offer are similarly routinized and scripted. From the standpoint of consumers, fast-food service organizations, just like self-service supermarkets, incorporate customers into the assembly-line process in that they are expected to collect and dispose of the products they purchase. By performing unpaid work customers are exploited to an even greater extent than the low-paid workers who serve them and are similarly dehumanized by the assembly line eating process and scripted interaction, most obviously in the drive-through 'restaurant' (Ritzer, 1996, 1998).

The expansion of fast-food corporations poses well-documented health and environmental hazards in the form of products that are high in salt, sugar and fat and therefore conducive to health problems such as obesity, and are often packaged in materials that are non-biodegradable such as polystyrene and therefore an environmental hazard (Ritzer, 1996; Schlosser, 2002). The global expansion of fast-food restaurant chains also threatens cultural diversity to the extent that the distinctive individuality of different countries is undermined by the successful transplantation of these Fordist service production systems. Ritzer (1998) in particular has emphasized the homogenizing consequences of the global growth of Fordist fast-food restaurants. As one of the most successful multinational corporations in the world, McDonald's has become a symbol

Table 6.2 Advantages and disadvantages of interactive service Fordism

	Society	Workers	Employers	Consumers
Advantages	Mass production, economies of scale, improved standard of living	Regular work	Increased productivity and profits	Inexpensive products and quick service
Disadvantages	Environmental and health hazards, cultural uniformity	Low-skilled, low-paid and alienating work	Absenteeism and high labour turnover	Exploitation, dehumanization, limited choice of low quality products

of American economic imperialism and perceived as a threat to local cultural identities, consequently it is a major target not just for anti-globalization protesters, but also for anti-capitalist, anti-obesity, and environmental social movements (Watson, 2006). Table 6.2 summarizes the main advantages and disadvantages of service Fordism in a manner that is comparable to that for industrial Fordism presented in Chapter 5 (Table 5.2).

Interactive service work: neo-Fordism and post-Fordism

In the context of noting that industrial Fordism started to decline in the 1970s, Ritzer (1996) discusses, again briefly, the prospects of Fordist McDonaldism changing in a post-Fordist direction. He argues that the growth of McDonaldism shows that there has not been a change from Fordism to post-Fordism, yet under pressure from competitors, critical consumers, environmentalists, and nutritionists, Fordist fast-food corporations have tried to adapt rather than contradict the basic premises upon which they built their success. Ritzer neglects to consider pressure for change emanating from the discontent of the workforce and the role of trade unions, although in a list of over two dozen ways 'actions individuals can take to cope with McDonaldization' he recommends that: 'If you work in such a system, organize your coworkers to create more humanized working conditions' (ibid.: 199–200). He also contends that although the post-Fordism thesis has been 'overblown', product diversity and higher quality products are potential threats to McDonaldization (1998: 180). Ritzer's analysis is limited by his either/or discussion of Fordism versus post-Fordism and although he asserts that 'there has been no clear historical break with Fordism', he does not consider the possibility of neo-Fordism (1996: 152). This section represents an attempt to rectify Ritzer's neglect of workplace resistance and to remedy his failure to discuss neo-Fordism in his account of interactive service work, both with reference to recent developments in fast-food service provision.

As was noted in the previous chapter, the spark that ignited the search for more efficient and less dehumanizing ways of organizing the production of higher quality goods and services was the crisis of profitability experienced by Fordist organizations in the 1970s, a period of growing competition, and increasing costs of production, worker discontent, and consumer dissatisfaction. The solutions to be considered are the same as for industrial work, namely the partial modification (i.e., neo-Fordism) and the total transformation of Fordism (i.e., post-Fordism) in terms of changes to the key features of Fordism outlined above (Table 6.1) and in Chapter 5 (Table 5.1).

Notwithstanding what Braverman has called the 'habituation' of the worker to the dehumanizing work conditions in fast-food restaurants, achieved primarily by 'manipulation' , for example, by 'training' programmes, but also by 'coercion' in the form of a lack of alternative jobs, worker discontent persists (1974: 150–1). Similarly, consumers, who might otherwise not be able to afford to eat out in a full-service restaurant, are 'trained' to conform to the rules of fast-food ordering and eating via advertising and restaurant design, yet still express dissatisfaction. For example, suggestive selling often irritated customers and was therefore disliked by window workers (Leidner, 1993). A good indication of worker discontent are the exceptionally high rates of labour turnover in fast-food restaurants, emphasized by Leidner who noted that labour turnover at McDonald's 'averaged 153 per cent in 1984, 205 percent in 1985' (1993: 51); Ritzer who found that 'the fast-food industry has the highest turnover rate – approximately 300 per cent a year – of any industry in the United States' (1996: 130–1); and Schlosser who reported that 'the turnover rate among assistant managers is extremely high' (2002: 74). Exceptions to this pattern are countries or regions where there are few other job opportunities, such as Germany and the south of Italy (Royle, 2000). It has also been suggested by Gould (2010) that not all workers at McDonald's are dissatisfied with its Taylorist system, especially the younger crew members whose life style is more compatible with the flexibility required by fast-food work organizations. For their part, customers, like the workers, are dehumanized by the extreme standardization of the fast-food assembly line service experience, consumer groups expressed dissatisfaction regarding the healthiness of the products, and communities around the world have resisted the establishment of fast-food restaurants in historically distinctive towns and cities, for example, Rome and Krakow (Ritzer, 1996).

In order to overcome these characteristically Fordist problems of worker and consumer dissatisfaction in an era of rising costs and increased competition, fast-food corporations introduced changes, particularly to their eating practices. In the case of worker discontent, it was noted above that the evidence for fast-food workers was not entirely unambiguous and that the typical response of a disgruntled fast-food worker was to resign rather than contest collectively the source(s) of the problem, hence the high labour turnover rate. There have been numerous attempts to unionize McDonald's workers in the USA, for example, four hundred in the early 1970s, but they were all unsuccessful, and the unions effectively gave up targeting such a renowned anti-union company (Love, 1995). However, in countries where legislation is more favourable to unions, McDonald's workers are more likely to be unionized, such as in Finland and Australia (Cobble, 1996). In the comparative study of working for McDonald's by Royle (2000), it is possible to discern ten inter-related reasons for the lack of successful collective resistance in McDonald's and other fast-food corporations:

1 McDonald's has a corporate culture that is historically rooted in anti-unionism. Although this is particularly salient for managers, Royle found that managers at McDonald's in the UK and Germany expressed anti-union views, and hence could be relied upon to ensure that the corporation continued to exclude trade unions (ibid.: 110–12).

2 The strength of this dimension of corporate culture was enhanced by the tendency for between one-third and half of all managers 'at McDonald's to be recruited from within the organization with the result that they were likely to share core company values, notably anti-unionism' (ibid.: 70).

3 McDonald's selects workers and especially managers and franchisees very carefully to filter out those with pro-union attitudes and used to require job applicants in the USA to take a lie detector test to help eliminate those with trade union sympathies before it was deemed illegal (ibid.: 61).

4 Training programmes at McDonald's are similarly rigorous and extensive, whether in-store or in regional centres. Managers and franchisees are socialized into the appropriate anti-union perspective at one of McDonald's campus based 'Hamburger Universities', founded in the USA in the 1960s and outside the USA in the 1970s (ibid.: 132).

5 The small-scale of fast-food outlets is less conducive to unionization than large-scale ones because managers and workers work more closely together (ibid.: 113).

6 The employment of young, old, foreign, or disabled workers who tend to be inexperienced or are too insecure to challenge managerial authority, termed 'recruited acquiescence' by Royle, makes it easier to enforce an anti-union policy (2000: 82).

7 The difficulty of unionizing young, part-time, temporary workers who tend to see unions as 'old fashioned' (ibid.: 118).

8 When the non-union employee relations policy is threatened by fast-food workers attempting to organize collectively to improve their conditions of employment, McDonald's responds vigorously by sending '"flying squads" of experienced managers' to help keep a restaurant union free, sacking union members, hiring non-union workers, or by closing the restaurant (ibid.: 86).

9 The decline of Keynesianism as a policy that legitimates state intervention and collectivism, and the rise of neo-liberalism that de-legitimates state intervention and collectivism, especially in the USA and the UK during the 1980s, provides an encouraging political-economic environment for the pursuit of more individualistic policies that exclude or marginalize unions (ibid.: 4–11).

10 In the light of these obstacles, it is understandable that unions have been reluctant to provide the resources necessary to recruit widely in the fast-food industry (ibid.: 110).

Royle concluded that with the exception of a few mainland European countries which had retained collectivist political culture and institutions despite continuing opposition by employers, McDonald's and other similar service sector corporations have been successful in resisting attempts to unionize fast-food workers. More specifically, the presence of supportive legislation and trade unions tends to result in improved wages and working conditions, especially in areas of low unemployment. Meanwhile McDonald's continues to attempt to thwart the efforts of any government and union to democratize the workplace. Put another way, excluding or marginalizing trade unions enables employers such as McDonald's to maintain managerial prerogatives, pay lower wages, and provide poorer working conditions such as holiday entitlement.

This analysis suggests that resigning is still one of the few ways to express job dissatisfaction for fast-food workers in most countries and that the fast-food corporations have been under very little pressure from their workers, other than the challenge of reducing the high labour turnover rate, to improve the intrinsic or extrinsic rewards of their workforce. The achievement of excluding or marginalizing unions by fast-food corporations also suggests that they have been successful in establishing and sustaining a 'unitary' managerial ideology that emphasizes co-operation rather than conflict and the right of managers to manage in the interests of everyone in the organization (Fox, 1966). The aim has been to ensure that everyone in the company implements the same technical and social standards and conforms to a management style that prioritizes the relationship between 'individual managers and individual employees', that defines work satisfaction in terms of social and psychological rewards, not material ones, and encourages workers to see themselves as part of a team ('crew'), and more broadly the '"McDonald's family"' (Royle, 2000: 64–5). Thus, in addition to an emphasis on practical and social skills, training courses at Hamburger University include one on team-building (Love, 1995). According to the UK training manual, McDonald's management style encourages workers to 'develop a sense of loyalty and pride ... [and] work harmoniously with management' (Royle, 2000: 64). The pervasiveness of this corporate ideology via a mixture of persuasion and coercion therefore not only discourages union activity, but motivates franchisees, managers and workers to the same corporate prescriptions around the globe.

In the late 1960s and early 1970s, McDonald's was faced with increasing competition in the USA and was keen to expand abroad, including Japan where the contrast in food cultures is greatest, namely rice and fish rather than bread and beef (Love, 1995). A senior McDonald's executive visited Japan and was impressed that workers in the new Japanese McDonald's 'followed the operating manual to the letter', although this is arguably unsurprising given the apparent congruence between McDonald's emphasis on uniformity and teamwork and Japanese work practices (ibid.: 426). As noted above, the team concept is central to the McDonald's method of managing and working, indicated most clearly by the term 'crew'. Within a restaurant team there is a degree of flexibility regarding the tasks crew members undertake in that they are required to clean the restaurant when they are not preparing or serving food, yet in practice 'kitchen workers usually remain in the kitchen and till workers on the till' (Royle, 2000: 57). Operating as a team is therefore crucial due to the tendency to minimize staffing and idle time, much the same as in a JLP car factory. Some monitored variation from otherwise highly standardized scripts is also allowed 'to avoid sounding like robots' (Leidner, 1996: 33). Crew members can attend monthly meetings at which the company conveys information to its employees, contribute to the (little used) suggestion scheme, complain in 'real approach to problems' (RAP) sessions that are held at the end of a shift two or three times a year, although they were not popular with restaurant managers and in some countries union members are excluded, and be part of 'quality action teams' that deal with specific issues such as health and safety (Royle, 2000: 122–3). Royle argues that these forms of 'McParticipation' focus mainly on communication and are more concerned with preserving managerial prerogatives than empowering workers (ibid.: 122). They constitute the McDonald's equivalent of teamwork and quality circles that are additions to a long-standing commitment to continuous improvement: 'We are continuously looking for a better way of doing things, and then a revised better way, and then a revised better way' (McDonald's executive, quoted by Love, 1995: 121).

In the late 1990s when its market share of the US fast-food market was declining, McDonald's introduced its version of just-in-time production called 'Made for You' that involved new technology to reduce labour costs and increase the speed at which food was served; 'advanced computer software essentially ran the kitchen assigning tasks to various workers for maximum efficiency, predicting future orders on the basis of customer flow' (Schlosser, 2002: 67). Also, since restaurant crews do not start assembling an order before it is placed, it means that every order can be customized, whereas previously special orders were discouraged because they disrupted the assembly line process (Cohen, 1998). Thus the achievement of individualized choice at low mass production prices, termed 'mass customization' (Pine, 1993), was made possible by the 'combination of two Japanese systems: the adaptable marketing system (AMS) and the flexible manufacturing system (FMS) or lean production' (Taylor et al., 1998: 109). These innovations enabled fast-food organizations to adapt their Fordist procedures in the sense that they could offer individualized products and respond quickly to the demand for a greater variety of products. For example, customers at McDonald's can request a burger with or without pickles and can select from an expanded menu that includes a wider range of products, such as eggs, fish, and chicken, albeit in a standardized form. McDonald's also 'adapted to the needs and demands of local markets' by offering customers McLaks in Norway and McSpaghetti in the Philippines, alongside the standard Big Mac and fries (Ritzer, 1998: 85). This suggests that the Fordist fast-food business has been modified in a manner comparable to the

Table 6.3   Key features of interactive service neo-Fordism

Neo-Fordism: type of interactive service system characterized by:

1   Qualified Taylorized work tasks and organization (e.g., limited job rotation, teamwork)

2   Assembly line process

3   Limited destandardization of parts, a slightly wider range of customized products, impersonal service

neo-Fordist JLP in order to be able to meet the new market conditions, namely increased competition and changing consumer preferences. Table 6.3 summarizes the key features of neo-Fordist interactive service work in a manner similar to that outlined in Chapter 5 for industrial work (Table 5.4).

These modifications to an otherwise essentially Fordist system of service production may be attributed more to labour shortages and competitive pressures than from the collective action of workers, although in those countries and regions where workers are supported by legislation and unions, pay and work conditions tend to improve despite the best efforts of global fast-food corporations to neutralize their power. However, these managerial methods of control and consent do not seem to have overcome the problem of worker dissatisfaction as indicated by a persistently high labour turnover rate. While interactive service workers are relatively powerless, individually except by resigning and collectively except where the state and unions in combination attempt to influence employers, the presence of customers represents a potential source of influence that management cannot ignore. The salience of consumer power has been noted above with reference to their supervisory role in the control of workers, additionally they can exert pressure on fast-food corporations individually by complaining and/or withdrawing their custom, and collectively by joining a protest group. The most famous case of the latter is the 'McLibel' trial in London that lasted from 1994–97, the longest in British history, in which two members of Greenpeace were sued by McDonald's for distributing leaflets that accused McDonald's of, among other things, selling unhealthy food (Schlosser, 2002). After several trials and appeals, in 2005, the case went to the European Court of Human Rights which found in favour of the activists. As a result of this long-running conflict between two individuals who could not afford legal representation and one of the most powerful corporations in the world, McDonald's attracted adverse publicity and the anti-McDonald's campaign attracted support.

A key selling point identified by nutritional and consumer critics concerns the size of fast-food meals, typically conveyed by the names given to products, such as 'Super-Size Fries' (McDonald's) and 'Whopper' (Burger King) (Ritzer, 1996: 60–1). The term 'supersize' was used against McDonald's in the film *Super Size Me* (2004) that highlighted the danger to health that prolonged consumption of fast-food posed (Watson, 2006). The size as well as the ill health-inducing content of fast-food is reflected by the widely used term 'junk food' to refer to highly processed meals that are high in fat, sugar and salt and low in essential vitamins and minerals (Kellner, 1999). McDonald's and other fast-food corporations have responded to their consumer and nutritional critics by introducing healthier foods, such as salads and white meat, and stopped selling extra large fries and drinks (Ritzer, 1996; Watson, 2006). However, the critical onslaught has continued in the form of calls for a 'fat tax' on junk food, which it is argued would encourage the consumption of healthier products by making unhealthier ones more expensive, thereby combating 'the growing problem of obesity (*Ecologist*, 2010). Nutritional critics have also become more provocative and still tend to focus on McDonald's as the fast-food global market leader. For example, a US television commercial paid for by the Physicians Committee for Responsible Medicine featured an overweight man on a mortuary trolley still holding a partly eaten McDonald's hamburger (*Guardian*, 2010). McDonald's also seems to be sensitive to environmental criticisms since it stopped using polystyrene packaging in the USA in the 1990s in response to the charge that such materials were polluting the environment (Ritzer, 1996; Schlosser, 2002).

Although fast-food corporations have responded positively to the criticisms of consumers, nutritionists, and environmentalists, it has not abandoned what continues to be in essence a Fordist way of mass producing a limited range of 'customized' products using standardized technology, labour, and interaction. The product range is less unhealthy and less environmentally damaging, but remains a threat to the health of consumers and the environment. Table 6.4 notes the main advantages and disadvantages of a neo-Fordist interactive service system from the standpoint of society, workers, employers and consumers, again in a manner similar to that discussed and outlined in Chapter 5 (Table 5.5).

The above analysis has suggested that the essentially Fordist character of interactive service work in fast-food production and consumption has been modified with respect to: (1) limited job rotation among team members, all of whom except union members in some countries, are given the opportunity to suggest ways of solving problems and improving service production; (2) increased consumer choice within an expanded but still narrow range of individualized products; and (3) slightly healthier products packaged

Table 6.4 Advantages and disadvantages of neo-Fordist interactive service system

	Society	Workers	Employers	Consumers
Advantages	Abundance	Slightly more varied range of social physical tasks	Higher productivity and profits	Mass customized products
Disadvantages	Environmental and health hazards	Low skill, low pay, and emotional alienation	Absenteeism and high labour turnover	Exploitation and dehumanization

in more environmentally friendly materials. These changes represent neo-Fordist adaptations rather than a post-Fordist transformation. The neo-Fordist modifications were introduced mainly due to pressure emanating from increased competition, high rates of labour turnover, changing consumer preferences, and the criticisms of nutritionists and environmentalists, not by the collective action of workers that fast-food corporations have been successful in discouraging or neutering via a range of anti-union strategies. Ritzer rejected the view that McDonaldism is post-Fordist and emphasized its continuities with Fordism. He concluded that: 'Fordism is alive and well in the modern world, although it has been transformed into McDonaldism' (1996: 152). Yet the evidence noted above of changes beyond Fordism suggests that interactive service work in fast-food restaurants is neither Fordist nor post-Fordist, but neo-Fordist. For it to become post-Fordist the production and consumption of fast-food would need to be characterized by genuinely multiskilled workers with expert knowledge, many of whom would not be performing routine tasks (e.g., chefs), operating in a non-assembly line system creating high-quality individual products. In other words it would cease to be a fast-food restaurant since it would be transformed into a slow-food one whose menu varied by the seasons, and whose dishes were made to order and took hours to prepare and consume rather than minutes. The next section will consider the growth of knowledge work and workers with reference to Castells' network enterprise thesis as a possible post-Fordist alternative.

Knowledge work and the Fordist model of change

The claim that during the second half of the twentieth century knowledge work expanded and was becoming more important in advanced industrial capitalist societies was discussed earlier (Chapter 4) in relation to Bell's post-industrial society theory of upskilling. To recap briefly, Bell suggested that a post-industrial society is a knowledge society and therefore the pivotal occupational groups are the professional and technical elites, especially scientists and engineers, whose economic power is based on knowledge, not property as in the past. He notes, but does not discuss for reasons of space, the issue of the 'changing organizational contexts of knowledge (e.g., the compatibility of hierarchical and bureaucratic work organization with the collegial and associational modes of status)' (Bell, 1976 [1973]: 262). In the past couple of decades others have addressed this important gap in Bell's analysis.

Prior to the development of the post-industrial or informational society perspective, expert workers were considered within the sociology of the professions, but the growth of new types of professional workers who were not members of independent professions rendered this approach less and less applicable. A helpful way of understanding the historical change from independent professional workers to contemporary knowledge workers is provided by Reed (1996) who has proposed a three-fold expert division of labour that complements and extends the phases of technological and organizational change outlined in Chapter 1 (Table 1.3). More specifically, Reed suggests that three major occupational groups are identifiable in terms of their 'respective knowledge bases, power strategies, and organizational forms' (ibid.: 582). The first expert group consists of liberal/independent professions such as doctors and lawyers, who were the most numerous knowledge workers during the rise of industrial capitalism, namely the pre-Fordist era. Their extensive education (theoretical knowledge) and training (skills) enabled them to claim high social status, great economic rewards, and considerable control over recruitment and performance. With the onset of the Fordist system, organizational/managerial professions, such as specialist administrators, expanded in line with the increased size and bureaucratization of private and public institutions but ceded control to their employers. The third and most recent expert group to emerge consists of knowledge workers/ entrepreneurial professions, such as financial and business consultants, whose 'expertise is directed to ... knowledge creation and development', which inclines them 'towards an organic or network type of organizational form' characterized by 'decentralized flexibility and autonomy' and enables them to regain effective control over their expertise (ibid.: 586). The origins and expansion of this group correspond to the neo- or post-Fordist era and are found in service organizations rather than in collegiate or bureaucratic structures associated more typically with liberal and organizational professions respectively. The key features of Reed's three expert groups are summarized in Table 6.5.

In the same way that Bell's contribution to the post-industrial society debate has been acclaimed as the most comprehensive (as noted in Chapter 4), Castells is regarded as the 'foremost sociological theorist of the information society' (Tonkiss, 2006: 110; Webster, 2002). His network enterprise thesis (NET) is the latest contribution to the debate about the transformation

Table 6.5 Key features of service work expert groups and the Fordist paradigm

Historical era	Expert groups	Knowledge base	Power strategy	Organizational form	Occupational type
Pre-Fordism	Independent/liberal professions	Abstract codified	Monopolization	Collegiate	Doctors, lawyers
Fordism	Organizational/ managerial professions	Technical, local	Credentialism	Bureaucracy	Managers
Neo-/Post-Fordism	Knowledge workers/ entrepreneurial professions	Esoteric, global	Marketization	Network	Financial, business consultants

Source: Amended version of Figure 1 in Reed (1996: 586).

of work. Although the NET thesis is within the tradition of post-industrial society theory, his contribution differs from Bell's in four important ways. First, Castells argues that it is not the theoretical character of knowledge that is crucial, since it is important in all societies, but the 'technology of knowledge generation, information processing, and symbolic communication' (2001: 17). Second, he contends that advanced (i.e., post-industrial) and less advanced (i.e., industrializing) economies are part of the same globalized system and that when considered as such manufacturing jobs did not decline during the second half of the twentieth century, but increased, which undermines the notion of post-industrialism. Third, he supports the polarization critique of Bell's thesis (discussed in Chapter 4) by noting that an emphasis on the expansion of professional occupations tends to neglect the growth of low-skilled service jobs. Fourth, and in Castells' view most importantly, the assumption that an increase in the economic significance of knowledge, services, and professions leads to one type of new post-industrial society is mistaken since there is diversity (e.g., the service and industrial economy routes represented by the USA and Japan respectively), as well as common trends (e.g., the rise in knowledge work) among different informational societies depending on their position in the globalized system. However, he concurs with Bell in the sense that he too claims that 'knowledge' and knowledge workers are central to productivity and that the current revolution in information technology gives rise to a new type of economic system that he calls the network society. This new type of society is capitalist and has three key elements: it is informational, global, and networked. That is to say, it is characterized by the production of knowledge and information on a global scale in which the business model is not the firm but networks of flexible firms. According to Castells, what is historically distinctive about the informational economy is that it is global 'with the capacity to work as a unit in real time, or chosen time, on a planetary scale' with 'globally integrated financial markets working in real time' at its core (ibid.: 101, 102). This new form of capitalism has the potential to increase productivity dramatically, but it is inherently unstable and therefore also 'brings with it the possibility of recurrent financial crises with devastating effects on economies and societies' (ibid.: 161). The implications of globalization for work and employment will be considered in Chapter 10.

Castells claims that in a network society work is transformed in three interrelated ways: production flexibility, organizational flexibility, and worker flexibility. First he argues that: 'We have entered *a new technological paradigm*, centred around micro-electronics-based, information/communication technologies', the key feature of which is maximum flexibility of production (2000: 9; italics in the original). In order to transcend the crisis of Fordism, move beyond its offspring lean production, and succeed in the ever-changing global competitive environment, flexibility is essential, especially technological. For example, to be able to assemble parts produced from very distant sources, it is necessary to have ... a micro-electronics-based precision quality in the fabrication, so that the parts are compatible with the smallest detail of specification; and ... a computer-based flexibility enabling the factory to program production runs according to the volume and customized character required by each order. (Castells, 2001: 123)

Second, the vertical bureaucracy associated with Fordism and neo-Fordism has been superseded by the horizontal structure 'characterized by seven main trends: organization around process, not task; a flat hierarchy; team management; measuring performance by customer satisfaction; rewards based on team performance; maximization of contacts with suppliers and customers; information, training, and retraining of employees at all levels' (Castells, 2001: 176). In other words, a post-bureaucratic organizational form (discussed in Chapter 1) characterized by autonomous, empowered, upskilled, flexible, co-operative knowledge workers is imperative if the full productive potential of the new technology is to be realized.

Third, although Castells subscribes to the polarization thesis (discussed in Chapter 4 and noted above), he suggests that the skill issue is of declining significance in the informational economy since all workers are subject to the flexibilization of work in terms of work tasks, working time, job stability, work location, and employment contract. Thus, though there is a division between a 'core labour force' of highly educated workers and a 'disposable labour force' whose work can be automated and who can be 'hired/fired/offshored, depending upon market demand and labour costs', management has the technological ability and the competitive incentive to require both to be flexible in every respect (ibid.: 295–6).

The main implication of these changes in work and employment is that to be able to benefit from all these flexibilities, Castells suggests that the corporation has to be transformed into a network enterprise, spelling the demise of individual (e.g., the entrepreneur) and collective (e.g., the corporation) units of capitalist economic activity. Castells notes that flexibility is not inevitable since the introduction of every kind of flexibility involves choices made by governments and businesses, which in the context of a 'hardening of capitalist logic since the 1980s' translated into a competitive pressure to be flexible or fail (ibid.: 280). Thus the network enterprise is totally flexible, the exemplar of which for Castells is the Californian-based Cisco Corporation. Castells concluded that a highly interdependent networked economy is characterized by the 'use of knowledge-based, information technologies to enhance and accelerate the production of knowledge and information in a self-expanding, virtuous circle' (ibid.: 10). According to Castells, the future of capitalism looks bright because it is informational, global and networked, especially for those parts of the world that are integrated into the informational global economy, far less so for those who are excluded.

Aside from noting that Fordism is 'an historical relic' in developed societies but extensive in developing ones, and that lean production is 'justifiably called by its critics "lean and mean"' since it is based on the assembly line and mass production, Castells' analysis indicates that the network enterprise form of production is post-Fordist in all respects since it involves flexible production, flexible multiskilled workers, and a flexible organization to deliver a wide range of high quality products (ibid.: 176).

There are several criticisms of the NET. First, generalizing from a model of work based largely on the possibly atypical experience of technologically advanced firms in California is problematic not least because as Castells points out, in Silicon Valley the scale of flexible or non-standard employment of knowledge and unskilled workers is distinctively high. Second, and following from the first point, the claim that the network enterprise is a post-bureaucratic organization is more of an assumption than an empirical fact since it has been estimated that 'few [companies] have actually moved more than a step or two from traditional [bureaucratic] structures' (Heckscher and Applegate, 1994: 2; Warhurst and Thompson, 1998; Boreham et al., 2008). Third, Castells' analysis of key production issues such as teamwork is superficial. For instance, a lack of information about teamwork in network enterprises precludes any firm judgement about whether it approximates to the Japanese or Swedish models of teamwork, as outlined by Berggren (1992). Moreover, research undertaken in what could be regarded as a nascent network society (Finland) addressed the issue of teamwork and produced mixed results in relation to Castells' NET (Blom and Melin, 2003). Fourth, Brophy has argued that Castells' NET underestimates the ongoing class struggle at work in the knowledge economy and her analysis of the 'revolt of the microserfs' shows that trade unions are adapting to and contesting the power of capital (2006: 623). Fifth, Head (2005) has demonstrated that most work, even for knowledge workers, is still Taylorized, although it is called 'reengineering' rather than scientific management mainly because it relies on information technology. Sixth, while Castells emphasizes discontinuity, others have shown that current socio-technical changes have a long history and are therefore not especially novel, after all, a network society is still capitalist (Kumar, 1995; Webster, 2002). In defence of Castells' extraordinarily comprehensive analysis it could be suggested that his NET is couched in ideal-typical terms, that many of the changes he analyses are emergent rather than established trends, and that he acknowledges that crises and conflict are endemic in a network society even though organized labour has been weakened by a combination of neo-liberal policies, new information technology, and globalization. Notwithstanding these qualifications, Table 6.6 summarizes the key features of a post-Fordist model of service work based on Castells' account of a network enterprise:

Table 6.6   Key features of a post-Fordist interpretation of service work

Post-Fordism: type of service system characterized by:

1   Flexible multiskilled work and organization
2   Flexible micro-electronic computer technology
3   Flexible parts and high-quality customized services

Castells' apparent admiration of the dynamism, efficiency, speed, and productive capacity of informational capitalism is tempered by his recognition that in such a society there are 'winners and losers' and that the 'losers pay for the winners' (2001: 503). Although he asserts that the identity of those who win and those who lose is changing all the time, it is clear from his account of the network society that the main pattern involves the familiar distinction between capital, which is concentrated, coordinated and global, and labour which is fragmented, divided and local. Within the non-capitalist classes, as noted above, there are highly educated, advantaged knowledge workers and the less well educated, disadvantaged, non-specialist workers, predominantly women, ethnic minorities, and immigrants. It is the latter whom Castells considers to be most vulnerable in terms of pay and security to the vicissitudes of the market, in marked contrast to the owners of capital and the relatively privileged knowledge workers who benefit from great profits and/or high pay. By way of compensation, as it were, Castells suggests although the 'social costs of flexibility can be high', social life may be enhanced and gender relations more egalitarian (2000: 290). In the case of unemployment (to be discussed in Chapter 8), Castells considers it a temporary problem since in this new type of network society, more jobs of a superior kind are created than destroyed globally. Just like people, different places are included or excluded from the bounty that derives from the economic growth created by informational capitalism depending on their relationship to the core financial global networks. Thus increasing inequality within and between classes and societies is a major consequence of the rise of the network society. Table 6.7 summarizes the main advantages and disadvantages of a post-Fordist service system from the standpoint of society, workers, employers and consumers.

Table 6.7 Advantages and disadvantages of a post-Fordist service system

	Society	Workers	Employers	Consumers
Advantages	Economic growth	Autonomy and empowerment	High productivity and profit	Product diversity and customization
Disadvantages	Financial/ economic crises	Job insecurity and economic exclusion	Increased competition and market volatility	Poverty and social exclusion

Summary and conclusions

The expansion of service work over the past one hundred years, especially in the advanced industrial capitalist societies, was accompanied by an increasing division between unskilled, low-paid interactive workers and highly skilled, well-paid knowledge workers. The Fordist model of change developed with reference to industrial work and was intended to apply to service work. Such work is now the main focus of empirical research, albeit not usually with reference to the Fordist paradigm.

The most common forms of pre-Fordist interactive service work were domestic labour, which declined dramatically during the early decades of the twentieth century, and retail sales work which expanded during the same period and continues to do so. The craft-like skills of the pre-Fordist retail interactive service worker were undermined by the successful application of Taylorism and assembly line principles, initially in the USA and subsequently in the rest of the industrialized world. This resulted in the now familiar Fordist self-service and fast-food retail systems which deskilled and disempowered the interactive service worker and upskilled and empowered the customer who was incorporated in an unpaid capacity into the work process. The presence of the customer in the service delivery system is thought to have been largely to the benefit of management since both are concerned to ensure a speedy and courteous service is provided consistently. The combination of a detailed division of labour, rigid scripts, and low pay contributed to a high labour turnover which is suggestive of extensive worker dissatisfaction and the view that working in a fast-food restaurant is as alienating as working on a car production line. Moreover, since interactive service work typically involves the performance of emotional and aesthetic labour, it has been argued, notably by Hochschild, that it is even more alienating because of the requirement by management to express false emotions. Neither Leidner nor Ritzer considered in detail Hochschild's thesis, though the thrust of their accounts of interactive service work were essentially negative from a worker's standpoint. Others have suggested that the complex social skills integral to interactive service work represent upskilling and multiskilling, and that younger workers find it satisfying. On balance, it was argued that the standardization of interactive service work tasks and scripts that are monitored closely in an assembly line system which prioritizes the speedy delivery of large volume of low-quality products, is indicative of an extreme form of Fordism. The parallels between the Fordism of service work and that of industrial work extend beyond the workplace to include its impact, both negative and positive, on consumers and society.

In response to the crisis of Fordism during the 1970s, service corporations in the fast-food industry instigated a range of changes to their production and consumption practices, including many of those associated with JLP, such as continuous improvement, just-in-time parts and labour, quality circles, and product diversity. It was found that these changes were often superficial, for example, the practice of suggestion schemes and job rotation was less impressive than that implied by the managerial rhetoric, and that these changes owed more to labour shortages, competitive pressures, and consumer dissatisfaction than to workers acting collectively. Explanations of why fast-food corporations have been largely successful in excluding independent unions range from the persuasive, such as propagating a unitary managerial ideology, to the coercive, such as sacking pro-union workers. While consumer critics, especially those concerned with health, the environment, and cultural diversity, have been highly critical of fast-food corporations, their influence has been limited. Once again the similarities between neo-Fordist industrial work and that of service work are marked not just in terms of how and what is produced, but also in terms of their malign and benign implications for consumers and society.

In the case of knowledge work in the service sector it was suggested that the independent professions were dominant in the pre-Fordist era, organizational professions in the Fordist era, and knowledge workers in the current neo-/post-Fordist era. Castells, the pre-eminent theorist of the information society, has advanced a NET which involves three elements; it is informational, global and networked, and emphasizes the key role of knowledge workers, especially those in financial networks. He argues that the emergence of a network society transforms the production process, the organization of work, and the occupational system, all in the direction of greater flexibility. His NET is optimistic in that he considers a network economy to be more efficient, productive, and innovative, but also warns, presciently in view of the global financial crash of 2008–09, that this new type of hyper-capitalism is unstable and increases inequality, and varies, especially in terms of place. Critics have argued that such a society is not new, that he underestimates the ability of organized labour to resist this form of deregulated informational capitalism, and that most corporations are not post-bureaucratic but remain essentially bureaucratic. Yet in view of the unprecedented flexibility of work processes, products, and workers it is clear that the network enterprise conforms to an ideal-typical model of post-Fordism.

Where once Fordism was considered to be a virtuous circle of production and consumption, Castells claims that informational technologies create a new virtuous circle that transforms work and life to the benefit of everyone in the long term. However, given the uneven growth and unequal impact of network enterprises, and the ever present risk of financial crises inherent in all production systems based on exploitation but pronounced in a network society, this assertion on behalf of a post-Fordist service system looks doubtful. The evidence and arguments advanced in this chapter (and Chapter 5) suggest that the demise of Fordism and the rise of post-Fordism have been exaggerated. In short, a continuation of past trends rather than a transformation of work. In his analysis of the transformation of work, Castells highlighted the growth of non-standard work, an issue that will be discussed in the next chapter.

Further reading

BOOKS Bear in mind that the Fordist model of change is a neglected theme in sociological studies of service work when you read the key books on this topic, such as: Ritzer (1996) *The McDonaldization of Society: An Investigation into the Changing Character of Contemporary Social Life*, Leidner (1993) *Fast Food, Fast Talk: Service Work and the Routinization of Everyday Life*, Macdonald and Sirianni (eds) (1996) *Working in the Service Society*, Hochschild (2003 [1983])

The Managed Heart: Commercialization of Human Feeling, Royle (2000) *Working for McDonald's in Europe: The Unequal Struggle*, and Castells (2001) *The Rise of the Network Society*. For critiques of these original contributions, see Webster (2002) *Theories of the Information Society* and Korczynski and Macdonald (2009) *Service Work: Critical Perspectives*.

ARTICLES
For a critique of Hochschild's thesis, read Brook (2009) 'The alienated heart: Hochschild's "emotional labour" thesis and the anticapitalist politics of alienation', *Capital and Class*, 33(2): 7–31 and Gatta et al. (2009) 'High touch and here-to-stay: future skills demands in US low wage service occupations', *Sociology*, 43(5): 968–89 considers the skill debate in relation to face-to-face interactive service work.

WEBSITES
For material on the gendering of emotional and aesthetic labour in the service sector, check out the *Warwick Institute for Employment Research*, www.2warwick.ac.uk/fac/soc/ier, and for material on the knowledge economy, see *The Work Foundation* website, www.theworkfoundation.com/

Questions for discussion and assessment

1 Compare and contrast pre-Fordist and Fordist interactive service work.
2 Assess critically Hochschild's emotional labour thesis.
3 Consider the claim that after the crisis of Fordism interactive service work developed in a neo-Fordist direction.
4 Account for the successful exclusion of independent trade unions by fast-food corporations.
5 Are there any redeeming features of contemporary interactive service work?
6 To what extent does Castells' network enterprise thesis conform to a post-Fordist model of work?
7 Evaluate the advantages and disadvantages of a post-Fordist service system.

7
NON-STANDARD WORK

Chapter contents

- The destandardization of work thesis
- Contractual destandardization: self-employment
- Spatial destandardization: homeworking
- Temporal destandardization: temporary/part-time work
- Critical evaluation of the destandardization thesis
- Summary and conclusions
- Further reading
- Questions for discussion and assessment

The historical analysis of the Fordist paradigm undertaken in the previous two chapters focused primarily on workplace flexibility or functional flexibility in terms of tasks and products/services, but it was also apparent that neo-Fordist and post-Fordist accounts of industrial and service work organizations agreed that there was a trend away from the standard Fordist model of permanent full-time work/employment (hereafter work) towards the growth of non-standard work or numerical flexibility. In short, the increasing flexibilization of the workplace was accompanied by the increasing flexibilization of the workforce. This is largely because JIT applies to the supply of labour as well as materials and parts if waste is to be eliminated and costs minimized. The idea of non-standard paid work, sometimes referred to as just-in-time labour, contingent work, is predicated therefore on the standard work pattern that emerged with the rise of industrial capitalism (discussed in Chapter 1) and reached its fullest development under Fordism (discussed in Chapter 5). The previous two chapters also showed that neo-Fordist and post-Fordist accounts of industrial and service work differed profoundly about the quality of contemporary work, with neo-Fordists arguing that it had deteriorated and post-Fordists that it had improved. The aim of this chapter is to consider the growth and quality of different types of non-standard work, which deviate from permanent full-time work that was the norm during the Fordist era, especially for men.

The destandardization of work thesis

According to Beck (1992) and Castells (2001), the standard form of paid work was based on high levels of standardization in terms of the labour contract, the location of work, and working time, all of which are in the process of being destandardized. The differences between the standard and non-standard models of work are summarized in Table 7.1.

Table 7.1 Key dimensions of standard and non-standard work/employment models

Dimensions	Standard work	Non-standard work
Contractual	Highly regulated* and collectively negotiated	Deregulated and individually negotiated
Spatial	Spatially concentrated, specialist site separate from home	Spatially variable, multiple sites
Temporal	Full-time, permanent	Variable time, impermanent
Gender system	Male breadwinner/female houseworker	Dual earner/variable houseworker

Note: *Regulations covering hours, pay, redundancy, health, safety, and benefits such as pensions, holiday and sick pay, etc.

The key features of standard work were referred to in Chapter 1 under the heading 'industrial' and were part of a wider conceptualization of work that included capitalist and patriarchal elements. From the perspective of the dominant conception of work, the standard worker was a male breadwinner who worked full-time on his employer's premises in exchange for regular pay and a range of benefits. With the demise of Fordism as a production system, the gender system associated with it also changed in the direction of dual-earner households. However, such was, and to some extent still is, the dominance of this model of paid work that other forms of paid work have been marginalized, and unpaid work, notably housework, has been under-valued. Part of the rationale of this book is to redress the balance by giving greater prominence to non-standard paid work and unpaid work than is usual.

Beck's and Castells' conceptions of non-standard work are similar in that Beck focuses on 'part-time work, inconsequential and temporary employment, and spurious forms of self-employment' (2000: 56), and Castells on 'part-time work', 'temporary work', and 'self-employment' (2001: 283). They also both note that the different types of non-standard work overlap and describe the new pattern of work and family systems in comparable ways. For example, Beck refers to the work 'revolution' in relation to 'lean production, subcontracting, outsourcing, offshoring, downsizing, [and] customization' (2000: 56), whereas Castells refers to the 'transformation' of work and that the 'emergence of lean production methods goes hand in hand with widespread business practices of subcontracting, outsourcing, offshoring, downsizing, and customizing' (2001: 282). Beck (1992; 2000) states that he is advancing the destandardization of work thesis in the form of hypotheses, though he illustrates them with the latest research including the same statistical source, namely the Organisation for Economic Co-operation and Development (OECD), that is used extensively by Castells (1997; 2001). Beck notes that the UK was at the forefront of the standardization of work and 'is now pioneering individualization' with about 40 per cent of work non-standard at the start of the 1990s, and refers specifically to the rapid growth of part-time work in the 1980s and 1990s in 'all the early industrializing countries' (2000: 56). Similarly, Castells (2000) shows that by the 1990s, in nine of the ten OECD countries he examined, over 30 per cent of the labour force were engaged in non-standard work, the exception was the USA where there is institutional labour flexibility and hence no need for non-standard forms of employment. They both portray the process of work destandardization as accelerating, albeit unevenly with some countries and regions, such as Spain and California, characterized already by the majority of the labour force involved in non-standard work. Beck and Castells also highlight the increase in the labour force participation of women and that they tend to be over-represented in non-standard work, especially part-time work, the largest single category. Castells provides far more detail on women's labour force participation than Beck and suggests that there are three main reasons for the 'massive' increase in women's labour force participation: they are cheaper to employ than men; they have the social skills demanded in an informational economy; and most importantly, because historically women are secondary earners and have retained primary responsibility for housework and child-rearing, they can offer the work flexibility needed in the 'new economy' (1997: 173). Thus, according to Castells, there is a 'good fit between the "flexible woman" [forced into flexibility to cope with her multiple roles] and the network enterprise' (2000: 20). The main consequences of the process of incorporating women into the labour force are that 'female bargaining power within the household increases significantly' and the patriarchal family is undermined (Castells, 1997: 173). Beck's analysis is comparable to Castells in that he too considers that women are well suited to the new world of non-standard work because unlike men, during the last decades of the twentieth century they have engaged in 'combinations of part-time work, casual contracts, unpaid work and voluntary activity' (2000: 92). However, in contrast to Castells, Beck regards the destandardization process as contradictory in that while 'demographic liberation, deskilling of housework, contraception, divorce, participation in education and occupations – express the degree of liberation of women from the dictates of their modern, female status', other conditions persist which 'reconnect women to their traditional role assignments' (1992: 111). Foremost among these limiting factors are child-bearing and child-rearing, although the thrust of Beck's account of destandardization is that class declines in importance and people 'within the same "class" can or even must choose between different lifestyles' (ibid.: 131). Finally, Beck concludes that the male breadwinner family concomitant with Fordism is being 'displaced by a family in which the roles of earner and provider, care-giver and child-rearer are shared and alternated, depending on phases and decisions' (ibid.: 134). Castells concurs in that he claims that the end of Fordism signals the decline of the male breadwinner which in turn weakens the 'material and ideological bases of patriarchalism' (1997: 27). Thus, the uniform and inflexible Fordist system of a standard work and family system is in the process of being destand-ardized, replaced by a more diverse and flexible pattern of work and family arrangements.

The clear implication of these analyses is that non-standard forms of paid work will soon be as prevalent or exceed standard work in contemporary soci-eties. For Beck and Castells, this is a momentous change that heralds a new type of society, the emergence of which is due mainly to the competitive pres-sure for flexibility and the global adoption of information technology: 'All around the world, flexible work and insecure terms of employment are grow-ing faster than any other form of work' (Beck, 2000: 84); 'Competition-induced, technology-driven trends toward flexibility underlie the current transformation of working arrangements' (Castells, 2001: 282). Central to both their explanations of the expansion of non-standard work is the role of information technology which enables employers to re-organize the produc-tion of goods and services and redefine the contractual, spatial and temporal dimensions of labour in the direction of increasing flexibility. Beck and Castells claim that the expansion of non-standard labour affects workers across all skill levels, involves increased specialization or upskilling, is in the interests of capital because it raises productivity and hence profits, increases the inequality between the knowledge- and income-rich and poor individuals and sectors of the global economy, improves the work–life balance, and reduces commuter traffic to the benefit of the environment. Moreover, although the problem of unemployment will persist in the short term, in due course more jobs will be created and unemployment will be transformed into different forms of under-employment, including informal work which will not be discussed because it is mainly undertaken by those in employment already. From the standpoint of workers the impact of the transformation of full-time, permanent, standard work to a diverse range of less than full-time, impermanent, non-standard forms of work is both positive and negative. On the plus side they gain a degree of freedom over how they organize their work and non-work lives, but they also have to contend with heightened employment insecurity and general vulnerability due to the decline of the institutional protection associated with Fordism. For example, without the safeguards provided by an employer, a trade union, or a welfare state, individual workers are in an even more unequal bargaining position vis-à-vis capital than before, which jeopardizes all the intrinsic and extrinsic rewards achieved over decades of collective struggle. In effect, as Beck notes, the risks have been transferred from institutions to indi-viduals. Unsurprisingly Beck's and Castells' conclusions are also remarkably similar, namely that the decline of standard work and the expansion of non-standard work involve the development of a 'risk-fraught system of flexible, pluralized, decentralized underemployment' (Beck, 1992: 144), or 'multifaceted, generalized flexibility for workers and working conditions, both for highly skilled and unskilled workers' (Castells, 2001: 296). Finally, whereas Beck emphasizes the growth of insecurity for all, and that: '[W]ork and poverty, which used to be mutually exclusive, are now combined in the shape of the *working poor*' (2000: 90, italics in original), Castells stresses that in the absence of corrective policies, extreme inequality, polarization and social exclusion are generated by the new work system. The key word in the destandardization thesis is flexibility; flexible production is complemented by flexible labour, which in turn begets flexible families.

The destandardization of work thesis is also advanced by Bauman in the context of his claim that there has been a change in the basis of identity from work to consumption: 'The role once performed by work in linking together individual motives, social integration and systemic reproduction, has now been assigned to consumer activity' (1998: 27). According to Bauman, under Fordism, work, and therefore identity, were built over a lifetime via regular full-time employment in one type of job, whereas today this type of work career is rare since new jobs tend to be temporary and/or part-time which renders occupational continuity impossible. Bauman (2001) reiterated his version of the destandardization of work thesis and surmises that capital has become highly mobile and global, which has enhanced its power over less mobile and more local labour, and governments, to the detriment of workers' conditions of employment.

In a similar vein, Sennett has argued that flexitime, the flexible scheduling of both full- and part-time work operates in 'about 70 percent of American corporations', tends to be used as a form of social control since it is a matter of reward from above rather than a right achieved from below, and that identity is less dependent upon work than in the past (1998: 58). In a later publication Sennett qualifies his account of the growth of flexibility by noting that the changes he describes 'refer only to the cutting edge of the economy: high technology, global finance, and new service firms with three thousand or more employees', yet he calculates that different forms of non-standard work add up 'to something like a fifth of the American labour force' (2006: 12, 49). He argues that in the new flexible organization of work, capital is liberated but workers are devastated, the identity they once obtained via work undermined by diminished loyalty, trust, and knowledge, which ironically impairs organizational efficiency, especially during an economic downturn.

Notwithstanding variations in terms of focus and depth of analysis, these four proponents of the destandardization of work thesis agree that non-standard forms of work are increasing, but disagree about how deleterious this is for workers. While Castells is arguably the most optimistic since he affirms the post-Fordist view that contemporary work for both standard and non-standard employees improves and suggests that inequality and unemployment can be mitigated by public policies, Bauman and Sennett are pessimistic, which is in line with the neo-Fordist expectation regarding the decline in job quality for all workers. Although Beck envisages advantages and disadvantages for workers, he tends towards the pessimistic perspective in that he suggests that poverty which was linked to a lack of work under Fordism, would be experienced by those in non-standard work who would become the new working poor, and that income insecurity would become endemic and affect all workers in the global economy. In order to assess the soundness of this thesis, data on the quantitative and qualitative aspects of the contractual, spatial, and temporal forms of non-standard work will be discussed with reference to self-employment, home-working, and temporary and part-time work respectively in the five largest and arguably most advanced economies (France, Germany, Japan, the UK, and the USA, hereafter the five), before an overall assessment and critique.

Contractual destandardization: self-employment

Self-employment epitomizes contractual destandardization because it is the exact opposite of standard employment in that typically it does not involve a contract of employment which specifies, among other things, working hours and pay, consequently the self-employed person is treated differently from an employee in relation to tax and social benefit entitlements. For example, in the UK the self-employed are not eligible for unemployment benefit, earnings-related additions to the state pension, invalidity benefit, sick pay, holiday pay and can claim for business expenses, such as transport costs, which reduces their tax liability (Eardley and Corden, 1994). Consequently, in contrast to the standard employee, the self-employed have to rely on private insurance to cover risks associated with working since they are excluded from the key areas of social protection achieved under the Fordist compromise between the employer, the employee, unions and the state. However, the category of self-employment is not unproblematic. Muehlberger (2007) has referred to work-ers who are formally self-employed but entirely dependent upon one company for work as the dependent self-employed and suggests that they represent a contradictory category that falls somewhere between being an employee and self-employed. This is similar to Felstead's notion of 'controlled self-employment' to describe the 'ambiguous' position of a franchisee (1991: 52). Conversely, there are those who are technically a dependent employee, for example, directors of limited companies, yet who are in control of their work. These anomalies are statistically important since it has been calculated that they can lead to very different estimates of the size of the self-employed workforce (Dale, 1991).

In ideal-typical terms, the self-employed own the means of production and consequently have autonomy in their work, hence the above references to control (Dale, 1986). This simple definition masks the diversity of this status, which ranges from part-time self-employment without employees, to full-time self-employment with (often unpaid) family workers and (typically paid) non-family labour, although the vast majority work alone. What unites the various manifestations of self-employment is the element of independence (or autonomy). This is the most distinctive feature of self-employment and the one that separates this employment status most clearly from that of dependent employee (Bechhoffer and Elliot, 1968). However, there is a gap between the ideology of autonomous self-employment and the reality of being at the beck and call of customers and/or at the mercy of bank managers. Typically the self-employed work long, unsocial hours, for uncertain, sometimes relatively low financial rewards, and often rely on other family members to contribute as unpaid workers (Hakim, 1988). Moreover, a study covering several European countries found that long hours and high work stress characterize the self-employed and create difficulties in the balancing of work–family needs as the demands of work take priority (Scherer and Steiber, 2010). Self-employment is inherently risky, hence insecure, especially during a recession since the self-employed and small firms lack the financial resources essential to survival (Wigley and Lipman, 1992), and high technology small firms are at risk permanently because they lack the capital to invest in research and development to enable them to innovate and compete successfully with larger, financially better resourced companies (Oakley, 1991). Thus the self-employed, with or without a small number of employees, may have escaped the alienation characteristic of being supervised closely as a dependent employee, but the self-employed are not only overworked and risk failure, but are 'indirectly controlled by others' (Scase and Goffee, 1982: 76). Hakim has summed up this finding by noting that the 'illusion of autonomy' is emphasized in order 'to rationalize a work situation that would otherwise be intolerable' (1988: 434).

Yet the idea of being in control, being one's own boss, is a 'deeply held belief' (Bechhofer et al., 1974: 114), a widely held 'aspiration' (Wright, 1997: 115), and the main reason that people in many advanced societies are attracted to self-employment (Nisbet, 1997). Self-employment is a more highly valued status than that of employee. The idea of independence is a key element of a nexus of what may be regarded as basic capitalist values, including self-reliance and initiative. Accordingly, the self-employed are regarded as the guardians of vital capitalist virtues who help to keep alive the idea that prosperity can be achieved via individual initiative and hard work, although they do not necessarily see themselves in this way (Scase and Goffee, 1982). Hence self-employment is important ideologically in that 'it buttresses the present system of inequality and offers it legitimation' (Bechhofer et al., 1974: 124). Given the historic tendency for multinational corporations to dominate economic activity, the political significance of the ideological function of self-employment cannot be underestimated.

Prior to the development of industrial capitalism the independent farmer, craft worker, shopkeeper, trader, and so on, was the norm. However, as the scale of production expands, there is a concomitant increase in the amount of capital needed to compete, which concentrates ownership among a few and limits the opportunities of the many to become business owners. Thus, self-employment or small-scale capitalism was typical of pre-industrial capitalism but thought to be increasingly atypical in advanced industrial capitalism. This transformation in the organization of production and the structure of competition was articulated by Marx in the first volume of *Capital* (1970 [1887]). Weber too outlined a similar process when he noted that before the advent of industrial capitalism 'every worker could be said to have been primarily interested in becoming an independent small bourgeois, but the possibility of realizing this goal is becoming progressively smaller' (1964 [1947]: 427). However, for Weber, the driving force behind the 'expropriation of the individual worker from ownership of the means of production' was the greater rationality and hence efficiency of a bureaucratic organization of production in a market system (1964 [1947]: 246). The Marx–Weber thesis that self-employment in particular, and small-scale capitalism in general, was destined for terminal decline corresponded to the historical trend in industrial capitalist societies – until recently. For example, Wright has calculated that in the USA the proportion of the labour force that were self-employed declined from over 40 per cent in 1870 to under 10 per cent in 1970, with a comparable though less steep decline in other societies (Wright, 1997). Unsurprisingly, the view that self-employment was in terminal decline became the dominant one, with education replacing entrepreneurialism as the conventional route to occupational success (Scase and Goffee, 1980).

Since the 1970s, there has been an unexpected reversal of this historical trend in many industrial capitalist societies, most notably the UK where self-employment had been static during the post-war era, but increased from 7.3 per cent of total employment in 1973 to 11.9 per cent in 1993, an increase of over 50 per cent (Robinson, 1999; Standing, 1997). It also increased to a lesser extent in the USA, but not in France, Germany and Japan. Table 7.3 (on p. 166) extends Standing's data on standard and non-standard types of work to include the latest OECD statistics on the five countries under discussion and shows that by 2009 it had risen to 13.4 per cent in the UK, and, with the exception of the USA where it declined slightly, had increased in France, Germany and Japan. Consideration of the five OECD countries shows that self-employment as a proportion of total employment increased only a little from an average of under 10 per cent in 1973 to over 11 per cent in 2009 (OECD, 2010). The self-employment rate for men is about twice that of women in most OECD countries. The expansion of self-employment since the 1980s, particularly in the UK, has been attributed to a range of interrelated economic and political/socio-cultural factors.

Economic factors include, first, deindustrialization, characterized by the decline of capital-intensive manufacturing, and the growth of labour-intensive services which require a smaller financial outlay, thereby encouraging self-employment (Scase and Goffee, 1980). There is empirical support from the

USA for the claim that 'the expansion of self-employment is significantly linked to post-industrialism' (discussed in Chapter 4 with reference to skill), in the sense that post-industrial occupations, such as business and professional services, tend to contribute hugely to the growth of self-employment (Wright, 1997: 135). Though women are under-represented in self-employment, they tend to be concentrated in the service sector, the growth of which partly explains the doubling of female self-employment in the UK between 1979 and 1987 (Casey, 1991).

Second, organizational restructuring, characterized by the conversion of employee jobs into self-employed jobs as part of the tendency for firms to seek numerical flexibility and reduce costs, was discussed in the context of the Fordism paradigm in Chapters 5 and 6. This can take various forms, two of the most prominent being self-employed subcontracting and self-employed freelance work. The former is associated with manual work whereas the latter is associated with knowledge work, and along with other types of non-standard work, such as part-time work and temporary work, they are considered as either highly risky forms of employment in Beck's version of the destandardization of work thesis discussed earlier, or highly rewarding flexible forms of employment in Castells' network enterprise thesis (discussed in Chapter 6 and above). Historically labour-only subcontracting has been widespread in the UK construction industry (Bresnen et al., 1985), but during the 1980s this form of self-employment spread to manufacturing industry (Fevre, 1987) and the service sector (Hakim, 1988). Freelancing also increased, such as in the production of television programmes in the UK, largely in response to the competitive pressure to reduce costs, and has involved the transfer of risks from employers to employees (Dex et al., 2000). Recent research has shown that although most subcontracters and freelancers are pushed into self-employment by organizational restructuring, work satisfaction was high and focused on the freedom to exercise initiative and use their abilities (Smeaton, 2003).

Third, technological innovations have encouraged self-employment by reducing the cost of setting up a business and by offering the advantage of flexibility or, as Castells has put it, 'as new technologies make it possible for small business to find market niches, we witness a resurgence of self-employment and mixed employment status' (2001: 236). For Beck, the teleworker in the electronic cottage is an 'extreme' example of 'decentralized', non-standard work, thereby emphasizing the temporal and spatial dimensions of destandardization of work rather than the contractual (1992: 147). Empirical research on the contractual aspect of telework in Britain found that in six cases only two involved self-employment and in both instances they were contracted to a single company, one of which provided support 'until full independence was established' (Stanworth and Stanworth, 1991: 41). Thus the majority of teleworkers are not self-employed in the sense of owning the means of production and working autonomously since teleworking tends to be initiated by companies with a concern for costs and flexibility rather than an individually inspired conversion to self-employment.

Fourth, according to the post-Fordist interpretation of industrial capitalist development, the change from mass consumption to more individualized consumption is thought to have encouraged small-scale production, hence self-employment, for example, by craft workers for niche markets (Burrows, 1991). Understandably, the fragmentation of consumption has been referred to as '"post-Fordist" consumption' (Lash and Urry, 1994: 174). The problem with this explanation of the expansion of self-employment is that it lacks any empirical evidence (Fine, 1995). This does not mean that this intuitive line of reasoning is totally without merit since Beck's individualization thesis implies not only the destandardization of work but also consumption, though research on the latter is less advanced than it is on the former.

Fifth, unemployment during the 1980s is thought to have stimulated entry into self-employment via a combination of limited opportunities for waged work, receipt of redundancy payments that can fund starting a business and the availability of relatively inexpensive equipment during a recession (Curran and Blackburn, 1991). There is evidence from the USA which shows that as unemployment rises so does self-employment (Wright, 1997), and from the UK which shows that unemployment does spur people on to enter self-employment (Bogenhold and Stabler, 1991). Hence unemployment is both cyclical and a 'push' factor, especially for men (Granger et al., 1995: 499) and ethnic minorities, who often turn to self-employment when they are unable to obtain work as an employee (Phizacklea and Ram, 1996). However, only a small proportion of entrants to self-employment were previously unemployed (Hakim, 1988), and even with the state financial support to help the unemployed become self-employed, a policy that was not unique to the UK (Yeandle, 1999), the move from unemployment to self-employment is a risky one that often ends in outright failure or a struggle to survive in an area of high unemployment (MacDonald, 1996). This was just one UK government initiative during the 1980s concerned with encouraging self-employment and reflects the political salience of both high unemployment and self-employment.

Political/socio-cultural factors include direct influences such as government policies to encourage self-employment and indirect influences to alter the political culture in a pro-enterprise direction. In the UK between 1979 and 1989 successive Conservative governments introduced 'over 200 legislative initiatives designed to make starting, running and expanding a small firm easier' (Burrows and Curran, 1991: 20). These measures included advice and training, loans and tax incentives, and a general relaxing of the regulations affecting the self-employed and small businesses in order to reduce their bureaucratic burden. Prominent among the measures introduced during the early 1980s were the Loan Guarantee Scheme (1981), to provide guarantees for bank loans, and the Enterprise Allowance Scheme (1982), to provide funds to facilitate the transition from unemployment to self-employment. The policy to encourage self-employment via direct legislative action was continued by post-1997 Labour governments.

Socio-cultural factors refer specifically to changes in attitudes and behaviour in relation to work and employment that favour self-employment over dependent employment and are typically summed up by the problematic concept of 'enterprise culture' (Keat and Abercrombie, 1991). From a right-of-centre political perspective, the enterprise culture denotes a distinct set of attitudes and values, notably risk-taking, self-reliance, and individualism, which contrast with a dependency culture characterized by risk-aversion, reliance on others, and collectivism (MacDonald, 1996). In the UK in the 1980s, successive Conservative governments sought to encourage an enterprise culture and discourage a dependency culture as a solution to the perceived long-standing problem of the relative inefficiency and lack of dynamism of the economy. The policy to foster an enterprise economy involved not just financial incentives and the support of the local and central arms of the state, but also spread to the state educational system. Enterprise education was incorporated into the national curriculum of secondary schools and into undergraduate and postgraduate programmes in higher educational institutions (Wigley and Lipman, 1992). This is entirely logical given that the aim was to inculcate a spirit of enterprise and that education is the main socialization agency under the control of the state. Once again, the policy to engender an enterprise culture, initiated by Conservative governments in the 1980s and early 1990s, was continued by subsequent Labour governments. There are good reasons to be sceptical of the impact of attempts to nurture an enterprise culture from above, including that it would have expanded for economic reasons irrespective of the alleged emergence of a more enterprising culture (Curran and Blackburn, 1991), that it does not account for employees who became 'reluctant entrepreneurs' at the behest of their former employers (Boyle, 1994), and that new entrants' experience of self-employment in a high unemployment area tends to be more a matter of economic survival than an expression of a resurgent enterprise culture (MacDonald, 1996).

This analysis of the increase in self-employment since the decline of Fordism in advanced industrial capitalist societies, with special reference to its exceptional growth in the UK, suggests that many inter-related economic and political/socio-cultural factors need to be taken into account, especially the former, and that there is a gap between the rhetoric and reality of self-employment. The lack of genuine autonomy and continued subordination to one employer among those who have been converted from an employee to self-employed status at the instigation and in the interests of capital have led Rainbird to argue that 'self-employment constitutes a form of disguised wage labour' (1991: 214). The increased quality of self-employed work is questionable given the long, unsocial hours, high risk, increased stress, and lack of state benefits and hence economic security, though there is the prospect of earning a higher income (profits) than if they had remained a standard worker (Kalleberg et al., 2000).

There are three possibilities regarding the future of self-employment (Edgell, 1993). First that the trend of self-employment could revert to the pre-1980s historical pattern of long-term decline (demise theory); second, that self-employment could stabilize at the current level of approximately 12 per cent of the labour force of industrial capitalist societies (marginalization theory); and third, that self-employment could continue to grow at the expense of standard wage labour (demarginalization theory). The first possibility (demise theory) is unlikely since the owners of small-scale businesses can 'pass on their capital assets to their children' (Scase and Goffee, 1982: 187), and because '[a] history of self-employment in a family is repeatedly found to be a significant factor in people taking up self-employment, and in success' (Hakim, 1988: 432). It is also a popular option with high levels of work satisfaction, notwithstanding the myth of autonomy, inherent insecurity and long working hours tendency. Moreover, with governments embracing the idea of an enterprise economy with practical and ideological support, the extension of self-employment to the public sector, employers converting employees into self-employed subcontractors of various kinds, further advances in technology which, among other things, reduces start-up costs, and the continued expansion of the service sector, the first possibility seems even more remote. Whether or not self-employment has peaked (marginalization theory) or will continue to grow (de-marginalization theory) depends partly upon one's definition of self-employment in that it could be argued that much of the recent growth of self-employment is spurious, and partly on the future strategies adopted by employers in an attempt to further enhance numerical flexibility and reduce their risks by transferring them to others.

Spatial destandardization: homeworking

Working at home was the norm prior to the rise of industrial capitalism. The introduction of the factory system, and its associated division of labour, necessitated the transfer of production to specialist sites (discussed in Chapter 1). Thereafter small-scale home-based work declined as the economic advantages of mass production rendered it relatively inefficient and therefore costly. The consequent spatial separation of work from home became a central element in the social construction of the standard form of work. However, this traditional type of homeworking or work that is located in the home, predominantly of a manual kind and undertaken primarily by women, persisted in less developed societies and never disappeared completely in the more developed ones where it survived hidden in the increasingly private sphere of the family (Boris and Prugl, 1996). For example, in nineteenth-century Britain it was prevalent in the clothing industry and the production of many other goods, such as boots and shoes (Pennington and Westover, 1989).

Homeworking by definition involves undertaking paid work at home, a workplace that is considered to be and still is an atypical spatial location in modern societies. Home-located work can and does vary in terms of time (permanent/temporary and/or full/part-time) and employment status (employer, self-employed, or employee), and as with self-employment, the employment status of homeworkers is problematic. For example, a study of routine blue- and white-collar homeworkers in Britain found that approximately one-third of homeworkers considered themselves as self-employed and an equivalent proportion thought that their work provider considered them to be self-employed (Felstead and Jewson, 1996). Thus approximately half of all home-workers in Britain were in the inherently risky category of 'self-employed' and consequently excluded from the range of employment protections applicable to employees, such as redundancy, lay-off, and maternity pay. The same research also reported that the remainder either did not know how their provider viewed them or could not specify their employment relationship! Also, incredibly, nearly 90 per cent of homeworkers studied by Felstead and Jewson did not have a written contract of employment, two-thirds do not receive an itemized pay slip and the vast majority were not entitled to various fringe benefits. The lack of protection from risks such as ill health and unemployment suggests that the vulnerability of homeworkers in Britain has changed little since the late nineteenth century when homework was 'one of the burning issues of the women's trade union movement up to the Trade Boards Act of 1909' (Pennington and Westover, 1989: 121).

Along with other types of non-standard work, homeworking is thought to have expanded in recent years, particularly in the USA and other modern societies, although compared to the contractual and temporal dimensions of destandardization, 'homeworking is one of the least researched and conceptually most difficult forms of employment' (Felstead and Jewson, 1997: 327). The data that is available varies the way it is defined and therefore measured which means that statistics on the incidence of homeworking should be treated with caution. For example, 'estimates based on whether any work is done at home widens the focus, while those based on whether work is done mainly at home narrow it' and the distinction between working at or from home is a further source of variation (Felstead and Jewson, 2000: 49). Notwithstanding this problem, Felstead and Jewson have noted that studies have estimated that homeworking increased by over 50 per cent in the USA between 1980 and 1990 to 3.4 per cent of the employed population, and by two-thirds in Britain between 1981 and 1991 to 5 per cent of the working population. More recently in the UK, homeworking increased from 9 per cent of the workforce in 1997 to 11 per cent in 2005, most of which was not traditional homeworking, but teleworking, that is working for pay mainly from home using computer and communication technologies (Ruiz and Walling, 2005). In other words, home-located telework doubled over this period whereas traditional homeworking declined in absolute terms and as a percentage of the workforce. Reports on the growth of telework reiterate that its measurement is problematic due to the lack of established definitions, though most agree that however it is defined, the number of teleworkers is at least twice as high in the USA than Europe (Gareis, 2010). The same study summarized the latest available data and noted that in the USA 18 per cent of the labour force worked mainly at home, a figure that included both teleworkers and other home-based workers, whereas in Europe it varied between 2 per cent and 8 per cent depending on the definition of telework used, and 4.5 per cent in Japan where the work culture values highly face-to-face interaction and homes tend to be too small for teleworking.

The main reasons for the increase in homeworking in advanced economies since the 1980s are technological innovations, notably information and communication technologies (ICT), and managerial strategies to enhance numerical flexibility in an attempt to reduce costs via outsourcing work to home-based production in the face of global competition (Felstead and Jewson, 2000). These two factors often operate together in the form of a cost-cutting restructuring of an organization, as in the case of Rank Xerox where managerial specialist staff were converted from conventional employees to self-employed new technology homeworkers during the early 1980s (Stanworth and Stanworth, 1991). Stanworth and Stanworth also suggested that the key factor is the development of new technology because it facilitates the spatial destandardization of work by allowing work to be undertaken in the home, thereby reversing the historical trend since the rise of industrial capitalism for work to be concentrated in specialist work spaces outside the home.

In terms of the qualitative dimension of homeworking, Felstead and Jewson (2000) and Felstead et al. (2001) distinguish between those who have considerable labour market power (non-routine high discretion professional and managerial staff or knowledge workers) and those who have minimal labour market power (routine manual and non-manual workers). They argue that this distinction 'should be conceptualized as a continuum rather than a dichotomy' and that it 'is of crucial relevance to the experience of home-located wage labour' (2000: 17–18). Studies of these two types of home-located workers have confirmed that low discretion homeworkers tend to be female, receive low pay and experience poor working conditions, including risks to their health and safety, whereas high discretion homeworkers are typically male, better paid with superior work conditions that reflect their greater access to dedicated workspaces and technologies (Felstead and Jewson, 2000; Felstead et al., 2005).

According to Felstead and Jewson, what is unique about all homeworkers is that 'they are engaged in a distinctive type of struggle, on a routine basis, to define and to bring into being aspects of their working lives that workplace producers rarely if ever encounter', namely 'the processes of the management of the self that are the bedrock on which the meaning and experience of home-located production rests' (2000: 112). They emphasize that homeworkers have to manage their work in terms of how it fits in within the emotional world of the household and their invisibility within the impersonal world of work. In practical terms this means that homeworkers have to organize the space they work in, their working time, and establish social boundaries while supervising themselves to ensure that the quantity and quality of their work are maintained and their occupational credibility is enhanced (Felstead et al., 2005). These distinctive features of homeworking apply to low and high discretion homeworkers and challenge the idea that paid work is something that takes place outside the home and creates difficulties in their work and family relationships. Homeworking therefore puts a premium on self-management skills, and in his respect there are clear parallels between self-employment and homeworking.

Time flexibility is considered to be one of the main advantages of homeworking for employees, although for male homeworkers it is mainly a matter of managing work and leisure time, whereas for women it is typically about managing work and domestic responsibilities (Felstead and Jewson, 2000). Thus men were concerned to establish a work routine and a separate space that mirrored working in a non-home environment, whereas women often organized their paid work around their unpaid house and child-care work and undertook their paid work in shared rather than dedicated space. This makes it easier for male homeworkers to work in an uninterrupted way and more difficult for female homeworkers to resist the perception that they are housewives. For both male and female homeworkers time flexibility may be undermined by a combination of an uneven supply of work, a piece-rate payment system, and the lack of a fixed working day/week, which can result in little control over their work pattern and a tendency to work intensively for long hours, plus the involvement of other family members as unpaid workers (Harvey, 1999). This suggests that although in theory homeworkers have the power to decide how, when and where to work, such decisions are often made with reference to their employer or supplier and/or other family members. Limited rather than total flexibility would seem to characterize homeworking, and just like the self-employed, they are 'relatively self-directed' rather than autonomous (Felstead and Jewson, 2000: 112).

From the perspective of an employer or supplier, homeworkers not only provide the advantage of numerical flexibility, often at a lower pay rate and without the costs associated with employment in a factory or office, such as heating, and employee benefits (Felstead and Jewson, 2000), ICT offers the prospect of a more flexible and egalitarian organization (Castells, 2001). However, homeworking is not without its difficulties for an employer since maintaining control over workers at a distance puts a premium on trust, and a manager's delegational and communication skills (Stanworth and Stanworth, 1991), and the technological potential of ICT seems to be constrained by the persistence of ideas about how to organize work, including Taylorism and hierarchy (Boreham et al., 2008). In practical terms, controlling and motivating workers at a distance is more difficult than doing so in a face-to-face situation (Pyoria, 2003) and may jeopardize teamwork (Dimitrova, 2003). For these reasons, both Stanworth and Stanworth, and Pyoria have suggested that a combination of home and office working would be an arrangement that suited both employers and employees. Potentially, the mixed location solution could also mitigate the problem of staff training and social isolation, which are considered to be two of the major disadvantages for homeworkers.

On balance, potentially, the advantages of homeworking for employees and employers seem to outweigh the disadvantages, yet homeworking in general, and teleworking in particular, constitute a small but expanding section of the workforce. This suggests that homeworkers appreciate that this type of non-standard work creates difficulties in both their work and family careers, and that employers are aware of discipline and trust problems concomitant with employing workers at a distance, hence their reluctance to relinquish their conventional control of workers. Also, perhaps the idea that work is something that is undertaken outside the home is more entrenched in organizational cultures and has been more thoroughly internalized by workers than is realized by those who advocate and celebrate homeworking.

Overly optimistic accounts of the transformation of work, especially by those who have a vested interest in its expansion, such as *The Telework Association* (www.telework.org.uk), tend to present ICT-facilitated home-working as an everyone wins development; workers improve their work–life balance, companies gain in flexibility, and for society there are environmental advantages, such as the time and energy saved by a decline in commuting to work. However, empirical research shows that there is a class and gender divide between high discretion, highly paid, predominately male homeworkers and low discretion, low-paid, predominantly female homeworkers, and that even the main winners suffer the social costs of increased home and work tensions. The gains to employers in terms of more flexible workforces and organizations have yet to be fully realized, and that consequently the environmental benefits are less than anticipated. Yet the factors that favour the continued expansion of homeworking, notably the increasing affordability and capability of ICT, exist already which suggests that this form of non-standard work is more likely to grow than shrink in the future.

Temporal destandardization: temporary/part-time work

Temporal non-standard work can take two forms: it can be for a fixed duration, namely temporary in contrast to permanent employment where the contract has no end-date, or it can be for a proportion of the standard working week, namely part-time instead of full-time. Although there is an overlap between these two forms of non-standard work and with self-employment (Casey, 1991), they will be considered separately because while temporary work is inherently insecure, part-time work is not, and as will become apparent, part-time work is highly gendered in that it is dominated by women and this has implications for explanations of its incidence and quality.

As with other types of non-standard work, it was widely but wrongly assumed that the development of the Fordist model of work, characterized by permanent contracts of employment and a range of 'rights, benefits and forms of protection', signalled the historical demise of temporary work (Campbell and Burgess, 2001: 171). Yet temporary work persisted, not least due to seasonal demand in agriculture and tourism.

Notwithstanding the usual definitional and measurement problems that afflict all forms of non-standard work, it has been shown that between 1983 and 1993 temporary work increased on average in the five economies from just under 6 per cent to just under 8 per cent (Castells, 2001; Standing, 1997). Moreover, even where the proportion of temporary work grew but remained relatively low at around 5 per cent or below, some forms of temporary work increased dramatically during this period, notably that for temporary agency workers in the USA and UK (Castells, 2001; Forde, 2001). Table 7.3 (on p. 166) includes the latest available statistics for the five countries and shows that between 1993 and 2009 temporary work expanded to an average of 9.4 per cent of total employment (OECD, 2010; US Bureau of Labour Statisics, 2011). Luo et al. (2010) argue that the rise in temporary work in the USA peaked around the turn of the century and the decline since was due mainly to the ease of disposing of this type of highly flexible non-standard worker during a recession. The incidence of temporary employment is similar for men and women in all the OECD countries noted above except Japan.

The period of major expansion of temporary work during the 1980s and 1990s has been attributed to three factors: (1) changes in the regulatory framework such as the deregulation of labour markets that enables employers to hire and fire more easily in the name of efficiency, most noticeable in the UK during the 1980s (Deakin and Wilkinson, 1991): (2) changes in employer strategies such as labour policies by private and public sector organizations to introduce more flexible employment relations thereby reducing labour costs (discussed in the previous two chapters and above, see also Carré, 1992; Conley, 2002): and (3) changes in employee preferences in the direction of more flexible working time and improved work–life balance (to be discussed in more detail below), although the evidence from studies of temporary workers in the UK and the USA, the countries with the weakest temporary employment level of regulation among the five (Rubery and Grimshaw, 2003: 166), shows that over 44 per cent of temporary workers in the UK and 60 per cent in the USA would prefer a permanent job (Atkinson et al., 1996; Rosenberg and Lapidus, 1999). This suggests that the expansion of the temporary workforce was in large part driven by the demands of employers in the context of deregulated labour markets rather than the preferences of employees and that it was used by employers as a cost-effective way of dealing with variable demand.

As far as the qualitative dimension of this type of non-standard work is concerned, the most recent OECD study of temporary work reported that: there was a 'wage penalty' for temporary workers in certain European Union countries which averaged 15 per cent; temporary workers often did not qualify for benefits such as holiday and sick pay due to time in employment eligibility rules; they were more likely to experience repetitive work tasks and inflexible work time schedules such as night and weekend shifts; and they 'tend to be less satisfied than permanent workers', especially in terms of pay and employment security (OECD, 2002: 131). Studies in specific countries have confirmed these negative findings. For example, research in the USA has found that temporary workers tend not to have access to health and retirement benefits, receive low pay, and have less opportunity for training than standard workers (Carré, 1992), while another US study found that temporary work contributed to 'long-term financial difficulties even for workers who ultimately enter permanent jobs' (McGrath and Keister, 2008; 201). For those who are employed intermittently in temporary posts, a Canadian study of 22 men and 30 women re-affirmed the immense economic and social significance of regular paid work and concluded that involuntary discontinuous employment had a detrimental effect on health and 'trapped workers in a vicious cycle of precariousness' (Malenfant et al., 2007: 31). On the plus side, the OECD noted that among European countries the majority of temporary workers experienced substantial continuity of employment, temporary contracts are sometimes a stepping stone to permanent work, and that the more highly educated the temporary worker, the greater the chances of receiving training and job tenure.

Studies of temporary agency workers, the fastest expanding subcategory of temporary workers in many countries, paint an even bleaker picture. For example, a study of two such agencies in the UK concluded that the interventions of agencies have 'facilitated, reinforced and regulated the employment of temporary workers' which 'exacerbated the contingent and insecure nature of temporary working for agency temps' (Forde, 2001: 642). Unlike a number of other European societies, the absence of regulations seems to have encouraged the growth and enhanced role of agencies in the UK labour market. Similarly, research into the operation of temporary employment agencies in Chicago found that their focus on the bottom end of the labour market was adding to the labour market insecurity and exploitation of the lowest-paid temporary workers (Peck and Theodore, 1998). In continental Europe and Japan, research has shown that temporary agency work tends to be dominated by women and the young, who receive little training and low wages (Burgess and Connell, 2004). Finally, in Germany it was shown that although temporary agency workers are no different from permanent workers from the standpoint of benefits such as holiday and sick pay, the six-month eligibility rule means that the majority of temporary workers are not 'covered by statutory dismissal protection' and that their pay is lower, their job tenure is shorter, and their career prospects are worse than standard workers (Weinkopf, 2009: 184). Weinkopf concluded that the growth of temporary agency workers was due mainly to the demand by employers for flexible labour and the deregulation of the labour market in 2003. These studies suggest that the growth of temporary employment agencies has a particularly deleterious effect on the pay and conditions of temporary workers to the clear advantage of employers in terms of increased flexibility and reduced costs. Temporary workers may be a small proportion of the labour force in many advanced economies, but temporary work is arguably one of the most precarious and least desirable forms of non-standard work and personifies just-in-time labour.

Turning to the other form of temporal destandardization, part-time work which can be either permanent or temporary and can range from a zero-hours contract in which the worker only gets paid when working yet available on-call, to 35 hours a week which is almost the same as many full-time workers. For example, the majority of part-time workers in the UK in the mid-1990s were in permanent employment (Purcell, 2000) and that 91 per cent of part-time workers in the USA in 2005 were in non-contingent (i.e., ongoing) employment (www.bls.gov/news.release/conemp.nr0.htm). There is no universally agreed definition of part-time work but the OECD defines it as 30 hours or less per week.

Part-time work was not unknown during the rise of Fordism, especially by married women in the service sector, but was boosted by the shortage of male workers in the UK during the Second World War and the 1950s (Beechey and Perkins, 1987). At the height of Fordism, namely from 1951 to 1971, male and female full-time work declined in Britain while female part-time employment expanded markedly from just over 10 per cent to nearly 40 per cent of female employment, with the female share in part-time employment at over 80 per cent (Hakim, 1996). Following the demise of Fordism, between 1973 and 1993 part-time work continued to expand in all the five economies from an average of just over 12 per cent in 1973 to 18 per cent in 1993 (Standing, 1997). It also continued to be female-dominated, ranging from 89 per cent of part-time employment in Germany to 66 per cent in the USA, with an average share of 78 per cent in the five countries (Castells, 1997). Table 7.3 (on p. 166) shows that by 2009 the incidence of part-time employment in the five countries increased very slightly to an average of 18.7 per cent of total employment and was still dominated by women whose share of part-time work had little changed little since 1993 at 74.5 per cent (OECD, 2010). The decline in the dominance of women in part-time work between 1973 and 2009 indicates a small increase in the proportion of men who work part-time, though women remain disproportionately involved in part-time work in all the five countries.

In order to explain why women are still over-represented in this type of non-standard work. Hakim (1991, 2000) has developed a three-fold typology of women's work-lifestyle preferences: (1) family-centred women who prioritize family over work and only engage in paid work in exceptional circumstances such as widowhood (20 per cent); (2) work-centred women who prioritize work over family and tend to work full-time continuously like men, except that men generally do not have a choice (20 per cent); and (3) adaptive women who prioritize neither work nor family (60 per cent) and prefer to work part-time in order to be able to achieve a balance between their paid work and family life. In Hakim's own words: 'Women's concentration in lower-paid and part-time jobs is the consequence, not the cause of most women's expectation of marriage and financial dependence on a man' (2000: 27). Hakim noted that the majority of female part-timers in Europe enter this type of non-standard work voluntarily, a point that has been confirmed for the USA (Tilly, 1992), that they report high levels of job and marital satisfaction, and that their low pay was due to their lack of qualifications and discontinuous work histories not discrimination. Hakim argues that female part-time workers are more like housewives than full-time workers because being a secondary earner does not increase their bargaining power in the household and there-fore does not threaten male domination in the home (Hakim, 1996). Women's work–family options are the result of five major social changes: (1) the contra-ceptive revolution which put women in control of their fertility; (2) the equal opportunities revolution which gave women access to all occupations; (3) the growth of white-collar work which appeals to women more than men; (4) the establishment of jobs for secondary earners which opened up the possibility of combining paid work with family life; and (5) the 'increasing importance of attitudes, values, and personal preferences in the lifestyle choices of prosper-ous, liberal modern societies' (Hakim, 2000: 3). These changes were achieved by the end of the last century in the USA and the UK, hence Hakim based her theory on studies in these two countries, but claimed that it applies in every country undergoing these social transformations. In effect, the social barriers constraining women's participation in paid work have been removed and the majority are in the adaptive category, whereas the majority of men are work-centred and therefore have little choice whether to undertake paid work or not, but as primary earners they have more choice about their participation in domestic work.

Hakim's preference theory was 'developed independently' of Beck's indi-vidualization perspective but it is 'consonant' with it in that it emphasizes individual choice over social constraints and claims that 'institutional con-straints remain, but they are becoming less important' and there are parallels between their lists of social changes that produced the diversity of lifestyle options for women (ibid.: 13, 175). Thus, preference theory has more in com-mon with Beck's account of destandardization than it does with Castells' one. The claim that women's work and family choices are largely voluntary and far less constrained by factors such as child-bearing and patriarchalism ruffled a few feminist feathers who responded by arguing that Hakim's preference theory is 'one-sidedly voluntaristic' and that 'male exclusionary practices have had a substantial impact on women's careers and occupational choices'

(Crompton and Harris, 1998: 131). Research by McRae came to a similar conclusion, namely that women's 'ability to overcome constraints is patterned by social structure/class whether manifested through differing qualifications, social networks or income' (2003: 334). On the basis of research using British data, Kan adopted a middle position, namely that preferences and constraints 'interact with each other and both play an important role in shaping women's employment careers' (2007: 459). Hakim did not deny that constraints still operate, but the evidence suggests that she underestimated their continuing influence.

In terms of the qualitative dimension of part-time work, despite improvements regarding the employment rights of part-timers in many countries (O'Reilly and Fagan, 1998), the OECD (2010) answer to the question 'How good is part-time work?' confirmed the findings of previous research that part-time workers continue to earn less than full-timers, have weaker job security and fewer opportunities for promotion, but an enhanced work–life balance. Specific country studies have also found that part-time work and the other form of temporal non-standard work, namely temporary work, are inferior to full-time work in a number of respects, notably in lifetime earnings and pension income in the UK, Germany and Denmark (Ginn and Arber, 1998), in the level of job security for these types of temporal non-standard workers in France and Britain (Paugam and Zhou, 2007), in terms of career progression for female full-time managers who switch to part-time work (Durbin and Tomlinson, 2010), and in pay, health insurance and pension benefits in the USA (Kalleberg et al., 2000). As Table 7.2 shows, a British study that replicated the aforementioned American one confirmed this pattern.

McGovern et al. (2004) concluded that despite the implementation in Britain of the European Union's Framework Directive on equality of treatment for part-time and temporary workers since they undertook their research, the comparative inferiority of these types of temporal non-standard work was unlikely to change because the new regulations excluded temporary agency workers and applied to only about 10 per cent of part-timers.

Table 7.2 Distribution of bad job characteristics by employment status (%)

	% of all employees	% with low wages	% with no sick pay	% with no pension	% with no career ladder
Full-time	77.2	22.3	31.1	31.1	46.3
Permanent	71.2	21.4	29.4	29.0	44.9
Temporary	6.0	32.0	53.7	57.4	64.4
Part-time	22.8	52.4	53.1	55.8	67.1
Permanent	20.1	52.7	50.3	54.3	68.2
Temporary	2.7	32.0	53.7	57.4	64.4
All	100.0	28.9	36.1	36.7	51.1

Source: Abridged version of Table 1 in McGovern et al. (2004: 236).

Critical evaluation of the destandardization thesis

Table 7.3 summarizes the incidence of non-standard from the end of Fordism to the present day, for the five countries under discussion throughout this chapter. The quantitative data presented in Table 7.3 show that non-standard work has increased since the demise of Fordism which broadly confirms the Beck and Castells destandardization thesis. However, the rate of increase has slowed down since 1993 and the pattern is uneven among the five countries that have been the main focus of this chapter. The USA and Japan stand out with the lowest and highest proportions of non-standard work as a percentage of total employment; the former because of its institutional flexibility (Castells, 2001), and the latter because of the strategy by Japanese management to jettison standard work (Kyotani, 1999). The overall picture, as far as the qualitative dimension of non-standard work is concerned, is that the pattern is more complex as some non-standard jobs are permanent and others involve highly paid knowledge workers, who do not conform to the non-standard jobs are all substandard generalization, though overall the evidence suggests that the pay and working conditions of the majority of non-standard workers are inferior to those of standard workers. However, these conclusions are subject to several qualifications and criticisms.

Table 7.3 Non-standard work in France, Germany, Japan, the UK, and the USA, 1973–2009

	Self-employed (% of non-farm employment)			Part-time (% of total employment)			Temporary (% of total employment)			Total non-standard (% of total employment)		
	1973	1993	2009	1973	1993	2009	1983	1993	2009	1973	1993	2009
France	11.4	8.8	9.0	5.9	13.7	13.3	3.3	10.2	12.5	20.6	32.7	34.8
Germany	9.1	7.9	11.7	10.1	15.1	21.9	9.9	10.2	13.5	29.1	33.2	47.1
Japan	14.0	10.3	15.8*	13.9	21.1	20.5	10.3	10.8	13.7	38.2	42.2	50.0
UK	7.3	11.9	13.4	16.0	23.3	23.9	5.5	5.7	5.7	28.8	40.9	43.0
USA	6.7	7.7	7.0	15.6	17.5	14.1	0.3	2.2**	1.8***	22.6	27.4	22.9
Average	9.7	9.3	11.4	12.3	18.1	18.7	5.9	7.8	9.4	27.9	35.3	39.5

Notes: *2008; **1995; ***2005.

Sources: Abridged version of Table 3 Standing (1997:20), updated from OECD (2010) and the US Bureau of Labor Statistics Contingent and Alternative Arrangements (2011).

First, all contributors to the debate about the destandardization thesis agree that the different types of non-standard work 'overlap' to a greater or lesser extent (e.g., Castells, 2000: 286). This means that by adding together each type of non-standard work as if they did not overlap, inevitably overstates the scale of non-standard work in any one country. When this is taken into account, it is not surprising that in the UK one survey found that: 'the overwhelming majority of paid jobs remain full-time and permanent and physically located in a specific place of work' (Taylor, 2003), and a study of the USA and European Union countries concluded that a 'stable core still accounts for the dominant form of employment' (Auer and Cazes, 2000: 405). This suggests that Beck and Castells' version of the terminal decline of the incidence of standard work is exaggerated and premature.

Second, if the employment of men and women are considered separately, it is clear that the majority of employed women are in non-standard forms of work and that this has been the case in the UK since 1987 when 52 per cent of women were in non-standard work (Hakim, 1996). This trend has continued with 62 per cent of employed women in non-standard jobs in the UK in 2010 (www.statistics.gov.uk). Thus the Beck and Castells' destandardization of work thesis applies far more to women workers than it does to men.

Third, during the rise of non-standard work, standard work has not remained static, it too has changed in various ways, some of which were discussed in the previous two chapters. Of most relevance to the issue of destandardization are the attempts by employers to introduce greater numerical flexibility within the standard workforce by varying the number of hours they work (Burchell et al., 1999), the decline in pension benefits in the UK and the USA, particularly the switch from defined benefits schemes in which the employer covers the costs, to defined contributions schemes in which the employee shoulders the risks (www.statistics.gov.uk/pensiontrends; Bernhardt and Marcotte, 2000), and the tendency for standard work to be less secure in terms of pay and employment (Heery and Salmon, 2000). These changes are to the advantage of employers because they reduce costs, and to the disadvantage of employees because they involve a deterioration in their employment situation. Thus, the distinction between standard and non-standard work is not as clear-cut as it was under Fordism. The convergence in the declining quality of standard and non-standard work is reflected in studies of full-time and part-time low-waged jobs that confirm Beck's worst fears about the rise of the working poor in two of the most prosperous economies, the USA and the UK, despite minimum wage legislation (Ehrenreich, 2001; Toynbee, 2003).

Although the destandardization of work thesis advanced by Beck and Castells is broadly supported by the evidence, subject to certain qualifications noted above, there are some contributors to the debate who have serious reservations about the credibility of the thesis. One of the earliest critiques of the destandardization thesis was Pollert (1988) who argued that non-standard forms of employment have deep historical roots, that transformation theorists tend to be selective regarding the evidence they adduce to show that it has increased dramatically, such as the focus on temporary work, and that there is a tendency to conflate the expansion of temporary work with that of part-time work. The most recent critique is that by Doogan who completely rejects the Beck and Castells' destandardization of work thesis on the grounds that 'the audacity of the vision is inversely related to the evidence provided to substantiate such claims' (2009: 146). Doogan argues first that it is 'illogical' to equate full-time work with stable employment since it 'can be both permanent and temporary', second, that the focus on the marked expansion of temporary work to 'epitomise the non-standard workforce as a whole' is misleading as it is only a tiny proportion of non-standard work and is therefore an inappropriate basis for generalization, and third, that temporary and part-time work should not be grouped together because the overlap is small except for male part-timers and the differences are great in terms of job stability (2009: 148). He concludes that non-standard work is too heterogeneous to allow simple generalizations about job quality, that the growth of non-standard work has been exaggerated greatly, especially the insecurity dimension, and drawing upon the research by Fevre (2007) suggests that the state has manufactured uncertainty via the spread of market forces to the public sector (Doogan, 2009: 202).

While Doogan's analysis covers North America and Europe, he focuses particularly on the lack of US statistical evidence that supports the destandardization thesis, yet as noted above, Castells emphasized that the USA is atypical in the sense that it is institutionally flexible and therefore there is no need to resort to non-standard forms of employment. Doogan's critique also tends to concentrate on temporal destandardization and neglects contractual and spatial, which considerably weakens his claim that Beck and Castells are mistaken about the growth of non-standard work. Thus Doogan's analysis is less than comprehensive and tends to underestimate the expansion of non-standard employment.

Summary and conclusions

The destandardization of work thesis is predicated on the idea that standard work is associated with the rise of Fordism and is usually conceptualized in terms of three key dimensions: the labour contract, the work site, and working hours. Two different perspectives, according to Beck's risk society thesis (1992, 2000) and Castells' network enterprise theory (2000, 2001), have advanced a destandardization of work thesis that claims that non-standard work is increasing at the expense of standard work and is characterized by flexibility, individualization and insecurity, but with potential social benefits for workers in terms of their work–life balance.

The destandardization of the work contract can refer to any aspect of an employment contract, but here self-employment was considered as its opposite since it lacks a contract of any kind. Homeworking was discussed as the embodiment of spatial destandardization, and temporary and part-time work to exemplify temporal destandarization. Problems of definition, and therefore measurement, afflict all forms of non-standard work. Historically, contractual, spatial and temporal forms of non-standard work had not disappeared completely with the rise of Fordist standard work. The overall trend of non-standard work in the five countries has been one of uneven growth since the demise of Fordism, unexpected in the case of self-employment and most marked in the case of female-dominated part-time work, though the rate of increase has slowed down in the recent past. In terms of the quality of non-standard work, the evidence is mixed but on balance shows that non-standard workers tend to receive lower pay, fewer benefits, and experience greater job insecurity than standard workers. This finding suggests that there is more support for pessimistic neo-Fordist interpretations of changes in job quality than for the optimistic post-Fordist view, although research on subjective perceptions rather than objective work conditions remained stable during the 1990s in the USA with the exception of job security (Handel, 2005).

There is also evidence that standard work itself has become less standard, especially in relation to working hours, job security, and pension benefits, thereby blurring the distinction between standard and non-standard work. Also, the different types of non-standard work tend to overlap, consequently, simply adding up each type is likely to overstate the scale of the destandardization of work process.

The uneven and limited growth of non-standard forms of work provides broad support for Beck and Castells' claim that non-standard work is expanding and the quality of such work is relatively poor, but their version of the destandardization thesis tends to exaggerate the extent of the change, especially the insecurity aspect. The over-representation of women in the largest category of non-standard work, part-time work, suggests that the destandardization of work thesis applies more to women than men. Some critics have argued that Beck and Castells are wrong about the scale of the growth of non-standard work and that the heterogeneity of non-standard work precludes generalizations about its quality.

A mixture of employee and employer-based reasons have been advanced for the growth of non-standard work, although the exact mix is not the same for every type of non-standard work. From the standpoint of employers, one factor seems to be present in every case, namely changes to the organization of production, some of which date from the crisis of Fordism in the late 1970s and are linked to the globalization of competition that constrained companies to introduce just-in-time labour to complement just-in-time production. The consequent managerial concern for increased numerical flexibility and lower costs of production has resulted in both the tendency for standard work to become less standard and for the types of non-standard work discussed in this chapter to expand, albeit unevenly. From the perspective of employees, the main motivation for undertaking non-standard work is to improve the work–life balance that flexibility allows and the main debate concerns the extent to which women prefer or are constrained to undertake non-standard work, especially part-time work.

The role of the state has also been influential in the growth of non-standard work: first, by its policies to encourage directly and indirectly certain types of non-standard work, as in the case of self-employment in the UK; second, by the absence of regulation, such as the operation of temporary employment agencies in the USA; and third, by the limited enforcement of regulations which favours the expansion of non-standard work. Government policies were an integral component of Fordism and they continue to play an important part ideologically via their advocacy of the flexibility of non-standard (and standard work) and, practically, by the presence or absence of regulations that affect the incidence and quality of non-standard work. Indeed, the unevenness of the expansion of different types of non-standard work may be due in large part to national variations in state legislation covering work conditions and rewards, which has influenced both individual and company decisions to embrace non-standard types of work.

Finally, an important element of both the Beck and Castells' versions of the destandardization of work thesis concerns unemployment, which is the focus of the next chapter.

Further reading

BOOKS The main proponents of the destandardization thesis are Beck (1992) *Risk Society: Towards a New Modernity* and (2000) *The Brave New World of Work*, and Castells (2001) *The Rise of the Network Society* (2nd edn). There are two good overviews of the debate; one that focuses on job security by Heery and Salmon (eds) (2000) *The Insecure Workforce*, and another on the different types of non-standard work by Felstead and Jewson (eds) (1999) *Global Trends in Flexible Labour*. On the gendered character of part-time work, consult Hakim (2000) *Work-Lifestyle Choices in the 21st Century* and follow up the criticisms by checking out the relevant references in the text, especially O'Reilly and Fagan (eds) (1998) *Part-Time Prospects: An International Comparison of Part-time Work in Europe, North America and the Pacific Rim*. The most sceptical view of the destandardization thesis can be found in Doogan (2009) *New Capitalism?: The Transformation of Work*.

ARTICLES For an analysis of non-standard work trends, consult Standing (1997) 'Globalization, labour flexibility and insecurity: the era of market regulation', *European Journal of Industrial Relations*, 3(1): 7–37, and for a review of the qualitative dimension of non-standard jobs, read McGovern et al. (2004) 'Bad jobs in Britain: non-standard employment and job quality', *Work and Occupations*, 31(2): 225–49.

WEBSITES The two key websites for the latest statistics on all aspects of work including non-standard work are the *Organisation for Economic Co-operation and Development*, www.oecd.org and the *International Labour Organization*, www.ilo.org

---
Questions for discussion and assessment
---

1   Account for the rise in self-employment in the UK since the 1980s.
2   Consider the work and family consequences of homeworking.
3   Is temporary agency work the least desirable form of non-standard work?
4   Why are women over-represented in part-time work?
5   Is all non-standard work sub-standard?
6   Assess the quantitative and qualitative dimensions of the destandardization of work thesis.
7   Examine the view that Beck and Castells exaggerate markedly the extent of the destandardization of work.

8

OUT OF WORK: UNEMPLOYMENT

Prior to the advent of industrial capitalism, self-provisioning of an essentially subsistence kind was of primary importance and regular paid work was of secondary importance for the vast majority. Hence, 'there was no unemployment because there was no norm of work' (Beck, 2000: 13). The revolutionary change inaugurated by industrial capitalism constituted a complete reversal of these priorities. In due course, as was noted in Chapter 1, the dominance of wage labour resulted in work becoming synonymous with employment. In such a society, to be without regular full-time employment, namely to be unemployed, involved exclusion from the main form of work and therefore from an income necessary for economic survival since all other legal avenues to alternative sources of income had more or less vanished.

It is entirely logical and fitting that the first society to industrialize on a capitalistic basis, the UK, was the first in which the twin issues of unemployment and underemployment in a time-related sense were raised politically by radicals as early as the 1820s (Thompson, 1970), and the first to introduce compulsory state insurance against unemployment in 1911 (Burnett, 1994). In between, the issues of unemployment and underemployment were theorized by Marx and Engels in the 1840s – the reserve army of workers theory (Marx and Engels, 1962 [1845]) – surveyed by Mayhew in the 1850s and Booth in the 1890s (Stedman Jones, 1984), and were the subject of an academic conference organized by the Sociological Society and held at the London School of Economics in 1907 (Burnett, 1994). The main lesson of these diverse contributions was that economic well-being in a market system was almost entirely dependent on avoiding being out of work, namely unemployment.

However, the economic theory that informed government policy between 1910 and 1940 considered unemployment to be an unavoidable consequence of the business cycle (Ashton, 1986). According to this view, there was little that a government could or should do except relieve the worst of its deleterious economic impact on the unemployed. Yet the political salience of mass unemployment often led governments to focus on the plight of the unemployed in a pragmatic way when faced with the threat of social unrest (McIvor, 2001). In the UK, the government offered tax incentives to companies to locate factories in areas of high unemployment and adopted an assisted migration policy to encourage the unemployed to move from depressed to prosperous parts of the country (Burnett, 1994). In the USA, in the aftermath of the stock market crash of 1929 and subsequent depression, in order to quieten political disorder, provide economic relief in the form of employment and inculcate the habit of work, an interventionist programme of public investment known as the New Deal was implemented (Piven and Cloward, 1974). A generation after it was pioneered in Britain, unemployment insurance was introduced in the USA in 1935 (Ashton, 1986).

In the light of these pragmatic policies, plus the experience of successful state regulation of labour during the Second World War, governments in the UK and the USA were eventually converted to the Keynesian idea that the state could do more than merely provide limited financial support, namely that it could create employment by attempting to influence the market via public investment (Ashton, 1986). By the 1950s the ideal of full employment was adopted as a policy objective and realized to a large extent in industrial capitalist countries. This was the culmination of the state dimension of Fordism that was part of what was referred to in Chapter 5 as the Fordist compromise between the interests of employers and employees. Thus, under the Fordist model of mass production and consumption, state policies tried to ensure that demand for goods and services remained relatively stable, despite the vicissitudes of the market.

The crisis of Fordism in the 1970s provoked another change in policy as rapid increases in inflation and unemployment reduced support for state intervention and strengthened the argument that market forces should operate without interference from governments or trade unions (Ashton, 1986). During the mass unemployment of the 1980s, the new orthodoxy was identical to that which had prevailed between 1910 and 1940, namely that unemployment was inevitable in a market society. The recrudescence of individualistic values and what were perceived as the twin virtues of free competition and minimal state intervention in the economy was complete when the Conservative governments of the 1980s abandoned the objective of full employment and substituted the primary policy aim of controlling inflation (Edgell and Duke, 1991). Governments in the UK and the USA have continued to follow essentially neo-liberal policies ever since, although opinions are divided on the inevitability of large-scale unemployment in the context of advancing technological change and increasing globalization; there are pessimists (e.g., Aronowitz and DiFazio, 1994) and optimists (e.g., Castells, 2001) regarding the scale of unemployment in the advanced economies this century.

From the standpoint of the unemployed, the two eras of mass unemployment in the twentieth century coincided with the dominance of the view that unemployment was a necessary consequence of a market economy and that the state should not intervene for fear of exacerbating the problem. Thus we find that, during both depressions, welfare benefits for the unemployed were cut (Edgell and Duke, 1991). Two other factors informed public policy during these mass unemployment eras; that the state could not afford to fund such large numbers when its income was shrinking and that generous unemployment benefits might undermine the incentive to work (Ashton, 1986). First, the cost argument is somewhat specious since fiscal prudence does not seem to apply to non-welfare state spending, such as defence (Edgell and Duke, 1991). Second, there is little evidence to support the theory of benefit-induced unemployment (Eichengreen, 1989; Sjoberg, 2000). On a positive note, in terms of the sociology of unemployment, the two major unemployment eras of the twentieth century stimulated extensive research on this issue.

More recently, Castells has argued (as noted in Chapter 7), that in the transition from a predominance of standard work to one of non-standard work, mass unemployment is not inevitable but that it depends in large part on the extent of the diffusion of information technology and public policies, although in the short term there will be 'painful adjustments' before the creation of new high technology jobs exceeds the loss of low technology jobs (2000: 281). The pattern of these 'painful adjustments' is the subject of this chapter on the sociological significance of unemployment.

Unemployment: meaning and measurement

There are major difficulties in comparing changes in the scale of unemployment over time in any one country and between countries. The main reason for both is that nation states frequently alter the way unemployment is measured, often for essentially political motives. For example, between 1979 and 1989, Conservative governments in the UK changed the way unemployment was measured in official statistics 30 times and virtually every one had the effect of reducing the unemployment total (Edgell and Duke, 1991). However, most governments increasingly measure unemployment using the International Labour Organization's (ILO), a specialist UN Agency, definition of unemployment, or one that is similar to it, which enhances the consistency of cross-national comparisons over time. The ILO classifies people as unemployed if they are: (1) without a job; (2) actively seeking employment; and (3) available for work. This is a less restrictive definition than the one also used by the current UK government that involves only counting those who are (1) jobless; (2) registered as unemployed; and (3) in receipt of unemployment-related state benefits, such as a Jobseeker's Allowance. Not unsurprisingly, given that they measure different things, the ILO measure typically produces a higher level of unemployment than the so-called 'claimant count', although more often than not they move broadly in the same direction (www.statistics.gov.uk 2004).

However it is measured, in the era of the Fordist compromise, unemployment was consistently low compared with the major pre-1940 and post-1980 recessions. For example, the unemployment rate (proportion of the labour force 'unemployed') in the 1950s and 1960s was typically below 2 per cent in the UK and under 5 per cent in the USA, whereas the unemployment rates in both countries were around 20 per cent in the early 1930s and 10 per cent in the mid-1980s (Ashton, 1986). The latest OECD (2010) figures on unemployment (which are based on the ILO definition) show that the average unemployment rate in the five most advanced economies (discussed in Chapter 7) was 7.8 per cent in 2009, with Japan recording the lowest rate of just over 5 per cent and the USA the highest at nearly 10 per cent. These unemployment rates suggest that the post-1945 Fordist era was a golden age as far as full employment was concerned since the relatively low unemployment rates during the 1950s and 1960s have not been achieved since Fordism started to decline.

From the perspective of the unemployed, the sociological significance of the recent high rates of unemployment in advanced industrial capitalist societies, which reached a peak during the major global recession of the 1980s, is that 'the economic and social consequences of job loss are much more severe for the individual than in times of full employment when other jobs are readily available' (Ashton, 1986: 37). Given that research into the impact of unemployment tends to be undertaken when unemployment rates are at their highest, the findings are likely to reflect the greater hardship experienced during such a period.

The 1980s resurgence of large-scale unemployment in advanced industrial capitalist societies has led some to argue that aside from professional workers, the work ethic was in decline (e.g., Gorz, 1999). There are also those who have expressed doubts about the pervasiveness of a work ethic during the development of industrial capitalism in the nineteenth century (Kelvin and Jarrett, 1985; Rose, 1989). Yet the continuing centrality of work is readily apparent from surveys, including those undertaken during a recession. For example, when the unemployment rate was at its highest in the UK in the mid-1980s, a representative survey found that the majority of respondents (92 per cent) expressed a strong commitment to work, reflecting the persistence of a secularized version of the Protestant work ethic (Mann, 1986). This study concluded: 'Even if work is boring or low paid, it is central to most people's notion of their own moral, as well as material, worth' (ibid.: 24). Moreover, even among those made redundant, commitment to the work ethic has been shown to remain high (Westergaard et al., 1989). For instance, another survey during the same recession found that the unemployed are 'more committed to employment than those in work' (Gallie and Vogler, 1994: 124). Similarly, surveys in the USA have shown that the decline of the work ethic is a myth. This is unsurprising given the emphasis placed on it by the capitalist state, corporations, the media and educational institutions (Beder, 2000). Thus, large-scale unemployment does not seem to undermine the work ethic since the unemployed retain a moral commitment to work in addition to an instrumental one. In sum, work is typically perceived as crucial not only to one's economic well-being, but also to one's sense of moral and social worth. It is invariably in this context that the effects of unemployment have been understood since the pioneering research of the 1930s.

Jahoda's deprivation theory of unemployment

The classic study of unemployment by Jahoda et al. (1974 [1933]) was a comprehensive in-depth account of the social impact of unemployment on the inhabitants of a small industrial community in Austria decimated by the economic crash of 1929. The fieldwork was undertaken between 1931 and 1932 when three-quarters of the families in Marienthal were dependent on unemployment relief for their economic survival. Apart from cultivating vegetables on an allotment and breeding rabbits, opportunities to make a living legally were minimal, hence the first and most obvious effect of unemployment was financial: 'The day on which the fortnightly payments of unemployment relief are made is more important than Sunday. The entire economic life moves in this fortnightly cycle' (Jahoda et al., 1974 [1933]: 17). The economic impact was more than a matter of not going out for a drink. Such was the extent of economic desperation in this unemployed community that '[w]hen a cat or dog disappears, the owner no longer bothers to report the loss; he knows that someone must have eaten the animal, and he does not want to find out who' (ibid.: 22).

In addition to a markedly reduced standard of living, unemployment was accompanied by a decline in social activities due as much to a feeling of resignation as straitened circumstances. For example, despite the growth of free time, the unemployed typically did not attend a library or borrow books despite the abolition of borrowing charges, and participated in social and political organizations less often than before even though some 'reduced their membership fees for unemployed members to a nominal level' (ibid.: 40). Thus the loss of confidence and sense of shame associated with unemployment seemed to contribute to the tendency to withdraw from social interaction outside the home.

For those among the study living on an income 'which averages just one quarter of normal wages', careful budgeting is vital, and it is significant that all the quotations used to illustrate this point are by women (ibid.: 31). This is indicative of the differential impact of unemployment on men and women, as the material on the use of time demonstrates clearly: 'For the men, the division of the day has long since lost all meaning' (ibid.: 67). They tended to idle away the time, doing virtually nothing, with the vast majority not wearing a watch. In marked contrast, the women, though strictly speaking they were not unemployed, they were extremely busy running the household. In other words, their 'day is filled with [domestic] work' (ibid.: 75). The data on time use revealed that for the men, the absence of paid employment meant that their daily lives, indeed weekly, monthly and annual routines, lost the time structure that was hitherto organized around work. Time no longer had any significance beyond the reference points of the physical needs to eat, sleep and get up, with punctuality of the unemployed men a source of marital conflict since the mealtimes were set by their wives. The problem of marital discord was also mentioned in the context of the general deterioration of personal relationships as hope of employment faded. At best, minor quarrels increased in frequency and at worst 'difficulties became more acute' (ibid.: 86). The sense of time for men had been disrupted severely, but this was not the case for the women of Marienthal.

Not unrelated to the loss of a sense of time was the tendency for the majority of the families, including the children and adolescents, to respond to unemployment with a feeling of resignation, characterized by the 'absence of long-term plans' and general 'aimlessness' (ibid.: 59). Although the initial reaction tended to be one of shock, even panic about the prospect of debt, it was followed by optimism, as reflected in the numerous job applications sent in the first few months of unemployment. However, failure to get a job and the inexorable deterioration in economic circumstances as any savings ran out, clothing and household items wore out, and unemployment benefits are 'superseded by emergency relief, which in turn is gradually reduced and can eventually be stopped altogether', optimism turns to pessimism (ibid.: 80). For some, eventually any lingering resilience tends to fade and apathy becomes the norm, the whole process 'intensified by the concomitant decline in health' (ibid.: 82). For others, such as those who had been relatively affluent in the past, experienced great difficulty in coming to terms with prolonged unemployment and seemed to be 'heading for individual disaster' culminating perhaps in suicide (ibid.: 97). Out of the one hundred families studied, 70 per cent were 'resigned', 7 per cent were 'broken', and only 23 per cent were 'unbroken', although some of the most proactive may have emigrated before the study commenced.

Aside from mentioning briefly that the young were more likely to leave the unemployed community and that if conditions deteriorate further, others may also migrate or even revolt, the vast majority studied experienced unemployment as an almost totally debilitating process, economically, socially, and psychologically, with variations in terms of age, gender and class.

The Marienthal research was the beginning of Jahoda's lifelong interest in the social impact of unemployment and during the next era of mass unemployment, the early 1980s, Jahoda built upon her earlier research and developed what has become known as the deprivation theory of unemployment (Haworth, 1997). The basic assumption of her theory is that the manifest function of work/employment is economic, but work also provides some unintended consequences or latent functions including, a time structure, social contact, collective purpose, identity/status, and regular activity (Jahoda, 1981, 1982). Unemployment, being out of work, results in deprivation of both the manifest and latent benefits of work and Jahoda argues that the latent consequences of work are the main reason 'why employment is psychologically supportive, even when conditions are bad' and 'why unemployment is psychologically destructive' (1981: 188). In other words, work is the crucial institution for the achievement of a sense of well-being in modern societies and its absence leads to a range of deprivations that other institutions, such as trade unions and religious organizations, have difficulty in addressing. Table 8.1 summarizes the key features of Jahoda's deprivation theory of unemployment and shows that when employment is the undisputed main source of various categories of experience, both manifest and latent, unemployment is experienced negatively in terms of a range of deprivations. More specifically, being deprived of income results in poverty and being deprived of a time structure, social contact, a sense of collective purpose and achievement, self-esteem derived from a work status/identity, and regular activity, results in a marked decline in socio-psychological well-being.

Table 8.1 Key features of Jahoda's deprivation theory of unemployment

	Categories of experience					
	Manifest	Latent				
	Income	Time structure	Social contact	Sense of purpose	Status/ identity	Regular activity
Employment	+	+	+	+	+	+
Unemployment	−	−	−	−	−	−

Jahoda et al.'s pioneering study of mass unemployment and Jahoda's subsequent elaboration of deprivation theory have had a major influence on the sociology of unemployment. First, contemporary reviews of research on the economic, social and psychological consequences of unemployment (e.g., Hakim, 1982) have confirmed that, notwithstanding the growth of the welfare state, prolonged unemployment involves a wide range of inter-related negative consequences and hence work in the form of employment is still the main way that individuals connect to the wider society. Unemployment therefore has the potential to threaten not just one's economic survival but also one's identity, even one's life. Thus the tendency to understand the human consequences of unemployment through the prism of paid work as employment is the lasting legacy of the Marienthal study of unemployment. Second, Jahoda's deprivation theory suggests that: 'Different groups of unemployed experience the absence of one category of experience or another with differing intensity' (Jahoda, 1982: 85). In the light of these two points it is necessary to consider the extent to which the social impact of unemployment is the same for various social categories.

Class, age and gender, and the impact of unemployment

Certain social categories in the working-age population are over-represented among the unemployed, especially during a recession, notably the working class, younger and older workers, women, and particular ethnic minorities, such as Pakistani and Bangladeshi groups in the UK and African-Americans in the USA. The social consequences of unemployment with respect to class, age and gender are discussed below since they are numerically the most important in industrial capitalist societies, with the exception of the USA where race or ethnicity is a major consideration.

Class

A recent study of 21 'affluent' OECD countries confirmed the historical pattern that the unemployment rate for the working class is higher than for any other class (Oesch, 2010). This is the main reason why sociological research on the impact of unemployment tends to focus almost exclusively on this class.

Ashton has argued that among the factors which influence the way in which unemployment is experienced are 'a person's status in the labour market, the extent to which their occupational identity is central to their self-image, their financial situation and their identity in the family' (1986: 122). Ashton is echoing Jahoda when he suggests that the '[t]ype of work experience is perhaps the most important factor influencing the experience of unemployment because it determines the level of income available and the opportunities for the development of an occupational identity' (1986: 124). On the basis of this systematic approach, and the conventional middle-class and working-class occupational model, Ashton has argued that professional and managerial careers maximize the tendency to 'develop an identity with an occupation' whereas relatively unskilled jobs minimize this possibility, and that, as a consequence, the threat to one's work identity is correspondingly greater for the former than the latter (ibid.: 124). Conversely, Ashton suggests that for the working class the biggest problem associated with unemployment is the abrupt and steep decline in income. The assumptions here are that the middle classes are more likely to have savings and identify with their work, and thus are likely to experience a greater sense of status loss if they become unemployed than the working class. However, research on occupational communities by Salaman (1974) has shown that identifying with an occupation is not an exclusively middle-class phenomenon. Hence the threat to one's work identity occasioned by unemployment is not necessarily restricted to professional workers.

Ashton's class analysis of the social impact of unemployment is supported by surveys of the unemployed, notably by the large-scale longitudinal survey of the unemployed undertaken by Daniel (1990). This showed that although the shortage of money was a problem for all unemployed people, it was a bigger problem for the manual working classes than for the non-manual middle classes, whereas a sense of shame was more significant for non-manual workers and skilled workers than for semi-skilled and unskilled workers. Research on white-collar unemployment by Fineman (1983) has also shown that the stigma of being unemployed was particularly acute among this social class. The main reason for this is that, for the middle class, employment represents a high social status and hence the loss of their occupational status is experienced as a major source of shame and therefore stress.

This was illustrated dramatically in the film, *The Full Monty* (1997), in which the most middle class of the redundant steelworkers featured in the firm continued to pretend to be employed. The class dimension of this reaction to unemployment is also apparent in Japan, where the shame of unemployment induces numerous 'salarymen' to 'haunt the business districts of downtown Tokyo, unable to stay home or in their neighbourhoods between the morning and evening rush hours' (French, 2000: 10). Attempts to conceal the discreditable status of being unemployed is fraught with difficulties, not least that it can lead to what has been termed 'derivative stigmata', such as feeling 'duplicitous or untrustworthy', which in turn can compound the problem of managing the original stigma (Letkemann, 2002: 511).

Not unrelated to the stigma experienced by the unemployed middle class is the finding that 'the parasuicide rate [attempted suicide] varies inversely with social class', suggesting that those most at risk are middle-class males (Platt, 1986: 160). This is in line with Ashton's theory that unemployment is more of a shock to those who had previously enjoyed a high status and relatively secure position in the labour market. However, less extreme forms of mental ill health, such as feeling depressed, seem to be experienced by all classes, although a slightly larger proportion of higher occupational classes than the lower ones, including those in the skilled manual category, reported feeling depressed (Daniel, 1990). This class pattern can be interpreted as showing that all males are attached to paid employment, but those who are most attached for both intrinsic and extrinsic reasons, which tends to be the middle class, are likely to experience unemployment even more negatively in terms of psychological well-being. This class pattern was confirmed by Anderson (2009) whose analysis of the British Household Panel Survey showed that the detrimental impact of job loss on subjective well-being was higher among the middle classes than the lower and higher classes. Anderson speculated that this was because unemployment for the lower classes involved the escape from unsatisfying work and for the higher classes it meant freedom from a stressful job, but for the middle classes whose previous work was satisfying in a non-stressful way, the negative impact on well-being was great.

On the basis of British data from the late 1980s, it was confirmed that the financial consequences of unemployment were understandably also more adverse for the working class than the middle class, especially for those in relatively low-paid and insecure jobs (Gallie and Vogler, 1994). This occupational class pattern is entirely consistent with Ashton's emphasis on the relevance of the kind of work undertaken prior to job loss that is crucial to the economic impact of unemployment. More generally, it has been found that the experience of unemployment increases significantly 'the probability of downward occupational mobility' and lessens 'the chances of moving to less vulnerable positions' (Layte et al., 2000: 170).

Age

Ashton does not systematically examine how the length of time in work affects the social consequences of unemployment except to note that for young people about to enter the labour market: 'Their financial needs are not of the same order as those of prime-age males or females with families to support' (1986: 131). Although young people and school-leavers in particular may not have the same financial responsibilities as adults, they are more likely to be unemployed during a recession and often do not qualify for unemployment benefits which are typically based on being in work for a certain length of time (Scarpetta et al., 2010). The same OECD study found that in addition to the negative effect on future pay and employment prospects, long periods of unemployment while young can result in permanent scars through the harmful effects on a number of other outcomes, including happiness, job satisfaction, and health, many years later (ibid.: 4). This research suggests that the financial impact of unemployment is not inconsiderable even for young people.

For adults, unsurprisingly the evidence shows that the impact of unemployment is particularly severe for middle-age, full-time workers, but far less so for those approaching retirement (Daniel, 1990). This does not imply that unemployment for those aged over 55 is unproblematic since employers are typically reluctant to recruit older workers (Gallie and Vogler, 1994). In other words, older people are likely to experience unfair discrimination on the basis of their age (ageism) in the labour market, not unlike several other segments of the working-age population, notably women and ethnic minorities. In the case of older men who are unemployed, many are reluctant to see themselves as retired and there is a clear class pattern with early retirement being more of a non-manual option than it is for former manual workers (Casey and Laczko, 1989).

According to Ashton's analysis of youth unemployment, the main social consequences for this age group are that their transition to adult status is delayed and becomes 'more problematic', while they remain dependent upon their family of origin for economic and social support (1986: 132). Aside from a study of male apprenticeship in the 1945–75 period, which argues that transitions in the past were also extended and not entirely unproblematic (Vickerstaff, 2003), these points have been broadly confirmed by research which shows that not only has the 'period of the transition … been lengthened', but that it has also 'become much more fluid and uncertain' (Coffield et al., 1986: 199). Similarly, the study by Allatt and Yeandle confirmed the delay and increased fluidity of the transition into adulthood thesis, and went further in attributing a wider form of social exclusion to prolonged youth unemployment by suggesting that 'young people who might never hold a job were consigned to a second order of citizenship, unable to contribute to the community' (1992: 145). Revealingly, in light of the link between unemployment and ill health, this study reported that the language of illness was often used by the young to describe their experience of unemployment.

The alleged fragmentation of the transition to adulthood during the recent past has not only been attributed to the growth of youth unemployment, a distinctive feature of the 1980s compared with the 1930s, but to the '"sexual revolution" of the 1960s and in the women's movement' (Hutson and Jenkins, 1989: 154). A similar line of argument has been advanced by Irwin, who has suggested that

[the] delay in household and family formation by young couples [is], in part, a consequence of the increased importance of the earnings of young women relative to young men in resourcing new households, and becoming parents at a standard of living commensurate with orientations towards general, societal levels of consumption. (1995: 312)

These contributions to the debate about unemployment and the transition to adulthood do not seem to be denying the relevance of youth unemployment, they are simply noting that it is not the only factor causing a delay.

Empirical research on the increased fluidity aspect of unemployment and the delayed transition to adult thesis has suggested that where there was once, at the height of Fordist full-employment, a relatively small range of 'smooth transitions' from education to employment, fractured particularly by class and to a lesser extent gender, this pattern became more complex during the decline of Fordism in the recession of the 1980s (Roberts, 1984: 43). In effect, during the 1950s and 1960s, the (male) working class left school and became manual workers, whereas their middle-class counterparts stayed on in full-time education before entering the labour market as non-manual workers.

The gender dimension was apparent in that young women typically entered the labour market with the expectation that they would leave it when they became mothers (Martin and Roberts, 1984). The decline of manual occupations following deindustrialization and the growth of non-manual occupations following the rise of the post-industrial service society, led to the creation of a greater variety of possible transitions into employment, including the distinct possibility that the young unemployed from disadvantaged class backgrounds were more likely to 'end up incarcerated (if male) or as a single parent (if female) as they mature' (Blanchflower and Freeman, 2000: 8).

Thus, in addition to the traditional transitions, which in the meantime have become less distinct as more young people stay on in academic and non-academic full-time education, at least two other possibilities have become apparent. These can be summarized as government training schemes and underemployment (Roberts and Parsell, 1988). With only a small minority of young people entering the labour market at the minimum school-leaving age, thereby reducing the scale of youth unemployment, the transition into adulthood has not only become more protracted, but also far more fragmented (Roberts et al., 1994). Despite the growth of options, the influence of class background has persisted into the new era in that it continues to have a cumulative effect on the selected route from education to employment broadly in the form of an academic trajectory for predominantly middle-class high achievers and vocational training for the rest, namely those from working-class social origins (Roberts and Parsell, 1992). Similarly for gender, studies have shown that 'as transitions into employment have been prolonged, despite equal opportunity policies, new schemes and courses have quickly become segmented into masculine and feminine tracks, just like older opportunities' (Roberts et al., 1994: 50). This suggests that, notwithstanding what has been called the 'destandardization of the lifecourse' (Brannen and Nilsen, 2002), the main routes from education into employment and their associated class and gender patterns, have changed little since the decline of Fordism and the expansion of options. Although there is evidence from a small-scale qualitative study in Bristol that the multiplicity and precariousness of young adults' pathways into the labour market do not faze them and that they retain an optimism founded on their adaptability (Bradley and Devadason, 2008).

Ashton's analysis of the distinctiveness of youth unemployment is qualified with reference to both class and gender in that he suggests that the threat to the realization of an occupational identity is greater for middle-class youths than working-class ones, and that for young males the impact of unemployment on their transition to adulthood is 'mediated by their involvement in peer group activities which can provide an alternative source of status and prestige' (1986: 132).

As indicated already, the influence of class, gender and age can be seen to converge in the controversy regarding the link between unemployment and crime. In a review of the research literature, Hakim concluded that 'parental

and youth unemployment increase juvenile delinquency' and that unemployment is particularly associated with property crimes, such as burglary and theft
(1982: 450). One way of interpreting the relationship between unemployment and crime is via Merton's famous 'anomie theory', which argues that
when legitimate opportunities to achieve success are blocked, namely employment, illegitimate means are adopted, namely crime (1957). It has been contended that young people, especially males, who are unemployed for a long
duration, are most likely to respond in a deviant manner (Box, 1987;
Blanchflower and Freeman, 2000). Youth unemployment is perceived as a
potential threat to social stability, hence it tends to be the main focus of government policies on unemployment (Jordan, 1982).

A review of the latest evidence on the incidence and social consequences of
unemployment found that the youth unemployment rate was consistently
high in the advanced economies that were the main focus in the previous
chapter, namely France, Germany, the UK and the USA, plus Italy, because
data for Japan was not available (Bell and Blanchflower, 2010). A comparison
of unemployment rates in these countries is presented in Table 8.2 and shows
that youth unemployment rates were high in all five countries, especially in
relation to overall rates, with a ratio of youth to adult rates that ranged from
3.3 in Italy to 1.3 in Germany with the UK in the middle of the group.

Table 8.2 Comparison of unemployment rates and youth to adult ratios in selected
countries, May 2010

Country	All (%)	Under 25s (%)	Ratio <25/all
France	9.9	22.6	2.28
Germany	7.0	9.4	1.34
Italy	8.7	29.2	3.36
UK	7.8	19.7	2.53
USA	9.7	18.1	1.87

Source: Abridged version of Table 2 from Bell and Blanchflower (2010: 5).

Bell and Blanchflower confirmed that youth unemployment 'lowered life
satisfaction, health status, job satisfaction and wages over twenty years later'
(2010: 13). Thus the long-term negative impact of unemployment on young
people suggests that this age group is not only more likely to be unemployed,
especially if they have no qualifications (i.e., working class), but they pay the
highest social and economic costs of a recession.

Gender

Until recently the issue of female unemployment had been neglected, possibly
a reflection of the pervasiveness of the idea that work outside the home is less
important to women than to men (Marshall, 1984; Sinfield, 1981). This form

of patriarchy was discussed in Chapter 1 with reference to the dominant conception of work. Yet, female unemployment is arguably more complex than male unemployment because, as was noted with reference to Hakim's preference theory in Chapter 8, in contrast to adult men, the vast majority of whom conform to the continuous employment pattern of work, there are three options for women: a full-time work career, a discontinuous work career, or a full-time home-maker career. The first two patterns of work history are most relevant to women's experience of unemployment since the home-maker career woman is unlikely to seek work outside the home except under economic duress.

The first large-scale study of female unemployment in Britain examined continuous and discontinuous work history patterns and noted that the former involved three elements: that 'paid employment is central, mandatory, and constant' and typically applies to virtually all adult males and some women, whereas in the case of the latter, paid employment is 'marginal, optional, and discontinuous' and typically applies to most women but rarely to men (Cragg and Dawson, 1984: 70). The contrast between the predominantly uniform male relationship to the labour market and the uneven female one, which varies from continuous to discontinuous, suggests that female unemployment is more of a 'continuum, rather than a discrete phenomenon with a comprehensive checklist of identifying characteristics' (ibid.: 70). Moreover, even among those women who were actively seeking paid employment, many did not consider themselves to be unemployed, partly because they were seeking part-time work which does not conform to the dominant male model of the unemployed breadwinner, and partly because 'most married women felt that their primary concern lay with their domestic responsibilities', and others did not register as unemployed because they were not eligible for unemployment benefit (ibid.: 71). Consequently, many unemployed women reject the label 'unemployed' especially if they are married, under no financial pressure to find work, and are constrained by domestic responsibilities.

In the Marienthal study it was clear from the use-of-time data that when women were made unemployed, the majority reverted to what they regarded as their primary responsibility, that of home-maker. This aspect of the Marienthal study has been confirmed by recent research in the sense that it found

> some support for the view that the more substantial responsibilities that women undertake in the domestic sphere provide a sense of identity and a patterning of activity that helps to offset certain of the psychological consequences of unemployment that have been identified in studies focussing on the male unemployed. (Gershuny, 1994: 216–18)

It has also been shown that women who had worked part-time in the past or had been a full-time housewife have extensive networks and the economic and social support they provide are not eroded by unemployment. This is in marked contrast to women who had worked full-time who 'experienced more social shrinkage following unemployment than unemployed men' (Russell, 1999: 219). This suggests that the impact of unemployment on men and women is different, especially in the case of women who had not been employed full-time prior to being made unemployed since their work identity is not threatened due to their lower commitment to a work career and their family role is not threatened because they can revert to their domestic role on a more full-time basis.

In Ashton's account of the various work and family factors that affect the experience of unemployment, he claims: 'It is in the household division of labour that the main source of women's distinctive experience of work and unemployment is to be found' (1986: 133). His argument seems to be that the more women identify with a family role, the more likely that this will constrain their labour market involvement and the less likely that their work identity will be threatened by unemployment. According to this analysis, women's experience of unemployment is different from that of men. However, Ashton also notes that even among women who work part-time to fit in with their family responsibilities, the loss of employment can have financial consequences for them and their family and reduce their sense of independence. This suggests that just because women's work history pattern is discontinuous and, for many, particularly those with young children, there is the option of enlarging their domestic role, it does not necessarily follow that their experience of unemployment is completely different from that of men.

Ashton's suggestion that women's experience of unemployment may not be too different from that of men is supported by surveys and case studies of female unemployment during the 1980s' recession in Britain. For example, the survey of unemployed women by Cragg and Dawson (1984) showed that, like men, they worked for economic and non-economic motives and that the loss of employment had a not dissimilar financial and social impact to that which it had on men in terms of the threat to their economic and social well-being. Coyle's (1984) study of women made redundant from two factories also showed that women were strongly attached to paid work, not just for financial reasons but for the status and satisfaction it provided. Consequently: 'As for men, unemployment for women means financial hardship, isolation, and depression', and 'women's domestic role is no compensation' (ibid.: 121). These studies suggest that women's and men's experience of unemployment are quite similar in that, for both, it has negative economic and social consequences. However, Coyle has also suggested that there was one major difference between male and female unemployment: for men, unemployment can trigger a 'crisis of gender identity' whereas for women, the option of an enlarged domestic role effectively precludes this possibility and instead unemployment for women often involves a 'crisis of autonomy' (ibid.: 121).

There are two other distinguishing features of women's unemployment. First, unemployed women are less willing to be geographically mobile in order to find work than unemployed men (Gallie and Vogler, 1994), and, second, unemployed women, especially if they are married and have children, are more likely to take a part-time job than unemployed men (Hakim, 1996; see also Cragg and Dawson, 1984). Hence, for women, the lack of a threat to their gender identity and their reluctance to be geographically flexible in their search for work, yet be more flexible than men in terms of the number of hours worked, suggest that women's labour market behaviour is still influenced by their domestic responsibilities.

Critical evaluation of Jahoda's deprivation theory of unemployment

Research on the social impact of unemployment is broadly supportive of Jahoda's deprivation theory in terms of both her assumption that an appreciation of the positive functions of employment is indispensable to understanding the negative consequences of unemployment and her contention that the negative consequences of unemployment vary in terms of class, age and gender. It is also apparent that the intensity of specific deprivations varies for different social groups, for example the loss of income was acute for the working class whereas the loss of status/identity was a major concern for the middle class; for young people unemployment typically delayed adulthood whereas for adults prolonged unemployment often meant economic hardship; and if women's work histories were similar to men's, their experience of unemployment was similar. More generally, a review of UK research on the mental health impact of unemployment (Warr et al., 1988), another on the rewards of work and the penalties of unemployment (Howarth, 1997), and specific tests of Jahoda's deprivation theory of unemployment in the UK (Gershuny, 1994), Germany (Paul and Batinic, 2010) and Europe (Ervasti and Venetoklis, 2010), have also confirmed the correctness of her approach to the analysis of the social impact of unemployment.

Notwithstanding all this supporting evidence, Jahoda has been criticized on two main grounds. First, Cole (2007) has argued that Jahoda's deprivation theory of unemployment is predicated on the proposition that paid work is crucial to human experience and that as a consequence being out of work deprives people of access to a range of experiences denoted by her five latent functions of employment, namely social contact, time structure, collective purpose, status and identity, and regular activity. Cole describes each of Jahoda's 'human needs that are provided by work' and suggests that they are 'contingent social constructs cut through with gendered and class based assumptions' (ibid.: 1143). He further claimed that the study of Marienthal 'reproduced a moral discourse of work that suppressed the material importance of poverty in deference to a theory of the psychological response', one that 'misread the activity of surviving unemployment as "doing nothing"'; that 'gendered the meaning of work' and 'eulogized work as such and thereby marginalized non-work experiences' (2007: 1145). Cole's critique of Jahoda chimes with the view that paid work no longer occupies the centrality it once did for people's lives and society in general, a thesis that has been advanced by Offe (1985) and other 'end of work' theorists. Granter's (2009) appraisal of theories of the end of work suggests that they tend to underestimate the continuing importance of paid work, not least because economic survival beyond a basic level as well as consumption depends largely upon income, the main source of which for the vast majority is regular employment.

The second criticism by Fryer and Payne (1984) concerns Cole's point regarding Jahoda's contention that the latent functions of work rather than the loss of income are the main factor for the well-being of those out of work. Fryer and Payne argue that Jahoda portrays unemployed people as essentially passive and overlooks their proactive potential and on the basis of 11 'atypical' unemployed people they argue that the unemployed 'are not mere pawns suffering the consequences of unemployment, they are agents causing things to happen' (ibid.: 290–1). Jahoda (1984) responded to this criticism by noting that their argument would have been stronger if they had considered a wider range of unemployed people than the unrepresentative highly proactive sample they studied. By the same token, it could be argued that the Marienthal study was similarly atypical in the sense that those investigated constituted the demoralized members of the community who had not migrated in search of work. Notwithstanding the class, age and gender variations in terms of the negative impact of unemployment, research on the political responses of the unemployed in the USA (Scholzman and Verba, 1980) and the UK (Edgell and Duke, 1991) shows that they tend not to be radicalized by their experience, a finding that is more in keeping with Jahoda's deprivation theory than Fryer and Payne's alternative agency theory. This is not to deny that some workers, particularly unionized ones, often resist redundancy collectively by occupying workplaces and establishing worker co-operatives, but such proactive responses are rare and often unsuccessful (Greenwood, 1977; Mellor et al., 1988; Morris, 2008). While the unemployed may not be spurred into political action which is suggestive of support for Jahoda's deprivation thesis, 'their political attitudes often move in the direction of increased support for collectivism' (Gallie, 1994), a tendency that is more in keeping with agency theory.

Summary and conclusions

Prior to industrial capitalism, various types of precarious work and therefore income prevailed and unemployment as we know it today did not exist. However, once alternative sources of income other than wage labour had virtually disappeared and work had become synonymous with employment, the issue of unemployment became a major social problem in the sense that it became associated with poverty and insecurity.

The two major eras of mass unemployment during the twentieth century, the 1930s and the 1980s, when the levels of unemployment reached around 20 per cent and over 10 per cent respectively in industrial capitalist societies, stimulated empirical research on the social consequences of unemployment. During the Fordist era in between these two twentieth-century peaks of unemployment, the unemployment rate was consistently well below 10 per cent in most industrial capitalist societies which suggests that the Fordist compromise was successful in limiting the scale of unemployment. The ILO definition of unemployment is now universally recognized and hence widely used, including by the OECD, which facilitates comparisons across time (historical) and space (cross-national). However, the measurement of female unemployment is less straightforward than it is for male unemployment due to women having the option of the less stigmatizing status housewife and their tendency not to register as unemployed if they are not eligible for unemployment benefit. The persistence of relatively high rates of unemployment, particularly among certain social groups, notably the young and the unqualified, indicates that Castells' optimism is not justified at the present time.

The most influential theory of the impact of unemployment was advanced by Jahoda, in embryonic form in the classic Marienthal community study in the 1930s and as a fully-fledged theory in the 1980s. Her deprivation theory of unemployment was based on the assumption that only permanent full-time work can provide an income (manifest function) and more importantly according to Jahoda, a time structure, social contact, sense of purpose, status/identity, and regular activity (latent functions), hence the loss of a job results in people being deprived of all these experiences, which in turn threatens their well-being. She also contended that the social consequences of unemployment varied in terms of class, age and gender, though its impact was and still is negative, despite the establishment of state welfare systems in most industrial capitalist societies during the Fordist era.

Research on the social impact of unemployment on different classes, age groups, and men and women broadly supports Jahoda's deprivation theory of unemployment in the sense that the precise impact of the various deprivations occasioned by the loss of a job varies among different social categories. In class terms, it was apparent that the financial implications of being unemployed was a major issue for the working classes, while the loss of status animated the middle classes. As far as age groups are concerned, although both the young and adults are affected by loss of income caused by unemployment, the middle-aged unemployed tend to be more concerned about maintaining their standard of living, whereas for the young unemployed, the highest risk of unemployment social group, it can involve a prolonged and more fluid transition to economic independence and therefore adulthood. The gender dimension of the experience of unemployment is complicated by the heterogeneity of women's involvement in the labour market. Thus, for women who conform to the male model of continuous employment, the impact of unemployment is likely to be similar to that for men, namely severe economic and social deprivation. Conversely, for women who participate discontinuously in the labour market, the economic impact of unemployment may not be so severe, especially if they are married and can opt for a life of secondary earner and/or primary home-maker. More general research comparing the economic and social well-being of employed and unemployed people has also verified Jahoda's deprivation theory of unemployment. Thus, the social consequences of unemployment are essentially negative for everyone but the precise pattern of the impact depends on a variety of factors, including class, age and gender, and how they combine in any one case. The degree of economic hardship experienced by the unemployed in contemporary societies will also be affected by the extent to which the social foundations of the Fordist welfare state have been eroded.

There have been root and branch criticisms of Jahoda's deprivation theory of unemployment. For example, at the base of Jahoda's deprivation theory of unemployment is the assumption regarding the primacy of regular employment and the main hypothesis that is developed on the basis of this assumption is that unemployed people tend to be demoralized more by the non-economic deprivations of job loss than by financial hardship. Both types of criticism have been contested. The first line of criticism is part of a wider debate about the end of work as the key social institution in modern societies and the second is part of the wider debate about agency versus structure in social theory. While unemployment can provoke some people, particularly the young, to migrate in search of work, and lead others, especially unionized workers, to contest redundancy, research suggests that the majority of those made unemployed find it a wholly depressing experience.

Ashton's claim that the main source of women's distinctive relationship to work and unemployment is the household division of labour was apparent in many of the discussions in the previous chapters, particularly the previous one which highlighted the issue of women and part-time work, as well as this one. The next chapter is concerned with the extent to which changes in the organization of unpaid domestic work have paralleled changes in paid work that have taken place since the rise and development of Fordism.

Further reading

BOOKS Ashton's (1986) *Unemployment under Capitalism: The Sociology of British and American Labour Markets* contextualizes the sociology of unemployment both historically and comparatively, and covers the class, gender and age variations in the experience of unemployment. The influential study by Jahoda et al. (1974 [1933]) *Marienthal: The Sociography of an Unemployed Community* is essential reading, alongside Jahoda's more fully developed deprivation theory of unemployment outlined in her book *Employment and Unemployment: A Social-Psychological Analysis* (1982). A summary of Jahoda's deprivation theory of unemployment and the personal agency critique can be found in Howarth (1997) *Work, Leisure and Well-being*, especially the early chapters. Empirical research on various aspects of the impact of unemployment is reported in Gallie et al. (eds) (1994) *Social Change and the Experience of Unemployment*.

ARTICLES
For pro- and anti-Jahoda views, consult Ervasti and Venetoklis (2010) 'Unemployment and subjective well-being: an empirical test of deprivation theory, incentive paradigm and financial strain', *Acta Sociologica*, 53(2): 119–38 and Cole (2007) 'Re-thinking unemployment: a challenge to the legacy of Jahoda et al.', *Sociology*, 41(6): 1133–49 respectively.

WEBSITES
For the latest data and analysis of unemployment by age and gender refer to the International Labour Office website at www.ilo.org. For an analysis of the impact of the 2008–9 recession in the UK on different occupations consult www.tuc.org.uk/extras/jsaclaims

---
Questions for discussion and assessment
---

1 Why is the Marienthal study of unemployment so highly regarded by sociologists?

2 Assess critically Jahoda's deprivation theory of unemployment.

3 Are the economic consequences of unemployment more important than the social consequences for well-being?

4 Discuss the view that the impact of unemployment is not the same for all classes.

5 Consider the claim that the impact of unemployment is the same for men and women.

6 What are the main social consequences of unemployment for young people?

7 Assess the generalization that the impact of unemployment is the same for everyone.

9
DOMESTIC WORK

In Chapter 1 it was argued that during the rise of industrial capitalism in Britain, in the absence of any restrictions on who could be employed and for how long, the opportunities for women to work outside the home were quite good, although they tended to undertake the relatively less skilled and less well paid types of work. However, the employment of large numbers of women outside the home, especially mothers, created problems for men whose authority was threatened, and employers whose supply of able-bodied workers was threatened. The solution was to limit the employment of women and children via a variety of practical and ideological forces that reduced a woman's role to domestic matters. The division of labour that developed involved men specializing in working for pay outside the home, enabling them to reassert their authority, and women working in an unpaid capacity inside the home, ensuring the maintenance and future supply of healthy workers. The male breadwinner and female home-maker model that evolved in Britain, and elsewhere to a greater or lesser extent but not universally, tended to be adopted far more by middle-class families than working-class ones who could less well afford a financially dependent wife, although support for this ideal was widespread. Ironically, the middle-class wife did not so much do the domestic work as employ and organize single working-class women to do it (Oakley, 1976).

The emergence of a dominant conception of work, with its emphasis on paid employment outside the home in the late nineteenth century, was reflected and affirmed in the Census categories in Britain which from 1881 onwards excluded unpaid domestic work (Hakim, 1980). Hakim noted that although the Census Report acknowledged the importance of such work, it was excluded for 'spurious methodological reasons' (ibid.: 558). Paid domestic workers continued to be counted as economically active, which shows that by this time only the production of goods and services exchanged in the market were deemed to be worthy of being included as work (Beneria, 1988). The long-term effect of not counting full-time unpaid domestic work from national statistics on work was to discount and hence undervalue women's economic contribution.

[handwritten margin note: only ↗producing ↗=work]

By the beginning of the twentieth century, largely as a consequence of the physical separation of the home from work, and in due course the relative exclusion of men from unpaid domestic work inside the home and women from paid work outside the home, the tradition of women being primarily responsible for the housework and children, referred to here as domestic work, was established, albeit in the form of an aspiration rather than a reality in working-class families. Taking his cue from Veblen's theory of women's subordination (1970 [1899]), Galbraith has suggested that '[t]he conversion of women into a crypto-servant class was an accomplishment of the first importance', and that thanks to the rise of industrial capitalism, 'the servant-wife is available, democratically, to almost the entire present male population' (1979: 49). Thus, instead of the gender-neutral term 'domestic worker', the widely held assumption in modern societies is that wives are primarily responsible for domestic work, hence the term 'housewife' (Martin and Roberts, 1984).

During the first half of the last century, aside from the exceptions of the two world wars when women entered the labour market in Britain temporarily as a matter of expediency and therefore did not challenge the dominant conception of work, the economic activity rate of adult women remained more or less static at around 33 per cent between 1901 and 1951, compared to a male rate that ranged from 84 per cent to 91 per cent (Hakim, 1996). In fact, in the UK, the gender dimension of the dominant conception of work was reinforced in Britain by the Beveridge-inspired post-war welfare state, which assumed that the wife's place was at home performing 'vital but unpaid labour' and that the husband's was at work full-time (Williams and Williams, 1987: 51). This gender division of labour was part of the Fordist compromise which privileged men in relation to standard work outside the home, thereby freeing them from major domestic responsibility, and 'constructed women's work in relationship to motherhood' (Gottfried, 2000: 239). Although the male breadwinner and female domestic worker ideal characterizes nearly all welfare regimes to a greater or lesser extent, there are variations in how it is operationalized (Warren, 2007) and how it developed (Janssens, 1997; Pfau-Effinger, 2004). Thus by the mid-to-late twentieth century, it was still clear who was expected to and actually did undertake most of the unpaid work inside the home. However, it is thought that during the latter decades of the last century the gendered pattern of domestic work started to change in an egalitarian direction. The extent to which this is the case and explanations of the degendering of domestic work are the subject of this chapter.

The sociology of domestic work

The gender-neutral term 'domestic worker' is misleading since it has been so thoroughly feminized and is synonymous with the role of a wife that the idea of a 'househusband' is greeted invariably with sniggers. Yet the historical association in theory and practice between married women and unpaid domestic work, encapsulated by the term 'housewife', dates only from the mid-to-late nineteenth century (Oakley, 1976). It was not until 100 years later that sociologists started to research it as a type of work, although general sociology textbooks still tend to discuss it under the heading 'gender' (e.g., Macionis, 2001), rather than in the context of work, with the notable exception of Giddens (1997). The first study of housework as an 'occupation' was undertaken by Lopata (1972) and based on data collected in the 1950s and 1960s from a sample of 568 Chicago housewives aged between 19 and 84, of whom 468 were full-time housewives. This was followed by Oakley (1974), who studied housework as 'work' and interviewed 40 full-time London housewives in 1971, all of whom were mothers aged between 20 and 30. The findings of these two pioneering studies were broadly similar regarding full-time housewives who were mothers, despite differences in the size and representativeness of their samples.

Both Lopata (1972) and Oakley (1974) noted the low social status of the 'job' of housewife and suggest that this is mainly due to the lack of payment, but also because preparation and recruitment to it are informal, entry is via marriage or cohabitation, and that it is ascribed on the basis of gender rather than achieved via formal training and testing. Employment outside the home does not negate the status of, and hence a wife's primary responsibility for, domestic work, although it may diminish the work load with other family and/ or non-family members undertaking more work. The low status of the housewife is indicated by commonly used words and phrases to refer to this unpaid work role, such as 'cabbage' or 'just a housewife' (Oakley, 1974: 47, 48), and is reflected in the 'dislike of the title "housewife" expressed by many of the women' interviewed by Lopata (1972: 78). The widespread denigration of the housewife role derives from the conventional representation of domestic work as a boring activity, and this epithet attaches to those who do it. In order to assess whether or not this image of housework is justified, the perspective advanced by Oakley (1974, 1976), and to a lesser extent Lopata (1972), will be adopted. This involves analysing unpaid domestic work in the same way as any paid work role, rather than as something that is intrinsic to femininity in modern societies. Thus unpaid domestic work will be analysed as far as possible in terms of the inter-related characteristics of work featured in the earlier chapters on paid work, including alienation, satisfaction, skill, hours and conditions, plus the impact of technological change on domestic work.

In Chapter 2 it was noted that Blauner operationalized alienation with reference to four dimensions: powerlessness, meaninglessness, social isolation and self-estrangement. Empirical research on domestic work shows that the power to exercise control over the scheduling of work tasks and how to accomplish them without direct supervision was extensive and valued highly by full-time housewives (Lopata 1972; Oakley, 1974). This freedom from interference in the work environment compared favourably with most paid work situations outside the home. However, the autonomy enjoyed by housewives was more 'theoretical than real' due to the 'obligation to see that housework gets done' (Oakley, 1974: 43), and the presence of children creates demands that cannot be ignored and leads to a sense of 'being tied down' (Lopata, 1972: 194). Other research has shown that housewives are constrained by the need to accommodate the demands of the husband's work since this is vital to the economic success of the family (Edgell, 1980), and that when husbands work at home, 'household routines get organized around the male breadwinner's work' (Finch, 1983: 55). These limitations on the freedom experienced by a housewife suggest that an unpaid domestic worker shares with the self-employed a sense of being one's own boss but in practice it is contradicted on a daily basis.

The evidence on meaninglessness and domestic work is also mixed in that some aspects are a major source of purposefulness, notably child-rearing, whereas domestic tasks such as washing-up are regarded as far less rewarding and endlessly repetitive. The housewives interviewed by Lopata and Oakley both reported considerable satisfaction with motherhood, although Lopata noted that '[t]he combination of being tied down and having a heavy workload leads many women in their twenties to wish for a maid or cleaning help' (1972: 196), and the majority of Oakley's sample expressed dissatisfaction with the monotony of housework. This pattern has been confirmed by subsequent research, notably in a study of 50 working-class and middle-class mothers which found that children 'gave them a purpose and in pursuing this purpose, they experienced their lives as meaningful', but also that they found it 'very demanding and frustrating' (Boulton, 1983: 104, 128). The parallels between rewarding child-care tasks and unrewarding housework and different types of paid work is instructive in that Blauner argued that '[w]orking on a unique and individuated product is almost inherently meaningful', whereas it is 'more difficult to develop and maintain a sense of purpose in contributing toward a standardized product since this inevitably involves repetitive work cycles' (1964: 23). In view of the relative autonomy of housework and satisfaction with particular tasks, Oakley's conclusion that 'housewives have more in common with assembly line workers than with factory workers engaged in more skilled and less repetitive work' is unconvincing (1974: 182).

At the child-rearing stage of the family cycle, social isolation has been found to be extensive, especially among housewives at the beginning of this stage. Lopata noted that child-care involves 'isolation from interaction and intellectual stimulation' (1972: 193), and according to Oakley, 'loneliness is an occupational hazard for the modern housewife, who is often cut off not only from community life but often from family life' (1974: 88). The main reason for the lack of social interaction is the house-bound nature of having a young child whose needs are paramount and the tendency for domestic work to be undertaken alone rather than as part of a work group. The problem of social isolation can be mitigated to some extent by living in a neighbourhood with lots of other young families (Lopata, 1972), and/or the same neighbourhood as one's kinship group (Oakley, 1974). Moreover, once the young child joins a pre-school play group or starts school, opportunities for social interaction are enhanced considerably as the housewife has an increased chance of meeting people and more free time to enjoy adult company. Other strategies that can reduce the social isolation of housewives include working part-time for pay or in a voluntary organization (Gavron, 1968; Lopata, 1972). Thus, although social isolation is potentially an acute problem for mothers with young children and a major source of discontent, the house-bound dimension for most is short-lived, but the inherently isolated nature of the domestic workplace endures.

Finally, with regard to self-estrangement or self-expression which refers to a lack of involvement in work, this is also applicable to domestic work. Lopata found that, on the one hand, the housewife who becomes a mother experiences an identity crisis due to the 'limitation of occasions to display a wide range of personality behaviours in a variety of social contexts which show the uniqueness of self', on the other hand, it 'is experienced as an increase in maturity, in capacities and abilities' (1972: 193). The tension between the potentially challenging, involving, and rewarding character of child-rearing, and the perceived boring nature of much of the housework associated with it, was apparent from Boulton's study of motherhood (1983). The positive and negative possibilities of domestic work were also outlined by Oakley who contrasted the routine character of ironing with the 'creative potential' of cooking, although the latter may be limited by the preferences and demands of husbands and children (1974: 58).

This review of the degree to which domestic work is alienating in Blauner's sense of the term suggests that there are some features of housework that are quite alienating, such as the more arduous and repetitive tasks, and that there are others which are far less so, notably child-rearing. In view of the mixed experience of domestic work, overall it could be argued that domestic work at the child-rearing stage of the family cycle is alienating to a medium rather than high or low degree. However, if the routine features of domestic work are separated from the mother role, the degree of alienation is higher. This has been confirmed by Oakley's likening of the experience of monotony, fragmentation and pace of work for housewives to that of assembly-line work, notwithstanding the greater autonomy and task variation characteristic of housework and valued by housewives. Domestic work is a dissatisfying activity in certain respects, and although child-care is a major source of meaning and purpose, it also contributes to a housewife's workload and restricts her freedom and social interaction.

As far as the other characteristics of work featured in the early chapters are concerned, domestic work encompasses a wide range of work roles and skill levels, including relatively unskilled manual work (e.g., cleaning), relatively skilled manual work (e.g., cooking), emotional work (e.g., child-care), service work (e.g., shopping), and a variety of non-manual work activities that put a premium on administrative and social skills (e.g., organizing work tasks and managing people). Clearly, domestic work involves a great variety of labour-intensive jobs, characterized by multiple tasks and skills, which can be rotated by choice within the constraints generated by the needs and demands of other family members. The 'heterogeneity' and import of the work activities undertaken by contemporary housewives are unmistakable and noted by both Lopata (1972: 364) and Oakley (1974: 183), though less impressive than in the pre-modern era when a knowledge of horticulture, animal husbandry, and making clothes were also an essential part of domestic work.

Domestic work: conditions and technology

Studies of the working hours of full-time housewives date back to the 1920s in the USA and show there was little change between the 1920s and 1960s, averaging about 52 hours in the mid-1920s and 55 hours a week in the mid-1960s, which 'is longer than the average person in the labour force' (Vanek, 1980 [1974]: 83). Oakley compared the surveys of housework hours in the USA, France, and Britain over a similar period and also found that, aside from small fluctuations, between 1929 and 1971 the average weekly hours spent on domestic work was reasonably stable with a slight increase over time (Oakley, 1974). In other words, while the average number of hours worked by factory workers each week decreased during this period by around 10 hours to 40 hours, those worked by the full-time housewives in her sample was 77 hours, which is nearly twice the hours worked in industry.

One explanation advanced by both Vanek and Oakley for the conundrum that despite the introduction of electrically powered technology in the form of labour-saving appliances into the home, such as washing and cleaning machines, the long working week of housewives has remained remarkably stable, and if anything has increased, focuses in large part on increased productivity and the related rise in standards of cleanliness and cooking. A good example of higher productivity and expectations concerns doing the laundry with the aid of a washing machine and tumble drier which enables this activity to be undertaken once or more a day rather than once or twice a week. Thus, in the more affluent contemporary society, 'people have more clothes now than they did in the past and they wash them more often' (Vanek, 1980 [1974]: 84–5). In addition to agreeing with the Vanek and Oakley thesis that domestic technology has increased the productivity and time spent on housework and their explanation, Cowan claims that, due to the introduction of complex industrial goods into households, 'houseworkers are as alienated from the tools with which they labour as assembly-line people' (1983: 7). More recent Australian time–use data has confirmed the tendency that 'owning domestic technology rarely reduces unpaid housework' and that in some circumstances it 'marginally increases the time spent on the relevant task' (Bittman et al., 2004: 412). These researchers also attributed this trend to the wish to improve the quantity and quality of domestic work outputs. Thus, technological change has not reduced the housewife's working week, although it has undoubtedly reduced the physical demands of domestic work.

A second possible explanation of the myth of time-saving electrical appliances suggested by Vanek concerns the under-valuation of domestic work in modern societies, which prompts those responsible for it to increase the quality and quantity of their output and hence expand the time spent on it in order to demonstrate the importance of their contribution. Vanek argues that the home-maker's contribution to the family economy is less clear 'compared to the more easily measurable and transparent significance of wages and that long working hours help to indicate the value of domestic work' (1980 [1974]: 88). A slightly different line of argument is offered by Oakley, who contends that the tendency for full-time housewives to set continuously exacting standards and routines is a form of 'job enlargement' that increases work satisfaction and working hours (1974: 111). Considered together, these explanations of the expansion of domestic work time could be construed as an attempt to legitimize what is conventionally regarded as an essentially mundane and unsatisfying job.

Another reason proposed by Vanek (1980 [1974]) for the constancy of the time spent on domestic work between the 1920s and 1960s by full-time housewives is that there has been a redistribution of time expended on various activities. For example, while less time is spent on food preparation, more time is devoted to shopping and child-care. The increase in shopping, including travelling, not only reflects the decline in producing one's own food and clothes (Cowan, 1983), but also the desire to escape the confines of the house and meet people, thereby alleviating the social isolation of domestic work (Oakley, 1974). The expansion of time spent on child-care activities, despite the historical decline in family size, is indicative of the increasingly child-centred character of modern societies (Oakley, 1976), and the tendency in Western culture to allocate primary responsibility for child-care to mothers rather than other relatives or non-family organizations (Boulton, 1983).

An alternative view on the issue of domestic work time in general, and the impact of technology in particular, has been put forward by Gershuny, who first of all qualifies Vanek's domestic work time thesis by arguing that in the UK the 'apparent constancy in the total' number of hours spent on unpaid domestic work is 'an artefact produced by the downwards effect of the new domestic technologies on working-class women, and the substantial increase in work caused by the loss of paid domestic service in middle-class households' (Gershuny, 2000: 67). Second, and following from the previous point, Gershuny shows that there was a 'strong middle-class bias' in the survey data used by Vanek which underpins the apparent growth in the time spent on domestic work (ibid.: 67). Third, although he agrees that the initial impact of domestic appliances is to increase productivity and hence the time spent on a particular activity, he also claims that as more efficient machines are made available, the time spent on 'the core housework tasks of cooking and cleaning' declines (ibid.: 67; see also Gershuny, 2004). Gershuny concluded that domestic appliances increased productivity but is very sceptical of the view that it results unambiguously in increased domestic work time.

There are several difficulties with the attempt to measure the amount of time spent on domestic work following the introduction and diffusion of electrical appliances into the home. First, there is the methodological problem of dividing the day up into specified time slots, such as half-hour periods, and asking respondents to record the main activity undertaken within each. This approach tends to overlook 'very short activities and secondary or concurrent activities' and therefore underestimates the total amount of domestic work and the fragmentation of such work (Thomas and Zmroczek, 1988: 107; see also Wajcman, 1995: 222). A similar point has been expressed by Hakim, who has noted that '[t]he number of hours of work can be misleading, given flexibility in the housewife's use of time' (1996: 47). This criticism raises serious doubts about the accuracy of this way of measuring domestic work participation. It is clear from Gershuny's 'Reflections on Time-Diary Methodology' that he is not unaware of this issue (2000: 249).

Second, it is difficult to isolate the time impact of one specific technological change, for example, the introduction of washing machines, from other related technological changes, such as the use of fabrics made from synthetic fibres and soaps made from synthetic detergents (Thomas and Zmroczek, 1988). It may be that the availability of clothes made from materials that are cheaper to buy and easier to wash and dry encouraged people to buy more clothes and wear them for shorter periods and this could account, in part, for the increase in time spent on laundry work. Once again, Gershuny is fully cognisant of this problem since he notes: 'It is very hard to disentangle the various strands of change' (2000: 181).

Third, technological developments do not occur in a social vacuum; 'fundamental social factors' are involved, notably the number of other people in a household and the amount of domestic work they create and undertake

(Wajcman, 1995: 222). In the Australian study cited above it was found that electrical kitchen appliances 'do not save women any time', whereas they do result in a reduction in the time men spend on domestic work (Bittman et al., 2004: 409). Cowan has suggested that this is 'partly because they believe that the work simply cannot be onerous, but also because some of the "extra" appliances actually relieve them of sex-related, or sex-acceptable chores' (1983: 200). Thus if men conventionally help with the washing-up, as is often the case, the impact of the purchase of a dishwashing machine would be to reduce their domestic work time contribution. Hence one of the major ironies of domestic appliances is that it saves men time and is implicated in the creation of more work for women. This is not meant to suggest that women have missed out completely on the time-saving potential of domestic technologies since, as Cowan also argues, the diffusion of washing machines, dishwashers, microwave ovens, frozen food, and so on were 'catalysts' of the increased participation of women in paid work (1983: 209). However, this development was a mixed blessing for women in terms of the total amount of time expended on paid and unpaid work by men and women, as the following section makes clear.

The symmetrical family thesis

One theory that links the development of industrial capitalism to the changing pattern of domestic work is Young and Willmott's symmetrical family thesis. They proposed a four-stage historical sequence starting with: (1) the eighteenth-century pre-industrial family in which men and women worked together as a unit of production; (2) the nineteenth-century early industrial family characterized by the physical and social segregation and inequality between men and women; (3) the less segregated, more equal and hence symmetrical twentieth-century (later) industrial family; and (4) the twenty-first-century multiple family types ranging from the asymmetrical to the symmetrical 'two demanding jobs for the wife and two for the husband' (Young and Willmott, 1973: 278).

From the standpoint of who is responsible for and undertakes domestic work the key stages are 2 and 3, since the first is no longer relevant to the vast majority of families and the fourth refers to a number of speculative possibilities that will be discussed in brief. The stage 2 family corresponds to the Fordist male breadwinner and female house-worker model discussed earlier and is characterized by a clear differentiation of roles within and outside the home. The husband's role was to earn money which he controlled, kept the total amount secret from his wife, and gave her a proportion for housekeeping. The wife's role was to do virtually all the domestic work, even if she worked out of necessity having overcome the practical and ideological barriers designed to prevent married women from obtaining paid work employment, and to spend the housekeeping on the family: 'There was a man's sphere and a woman's sphere, in spending as in other functions' (Young and Willmott, 1973: 82). In the highly segregated and gendered division of labour, '[i]f the husbands did any "work" at all at home the tasks that they, and their wives, thought proper to them were those to which male strength and male manual skill lent themselves' (ibid.: 94). In industries with multiple shift systems, such as coal mining, the gendered character of domestic work was especially crucial to the organization of industrial work (Beynon and Austrin, 1994).

This changed during the second half of the twentieth century with the rise of the stage 3 symmetrical family, which, via the 'Principle of Stratified Diffusion', spread from the middle classes to the working classes so that by 1970 it was the predominant pattern among Young and Willmott's large London area research sample (1973: 19). The three defining features of this new type of family are that it is home-centred, focused on the nuclear family and, most importantly from the perspective of the sociology of work, a less segregated and more equal relationship characterized by 'financial partnership' (ibid.: 84). In practical terms this translates into a husband doing more unpaid domestic work, although primary responsibility is retained by the wife, and a wife doing more paid work with the husband retaining the major responsibility for economic support. Young and Willmott qualify their thesis, such as when they note that this 'egalitarian tendency works with a time lag', use the phrase 'more symmetrical', and emphasize that '[w]e are only talking of trends' (ibid.: 20, 32, 265). Yet there is no escaping the main thrust of their argument, namely that in modern Britain there is now a more equal division of paid and unpaid work which started at the top and worked its way down the class structure to the point where the 'great majority of married people in our sample were members of the dominant type of new family' (ibid.: 94).

Young and Willmott suggest that a variety of factors caused the change from the male-dominated and highly segregated nineteenth-century family to the more equal and less segregated twentieth-century family, including affluence, migration, establishment of the welfare state, the reduced paid working hours of men, and the employment of married women outside the home, but seem to place particular weight on technology and feminism. The rise of feminism was successful to the extent that it improved the status of women, legally, economically, politically and socially, and the role of technology was similarly multifaceted in that it helped to improve the quality of home life via smaller families (i.e., contraceptive technology), better housing (i.e., access to clean water plus new sources of energy), and the availability of consumer goods (i.e., washing machines). The idea that technology transforms work and family largely for the better, to the extent that it upskills paid jobs and improves the quality of home life, corresponds to Bell's post-industrial society thesis (discussed in Chapter 4) and is acknowledged as a 'major influence on their thinking' (Young and Willmott, 1973: 19). Thus, the symmetrical family thesis is infused with the same optimism that is apparent in the writing of post-industrial theorists, except in this case the focus is unpaid domestic work rather than paid work.

The symmetrical family thesis is concerned with trends in the late twentieth century whereas the stage 4 family is essentially about changes at the beginning of the twenty-first century. In keeping with their 'Principle of Stratified Diffusion', Young and Willmott begin their speculations about stage 4 families by considering 'the impact upon the top strata of the two chief forces', namely technology and feminism (1973: 271). First, they argue that the introduction of technology into the paid workplace will reduce the number of physically demanding and monotonous jobs, there will be an expansion of more interesting jobs and 'the greater attachment to work of middle-class people will extend downwards' (ibid.: 271). This will mean more intrinsically rewarding and therefore satisfying jobs for men and women, with possibly longer working hours outside the home. Second, feminism would reinforce this trend, encouraging women to expect and achieve work satisfaction outside as well as inside the home. Young and Willmott summarize the implications of the combined impact of technology and feminism on the paid and unpaid work roles of men and women by noting: 'By the next century – with the pioneers of 1970 already at the front of the column – society will have moved ... to two demanding jobs for the wife and two for the husband. The symmetry will be complete' (ibid.: 278). Young and Willmott suggest that this is a prospect fraught with problems, notably a high rate of marital breakdown, which risks the well-being of children, and 'if people by their own hyper-activity threatened their own inner stability, they would slowly turn the line of the march in another direction' (ibid.: 282). They speculate that this could lead to less emphasis on paid work, such as shorter and/or more flexible working hours, and the transfer of paid work to the home, all of which would enable people to reconcile the competing demands of work and home. The material presented in Chapters 5 and 6 suggests that Young and Willmott's speculations are more post-Fordist than neo-Fordist and as such their analysis is overly optimistic.

A second possibility is that there will be an increase in shiftwork and weekend work due to the growth of technology and 24-hour production, and the growth of the service sector and 24-hour consumption. Young and Willmott suggest that this will constrain husbands and wives to work at different times and, consequently, '[t]he life of the family can hardly be enhanced', specifically, 'the family's joint life is challenged' (ibid.: 273). At the time of their research, this development mostly affected manual workers, but was expected to spread to non-manual workers; in other words, 'in a manner directly contrary to the Principle [of Stratified Diffusion]' (Young and Willmott, 1973: 273). This possibility potentially undermines symmetry in the sense that a shared social life is difficult if couples work different shifts and, according to Young and Willmott's analysis of unsocial working hours, it disrupts family life and creates extra work, such a cooking meals for family members at different times. Recent research in Britain on flexible paid work and household arrangements found that working nights was very unpopular with both men and women, and that women particularly disliked working weekends and that men disliked working evenings (Horrell et al., 1994). The main reasons for these preferences were that it created difficulties for child-care, especially for women, and both men and women were concerned about the impact of working nights and weekends on their social life. Men and women were open to flexible working so long as it was 'under their control not the employer's' (ibid.: 129). Although this research did not address the issue of symmetry, it did show that resistance to flexibility was founded on a concern to minimize the disruption to prevailing household arrangements, especially in terms of the women's responsibility for child-care.

Finally, the idea that wives experience a triple burden, which is implicit in Young and Willmott's analysis of the work-centred rather than home-centred family life of managing directors, has been advanced by Finch's theory of wives' incorporation in men's work. She argues that employed wives often 'end up doing *three jobs*' in that in addition to their paid work and unpaid domestic work, they contribute in various ways to the husband's paid work career (Finch, 1983: 149; italics in the original). For example, if a husband works at home and/or is self-employed, his wife is likely to be recruited as an unpaid receptionist, and if his work involves entertaining colleagues, she will be expected to act as a hostess. In these and other ways, Finch suggests that the hierarchy of priorities that assigns primacy to the male breadwinner's work career ensures the wife's incorporation into her husband's work. Thus the asymmetry of many middle-class couples is traced to the enduring asymmetry of the work–family nexus, highlighted by Edgell (1980). Not to be outdone, as it were, Castells has argued that due to the increased involvement of women in paid work, the burden carried by women in their everyday lives correspondingly increased to a 'quadruple shift (paid work, home-making, child-rearing, and night shift for the husband)' (1997: 125). However the roles of working mothers are conceptualized and counted, the general point is that such women tend to shoulder a greater paid and unpaid work burden than their husbands.

Critical evaluation of the symmetrical family thesis

The main strengths of the symmetrical family thesis are that it was based on theoretically informed large-scale survey research with a high response rate and that the findings were historically contextualized. Moreover, the project utilized a variety of research methods and was wide-ranging in that it included a sub-sample who completed time budget diaries, plus two small-scale samples of active sportsmen and managing directors, two case studies of factory workers, and two other studies of shift workers. Unfortunately, it was also London-centric which disqualifies any claim to being representative of anything other than the London Metropolitan Region, the time budget survey response rate was low, and the other small-scale studies only included men, which undermines further the representativeness of the project.

However, the main weakness of the symmetrical family thesis is the lack of convincing empirical evidence, even from Young and Willmott's own data. First, although they present qualitative and quantitative data that purports to show increasing symmetry, their analysis does not provide unequivocal support for their thesis. For example, Oakley has noted that there was only one question on the domestic division of labour out of an interview schedule of over 100 and the table (No. 8) that summarizes the answers to this 'poorly worded question' reveals a limited degree of male domesticity (1974: 164). The same key table also demonstrates the weakness of the class diffusion dimension of their symmetrical family thesis since it shows that husbands in clerical jobs assist in the home more than any other occupational class, including the more unambiguously middle-class professional and managerial categories. Young and Willmott concede that among their respondents, 'it was in virtually all not expected that men should do more than *help* their wives' and that wives 'retain primary responsibility for domestic work' (1973: 96; italics in the original). However, rather than revise their theory about increasing symmetry, they maintain that 'the extent of sharing is probably still increasing' (ibid.: 94).

The results of empirical research in the UK, the USA, and other modern societies since Young and Willmott's study was first published in 1973 were no more encouraging for the symmetrical family thesis in that study after study revealed little evidence of behavioural symmetry, even among the strategic case of middle-class couples (e.g., Berk, 1985; Brannen and Moss, 1991; Edgell, 1980; Gregory and Windebank, 2000; Martin and Roberts, 1984; Morris, 1990; Picchio, 2003; Wajcman, 1996). Although these and other studies found some evidence of less traditional attitudes towards the division of domestic work, they also found that the majority of husbands did not share it equally, and most importantly, research on two of the main inter-related pillars of the symmetrical family thesis, sharing power and money, tend not to support the thesis. In the case of power, in terms of who has most say in decision-making, Edgell's (1980) study of middle-class couples found that the major strategic decisions, such as moving, finance, and car-buying were made by the husband, whereas the less important operational decisions, such as what to eat, which clothes to buy the children and how to decorate the house, were made by the wives; a male-dominated pattern that has been confirmed by subsequent research (Hardill et al., 1997). These two studies may have been small-scale but they are critical given that the symmetrical family thesis contends that the middle class are in the vanguard of increasing marital egalitarianism. As far as the organization of money is concerned, although there is evidence from a large UK survey of a decline in the housekeeping allowance system associated with stage 2 families, and that pooling was the most prevalent system (50 per cent

Table 9.1 The incidence of different household allocative systems

	Allocative system	(%)
Pooling systems	Female-managed pool	15
	Joint pool	20
	Male-managed pool	15
Segregated system	Female whole wage	27
	Male whole wage	10
	Housekeeping allowance	13
Total %		100

Source: Adapted from Table 2 in Vogler and Pahl (1993: 77).

of respondents), as Table 9.1 shows, a mere '20 per cent of respondents used the egalitarian joint pool system', a 'moderate 14 per cent' increase between the generations (Vogler and Pahl, 1993: 92). Symmetrical families are still a minority according to these studies, although the Vogler and Pahl study confirmed that joint pooling was more prevalent among the middle classes.

The symmetrical family thesis places great weight on the rise in married women's employment and the tendency for husbands to do more domestic work: 'In the interests of symmetry it was only fair, as husbands and wives saw it, for the men to do more so that their wives could do less' (Young and Willmott, 1973: 114). The crucial question is, how much more? According to Young and Willmott, when a wife works part-time, her domestic working hours each week are reduced by about ten hours, and when she works full-time they are reduced by just over another ten hours. In terms of total paid and unpaid working hours, women who are employed full-time outside the home work on average four hours each week longer than their husbands, and those who are employed part-time work two hours a week longer. In a year, this adds up to married women working over 200 or 100 hours more than their husbands if they are employed full-time or part-time respectively. If an average working week for men, including travel to work time, is approximately 50 hours a week, as was the case in Young and Willmott's sample, then married women work about a month or two weeks longer than married men. Clearly, married men are doing more, as Young and Willmott put it, but if their wives have a paid job, they still work longer hours in total each week/year.

A similar calculation has been made by Hochschild on the basis of 1960s and 1970s time–use studies which showed that 'women worked roughly fifteen hours longer each week than men', or 'an extra month of twenty-four-hour days a year' and concluded that 'most women work one shift at the office or factory and a "second shift" at home' (1990: 3–4). The marked difference between the two estimates may be due to sampling in that Young and Willmott's figures refer to 'married men and women aged 30 to 49' whereas the Hochschild ones only include two-earner families with children. Both calculations are well below the 77-hour average working week of Oakley's sample of housewives, all of whom were mothers of young children (1974), yet still provide evidence of an extra domestic work burden for married women who undertake paid work, and that this ranges from four to 15 hours each week depending on circumstances such as the number and age of children in the family, and of course, 'upon how much of it the husband will share' (Young and Willmott, 1973: 277).

What is crucial to an evaluation of the symmetrical family thesis is the extent to which husbands increase their participation in domestic work when their wives go out to work on a part- or full-time basis. In other words, if, according to Young and Willmott, wives reduce their domestic work time by approximately 25 per cent when they work part-time and by 50 per cent when they work full-time, do husbands increase their domestic work time by similar proportions? Young and Willmott answered this question indirectly and imprecisely when they reported, on the basis of a flawed question, highlighted by Oakley and noted above, that more husbands 'help in the home' when their wives go out to work part-time, and slightly more when they work full-time (1973: 115). Using a different but similarly indirect and imprecise measure, Hochschild's data on the participation of husbands in domestic work found that '[o]f the men who earned more than their wives, 21 per cent shared housework. Of the men who earned about the same, 30 per cent shared. But among the men who earned *less* than their wives, *none* shared' (1990: 221, italics in the original). Hochschild concluded that since only a small minority of husbands share equally the domestic work when their wives go out to work, this represents a 'stalled revolution', one that 'is in danger of staying stalled' (1990: 362, 267). Thus, neither of these studies, nor the others cited earlier, afford support for the symmetrical family thesis, although they do show that husbands undertake more domestic work when their wives go out to work. The optimism of the symmetrical family thesis is punctured by these more pessimistic findings which found that symmetry did not even characterize the middle-class vanguard.

It is not all bad news for Young and Willmott's symmetrical family thesis, however. There is some evidence of a change in attitudes and behaviour with middle-class husbands expressing the view that they should and did do more child-care domestic work, which they preferred to cleaning or ironing, at certain stages of the work and family career cycles (Edgell, 1980). However, this was a temporary modification to an otherwise segregated and unequal division of domestic work participation by husbands and wives, and consequently did not threaten the primacy of their respective breadwinner and domestic worker roles. Less traditional attitudes were also found in a large-scale representative survey of adults living in the UK in the mid-1980s (Witherspoon, 1985). This study showed a marked inequality of participation in various household tasks, but less inegalitarian attitudes regarding who should do them. For example, the married and the never married consistently favoured a more equal division of domestic labour, with 62 per cent of the former and 68 per cent of the latter expressing the view that shopping should be shared equally, compared to 39 per cent that actually did, and 45 per cent of the married and 56 per cent of the never married reporting that household cleaning should be shared, compared to 23 per cent that actually did. The less inegalitarian attitudes revealed by this survey, especially among the younger never married and married women who worked full-time outside the home, is a small crumb of comfort for those who are looking for evidence of symmetry.

More encouragement for the symmetrical family thesis is provided by the higher percentages of married and cohabiting couples who actually shared various domestic tasks and thought that they should be shared in the UK in 1991 (Whitmarsh, 1995) and elsewhere (Crompton and Harris, 1999). In terms of the core domestic tasks referred to above, the 'actually shared' percentage was up to 47 per cent for shopping and 27 per cent for household cleaning, and the 'should be shared' percentages were up to 76 per cent and 62 per cent respectively for the same tasks, although some domestic tasks were still markedly gendered, notably the female-dominated activity of ironing and the male-dominated one of repairing equipment (Whitmarsh, 1995). There was also a decline in the percentage of adults who agreed with the idea of male breadwinning and female domestic workers between 1987 and 1994 in the UK. Thus between the mid-1980s and the early 1990s there was a clear trend of increasing egalitarianism in terms of both behaviour and attitudes, especially the latter. This trend was also apparent in a large-scale postal survey of young couples in Sweden and Norway, considered to be at the forefront of egalitarianism, which although it revealed a gap between ideals and practices, the extent of the equal sharing of housework was at or above 50 per cent as Table 9.2 shows (Bernhardt et al. 2008).

Further support for the symmetrical family thesis has been provided by UK time–budget data which shows that husbands were doing more domestic work in 1987 than in 1975, although the husbands of wives who worked full-time for pay outside the home were still doing a 'substantially smaller proportion of the total work of the household' (Gershuny et al., 1994: 179; see also Horrell, 1994). This pattern was not unique to the UK but was apparent in all modern societies for which time–use survey data is available for this period. Gershuny et al. concluded that 'married men's proportion of the total of

Table 9.2 Egalitarian ideals and equal sharing of housework among young couples in Sweden and Norway

		Sweden (%)	Norway (%)
Egalitarian ideals	No	24	38
	Yes	76	62
Equal sharing of housework	No	41	51
	Yes	59	49

Source: Abridged version of Table 1 in Bernhardt et al. (2008: 281).

domestic work time has a regular and substantial growth over the past three decades', and that 'the women's proportion of the total of paid and unpaid work increases in most countries over this period' (1994: 185–6). This is interpreted as a case of 'lagged adaptation', changes to the domestic division of labour slowed down by a process of negotiation between couples, which implies that it is only a matter of time before men compensate fully for the entry of women into paid work. Gershuny et al. commented that

> even if lagged adaptation does lead to a 'symmetry' in the Young and Willmott sense that the total of work may in the longer term tend towards equality between husband and wife, still the differential pattern of responsibilities for paid and unpaid work provides substantial advantages to the husband in terms of earnings and status. (1994: 188)

This is an important qualification since it suggests that meaningful symmetry in the sense of gender equality in paid and unpaid work is a long way off. It should also be borne in mind that time–budget data underestimates women's unpaid work time and overestimates men's paid work time because short rest-breaks tend to be recorded for unpaid domestic work but not for paid work away from home (ibid.). The contention of Gershuny et al. that as more women are employed outside the home, men will eventually increase their participation in domestic work has been criticized, on the basis of empirical research on dual-earner couples in the UK and France, for being 'somewhat optimistic, if not totally unfounded' (Windebank, 2001: 286). More promisingly for the Gershuny theory of lagged adaptation is the finding that women in particular occupations have the relational resources, notably interpersonal skills which enable them to challenge successfully the traditional domestic division of labour (Benjamin and Sullivan, 1999). UK time–use data that extends Gershuny's analysis to 1997 is presented in Table 9.3 and shows that husbands increased their contribution to domestic work between 1975 and 1997, especially if their wives worked.

Table 9.3 appears to endorse the symmetrical family thesis by showing that over the 20-year period there was an increase in egalitarianism, but the pace of

Table 9.3 Percentage of couples in domestic division of labour categories by employment status of partners

% done by woman	Both ft			Husband ft, wife pt			Husband ft, wife ne		
	1975 (%)	1987 (%)	1997 (%)	1975 (%)	1987 (%)	1997 (%)	1975 (%)	1987 (%)	1997 (%)
0–49	15	20	32	3	6	1	2	6	4
50–69	37	47	40	19	43	4	15	30	39
70+	47	39	21	62	74	41	64	85	54

Key: ft = full-time, pt = part-time, ne = not employed.
Source: Abridged version of Table 2 in Sullivan (2000: 449).

change is slow, which is supportive of the theory of lagged adaptation, and women continue to undertake most of the housework even in dual-earner families which is indicative of the persistence of the highly gendered and unequal division of domestic work. Sullivan's research also showed that there was a trend of egalitarianism originating in the middle classes and percolating down to the class structure which is in keeping with the symmetrical family thesis.

Explanations of the unequal division of domestic work

Morris (1990) has suggested three interconnected explanations for the lack of change regarding the persistence of female-dominated participation in unpaid work: (1) institutional constraints; (2) normative constraints; and (3) power inequalities within the household (1990: 190). The first includes a labour market in which women still tend to be secondary earners and this makes it difficult for them to challenge, let alone alter in a radical way, a traditional division of labour that assigns primary responsibility for domestic work to women. Institutional constraints also refers to welfare regimes that range from strong (e.g., the UK), to modified (e.g., France), and weak (e.g., Sweden) male breadwinner models of state welfare and therefore reinforce to a greater or lesser extent a gendered and unequal division of domestic work (Lewis, 1992). Policies based on the male breadwinner model are in decline but the change often involves modification in the form of the male breadwinner/female part-time worker model (Charles and James, 2005; Solera, 2009), although the introduction of statutory work–life balance measures provides an opportunity for further change (Gregory and Milner, 2008). Moreover, although welfare regimes are in the process of changing in the direction of the dual-earner/carer model, the lack of gender equality 'put women at a disadvantage in paid work and pensions, and discourages men's participation in care work' (Pascall and Lewis, 2004: 375). While this explanation of the persistence of a female-dominated pattern of domestic work may well apply to most couples, even middle-class ones, the tendency for unemployed husbands to shun domestic work indicates that ideas about masculinity and femininity are also relevant (Morris, 1990).

Second, although there is evidence that gender norms are changing to the extent that fewer people support the idea that men should be the primary breadwinners and women the primary domestic workers, there is also evidence which shows that gender norms have become more implicit and therefore less easy to contest (Beagan et al., 2008), that more women than men express non-traditional attitudes and that women continue to undertake most domestic work (Griffin et al., 1998; Morris, 1990). One possible interpretation of the tendency for women to do less domestic work when they enter the labour market and for men to resist undertaking proportionally more domestic work is that women operate with reference to the economics of the household, which results in a reduction of their unpaid domestic work burden, whereas men operate with reference to a gender framework which constrains them to resist doing more domestic work for fear of losing their masculinity. This theory has been advanced by Brines who has summed it up by noting that 'she gets to do less house-work as she provides, while he gets to do gender while she provides' (1994: 684). In the aforementioned study by Hochschild, the findings were not interpreted explicitly in terms of the operation of economic forces and gender norms, although the limitations of the 'logic of the pocketbook' was noted and it was contended that it was a matter of 'balancing' the loss of one form of power by relying on another form of power (1990: 221). This study concluded that men and women engage in power balancing and that 'the political struggle behind a cultural shift and not the timeless logic of the pocketbook seems to determine how much men help in the home' (ibid.: 225). The importance of gender-role attitudes was confirmed by a study carried out in Norway, the UK, and the Czech Republic which showed that attitudes have more of an influence on the domestic division of work than women's employment, yet insisted that this does not imply that economic factors are unimportant (Crompton and Harris, 1999). When this research was repeated eight years later there had been an increase in non-traditional gender role attitudes but little change in the domestic division of work in all three countries, which led to the conclu-sion that the pace of change was 'glacial' (Crompton et al., 2005: 228).

The third explanation for the lack of fundamental change in the division of domestic work concerns the distribution of power within a family, especially economic power, a factor that is readily apparent from the persistence of income inequalities between men and women outside and inside the home (Allen, 1999; Arber and Ginn, 1995; Pahl, 1989), even in highly egalitarian societies such as Sweden (Nyman, 1999). The significance of this point is indicated by two UK studies; one which showed that 'men who contribute a greater share of paid work hours or have a greater earnings power than their wives do a much smaller share of housework' (Harkness, 2008: 265), and another which found little support for the 'claim that "gender trumps money"' (Kan, 2008: 62). The studies by Sullivan (2000) and Bernhardt et al. (2008) referred to above also confirm the impact of women's paid work on the distri-bution of domestic work suggesting that the greater the women's involvement in the labour market, the less domestic work she undertakes and the more her partner does.

Several studies indicate that these conceptually distinct influences on the division of domestic work operate together in practice. For example, Gershuny (1994) concluded that early socialization regarding gender norms plus a wife's employment status were the main factors, plus the institutional framework regarding employment and child care, and Kan (2008) concluded that atti-tudes to gender and economic resources both influence the domestic division of labour. A further possibility, advanced by Vogler (1998) and by Breen and

Cooke (2005) is that the division of domestic work depends most importantly upon male gender norms plus female economic resources, which suggests that the main obstacle to symmetry is male reluctance to eschew a patriarchal ideology that is past its sell-by date.

Outsourcing domestic work

One potential solution to the problem of a woman's heavier domestic work load is to pay someone else to do it, known as domestic outsourcing or con-tracting out housework. This includes direct substitution in the form of paid labour (e.g., a cleaner or child-carer), and indirect substitution in the form of manufactured goods (e.g., ready-made meals), or appliances that aid produc-tivity (e.g., vacuum cleaners) (Bittman et al., 1999). The focus here will be almost exclusively on the first type since the second has been covered to some extent above with reference to technology and domestic work.

As noted above, Gershuny (2000) has suggested that the decline of paid domestic servants between the 1930s and 1960s in the UK increased consider-ably the domestic work time of middle-class housewives. For many middle-class families in 1980s' UK, this problem was solved to some extent by paying someone else to undertake the particularly labour-intensive domestic work. The resurgence in demand for paid domestic workers has been attributed pri-marily to the increase in paid work among middle-class women, plus a concern with '"leisure time" and "quality time"' (Gregson and Lowe, 1994: 95). In the case of the decision to employ a cleaner, it was the demanding nature of such work that created a time difficulty in dual-career households, plus a reluctance among middle-class husbands to increase their already minimal contribution to domestic work, and for some couples it helped to avoid con-flict over a husband's relative lack of participation in this domestic work task. In the case of the employment of someone to undertake child-care work, Gregson and Lowe argue that this was 'essential' if a dual-career couple with pre-school-aged children wanted to 'maintain this employment pattern' (1995: 157).

While the employment of cleaners and child-carers conforms to the social relations of waged labour, Gregson and Lowe argue that cleaners enjoy a degree of autonomy and that the relationship between child-carers and their employers is distinctive in that it is 'shaped by both wage and false-kinship relations', with the latter dominating everyday interaction (1995: 159). In both forms of substitution, though, the typically female employee relates pri-marily to the wife in middle-class dual-career households since domestic work is regarded by both parties as women's work. Hence, the employment of paid domestic workers amplifies the managerial dimension of the middle-class wife who also undertakes paid work outside the home. Gregson and Lowe con-cluded that from the standpoint of the dual-career family it solves the problem of getting essential domestic work done, but at the cost of a higher work load for wives than husbands.

A study of the domestic work arrangements of male and female managers found that in contrast to male managers, who tend to be 'serviced by their wives' even when the wife works part-time, 'women managers are serviced by housewife substitutes in the form of other women's labour' (Wajcman, 1996: 626). Thus, this research confirmed that in addition to undertaking a disproportionate volume of domestic work, working wives organize and supervise paid domestic workers. The lack of symmetry among this middle-class sample studied a generation later than Young and Willmott's sample shows that husbands have yet to adapt to the domestic work implications of the employment of their wives, other than to agreeing to the hiring of substitute labour.

The generalization that paid domestic work invariably involves hard work, long hours, and relatively low pay and status has been widely confirmed, as Gregson and Lowe note, but a number of criticisms have been directed at their study. First, their claim that the outsourcing of house-cleaning and child-care domestic work has expanded markedly in the UK since the 1980s has been shown to be an exaggeration based on a flawed method of estimating the demand for these services, namely advertisements in a journal (Bittman et al., 1999). Second, Australian household expenditure data for the mid-1990s found that the outsourcing of food preparation at nearly 90 per cent of households exceeded that of all other types of outsourcing added together, including laundry (10 per cent) and child-care (10 per cent), and that the outsourcing of male-dominated tasks such as gardening at 9 per cent occurred over twice as often as the outsourcing of the female-dominated task of cleaning at 4 per cent (Bittman et al., 1999). Third, Gregson and Lowe have been criticized by Anderson (1996) for neglecting black and migrant domestic workers on the grounds that 'in contemporary Britain, no such close association exists between ethnicity, female migration and waged domestic work' (Gregson and Lowe, 1994: 123). Anderson claims that Home Office figures show that this is not the case and argues that Gregson and Lowe's crucial cleaner/nanny analytical distinction 'does not hold for migrant women' (Anderson, 1996: 581). Following from this point, it could also be argued that Gregson and Lowe neglected the informal dimension of paid domestic work, yet it has been shown that off-the-books workers often undertake domestic work, including child-care, and the employment of such vulnerable workers increases the power of the employer and reduces that of the employee, especially if the workers lack documentation (Leonard, 1998: 130). This dimension has implications for the work conditions in general, and the autonomy of cleaners in particular, since in contrast to Gregson and Lowe's account, such workers tend to experience greater exploitation and, specifically, may find it more difficult to control for whom, when and what they clean.

At best, outsourcing domestic work is a partial solution to the problem of a lack of time among some dual-earner couples at a particular stage of the family cycle; at worst, it increases the work load of wives and is an expensive option that is available only to the relatively affluent.

Summary and conclusions

The gender-neutral terms of unpaid domestic work and housework conceal the ascriptive tendency for women to undertake the bulk of this type of work. Yet the rise of the full-time housewife is a relatively recent development that was associated with the rise of the male breadwinner as an idea and practice in the late nineteenth century in the UK and other industrial capitalist societies. This model prevailed to a greater or lesser extent in virtually all modern societies during the twentieth century and involved relative exclusion from paid work and economic dependency for wives and relative exclusion from unpaid domestic work and economic independence for husbands. Although the male breadwinner and female houseworker model is on the wane, it has yet to be eclipsed totally by alternative arrangements, even among dual-career couples.

Domestic work is not only unpaid, but essentially a form of deskilled manual work involving a multitude of tasks, although the managerial dimension has arguably increased in the recent past, especially if domestic work is outsourced. The combination of no pay and hence financial dependency, and repetitious and hence monotonous physical work, ensures that domestic work is perceived widely, including by those who undertake most of it, as a low-status and dissatisfying job. The studies of domestic work as an occupational role by Lopata and as work by Oakley revealed that is was comparable to factory work in terms of Blauner's operationalization of alienation. First, control was highly valued, especially the lack of close supervision, but elusive due mainly to the demands of others, especially husbands, upon whose agenda-setting primary paid work the household depends for its economic survival. Second, domestic work involves some meaningful activities, notably child-rearing, but mostly many routine ones that tend to be repeated, often several times a day or week. Third, social isolation was inherent in the sense that domestic work was typically undertaken alone, and in some circumstances it was acute, for instance, during the early years of the child-rearing stage, although it could be mitigated by developing a network of family, friends and neighbours. Fourth, opportunities for self-expression are limited since the majority of domestic tasks tend to be repeated in a routine way on a relentless basis. Even the creative potential of some domestic work tasks, such as cooking, was more apparent than real, as the data on technological short-cuts in food preparation testifies. Overall, while domestic work may not be as highly alienating as assembly-line work, it seems to be moderately alienating at the very least.

The impact of technological change on domestic work, including the introduction of electrical appliances and other technological innovations, such as non-iron materials and ready-made meals, has reduced the physical demands of domestic work but does not seem to have led to a marked reduction in the amount of time spent on domestic work, especially by full-time house-wives. This has been explained with reference to the higher productivity and standards facilitated by the diffusion of domestic technologies, and to the increased time spent on buying, operating, cleaning and maintaining the new technologies. Ironically, some domestic technologies may have reduced the time men spend on domestic work, dishwashing machines being the favoured example. The alternative view, advanced by Gershuny among others, is that the decline of domestic servants increased the domestic work load for mid-dle-class housewives and technology reduced the time spent on core domes-tic tasks, namely cleaning and cooking, although he does concede that domestic technology increased productivity and in the short term this may have led to an increase in domestic work time. Critics of this account of the impact of technology on time spent on domestic work have pointed out that it is based on time–budget data, which is unreliable and tends to underesti-mate domestic work time. Although it is difficult to separate out the impact of technology from other influences on domestic work, there are some cir-cumstances in which the use of technology does result in less time being spent on domestic work, for example, in dual-earner households, and there are others when it does not, for example, when it stimulates an increase in certain domestic activities, such as laundry work. Directly or indirectly, domestic technology tends not to be the time-saving panacea of marketing rhetoric.

The symmetrical family thesis also highlighted the impact of technological change on domestic work, along with the role of feminism and the growth of women's work outside the home, as factors that contributed to the change from segregated and unequal marital relationships to more desegregated and equal ones during the last century. The problematic data that Young and Willmott provided, ostensibly in support of their thesis, has been found to be flawed, and subsequent empirical research in the UK and similar societies has tended to show that while attitudes have become less traditional, domestic work behaviour remains less than symmetrical, with the exception of young couples in Sweden and Norway. Other evidence, particularly when derived from time–budget diaries, show that there has been an increase in the sharing of domestic work between couples and that this trend can be expected to continue in the future in accordance with the theory of lagged adaptation. The inconsistency of findings on this issue may be due to variations in the measure-ment and interpretation of domestic work patterns, although when this pos-sibility was taken into account, little change was found, thereby confirming that the revolution had stalled (Warde and Hetherington, 1993). One way to reconcile the conflicting evidence regarding the symmetrical family thesis is to conclude that there is weak support for a strong version of the symmetrical family thesis and strong support for a weak version.

Various explanations have been advanced for the lack of any radical change in the tendency for women to continue to be primarily responsible for domestic work and men for the economic prosperity of the household. These include the persistence of institutional, cultural and politico-economic (in the sense of power) advantages of men over women outside and inside the household. Thus, no one factor alone can account for the continued inequitable distribution of unpaid domestic work between men and women in the same household, and while women have taken more responsibility for breadwinning, men have yet to match this change by taking a commensurate degree of responsibility for domestic work.

Young and Willmott discussed three possible future developments with reference to the fate of the symmetrical family in the twenty-first century. The first was predicated on a general upskilling of paid work, which is thought to lead to increasing involvement in such work. The second assumes that temporal flexibility will characterize more and more jobs as the economy continues to deindustrialize and become dominated by service work. The third is a variation of the first in that it focuses on the exceedingly work-centred lives of managing directors. All three eventualities are problematic for the prospects of symmetry since they imply that paid work is likely to be more of a priority in the future than in the past for both men and women in general and especially for those with demanding paid work careers. This suggests that paid work trends seem to favour the growth of asymmetry rather than symmetry in the domestic division of labour in the longer term.

One possible solution to the discordant issue of who does the unpaid domestic work is to outsource some or all of it, especially the more labour-intensive and routine tasks like cleaning and the laundry. For a wife or female partner in a dual-career household this strategy is often vital to the success of her paid work career and can reduce conflict over who does certain domestic tasks. In effect, for a women, the employment of someone else, usually another women, to undertake the more time-consuming domestic activities is a damage limitation exercise in terms of her work and family careers. However, this option is only available to relatively affluent couples and even then the female partner tends to be responsible for organizing and supervising the employee(s).

Throughout the analysis of unpaid domestic work, the nub of the issue of who does it is male resistance to sharing this type of work equally. According to Beck, while women have raised their expectations of increased equality outside and inside the family, 'men have practiced a *rhetoric of equality*, without matching their words with deeds' (1992: 104; italics in the original). For Beck, the current antagonism between men and women is rooted in the development of industrial society which created the separate spheres of public paid work for men and private domestic work for women. As a consequence of this arrangement, gender roles and statuses were ascribed, but whereas men were assigned primary responsibility for paid work and can obtain a sense of economic independence, women were assigned primary responsibility for domestic work and were consigned to dependence upon others. The increasing feminization of paid work has helped to free men 'from the yoke of being *sole* supporter of the family', and various social factors have freed women to some extent, but not entirely, from their 'gender fate', including longer life expectancy, family planning, the technological restructuring of domestic work, and the trend towards the equalization of educational and occupational opportunities (Beck, 1992: 110, 112). The ensuing gap 'between women's expectations of equality and the reality of inequality in occupations and the family', prompted Beck to predict that conflict between men and women in their private relationships will increase and 'fill the corridors of the divorce courts or waiting rooms of marriage counsellors and psychotherapists' (1992: 120, 121). To paraphrase Beck, women are still struggling to lessen the yoke of being mainly responsible for domestic work, but in the meantime they continue to carry a dual, triple, quadruple burden!

Further reading

BOOKS The classic studies of domestic work by Oakley cover both the history of housework with reference to the rise of industrial capitalism, *Housewife* (1976), and domestic work as work, *The Sociology of Housework* (1974). The pre-eminent study of technology and domestic work is Cowan's (1983) *More Work for Mother: The Ironies of Household Technology from the Open Hearth to the Microwave*. For a critique of and an alternative to the view that technology does not reduce the time spent on domestic work, consult Gershuny (2000) *Changing Times: Work and Leisure in Postindustrial Society*. Young and Willmott (1973) *The Symmetrical Family: A Study of Work and Leisure in the London Region* should be read carefully and critically. A summary of the relevant theories and data can be found in Morris (1990) *The Workings of the Household: A US–UK Comparison*. A useful collection of theoretically informed empirical research on various aspects of the changing pattern of domestic work is Anderson et al. (eds) (1994) *The Social and Political Economy of the Household*.

ARTICLES The key issues of how money is managed and who does the domestic work are covered by Volger and Pahl (1993) 'Social and economic change and the organization of money within marriage', *Work, Employment and Society*, 7(1): 71–95, and Sullivan (2000) 'The division of domestic labour: twenty years of change?', *Sociology*, 34(3): 437–56.

WEBSITES The most up-to-date UK Economic and Social Research Council funded research findings on gender quality in the form of two working papers published in 2011 by P. Schober can be found at www.esrc.ac.uk. For an analysis of how Australian men and women balance their work and family responsibilities consult the paper by S. Squire and J. Tilly (2007) `It`s about time: women, men, work and family` at www.humanrights.gov.au/sex_discrimination/its-about-time/

Questions for discussion and assessment

1 Consider the view that domestic work is as alienating as factory work.
2 Does technology reduce the time spent on domestic work?
3 Examine the strengths and weaknesses of the symmetrical family thesis.
4 Explain the apparent reluctance of husbands to share domestic work equally.
5 Why is domestic outsourcing only a limited solution to the domestic work load problem?
6 Assess Gershuny's theory of lagged adaptation.
7 To what extent and why has domestic work remained highly gendered and unequal?

10

GLOBALIZATION: PAID AND UNPAID WORK

Chapter contents

- Globalization
- Causes of globalization
- Globalization in action: call centres
- The transformation of paid work?
- The transformation of unpaid work?
- Summary and conclusions
- Concluding remarks: continuity and change and 'work'
- Further reading
- Questions for discussion and assessment

In the journey from what is often regarded as non-alienating work in hunting and gathering societies, to the most alienating Fordist factory work in industrial capitalist societies, and finally to the promise of less alienating forms of work thought to accompany the move from neo-Fordism to post-Fordism, the concept of globalization has been an intermittent presence, explicitly or implicitly. Yet, as recently as the late 1980s some dictionaries of sociology (e.g., Abercrombie et al., 1988) did not include an entry for globalization, and even in the early 1990s some textbooks on the sociology of work (e.g., Hall, 1994) treated the issue of globalization in a cursory manner. However, it would be remiss not to discuss it in reasonable depth at the beginning of the twenty-first century, such is the prominence of these concepts in public discourse and sociological analysis (e.g., Cohen and Kennedy, 2007).

At various points in the earlier analysis, the issue of globalization was particularly pertinent, such as in the discussions of the globalization of car production (Chapter 5) and the global network enterprise (Chapter 6). Likewise in the contributions of Beck (1992, 2000) and Castells (1997, 2001), broached at many junctures in the earlier chapters, the idea of globalization was referred to but not discussed in detail. In view of the current estimation of the importance of globalization, it is now time to consider the meaning, causes and implications of this process for both paid and unpaid work. Thus the aim of this chapter is to consider globalization in theory, and in practice with reference to call centre work and the Fordist paradigm, plus the impact of globalization on different types of paid and unpaid work and the implications of this process for the dominant conception of work (discussed in the first chapter).

Globalization

Marx and Engels were among the first social theorists to refer to the global character of industrial capitalism: 'The need of a constantly expanding market for its products chases the bourgeoisie over the whole surface of the globe. It must nestle everywhere, settle everywhere, establish connexions everywhere' (n.d. [1848]: 54). Thus capitalism was the spur to the globalization of production and exchange, and in the process capital sought to 'tear down every spatial barrier to intercourse' and 'annihilate this space with time' (Marx, 1973 [1857–58]: 539). Among other things, Marx (and Engels) was suggesting that globalization was an economic process with major political and social ramifications and that it was not a natural force but a capitalist imperative rooted in the need to accumulate capital, aided and abetted by political policies that favoured capitalist expansion or risk decline in the face of increasingly international competition. These themes are still apparent in contemporary discussions of globalization which typically refer to the 'widening, deepening and speeding up of worldwide interconnectedness in all aspects of social life' (Held et al., 1999: 2).

Three approaches to contemporary globalization have been identified: hyperglobalists, such as Albrow (1996), for whom it represents something totally new; sceptics, such as Hirst and Thompson (1996), for whom it is not new but merely a continuation of past developments; and transformationalists, such as Scholte (2005) and Castells (2001), for whom it is 'historically unprecedented such that states and societies across the globe are experiencing a process of profound change as they try to adapt to a more interconnected but highly uncertain world' (Held et al., 1999: 2). In contrast to the 'everything is new', 'nothing is new' perspectives, transformationalists adopt a middle position which acknowledges that contemporary globalization is characterized by both continuities and distinctive features. The main continuity with past phases of globalization is the movement of people, goods and ideas across the world, whereas the main distinctiveness of contemporary globalization is the time–space compression noted previously (Chapter 6) with reference to transnational call centres. A precise definition of globalization that takes into account 'spatial-temporal processes of change' defines it as

> a process (or set of processes) which embodies a transformation in the spatial organization of social relations and transactions – assessed in terms of their extensity, intensity, velocity and impact – generating transcontinental or interregional flows and networks of activity, interactions, and the exercise of power. (Held et al., 1999: 16)

In light of this approach, Scholte (2005) has distinguished between three distinct phases of globalization:

1 Global imagination: to the eighteenth century.
2 Incipient globalization: 1850s to 1950s.
3 Full-scale globalization: 1960s to the present.

In terms of the historical periodization outlined in Chapter 1 (see Table 1.2), these three phases correspond to pre-modern, early modern, and late modern globalization, and in terms of the Fordist paradigm discussed in relation to industrial and service work in Chapters 5 and 6, contemporary globalization is associated with the demise of Fordism and its replacement by neo- and post-Fordism. Scholte's model implies that globalization is a complex historical process in the sense that initially it was essentially a matter of consciousness and international connections among a minority, also referred to as proto-globalization (Cohen and Kennedy, 2007). Second, it developed from mere ideas to global relationships which were manifested in the cross-border character of communications, markets, organizations and production, as well as consciousness. Third, contemporary globalization is considered to be quantitatively and qualitatively different since transworld relations have expanded in every respect.

The conceptual framework advanced by Held et al. 'provides the basis for both a quantitative and qualitative assessment of the historical patterns of globalization' (1999: 17). Thus, contemporary globalization is characterized by extensive networks, intensive flows within networks, speedy, frequent instantaneous global interactions, all of which impact on all areas of economic, social and political life, and affect everyone in the world to a greater or lesser extent. Somewhat more prosaically, there is a tendency to refer to the expansion of the global scale of interconnections in terms of global communications (e.g., electronic mass media), global markets (e.g., global products), global production (e.g., global production chains), global money (e.g., global credit cards), global finance (e.g., global banking), global organizations (e.g., global companies and agencies), and global consciousness (e.g., global events). The acceleration of global relations is indicated similarly by data that shows a marked and sometimes spectacular increase over the past few decades of transborder relations, such as the growth of transnational corporations (e.g., IBM), international governmental organizations (e.g., the United Nations), international non-governmental organizations (e.g., Greenpeace), the consumption of global products (e.g., Coca-Cola), and global communications devices (e.g., computers) (Castells, 2001; Cohen and Kennedy, 2007; Scholte, 2005).

The revealing thing about such lists, and the statistics that accompany them, is that many of the indicators pre-date full-scale or contemporary globalization dating from the second half of the twentieth century, including those which transcend geographical space such as the telegraph, the fax and the computer.

Moreover, even the most fervent advocates of the idea that the global economy is here already, and differs from previous forms of globalization, admit that 'not everything is global in the economy: in fact most production, employment, and firms are, and will remain, local and regional' (Castells, 2001: 101). Although such data tends to confirm the view that contemporary globalization has roots in the past, involves distinctive ways of organizing activities in terms of space and time, and is ongoing, some words of caution are appropriate. First, there is the possibility of confusing 'economic globalization with internationalization of the economy' (Beck, 2001: 120). Second, economic trends still have to be interpreted carefully – such data is not unambiguous evidence of globalization (Held et al., 1999). Third, quantitative evidence cannot, by itself, 'confirm or deny the "reality" of globalization' since qualitative changes are also essential, for example, the 'exercise of power', and such 'shifts' are 'rarely captured by statistical data' (Held et al., 1999: 11).

There are two other concepts, which are related to the process of globalization, that are relevant to the analysis and therefore worthy of comment: globality and globalism. Robertson (1992) is credited by Beck with being the first to distinguish between globalization as an external process and globality as the 'extent to which people are conscious of living in the world as one place' (Beck, 2001: 88). In effect, globalization refers to objective reality and globality to the subjective awareness of that reality and for most people local ties are still far more salient than global ones (Kennedy, 2010). Buying products over the internet illustrates perfectly the external or objective reality of globalization, and events as diverse as international sporting competitions and humanitarian disasters that prompt a global response raise consciousness of the world as a single place. Globalism is usually taken to mean the 'neo-liberal ideology of world market domination' and as such is the political-economic dimension of the contemporary phase of globalization (Beck, 2001: 118). Beck has criticized contemporary globalism on the grounds that it is based on 'an antiquated economism projected on a gigantic scale', not least because the idea of free world trade is a myth, yet policies based on this premise often lead to increased inequality (ibid.: 117; see also Gray, 1998). In the following analysis, the primary focus is the economic aspects of globalization since these are the most pertinent to the sociology of work.

Causes of globalization

Four main inter-related factors are thought to have caused the expansion of globalization: rationalism, capitalism, technology, and regulation (Scholte, 2005). No one factor is considered causally paramount in the following account, though this is not always the case since those writing within the Marxian tradition highlight the decisive role of capitalism, whereas neo-Weberians emphasize the influence of rationalism.

Rationalism refers to a type of knowledge that is thought to have assisted the growth of global thinking and hence globalization. Rationalist knowledge does not recognize boundaries based on nationhood, religion, ethnicity, and so on, and in this sense is thought to have encouraged globalization.

Capitalism refers to a distinctive way of organizing economic activity oriented to making a profit and this aspect of capitalism is regarded as a key force behind globalization. The unceasing concern to accumulate a surplus or fail constrains capital to seek out cheaper production sites and new markets for their products, which in practical terms means the world.

Technology refers to the application of knowledge, typically scientific knowledge, to solve practical problems, which, from the standpoint of the sociology of work, means problems to do with the production and consumption of goods and services. Technological innovations in production and transportation were prominent during the early modern phase of globalization, while technological innovations in information and communication were particularly important during the late modern phase of globalization. In both cases technology enables individuals and companies to develop global connections.

Regulation refers to the politico-legal framework that provides the rules and procedures which govern global relationships without which globalization could not develop, let alone prosper. In the early modern phase the relevant rules and procedures emanated from individual nation states which were prominent in promoting globalization, such as the UK in the second half of the nineteenth century and the USA in the first half of the twentieth century. In the late modern phase of globalization, international government organizations (e.g., the United Nations), and international non-governmental organizations (e.g., the International Organization for Standardization) have tended to become more influential. International agreements on cross-border socio-economic relations have created a regulatory framework within which globalization has flourished.

Castells' theory of the network society (discussed in Chapter 6) illustrates the inter-related character of the driving forces behind globalization. Castells gives pride of place to the revolution in information technology because it 'provided the indispensable, material basis' for the creation of the new global economy (2001: 77). Yet he emphasizes that firms do not invest in 'technology for the sake of technological innovation', they do so in the hope that they will be rewarded in terms of improved competitiveness and greater profitability (ibid.: 94). Moreover, Castells argues that globalization emerged towards the end of the twentieth century, originally in America, as part of the neo-liberal-inspired restructuring of companies and financial markets following the economic crisis of the 1970s, which in turn prompted the diffusion of the then new information and communication technologies, and that the 'decisive agents in setting up a new, global economy were governments', led by the USA, and 'their ancillary international institutions', such as the International Monetary Fund (ibid.: 137). There were three inter-related parts to the neo-liberal project that laid the foundations for the contemporary phase of capitalist globalization: deregulation, the liberalization of trade, and privatization. Thus, Castells embraces the neo-Marxist emphasis on profit-seeking capitalism and the neo-Weberian emphasis on the efficacy of rational knowledge in that he considers globalization to be a complex capitalist and technological phenomenon that was promoted actively by the most advanced capitalist states acting in a rational self-interested manner in accordance with a revived neo-liberal ideology. The evidence from one of the most detailed accounts of the development of globalization is that multi-causal explanations are superior to mono-causal ones, hence it concluded that the contemporary process of globalization is a 'product of a unique conjuncture of social, political, economic and technological forces' (Held et al., 1999: 429). Contemporary globalization is therefore the product of certain mutually reinforcing processes, most importantly the capitalist search for lower costs and higher profits that is encouraged by capitalist states and facilitated by advanced technologies that shrink space and time.

Globalization in action: call centres

Call centres that provide services to large numbers of customers globally and that can be located anywhere in the world, though usually in low wage countries where unions are weak or absent, epitomize contemporary globalization in three ways. First, the transfer of work from one country to another, known as offshore outsourcing, is made possible by advances in information and communication technologies. Second and third, this technological capability enables the work undertaken to transcend space and time as if geographical distance and time zones did not exist. In other words, call centres are not only high technology work organizations but represent the ultimate 'time–space compression' thought to be distinctive of contemporary globalization (Harvey, 1989: 240). They are a form of voice-to-voice interactive service work characterized by emotional labour discussed in Chapter 6 with reference to face-to-face interactive service work and employ an increasing proportion of non-standard workers (discussed in Chapter 7), especially women part-time (Houlihan, 2004). Call centre work is a new occupational category that made its first appearance in official statistics in the UK in 2000 (Huws, 2009). This type of work is expanding globally in both advanced industrial capitalist countries such as the UK (Heckley, 2005) and developing countries, notably India (O'Connor, 2003), although the majority of call centres serve national rather than international markets (Holtgrewe et al., 2009). As in the case of face-to-face interactive service work, this analysis focuses on the extent to which the organization of call centres conforms to the Fordist model of production or has developed in a neo-Fordist or post-Fordist direction.

The production models used in call centre research often start by noting the mass production character of call centre work, but conceptualize the diversity of call centres by departing from the Fordist paradigm and drawing upon human resource management and/or organizational theory. For example, Batt and Moynihan (2004) have proposed a three-fold typology of call centre service production models that includes: (1) classic mass production based on Taylorist principles with an emphasis on the standardization of the whole work process; (2) hybrid mass customization in which there is an attempt to go beyond pure Taylorism by paying more attention to the quality of the work and the service provided; and (3) the professional-service model that involves specialist workers providing high quality service. This typology corresponds to the Fordism, neo-Fordism, and post-Fordism systems as discussed in the earlier chapters.

With supreme irony, the first company to establish a call centre was in manufacturing, namely Ford in the USA in the 1960s to deal with a recall problem using a toll-free telephone number (Shire et al., 2002). In due course the telephone was combined with computer technology that automatically distributed calls via filters and assigned them to an appropriate and available agent, and further advances in information and communication technologies allowed agents to access callers' details, including their customer records, and contact them by email (Head, 2005). The combination of telephone, computer, and information and communication technologies has, according to Fernie and Metcalf, significantly augmented the managerial power to such a degree that the organization of a call centre resembles a prison or 'panopticon' and that 'the "tyranny of the assembly line" is but a Sunday school picnic compared with the control management can exercise in computer telephony' and in support of this claim cite an advertisement for call centre software entitled 'Total Control Made Easy' (1998: 2). The image of call centres as white-collar factories caught the imagination of the press (e.g., *Guardian*, 1998) and was confirmed to some extent by research. In terms of the key features of Fordism analysed with reference to industrial and service work (Chapters 5 and 6), namely Taylorized tasks, assembly line production, and mass standardized products, research on call centre work has shown that it involves performing an endless stream of short job cycle routine tasks characterized by software-driven scripted conversations and the fulfilment of quantitative (e.g., number of calls answered) and qualitative (e.g., rapport) performance targets to deliver a standard service to as large a number of customers as speedily as possible. This is all achieved in the presence of customers that requires call centre workers to perform standardized emotional labour, and the surveillance and monitoring by supervisors armed with specialist software, which prompted Taylor and Bain to describe such work as 'an assembly line in the head' (Taylor and Bain, 1999; see also Bain et al., 2002; Head, 2005; Zapf et al., 2003). Meeting target times is a particular problem since managers, often unconstrained by the presence of unions, increase the speed of the process by reprogramming the software in an instant in a manner reminiscent of classic Fordism and neo-Fordist lean production (Head, 2005). This adds to the stress of the work, especially under a lean staffing policy (Baldry et al., 2003). Unsurprisingly, call centres are unhealthy workplaces (Bakker et al., 2003; Taylor et al., 2003), absenteeism and labour turnover rates tend to be high (Deery and Kinnie, 2004), and individual and collective resistance widespread, despite the anti-union policy of many call centres (Muholland, 2004; Taylor and Bain, 1999). The power of trade unions, even in a hostile environment in which union density was low and there was no agreement between the union and the company, was demonstrated when managers at a UK call centre proposed that workers who failed to meet targets should suffer the indignity of wearing a dunce's cap, but following union objections it was not implemented (Taylor and Bain, 2001). Once again the parallels with industrial and service Fordism are unmistakable. This suggests that call centres are a manifestation of Fordism: 'The massed cubicles of the call centre are digital assembly lines on which standardization, measurement, and control come together to create a work-place of relentless discipline and pressure' (Head, 2005: 98).

However, there are limitations to managerial control that stem from what has been referred to as the contradictory logics of call centre work, the need to be customer-friendly, a major source of job satisfaction, and cost-efficient, a major source of job dissatisfaction (Korczynski et al., 2000; Korczynski, 2001). From the standpoint of capital, the managerial concern with service quality is no different from their concern with efficiency costs, since both are rooted in the need to maximize profits or fail in the competitive market (Taylor and Bain, 2005). Moreover, in combination they contribute to the relentless emotional intensity of the work which stresses workers out, increases absence due to sickness, increases labour turnover, lowers performance, and reduces the call centre workers' capacity to engage positively with customers. In an attempt to resolve these problems management have adopted a range of 'employee involvement techniques', such as teamwork, job rotation, suggestion schemes and quality circles (Taylor and Bain, 1999: 110). However, the same research found that there was often a gap between the unitary managerial rhetoric and the practices of participation, for example, teams were often supervisor led and associated with peer pressure, team meetings were often brief or not held, and quality circles lacked authority and autonomy. Other research has found that increasing the involvement of workers, reducing electronic monitoring, spending more time with each customer, and diversifying tasks and devolving them to teams, improved productivity and lowered turnover (Batt and Moynihan, 2004). Yet workers continued to be monitored, enjoyed minimal task discretion and experienced extreme pressure to keep answering calls from potentially dissatisfied customers, hence the creation of 'de-stress zones' and 4-hour shifts by part-time workers (Houlihan, 2004). Also they did not cease contesting managerial control (van den Broek, 2004; Taylor and Bain, 2001), and as far as customers are concerned, this issue is potentially tricky, notwith-standing the sophistication of the software that creates branches automatically in scripts to encompass the variability of customer responses. After navigating the automated number system, waiting for an appropriate call centre agent, a customer who discerns insincerity in the voice of the worker may express anything from mild irritation to phone rage (Deery and Kinnie, 2004). Also, since customers are not part of the organizational hierarchy, they cannot be relied upon to conform to managerial attempts to standardize voice-to-voice interaction and play their part in the 'co-production' of service work (Rieder et al., 2002). The prevalence of worker and customer resistance suggests that managerial control is neither 'total' nor 'easy' as claimed in the advertisement quoted above, and points in the direction of neo-Fordist modifications to an otherwise Fordist system. This neo-Fordist type of call centre has been called a 'mass customized bureaucracy' in that it represents a hybrid system involving Taylorized bureaucratic control with an element of worker empowerment (Frenkel et al., 1999: 270) and the widespread use of part-time workers to achieve the numerical flexibility demanded by variable call volumes (Belt, 2004; Houlihan, 2004).

In call centres that deal with more complex problems, such as technical support that requires the employment of knowledge workers (discussed in the previous chapter), tasks are less routinized, specialists work together to resolve queries, and enjoy more discretion within a post-bureaucratic network organization (Frenkel et al., 1999). Call centres in which non-standard problems are the norm, operate in a knowledge-intensive environment characterized by 'learning, problem solving and sharing of contextually specific tacit knowledge' designed to provide a high quality customized service (Batt and Moynihan, 2004: 29). Yet, even in such empowered, high trust work situations, knowledge workers experience peer pressure and have to complete tasks and projects on time and within budget as specified by the targets set by managers, and were monitored (Mueller et al., 2008), though to a lesser extent than non-specialist workers (Frenkel et al., 1999). However, a comparative study of professional call centre work showed that in Canada nurses retained their autonomy, whereas in England they were subordinated to the software that controlled the work process (Collin-Jaques, 2004). This research suggests complexity alone does not ensure that the organization of call centre work will tilt in the direction of the professional service model since much depends on the historical politico-economic context and type of software chosen by managers. Thus knowledge-intensive call centres tend to conform to the post-Fordist ideal type. Table 10.1 summarizes the key features of work in Fordist, neo-Fordist, and post-Fordist call centres.

Table 10.1 Key features of Fordist, neo-Fordist and post-Fordist call centres (CCs)

Key features	Fordist CC	Neo-Fordist CC	Post-Fordist CC
Standardized tasks (scripted and timed)	Tight	Variable	Loose
Assembly line volumes	High	Medium	Low
Service customization	Low	Medium	High

The analysis has suggested that not all call centres are the same, they can range from Fordist, to neo-Fordist and post-Fordist ways of organizing work; the key question therefore is, which model is most prevalent? The organization of call centre work can vary within and between call centres (Taylor and Bain, 2001) and much depends upon the complexity of the work (Frenkel et al., 1999), the segment of the market served (Batt and Moynihan, 2004), where it is located since market and employment conditions vary between countries (Holtgrewe et al., 2009), or a combination of two of more of these factors (Taylor and Bain, 2005). Several studies have claimed that the majority of call centres veer towards the Fordist rather than the post-Fordist end of the range; in the words of Taylor and Bain, 'the technologically driven, low-cost, lean production model' tends to 'dominate' (2007: 354–5; see also Houlihan, 2004). This is especially the case of call centre work that is outsourced to Indian call centres 'where standardization occurs *in extremis*, employee exit and burnout appear to be commonplace' (Taylor and Bain, 2005: 271; italics in the original). Thus call centres in India tend to conform to the Fordist mass production model, including those that employ knowledge workers, which is indicative of the tendency to outsource high skill work (D'Cruz and Noronha, 2009; Upadhya, 2009). Taylor and Bain (2005) advance four main reasons why India has become the most popular destination for call centre outsourcing; most importantly major cost savings, plus the availability of English-speaking staff, the absence of trade unions, and a favourable politico-economic environment in the form of tax incentives and a willingness to relax regulations, for example, to allow women to work at night – a clear indication of the global power of capital. 'Indian call centre work is promoted by management as a high skilled, high status, well paid career with perks such as free transport and food' (Mirchandani, 2004).

Despite these major advantages and the use of the same informational and communication technologies, outsourcing call centre work is beset with distinctive challenges that add considerably to the familiar range of problems associated with Fordist mass production such as absenteeism and workers resistance. First Mirchandani (2004) raises the issue of synchronicity in that time–space compression is experienced by Indian call centres workers as time–space expansion, a concept developed originally by Katz (2001), since they are required to adjust their lives to US or UK holidays and time zones, including working nights which excludes them from local social life. Thus the much vaunted time–space compression serves the interests of global capital, not workers. Second, shift work poses an acute problem for female call centre workers in a patriarchal culture that considers women working at night to be socially unacceptable and although call centre companies provide transport between home and work, the reputation and safety of women workers are at risk. In order to mitigate these dangers, Basi reported that women police their own dress by adopting three 'veiling regimes', one for home, one for travelling to work, and one for work (Basi, 2009: 142). Third, locational masking via the adoption of Westernized pseudonyms and attempts to conceal the location of the call centre in order to manage hostility from customers who may resent the export of jobs, though deceiving customers in this way can lead to increased tension and provoke hostility (Mirchandani, 2004). Fourth, compulsory language and cultural training to neutralize workers' accents and familiarize them with various aspects of the customers' society with the aim of facilitating interactional rapport and lessening the potential of customer abuse (D'Cruz and Noronha, 2009). For example, cultural misunderstandings, such as the UK customer who said, 'I've got a hatchback' and the agent in India responded, 'I'm terribly sorry, I hope you get better soon' (Keating, 2008). According to Mirchandani, the mandatory language and cultural training programmes represent a form of 'cultural imperialism' (2003: 8). These distinctive features of transnational call centre work in India exacerbate an already stressful job by requiring workers not only to meet Taylorized targets while faking empathy, but to do so using a fake name, fake accent, and concealing the location of their work. Constructing a false cultural identity is an extreme form of flexibility. In contrast to management rhetoric about prestigious work, although it is relatively well paid by local standards, workers tend to view it as a temporary job rather than a permanent career (Basi, 2009; Taylor and Bain, 2005). The difficulties for Indian call centre workers and customers have led several companies to either reverse their policy of exporting their call centre work or to decide not to relocate abroad (Keating, 2008). The rapid expansion of transnational call centres is unlikely to continue if it threatens service quality and customer loyalty.

The transformation of paid work?

Industrial and service work have both been reorganized partially rather than totally, which suggests that the problems associated with Fordism, such as work alienation and intensification which contribute to worker discontent, and the mass customization of products and services that nourishes consumer dissatisfaction, have not been solved, but if anything, added to, for example, by the growth of non-standard jobs of a lower quality than standard ones. The decline of Fordism and the growth of neo-Fordism in both industrial and service work, especially in what has been called the call centre 'digital assembly line', is evidence of the continuing influence of Taylorism on the organization of work (Head, 2005: 100).

Many of these changes in the patterning of work can be understood through the prism of globalization, a perspective that has been well summarized by Debrah and Smith: 'Faced with the imperative of globalization, management constantly seek greater wage flexibility, functional and numerical flexibility. Thus, the competitive pressures associated with economic globalization induce shifts in workforce composition, labour demand, and the inter-temporal deployment of workers' (2002: 9). For example, it will be recalled that in the discussion of Castells' network enterprise thesis (Chapter 6), he argued that the three key interrelated features of the new type of economy are that it is informational, global and networked, as well as capitalist, and that the network enterprise was its characteristic organizational form, in which 'internal adaptability and external flexibility' are paramount (2001: 258). Similarly, in the discussion of non-standard paid work (Chapter 7), the contributions of Castells (2001) and Beck (1992, 2000) suggested that globalization was heavily implicated in the (uneven) growth of different types of non-standard paid work. Also, in the above discussion of transnational call centres, it was shown that they are a product of contemporary globalization and that the technological ability to shrink time and space was to the advantage of capital but to the disadvantage of labour who experienced it as an expansion of time and space. Moreover, there is evidence that it is not just routine work that is being deskilled and outsourced. The trend is for knowledge work to be Taylorized which makes it easier to export from the USA and the UK to India and China to take advantage of lower wages and non-union workplaces, which in turn increases unemployment and income inequality in the exporting countries (Brown et al., 2011; Hytrek and Zentgraf, 2008). While work may not have been transformed to the extent that Castells suggests, contemporary globalization has certainly put additional competitive pressure on capitalist enterprises to lower costs and be flexible in every sense, although there are major social costs and hence limitations to this neo-liberal economic project.

Globalization is not the only process involved in the transformation of paid work, the feminization of the labour force is also an integral factor. Castells argues that although women are less well paid than men for similar work, are over-represented in social and personal services work, and in part-time employment, they are increasingly employed at the higher levels of multi-skilled informational work – the fastest-growing area of employment. Therefore, they 'are not being relegated to the lowest skilled service jobs' (1997: 165). However, Beck's reference to 'precarious feminization' indicates that he is more aware that the feminization of work is not all good news for women (2000: 64). Women remain under-represented at the top of the standard jobs hierarchy and over-represented in lower-paid and lower-quality non-standard work, which suggests that the revolution in women's position in the labour market is far from complete.

Arguably the most profound transformation of work concerns the relationship between capital and labour in a globalizing economy since it affects all aspects of work. On this point Beck and Castells are in broad agreement, and even use similar language to articulate the strengthening of capital and the weakening of labour as a result of the free market character of contemporary capitalist globalization. Thus, Beck has noted that: '[c]apital is global, work is local' (2000: 27), while Castells has written that '[a]t its core, capital is global. As a rule, labour is local' (2001: 506). Castells elaborates the argument by summarizing the impact of the current phase of globalization on the two main protagonists in the capitalist system: 'Labour is disaggregated in its perform-ance, fragmented in its organization, diversified in its existence, divided in its collective action', whereas, 'Networks converge toward a meta-network of capital that integrates capitalist interests at the global level and across sectors and realms of activity' (ibid.: 506). In short, capital is well organized and therefore powerful, but labour is disorganized and therefore weak.

In the case of labour, Beck claims that, as a result of globalization and related social processes, class will fade in significance 'beside an individualized society of employees' (1992: 100), and Castells states that the combination of organi-zational restructuring facilitated by information technology, 'and stimulated by global competition, is ushering in a fundamental transformation of work: *the individualization of labour in the labour process*' (2001: 282; italics in the origi-nal). By this, Castells means that each employee's role is defined individually and that s/he has to negotiate the terms and conditions of his/her employment individually. Hence, under the 'new management rules of the global economy … labour lost institutional protection and became increasingly dependent on individual bargaining conditions in a constantly changing labour market' (ibid.: 301–2). Thus, confronted by the growing wealth and mobility of capital in the form of global firms and global networks of firms, supported by national gov-ernments and international non-governmental organizations, labour has become more vulnerable to the vicissitudes of the global capitalist market.

The increased power of capital and the reduced power of labour can be explained with reference not only to the trend noted by Beck and Castells for capital to be organized on a global scale and labour to be organized on a national scale, but to several other related tendencies. First, government poli-cies informed by neo-liberal economic policies support transnational corpora-tions by offering financial incentives in the form of grants and tax concessions and/or by modifying or even suspending labour legislation, in the hope that these policies will persuade transnational corporations to set up in business and create more jobs (Sklair, 2002). Second, transnational corporations have the ability to relocate their business(es) to countries where labour is available most cheaply, and/or is least regulated (Gray, 1998). Third, the historic ten-dency for capital to be concentrated among fewer and fewer companies has increased markedly due to globalization, and this has enhanced the power of capital in relation to both individual employees and individual governments (Scholte, 2005). As a result of the increased power of capital in the 'new inter-national division of labour' (Fröbel et al., 1980), it is argued that flexibility is invariably on the employer's terms and that this is to the disadvantage of employees.

An extreme example of the global power of capital and the local powerless-ness of labour is afforded by free-trade areas known as Export Processing Zones (hereafter EPZs), located mainly in the less developed part of the world. EPZs are notorious due to the tendency for transnational corporations to relocate production in such areas to take advantage of tax breaks, cheap, non-unionized, flexible and mostly female labour, and minimal health, safety and environmental regulations (Fröbel et al., 1980; Sklair, 2002). The highly exploitative, sweatshop conditions of factories in EPZs have been described in detail by Klein (2000), who, along with other politically concerned individuals and groups, has used naming and shaming plus consumer boycotts in an attempt to persuade global manufactures, such as Nike, to improve their employment practices. There is also the evidence of the extreme exploitation and oppression that characterize the flexibilization of work at the end of the subcontracting supply chain in EPZs. This picture of seriously empowered capital and disempowered labour is reflected by the pervasive dominance of a neo-liberal ideology among political and business leaders that informs contemporary globalization and which considers trade unions and welfare benefits as impediments to enterprise and the efficient operation of the market. It is also reflected by the trend of growing class inequality within and between countries (Castells, 2000) and by the ability of global corporations to avoid high tax locations in favour of low tax ones, namely offshore tax havens (Dicken, 2011), a process that is not unconnected to the decline in tax paid by US corporations between 1954 and 1998 (Klein, 2000). In Veblen's terminology, global capitalism has become more predatory, a view endorsed by Castells who noted that: 'The hardening of capitalist logic since the 1980s has fostered social polarization in spite of occupational upgrading' (2000: 280).

This does not mean that the ideological and economic power of global capital is not being challenged. There is evidence that: (1) governments are beginning to place restrictions on transnational corporations (Dicken, 2011); (2) the International Monetary Fund which insists on economic liberalization in exchange for aid (Kiely, 2005) is now recommending increased financial regulation to prevent future economic crises (Kodres and Narain, 2009); (3) union membership has stabilized and national unions are beginning to organize transnationally and co-operate with social movements that share their concerns (Beynon, 2003); and (4) consumers, empowered by the internet, are forcing corporations to change some of their policies (Smithers, 2008). The alliance of workers and consumers to put pressure on the owners and managers of capital pre-dates the rise of Fordism in the USA and although the combination of the collective power of labour and the consumer power of predominantly middle-class activists contains a hierarchical dynamic that is fraught with difficulties (Frank, 2003), in the era of the internet it also constitutes a major threat to capitalist hegemony.

The transformation of unpaid work?

Arguably, the patterning of unpaid domestic work has changed far less than that of paid work, though it has not been entirely immune to external pressures for change. Two theories that deal with the potentially transforming influences on unpaid work in a historically informed way are Beck's (1992) account of the detraditionalization of the nuclear family, and Castells' (1997) analysis of the rise of the informational global economy, both of which consider that the patriarchal nuclear family is in crisis. According to Beck, the acrimonious state of contemporary gender relations can be traced back to the partial modernization of industrial capitalism in that men were freed from traditional constraints rooted in the family, class and community, which enabled them to participate fully and equally in the public sphere of paid work, but women were not. In fact, it was women's lack of freedom from unpaid domestic work that allowed men to achieve independence, and research on the domestic basis of the managerial career indicates that this still applies (Wajcman, 1996). However, the male breadwinner and female house-worker model, though never universally accepted or practised, particularly by those who could not afford to conform to it, is in decline (Crompton, 1999). Beck's explanation of the loosening of women's 'feudal' ties includes, among other things, the equalization of educational and employment opportunities, which have changed women's economic condition, and the revival of feminism, which has raised their consciousness of the persistence of gender inequalities. These changes are part of a more general process of individualization that is associated with globalization, especially in relation to the individualization of work. With more and more women entering the public sphere of paid work, they too are becoming part of the 'individualized society of employees' (Beck, 1992: 99). Although it is still the case that while women participate in paid work in increasing numbers, men have not increased their participation in unpaid domestic work to the same extent. Hence, for Beck, the crux of the issue of the highly gendered pattern of unpaid domestic work is how to resolve the conflicting demands of paid work outside the home and unpaid work inside the home, and the persistence of gender inequalities associated with them.

According to Beck, there are three, 'by no means mutually exclusive', possible outcomes to this contradiction: 'return to the family in its traditional from; equalization according to the male model; and experimentation with new forms of living beyond male and female roles' (1992: 119). Beck considers the first two options to be 'pseudo-alternatives' which either reaffirm the traditional family or acknowledge the dominance of the needs of the market (ibid.: 124). Specifically, the first would undermine the modernization of the public sphere of employment by re-consigning women to the private sphere of the family, and the second would undermine the private sphere of family relationships by prioritizing the public sphere of paid work, the logical conclusion of which is 'not harmony with equal rights, but isolation in courses and situations that run counter and apart from each other' (ibid.: 123). It is only the third option that offers the possibility of reconciling the demands of the two (currently) diametrically opposed institutions. This will only be achieved 'if arrangements are made enabling both functions to be combined throughout the couple's life together' (Beck and Beck-Gernsheim, 1995: 163). Thus, the organization of paid work and family life will have to be modified so that the social and economic needs of individuals can be met satisfactorily, such as more family-friendly paid work arrangements and more unpaid work friendly-family arrangements. Beck suggests that couple mobility could replace, where appropriate, individual mobility and that several families could share child-rearing instead of arranging it on an individual family basis. In these and other ways, paid work and family life could be reunified without destroying either institution.

In the case of Castells' analysis of the transformation of unpaid work, it is framed by his account of the rise of the informational global economy, featuring all the usual suspects, namely the feminization of work, feminism, and technological advances in contraception and family planning. Castells is in no doubt that in virtually all societies, but especially the most advanced ones, the patriarchal family is in crisis, by which he means that the traditional male breadwinner and female house-worker model has been seriously weakened by the above forces and that this is reflected in the statistical trends in such things as divorce, separation, marriage rates, non-marital births, and single-parent households. Of all the forces affecting the decline of the male breadwinner and female house-worker model, Castells places great weight on globalization and the 'expansion of women's employment in the 1990s' at all levels and skills, which he attributes in large part to 'their flexibility as workers' plus their relative cheapness and social skills (1997: 173). Castells claims that the congruence between the need of the new economy for flexible labour also 'fits the survival interests of women who, under the conditions of patriarchalism, seek to make compatible work and family, with little help from their husbands' (ibid.: 173). This has two consequences for the family: 'female bargaining power in the household increases significantly' and patriarchal ideology is 'decisively undermined' (ibid.: 173). In the absence of supportive welfare services, women's consciousness of their difficulty in juggling paid and unpaid work is raised further by the growth of feminist ideas and movements.

The almost universal crisis of the patriarchal family 'manifests itself in the increasing diversity of partnership arrangements among people to share life and raise children', illustrated by Castells with reference to American data (1997: 221). Hence, in many cases, the patriarchal family is history already, notably in the 'growing proportions of female-headed households, and seriously challenged in most other families' (Castells, 1997: 228). Moreover, in the growing proportion of non-family households, estimated by Castells to be approaching 40 per cent, the issue of patriarchalism is avoided altogether. Thus, for Castells, the crisis of the patriarchal family seems to have been resolved in many households in the sense that the taken-for-granted role structure of the traditional family no longer applies, although the possibility of a conservative backlash cannot be ruled out. In the current complex diversity of family relationships, no one standard family form predominates as in the past, hence the patterning of gender relations in the future is uncertain.

In order to examine the progress of the gender revolution historically and cross-nationally, various conceptual models have been advanced that specify different

Table 10.2 Historical and cross-national gender models of paid and unpaid work in households

Gender models	Paid work			Unpaid work*		
	Men	Women	Other**	Men	Women	Other**
PATRIARCHAL e.g., USA, UK and Western Europe 1900c to 1950s	sole	excluded	I/M	excluded	sole	I/M
TRANSITIONAL e.g., USA, UK, Germany, France and Netherlands 1950s to late 20th century	primary	secondary	I/M/S	secondary	primary	I/M/S
EGALITARIAN e.g., Scandinavia late 20th to early 21st century	shared	shared	I/M/S	shared	shared	I/M/S

Notes: *Unpaid work includes both housework and caring.

    **Other includes informal (I), market (M), and state (S) provision of income and/or services.

combinations of gendered arrangements for the accomplishment of paid and unpaid work undertaken by couples within an individual household. (e.g., Crompton, 1999; Ellingsaeter, 1998; Lewis, 1992; Pfau-Effinger, 1993; Warren, 2007). Excluding the pre-modern family economy system, most models start with the male breadwinner/provider model associated with Fordism (note modifications to this gender arrangement (neo-Fordism?)), and end with the equivalent to the symmetrical family involving dual earners/domestic workers (post-Fordism?). The various models show that the paid and unpaid work needed to support a family can be provided by men, women, and by sources external to the household, namely a social network (i.e., kin, friends, and neighbours), the employment of others on a private basis, and/or the state (local and national). Table 10.2 is a more gender-neutral composite of these models and shows that the combination of providers varies in terms of time and space from a patriarchal gender division of paid and unpaid work, to a transitional, and an egalitarian arrangement.

First, Table 10.2 indicates that during the first half of the twentieth century the predominant gender division in most industrial capitalist societies was essentially patriarchal in that men were expected to be the sole providers (breadwinner) and women the sole unpaid workers (domestic worker), backed up by informal and/or private support due to the absence of state welfare benefits and services. This pattern was more of an ideal than a reality for working class couples since women often worked out of necessity, a class dimension that is still apparent today (Warren, 2007). Similarly, regional pockets of patriarchalism may persist long after traditional gender practices have been modified by the majority of a national population (Charles and James, 2005). Second, with the exception of a few countries (e.g., Ireland and Italy), a less unequal gender division of work developed in most countries from the 1950s onwards and was occasioned by the trend for women to work outside the home, especially part-time in the expanding service sector, and by the creation of a gendered state welfare system that reflected and reinforced the amended patriarchal division of work. This transitional arrangement, sometimes referred to as the modified male breadwinner (Lewis, 1992) or the one and a half income model (Plantenga, 2002), developed towards the end of the Fordist era. The egalitarian model or dual income model only applies to Norway, Sweden, Finland and especially Denmark and is associated with greater gender employment equality and a more family-friendly state welfare system that undermines patriarchy via flexible working hours and child-care policies that encourage women to enter the labour market (Ellingsaeter, 1998; Warren, 2007). However, even if both partners undertake full-time paid work, this does not necessarily translate into equal dual breadwinning or equal dual domestic working (Warren, 2007), which is in keeping with Ellingsaeter's view that these countries confirm to a modified dual breadwinner model. The overall trend is that patriarchalism has declined and gender egalitarianism has increased over the past century, but full gender equality in terms of both paid and unpaid work has not been achieved in most advanced capitalist societies.

Summary and conclusions

Globalization is a highly contested concept although there seems to be an emerging consensus that the essence of contemporary capitalist globalization concerns the compression of time and space. The focus of the analysis has been on economic globalization more than on the political or socio-cultural aspects of this complex historical process since this dimension is the most relevant to the impact of globalization on different types of paid and unpaid work.

Historically, three main phases of globalization have been identified: pre-modern, modern, and late modern or contemporary globalization corresponding to the progressive deterritorialization of space culminating in the compression of space and time. The key indicators of the current globalization phase include the global interconnections between people, societies, and institutions, especially economic and political ones.

The major causes of globalization include ideas (e.g., rationalism), economic forces (e.g., capitalism), technological factors (e.g., information and communication technologies), and regulatory frameworks (e.g., liberalization of the international movement of capital). In view of the complexity of the globalization process, and hence the difficulty of separating out one cause from another, it is widely thought that multi-causal explanations are the most appropriate. There is also general agreement that the growth of contemporary globalization was not inevitable but was promoted actively by the governments of the most advanced industrial capitalist societies, notably the USA, and the leading international corporations, hence its neo-liberal political-economic character. However, once the process of globalization has advanced to the stage where transworld interconnections are so extensive that virtually everyone is affected by them directly or indirectly, it has effectively become an irreversible process.

The growth of the global economy during the second half of the twentieth century coincided with parallel developments on a world-wide scale, such as social movements, including feminism, and global trends, such as the feminization of work. These and other factors, such as biological technologies, contributed to the ability of networks of women to challenge patriarchalism, and influence the nature and direction of globalization.

Call centres are a new and expanding type of voice-to-voice interactive service work organization that epitomize the globalization of paid work in that they transcend space and time thanks to the widespread use of advanced information and communication technologies. Originally they were based on the Fordist production work model involving an assembly line of a large volume of short cycle tasks that were target-driven and characterized by closely supervised (i.e., monitored) standardized scripts. This type of service production system was worker-unfriendly and resulted in high levels of stress, absence due to ill health, and labour turnover, all of which detracted from the quality of service provision. In order to mitigate these problems, teamwork, quality circles, and de-stress zones were introduced, although the essential Fordist character of call centres remained, notably standardized tasks and targets. Thus contemporary call centres are neo-Fordist, although those that employ knowledge workers to deal with more complex customer issues tend to be organized in a more collaborative, post-Fordist manner. When call centre work was offshored and outsourced, mostly to India to take advantage of cheaper, non-union English-speaking labour, they tended to conform to the Fordist service production model to an excessive degree and faced distinctive problems additional to those normally associated with this way of organizing work. These include the issue of synchronicity or space–time compression in the interests of capital and space–time expansion for call centre workers which leads to their exclusion from local social life. Second, the pervasiveness of night work is a particular problem for women in a profoundly patriarchal society since it puts their safety and reputation at risk – threats that are not entirely eradicated by the provision of transport between home and work and the practice of veiling regimes. Third, the practice of locational masking by concealing the location of the call centre and the use of Westernized pseudonyms is designed to minimize customer hostility but tends to increase rather than decrease it. Finally, language and cultural training is mandatory in order to enhance rapport and minimize misunderstanding though it involves the constructing of a fake identity which exacerbates an already difficult job. Transnational call centres are not popular with UK and US customers, hence the trend of rapid expansion is likely to slow down or even go into reverse.

Paid work has been affected by globalization and associated factors, notably new information and communication technologies, feminism, and the feminization of work, in that standard work has not only changed in terms of flexibility in every sense, but it has also declined relative to non-standard work. Women tend to be over-represented in most types of non-standard work, especially part-time and home-based work, which also happen to be less well paid with less desirable conditions of employment. Castells claims that the feminization of work does not involve women being channelled into the low-skilled jobs, although he does note that they are paid less than men for similar work. Beck argued that the feminization of work mainly affects non-standard work and suggests that the growth of this type of low-paid and insecure work relative to well-paid and secure standard work is inextricably associated with unrestrained capitalist globalization

A major debate surrounding contemporary globalization concerns the enhanced power of capital organized transnationally relative to the power of labour which tends to be organized locally. While acknowledging the economic advantages of globalization, in terms of increased employment and the diffusion of inexpensive quality goods and services, the social costs, in the form of dramatic levels of work oppression and exploitation, represent the unacceptable face of capitalist globalization. The increased power of global capital, largely beyond the control of any one nation state, and the decreased power of local labour, largely within the control of individual nation states, is illustrated clearly with reference to EPZs where female-dominated jobs have often reduced the scale of unemployment at the cost of repressive labour practices. However, there is some evidence that governments, unions, consumers and various social movements are beginning to challenge and limit the worst excesses of unbridled global capitalism. The weakness of labour during the rise of neo-liberal global capitalism is comparable to the situation confronted by workers during the rise of industrial capitalism, or the early modern phase of globalization, in that this was also an era of free trade and unconstrained competition. In both cases, independent trade unions and state intervention designed to regulate excessive exploitation and provide an economic safety net were/are regarded as obstacles to free enterprise.

The transformation of unpaid domestic work has progressed more slowly than that of paid work, notwithstanding the decline during the twentieth century of the male breadwinner and female house-worker model, due to a variety of factors including the usual suspects of feminism and the feminization of work. Consequently, women still tend to do the bulk of the domestic work, including child-care, if they work outside the home for pay on a part-time basis, and still retain primary responsibility for it when they work full-time, in which case private or public substitute domestic workers are often used. Thus, patriarchalism is still pervasive and paid and unpaid work has yet to be transformed totally since egalitarianism is evident in very few countries.

Concluding remarks: continuity and change and 'work'

It is now time to revisit the dominant conception of work outlined in the first chapter and consider to what extent and why its key dimensions – capitalist,

Table 10.3 Dominant conception of work (DCW) revisited

DCW	Status of each dimension at the beginning of the 21st century
Capitalist	Strengthened markedly by neo-liberal globalization but still contested by radical trade unionism and anti-capitalist social movements
Industrial	Weakened moderately by flexibilization & by information & communication technology
Modern	Weakened marginally by growth of self-employment
Patriarchal	Weakened moderately by feminism & the feminization of paid work and to a lesser extent by the masculinization of unpaid domestic work

industrial, modern and patriarchal – have changed since its establishment at the beginning of the twentieth century. Table 10.3 summarizes the contemporary state of the four dimensions of the dominant conception of work.

First, the analysis presented throughout this text suggests that the capitalist dimension has been strengthened during the process of neo-liberal globalization to such an extent that contemporary capitalism justifies fully Head's designation that it constitutes 'the new ruthless economy' (2005: 109). The market system has been extended to most sectors of the economies of advanced societies, from the provision of services that were once considered natural state monopolies (e.g., water and gas), to public services that were previously untouched directly by capitalism (e.g., health and education). As a consequence, currently capitalism is virtually universal in practice and hegemonic ideologically. Yet it continues to be a crisis-prone system, hence opposition to capitalism can never be discounted. Capitalism has become more extreme and ubiquitous.

The combined forces of globalization, flexibilization, technological innovation, feminism, and the feminization of paid work, and the masculinization of unpaid domestic work have changed to some extent the industrial, modern and patriarchal dimensions of the dominant conception of work. In the case of the industrial dimension, the flexibilization of industrial and service production systems and the global diffusion of technological innovations in information and communication have changed it to a moderate degree in the sense that the contractual, spatial and temporal elements of paid work have been destandardized, albeit unevenly. The main social costs of the weakening of the industrial dimension have fallen on workers, especially women, and the main beneficiaries have been the owners and senior executives of global corporations. As far the modern dimension is concerned, this has been weakened marginally by the unexpected expansion of self-employment, spurious or otherwise, formal or informal. This trend is not unconnected to the processes of flexibilization and technological innovation, and involves the recrudescence of ascription on the basis of family membership, or other types of high trust groups, which contrasts with the modern principle of universalistic achievement. Finally, patriarchalism has been weakened moderately by feminism and the feminization of paid work in the global economy, and to a lesser extent by the masculinization of unpaid domestic work. However, it is apparent from the material presented above and in the earlier chapters that paid work and unpaid domestic work remain highly gendered and unequal, and that women continue to take the strain, though less so than when the male breadwinner/female domestic worker model prevailed. Overall, continuity more than change characterizes the recent history of the dominant conception of work that developed with the rise of industrial capitalism, and, while there have been some changes, neither paid work nor unpaid work have been transformed.

Finally, this sociological analysis of work has shown that variations in the patterning of paid and unpaid work need to be historically and geopolitically located. Second, all forms of work also need to be understood with reference to the increasing globalization of economic life. Third, that each type of work impacts on every other type of work and therefore no one type of paid or unpaid work can be understood in isolation. Furthermore, and following from this point, the hope of a more symmetrical or 'egalitarian' family pattern, expressed in their different ways by, among others, Castells (1997: 242), Beck (2000), and of course Young and Willmott (1973), depends in large part upon changes in the nature and distribution of paid work. While it is good to have a vision of a more democratic and balanced pattern of paid and unpaid work, it is more likely to become a reality if all dreamers participate in trying to bring about the desired changes.

Further reading

BOOKS A good introduction to globalization is Scholte (2005) *Globalization: A Critical Introduction.* An up-to-date overview of globalization, albeit from a geographical perspective, that covers the recent financial crisis is Dicken (2011) *Global Shift: Mapping the Changing Contours of the World Economy.* The most detailed account of the Fordist character of call centres can be found in Head (2005) *The New Ruthless Economy: Work and Power in the Digital Age.* Deery and Kinnie (2004) *Call Centres and Human Resource Management: A Cross-National Perspective* contains an excellent range of material on call centre work. The most comprehensive, theoretically informed empirical analysis of globalization and related transformations in relation to work is Castells (2001) *The Rise of the Network Society* (2nd edn) and (1997) *The Power of Identity.* Beck's *Risk Society: Towards a New Modernity* (1992) and *The Brave New World of Work* (2000), also discuss globalization, plus the destandardization of paid work and the detraditionalization of the family in interesting and provocative ways. The monograph edited by Crompton (1999) *Restructuring Gender Relations and Employment: The Decline of the Male Breadwinner* covers national variations in Europe in the patterning of women's employment.

ARTICLES Taylor and Bain (2005) '"India calling to the far away towns": the call centre labour process and globalization',

Work, Employment and Society, 19(2): 261–82, covers call centre work in general and the distinctiveness of Indian call centres, and for an account of workers' dissent and resistance consult Taylor and Bain (2001) 'Trade unions, workers' rights and the frontier of control in UK call centres', *Economic and Industrial Democracy*, 22(1): 39–66.

WEBSITES For research reports on call centre work, consult www.callcentres.net/. Mirchandani's studies of Indian call centres including her 2004 article can be downloaded from the University of Toronto website; www.aecp.oise.utoronto.ca/main/faculty/mirchandani

—————— Questions for discussion and assessment ——————

1 What is globalization and how has it changed historically?
2 Account for the rise and distinctiveness of contemporary globalization.
3 Evaluate the neo-Fordist character of call centres.
4 Assess the implications of the distinctiveness of Indian call centre work.
5 Consider the impact of globalization on paid work.
6 How has unpaid domestic work changed since the advent of the global economy?
7 In what ways and to what extent is the dominant conception of work still valid?

GLOSSARY

Cautionary note: Definitions of social science terms are invariably contested. It is therefore imperative to consult the relevant section(s) of the text, making a note of any variations. In other words, do not be deceived by the apparent simplicity of the definitions and read carefully the sources cited.

Agrarian society: An advanced (third) type of pre-industrial human society characterized by the use of animal power for farming and transport, such as horses for ploughing and riding.

Alienation: A concept used by Marx to describe the exploited and oppressed condition of labour under an industrial capitalist mode of production, and operationalized by Blauner in order to examine empirically the impact of different types of technology. The latter's conceptualization emphasized a worker's powerlessness, the meaninglessness of work, social isolation and self-estrangement.

Bureaucracy: A type of organization characterized by a hierarchical structure of authority, a set of written rules, clearly defined division of specialist labour, with office holders recruited and promoted on the basis of ability and technical knowledge. The concept was developed by Weber who considered that an impersonal bureaucracy was the most rational, impartial and therefore efficient way of achieving complex goals such as collecting taxes or making cars.

Capitalism: A type of economic organization oriented to the accumulation of profit involving the private ownership of the means of production and the employment of free wage labour.

Commodification: A process by which goods and services are produced by profit-oriented organizations and exchanged for money under a market system.

Conspicuous consumption: A concept developed by Veblen that refers to a zero sum game involving the competitive, conspicuous consumption of leisure (time), goods and services (money), and resources (waste) in order to demonstrate one's economic prowess and high social status.

Continuous improvement or *kaizen*: The idea that organizations should never stop seeking ways to improve the quantity and quality of production; associated with Japanese lean production.

Cultural lag: When two previously harmonious features of society become dissociated over time due to one changing more radically than the other.

Domestic work: A form of unpaid work involving tasks undertaken in and around the home, including child-care, also referred to as housework and domestic labour.

Dual earner/variable house-worker model: The idea that no one adult member of a household should be solely responsible for economic provision or domestic work.

Emotional labour: A concept developed by Hochschild that refers to the expression of feelings by workers required by their employers, such as friendliness, during service interactions. Emotional labour in exchange for pay often involves an aesthetic dimension, either visual and/or aural, such as smartness and smiling, and is sometimes referred to as aesthetic labour.

Enterprise culture: Ideas and practices concerned with initiative and self-reliance oriented to making a profit.

Expert systems: A computer programme based on the specialized knowledge of a group of experts collected by knowledge engineers, that can make decisions that would otherwise be made by a human expert.

Family wage: A male wage sufficient to support a family without financial contributions from other family members that was based on the model that the ideal family comprised a male breadwinner and dependent full-time housewife.

Feminism: A social movement/set of ideas concerned with challenging male domination, thereby improving the condition of women and achieving equality.

Flexibility: The ability to change production easily by altering the size of the workforce (numerical flexibility), the roles of the workforce (functional flexibility), and/or the output of the workforce (product flexibility).

Flexible specialization: A model of work organization associated primarily with Piore and Sabel that involves the combination of craft skills and advanced technology which enables companies to supply high-quality customized products to diversified markets.

Fordism: A system of mass production and consumption pioneered by Henry Ford in America at the beginning of the twentieth century. The main features include the fragmentation and simplification of tasks, the moving assembly line, and the standardization of interchangeable parts and low-quality products.

Globalization: A complex historical process characterized by increasing economic, political and socio-cultural interconnections that compress time/space.

Guild: A pre-modern organization of urban skilled workers set up to control entry, training (apprenticeship), standards, and competition.

Hegemony: The consensual dimension of ruling class ideas that legitimate the existing social system and that are internalized by subordinate classes.

Home-working: Income-generating economic activity derived from working at and/or from home.

Horticultural society: A (second) type of human society which evolved from semi-nomadic hunting and gathering societies to become a settled horticultural one based on the use of metal tools for the production of food.

Hunting and gathering society: The earliest known (first) type of human society dominated by the use of stone weapons and tools for hunting animals and the gathering of food, such as berries, and hence nomadic.

Individualization: A concept developed by Beck that refers to the tendency for individuals in late modern society to be set free from traditional sources of collective identity rooted in early modern society, such as class, family and community.

Industrial capitalism: A fourth type of society in which economic organizations are privately owned and use large-scale machinery powered by inanimate sources of energy.

Industrialization: The transformation of an essentially agrarian economy into a manufacturing one characterized by the use of inanimate sources of energy such as steam to power large-scale machinery, epitomized by factory production.

Informal work: Work that is legal or illegal but undeclared to the tax and other regulatory authorities.

Interactive service work: A concept developed by Leidner that refers to work that involves interacting with service recipients (e.g., customers, clients, etc.) either face-to-face or voice-to-voice.

Japanese lean production (JLP): A method of organizing work that was pioneered by Toyota, associated with Japanese companies, and has been adopted by Western companies. It seeks continuous improvement via just-in-time (JIT) production (the supply of parts, materials and labour when they are needed), total quality control (TQC) (the emphasis on zero defects), and teamwork (TW) (groups working together flexibly with a team leader).

Just-in-case production: The supply of materials, parts, and labour in advance of when it is needed; associated with Fordism.

Just-in-time production: The supply of parts, materials and labour when it is needed; associated with Japanese lean production.

Knowledge work/ers: Contemporary manifestations of what were known as professional and technical work/ers during the pre-Fordist and Fordist eras. Work that involves specialist knowledge that is created and/or applied, and/or transmitted, by well qualified and/or experienced workers.

Leisure class: A parasitic class which abstains from useful work because it regards it as demeaning and instead engages in the conspicuous consumption of time (leisure), money (expensive goods and services) and resources (waste). The leisure class was analysed in detail by Veblen.

Male breadwinner/female domestic worker model: The idea that men should be the primary economic providers in a household, and that women should be the primary unpaid domestic workers.

Marriage bar: A prohibition on the hiring of women workers, often operated in conjunction with a retain bar, which prohibited the retention of women when married.

McDonaldism: A neo-Fordist form of service production system characterized by qualified Taylorized social and manual work tasks, a modified assembly line, and limited destandardization of parts and medium-quality products.

Modernization: The social and cultural dimensions of (Western) industrialization involving the decline of traditionalism and characterized by literacy, rationality and urbanization.

Neo-Fordism: A reformed version of Fordism involving qualified Taylorized work tasks, a modified assembly line, a limited destandardization of parts and a wider range of higher-quality products.

Neo-liberalism: An economic (and political and social) set of ideas that dates from the rise of capitalism which stresses the importance of a free market and unrestrained competition. When this doctrine was revived in the 1990s, it was sometimes referred to as New Right ideology.

Network enterprise: A business model made up of companies or sections of companies thought by Castells to have superseded individual and collective capitalist units.

Network society: A concept developed by Castells to refer to a new type of society that is informational, global and networked.

Non-standard work: Forms of paid work that deviate contractually, spatially, or temporally from what had become standard by the mid-to-late twentieth century in Western industrial capitalist societies, namely regular, full-time employment based on a contract specifying wages, hours and benefits. Also known as contingent work or flexible work.

Patriarchy: Ideas and practices by which males dominate females.

Post-bureaucracy: An emergent, less impersonal organizational form character-ized by a lack of hierarchy, reduced functional specialization, with roles guided by principles rather than rules. It is thought that such an organization is better suited to a work environment in which technological and economic change are acute by virtue of its greater adaptability. Post-bureaucracy and bureaucracy are not mutually exclusive; mixed organizational forms are possible.

Post-Fordism: A radical alternative to Fordism involving flexible multiskilled work, flexible computer technology, flexible parts and high quality customized products.

Post-industrial society: A (fifth?) type of society in which services and service work (white-collar) rather than manufacturing and factory work (blue-collar) dominate the economy.

Pre-industrial society: Any type of society dominated by non-manufacturing economic activities, including hunting and gathering, horticulture and farming.

Protestant work ethic: The idea that work is a virtuous activity (a sign of election among Calvinists) and that one should work conscientiously, consume ascetically, and eschew idleness. The Protestant source of this idea was examined by Weber.

Self-employment: Workers who own and operate the means of production either alone or in combination with others.

Skill: One or more competences required by a specific job, possessed by an individual, or associated with particular types of work or occupation. A decline in skill is usually termed deskilling and an increase in skill is usually termed upskilling, whereas a tendency for both to occur is termed polarization.

Standard work: Work in the form of full-time employment involving a contract that typically includes regular pay for a specified number of hours and a range of benefits, notably sick pay and a pension. This form of work is thought to have become the norm by the mid-to-late twentieth century in Western industrial capitalist societies as a result of what some have called the Fordist compromise to match mass production and mass consumption.

Taylorism (or scientific management): Principles of work organization advocated by Taylor, notably the transfer of all discretion from workers to management and the fragmentation and simplification of tasks.

Teamwork (TW): Working flexibly as part of a group under a team leader instead of individually; associated with Japanese lean production.

Technological determinism: The assumption that technology – productive technique including both the material objects and their social organization – determines social relationships.

Technology: The application of scientific knowledge to solve practical problems. A narrow definition tends to focus on material objects whereas a broad definition tends to include how the materials are operated and organized.

Temporary work: Employment that is regarded by employers and employees to be of a limited duration that can range from casual work lasting a few hours to contract work lasting a few years.

Total quality control (TQC): The adoption of a holistic approach to maximizing the quality of every aspect of production aiming at zero defects; associated with Japanese lean production.

Trade unions: Associations of employees who combine together to maintain and improve their pay and working conditions.

Traditionalism: Ideas and practices handed down from one generation to another.

Unemployment: A situation of being without paid employment. A concept that is inextricably associated with the development of industrial capitalism which involved the demise of alternative sources of income.

REFERENCES

Abercrombie, N., Hill, S. and Turner, B. (1988) *Dictionary of Sociology* (2nd edn). London: Penguin.

Abernathy, W., Clark, K. and Kantrow, A. (1983) *Industrial Renaissance: Producing a Competitive Future for America*. New York: Basic Books.

Adler, P. (1995) '"Democratic Taylorism": The Toyota production system at NUMMI', in S. Babson (ed.), *Lean Work: Empowerment and Exploitation in the Global Auto Industry*. Detroit: Wayne State University Press, pp. 207–19.

Aglietta, M. (1987 [1976]) *A Theory of Capitalist Regulation: The US Experience*. London: Verso.

Aguren, S., Hansson, R. and Karlsson, K. (1976) *The Volvo Kalmar Plant: The Impact of New Design on Work Organization*. Stockholm: The Rationalization Council SAF–LO.

Albrow, M. (1996) *The Global Age*. Cambridge: Polity.

Alexander, D. (1970) *Retailing in England during the Industrial Revolution*. London: Athlone Press.

Allan, E. and Steffensmeier, D. (1989) 'Youth, unemployment and property crime: differential effects on job availability and job quality on juvenile and young adult arrest rates', *American Sociological Review*, 54(1): 107–23.

Allatt, P. and Yeandle, S. (1992) *Youth Unemployment and the Family*. London: Routledge.

Allen, J. and du Gay, P. (1994) 'Industry and the rest: the economic identity of services', *Work, Employment and Society*, 8(2): 255–71.

Allen, S. (1999) 'Gender inequality and divisions of labour', in H. Beynon and P. Glavanis (eds), *Patterns of Social Inequality*. London: Longman, pp. 20–55.

Amin, A. (ed.) (1994a) *Post-Fordism: A Reader*. Oxford: Blackwell.

Amin, A. (1994b) 'Post-Fordism: models, fantasies and phantoms of transition', in A. Amin (ed.), *Post-Fordism: A Reader*. Oxford: Blackwell, pp. 1–39.

Anderson, B. (1996) 'Review of *Servicing the Middle Classes*, by N. Gregson and M. Lowe', *Work, Employment and Society*, 10(3): 581–3.

Anderson, M. (1971) *Family Structure in Nineteenth-Century Lancashire*. Cambridge: Cambridge University Press.

Anderson, M., Bechhofer, F. and Gershuny, J. (eds) (1994) *The Social and Political Economy of the Household*. Oxford: Oxford University Press.

Anderson, S. (2009) 'Unemployment and subjective well-being: a question of class?' *Work and Occupations*, 36(1): 3–25.

Anthony, P. (1977) *The Ideology of Work*. London: Tavistock.

Appelbaum, E. and Batt, R. (1994) *The New American Workplace: Transforming Work Systems in the United States*, Ithaca, NY: ILR Press.

Applebaum, H. (1992) *The Concept of Work: Ancient, Medieval and Modern*. New York: State University of New York Press.

Arber, S. and Ginn, J. (1995) 'The mirage of gender equality: occupational success in the labour market and within marriage', *British Journal of Sociology*, 46(1): 21–43.

Aronowitz, S. and DiFazio, W. (1994) *The Jobless Future: Sci-Tech and the Dogma of Work*. Minneapolis: University of Minnesota Press.

Ashton, D. (1986) *Unemployment under Capitalism: The Sociology of British and American Labour Markets*. Brighton: Wheatsheaf.

Atkinson, J., Morris, R.J. and Williams, M. (1996) *Temporary Work and the Labour Market*. Brighton: University of Sussex, Institute of Employment Studies.

Attewell, P. (1987) 'The deskilling controversy', *Work and Occupations*, 14(3): 323–46.

Attewell, P. (1989) 'The clerk deskilled: a study of false nostalgia', *Journal of Historical Sociology*, 2(4): 357–88.

Auer, P. and Cazes, S. (2000) 'The resilience of the long-term employment relationship: evidence from the industrialized countries', *International Labour Review*, 139(4): 379–408.

Babson, S. (1995) 'Lean production and labour: empowerment and exploitation', in S. Babson (ed.), *Lean Work: Empowerment and Exploitation in the Global Auto Industry*. Detroit: Wayne State University Press, pp. 1–37.

Bain, A. (2005) 'Constructing an artistic identity', *Work, Employment and Society*, 19(1): 25–46.

Bain, P. and Taylor, P. (2000) 'Entrapped by the "electronic panopticon": worker resistance in the call centre', *New Technology, Work and Employment*, 15(1): 2–18.

Bain, P., Watson, A., Mulvey, G., Taylor, P. and Gall, G. (2002) 'Taylorism, targets and the pursuit of quantity and quality by call centre management', *New Technology, Work and Employment*, 17(3): 170–85.

Bakker, A., Demerouti, E. and Schaufeli, W. (2003) 'Dual processes at work in a call centre: an application of the job demands-resources model', *European Journal of Work and Occupational Psychology*, 12(4): 393–417.

Baldry, C., Bain, P. and Taylor, P. (1998) '"Bright satanic offices": intensification, control and team Taylorism', in P. Thompson and C. Warhurst (eds) *Workplaces of the Future*. Basingstoke: Macmillan, pp. 163–83.

Bales, K. (2000) *Disposable People: New Slavery in the Global Economy*. Berkeley: University of California Press.

Baran, B. (1988) 'Office automation and women's work: the technological transformation of the insurance industry', in R. Pahl (ed.), *On Work: Historical, Comparative and Theoretical Approaches*. Oxford: Blackwell, pp. 684–706.

Basi, J. (2009) *Women, Identity and India's Call Centre Industry*. London: Routledge.

Bauman, Z. (1998) *Work, Consumerism and the New Poor*. Milton Keynes: Open University Press.

Bauman, Z. (2001) *The Individualized Society*. Cambridge: Polity.

Beagan, B., Chapman, G., D'Sylva, A. and Bassett, B. (2008) '"It's just easier for me to do it": rationalizing the family division of labour', *Sociology*, 42(4): 653–71.

Bechhofer, F. and Elliot, B. (1968) 'Small shopkeepers and the class structure', *European Journal of Sociology*, 9: 180–202.

Bechhofer, F., Elliot, B., Rushforth, M. and Bland, R. (1974) 'The petits bourgeois in the class structure: the case of the small shopkeepers', in F. Parkin (ed.), *The Social Analysis of Class Structure*. London: Tavistock, pp. 103–28.

Beck, U. (1992) *Risk Society: Towards a New Modernity*. London: Sage.

Beck, U. (2000) *The Brave New World of Work*. Cambridge: Polity.

Beck, U. (2001) *What Is Globalization?* Cambridge: Polity.

Beck, U. and Beck-Gernsheim, E. (1995) *The Normal Chaos of Love*. Cambridge: Polity.

Beck, U. and Beck-Gernsheim, E. (2002) *Individualization: Institutionalized Individualism and its Social and Political Consequences*. London: Sage.

Beder, S. (2000) *Selling the Work Ethic: From Puritan Pulpit to Corporate PR*. London: Zen Books.

Beechey, V. and Perkins, T. (1987) *A Matter of Hours: Part-time Work and the Labour Market*. Cambridge: Polity.

Bell, D. (1976 [1973]) *The Coming of Post-industrial Society: A Venture in Social Forcasting*. London: Penguin.

Bell, D. (1980) 'The information society: the social framework of the information society', in T. Forester (ed.), *The Microelectronics Revolution: The Complete Guide to the New Technology and Its Impact on Society*. Oxford: Blackwell, pp. 500–49.

Bell, D. and Blanchflower, D. (2010) 'UK unemployment in the great recession', *National Institute Economic Review*, 214(1): 3–25.

Belt, V. (2004) 'A female ghetto?: women's careers in telephone call centres', in S. Deery and N. Kinnie (eds), *Call Centres and Human Resource Management*. Basingstoke: Palgrave Macmillan, pp. 174–97.

Beneria, L. (1988) 'Conceptualizing the labour force: the underestimation of women's economic activities', in R. Pahl (ed.), *On Work: Historical, Comparative and Theoretical Approaches*. Oxford: Blackwell, pp. 372–91.

Benjamin, O. and Sullivan, O. (1999) 'Relational resources, gender consciousness and possibilities of change in marital relationships', *Sociological Review*, 47(4): 794–820.

Benner, C. (2002) *Work in the New Economy: Flexible Labour Markets in Silicon Valley*. Oxford: Blackwell.

Benson, J. and Shaw, G. (eds.) (1992) *The Evolution of Retail Systems: c1800–1914*. Leicester: Leicester University Press.

Berg, M. (1988) 'Women's work, mechanization and early industrialization', in R. Pahl (ed.), *On Work: Historical, Comparative and Theoretical Approaches*. Oxford: Blackwell, pp. 61–94.

Berg, M. (1994) *The Age of Manufactures 1700–1820: Industry, Innovation and Work in Britain* (2nd edn). London: Routledge.

Berggren, C. (1992) 'New production concepts in final assembly – the Swedish experience', in S. Wood (ed.), *The Transformation of Work: Skill, Flexibility and the Labour Process*. London: Routledge, pp. 172–203.

Berggren, C. (1993) 'Lean production – the end of history?', *Work, Employment and Society*, 7(2): 163–88.

Berk, S. (1985) *The Gender Factory: The Apportionment of Work in American Households*. New York: Plenum.

Bernhardt, A. and Marcotte, D. (2000) 'Is "standard employment" still what it used to be?', in F. Carré, M. Ferber, L. Golden and S. Herzenberg (eds), *Nonstandard Work: The Nature and Challenges of Changing Employment Arrangements*. Champaign, IL: Industrial Relations Research Association, University of Illinois at Urbana-Champaign, pp. 21–40.

Bernhardt, E., Noack, E. and Lyngstad, T. (2008) 'Shared housework in Norway and Sweden: advancing the gender revolution', *European Journal of Social Policy*, 18(3): 275–88.

Besser, T. (1996) *Team Toyota: Transplanting the Toyota Culture in the Camry Plant in Kentucky*. Albany, NY: State University of New York Press.

Beynon, H. (1975) *Working for Ford*. Wakefield: E.P. Publishing.

Beynon, H. (2003) 'Globalization, trade union organization and workers' rights' in P. Fairbrother and C. Yates (eds) *Trade Unions in Renewal*. London: Routledge, pp. 263–81.

Beynon, H. and Austrin, T. (1994) *Masters and Servants: Class and Patronage in the Making of a Labour Organization*. London: Rivers Oram Press.

Beynon, H. and Nichols, T. (2006) 'Introduction' to H. Beynon and T. Nichols (eds), *Patterns of Work in the Post-Fordist Era: Fordism and Post-Fordism*. Cheltenham: Edward Elgar, Vol. 1, pp. ix–xxiv.

Bittman, M., Matheson, G. and Meagher, G. (1999) 'The changing boundary between home and market: Australian trends in outsourcing domestic labour', *Work, Employment and Society*, 13(2): 249–73.

Bittman, M., Rice, J. and Wajcman, J. (2004) 'Appliances and their impact: the ownership of domestic technology and time spent on household work', *British Journal of Sociology*, 55(3): 401–23.

Blackburn, R. and Mann, M. (1979) *The Working Class in the Labour Market*. London: Macmillan.

Blanchflower, D. and Freeman, R. (eds) (2000) *Youth Unemployment and Joblessness in Advanced Societies*. Chicago: University of Chicago Press.

Blauner, R. (1964) *Alienation and Freedom: The Factory Worker and His Industry*. Chicago: University of Chicago Press.

Blom, R. and Melin, H. (2003) 'Information society and the transformation of organizations in Finland', *Work and Occupations*, 30(2): 176–93.

Blyton, P., Lucio, M., McGurk, J. and Turnbull, P. (2002) 'Globalization, restructuring and occupational labour power: evidence from the international airline industry', in Y. Debrah and I. Smith (eds), *Globalization, Employment and the Workplace: Diverse Impacts*. London: Routledge, pp. 24–40.

Bogenhold, D. and Staber, U. (1991) 'The decline and rise of self-employment', *Work, Employment and Society*, 5(2): 223–39.

Booth, A. (1995) *The Economics of Trade Unions*. Cambridge: Cambridge University Press.

Boreham, P., Parker, R., Thompson, P. and Hall, R. (2008) *New Technology @ Work*. London: Routledge.

Boris, E. and Prugl, E. (eds) (1996) *Homeworkers in Global Perspective: Invisible No More*. London: Routledge.

Boserup, E. (1970) *Women's Role in Economic Development*. London: Allen and Unwin.

Boulton, M. (1983) *On Being a Mother: A Study of Women with Pre-school Children*. London: Tavistock.

Bowles, S. and Gintis, H. (1976) *Schooling in Capitalist America*. London: Routledge and Kegan Paul.

Box, S. (1987) *Recession, Crime and Punishment*. London: Macmillan.

Boyle, E. (1994) 'The rise of the reluctant entrepreneurs', *International Small Business Journal*, 12(2): 63–9.

Bradley, H. (1989) *Men's Work, Women's Work: A Sociological History of the Sexual Division of Labour in Employment*. Cambridge: Polity.

Bradley, H. and Devadason, R. (2008) 'Fractured transitions: young adults' pathways into contemporary labour markets', *Sociology*, 42(1): 119–36.

Brannen, J. and Moss, P. (1991) *Managing Mothers: Dual Earner Households after Maternity Leave*. London: Unwin Hyman.

Brannen, J. and Nilsen, A. (2002) 'Young people's time perspective: from youth to adulthood', *Sociology*, 36(3): 513–37.

Braverman, H. (1974) *Labour and Monopoly Capital: The Degradation of Work in the Twentieth Century*. New York: Monthly Review Press.

Bresnen, M., Wray, K., Bryman, A., Beardsworth, A., Ford, J. and Keil, E. (1985) 'The flexibility of recruitment in the construction industry; formalization or re-casualization?', *Sociology*, 19(1): 108–24.

Bright, J. (1958) 'Does automation raise skill requirements?', *Harvard Business Review*, 36(4): 85–98.

Brines, J. (1994) 'Economic dependency, gender and the division of labour at home', *American Journal of Sociology*, 100(3): 652–88.

Brook, P. (2009) 'The Alienated Heart: Hochschild's "emotional labour" thesis and the anticapitalist politics of alienation', *Capital and Class*, 33(2): 7–31.

Brophy, E. (2006) 'System error: labour precarity and collective organizing at Microsoft', *Canadian Journal of Communication*, 31(3): 619–38.

Brown, P., Lauder, H., Ashton, D. (2011) *The Global Auction: The Broken Promises of Education, Jobs, and Incomes*. Oxford: Oxford University Press.

Brown, R. (1992) *Understanding Industrial Organizations*. London: Routledge.

Brynin, M. (2002) 'Overqualification in employment', *Work, Employment and Society*, 16(4): 637–54.

Burawoy, M. (1979) *Manufacturing Consent: Changes in the Labour Process under Monopoly Capitalism*. Chicago: University of Chicago Press.

Burawoy, M. (1996) 'A classic of its time: review of *Labour and Monopoly Capital* by H. Braverman', *Contemporary Sociology*, 25(3): 296–9.

Burchell, J., Day, D., Hudson, M., Ladipo, D., Mankelow, R., Nolan, J.P., Reed, H., Wichert, I.C. and Wilkinson, R. (1999) *Job Insecurity and Work Intensification*. York: Joseph Rowntree Foundation.

Burgess, J. and Connell, J. (2004) *International Perspectives on Temporary Agency Work*. London: Routledge.

Burnett, J. (1994) *Idle Hands: The Experience of Unemployment, 1790–1990*. London: Routledge.

Burrows, R. (ed.) (1991) *Deciphering the Enterprise Culture: Entrepreneurship, Petty Capitalism and the Restructuring of Britain*. London: Routledge.

Burrows, R. and Curran, J. (1991) 'Not such a small business: reflections on the rhetoric, the reality and the future of the enterprise culture', in M. Cross and G. Payne (eds), *Work and the Enterprise Culture*. London: Falmer, pp. 9–29.

Callender, C. (1985) 'Unemployment: the case for women', in C. Jones and M. Benton (eds), *Yearbook of Social Policy in Britain 1984/5*. London: Routledge, pp. 47–73.

Campbell, I. and Burgess, J. (2001) 'Casual employment and temporary employment in Europe: developing a cross-national comparison', *Work, Employment and Society*, 15(1): 171–84.

Carré, F. (1992) 'Temporary employment in the eighties', in V. duRivage (ed.), *New Policies for the Part-time and Contingent Workforce*. New York: M.E. Sharpe, pp. 45–87.

Casey, B. (1991) 'Survey evidence on trends in "non-standard" employment', in A. Pollert (ed.), *Farewell to Flexibility?* Oxford: Blackwell, pp. 179–99.

Casey, B. and Laczko, F. (1989) 'Early retired or long-term unemployed: the situation of non-working men aged 55–64 from 1979–1986', *Work, Employment and Society*, 3(4): 509–26.

Castells, M. (1997) *The Power of Identity*. Oxford: Blackwell.

Castells, M. (2000) 'Materials for an exploratory theory of the network society', *British Journal of Sociology*, 51(1): 5–24.

Castells, M. (2001) *The Rise of the Network Society* (2nd edn). Oxford: Blackwell.

Charles, N. and James, E. (2003) 'The gender dimensions of job insecurity in a local market', *Work, Employment and Society*, 17(3): 531–52.

Charles, N. and James, E. (2005) '"He earns the bread and butter and I earn the cream": job insecurity and the male breadwinner family in South Wales', *Work, Employment and Society*, 19(3): 481–502.

Clark, A. and McCurry, J. (2010) 'Toyota boss "regrets" faulty accelerators', *Guardian*, 25 February.

Clark, J., McLoughlin, I., Rose, H. and King. R. (1990) *The Process of Technological Change: New Technology and Social Choice in the Workplace*. Cambridge: Cambridge University Press.

Clarke, S. (1992) 'What in the F—'s name is Fordism?', in N. Gilbert, R. Burrows and A. Pollert (eds), *Fordism and Flexibility: Divisions and Change*. London: Macmillan, pp. 13–30.

Cobble, D. (1996) 'The prospects for unionism in a service society', in C. MacDonald and C. Sirianni (eds), *Working in the Service Society*. Philadelphia: Temple University Press, pp. 333–58.

Cockburn, C. (1983) *Brothers: Male Dominance and Technological Change*. London: Pluto.

Coffey, D. (2006) *The Myth of Japanese Efficiency: The World Car Industry in a Globalizing Age*. Cheltenham: Edward Elgar.

Coffield, F., Borrill, C. and Marshall, S. (1986) *Growing up at the Margins: Young Adults in the North East*. Milton Keynes: Open University Press.

Cohen, D. '(1998) 'McDonald's new system is "Made for You"', *Journal Record, The (Oklahoma City)*, June 4.

Cohen, R. and Kennedy, P. (2007) *Global Sociology* (2nd edn). London: Palgrave Macmillan.

Cole, M. (2007) 'Re-thinking unemployment: a challenge to the legacy of Jahoda et al.', *Sociology*, 41(6): 1133–49.

Collin-Jacques, C. (2004) 'Professionals at work: a study of autonomy and skill in nurse call centres in England and Canada', in S. Deery and N. Kinnie (eds), *Call Centres and Human Resource Management: A Cross-National Perspective*, Basingstoke: Palgrave Macmillan, pp. 153–73.

Collins, R. (1979) *The Credential Society: An Historical Sociology of Education and Stratification*. New York: Academic Press.

Collins, R. (1992) 'Weber's last theory of capitalism: a systemization', in M. Granovetter and R. Swedberg (eds), *The Sociology of Economic Life*. Boulder, CO: Westview Press.

Collinson, D. and Knights, D. (1986) '"Men only": theories and practices of job segregation in insurance', in D. Knights and H. Willmott (eds), *Gender and the Labour Process*. Aldershot: Gower, pp. 140–78.

Collinson, M. and Collinson, D. (1996) '"It's only Dick": the sexual harassment of women managers in insurance sales', *Work, Employment and Society*, 10(1): 29–56.

Conley, H. (2002) 'A state of insecurity: temporary work in the public services', *Work, Employment and Society*, 16(4): 725–37.

Cooley, M. (1987 [1980]) *Architect or Bee? The Human Price of Technology*. London: Hogarth Press.

Coombs, R. (1985) 'Automation, management strategies and labour-process change', in D. Knights, H. Willmott and D. Collison (eds) *Job Redesign: Critical Perspectives on the Labour Process*. Aldershot: Gower, pp. 142–70.

Cooper, C., Stewart, M. and Taylor, P. (1998) ' From Taylor to Mrs Taylor: The transformation of the accountancy craft'. www.commerce.adelaide.edu.au/research/aaaj/apira_1998/archives/pdfs/47.pdf.

Coops, A. (2000) 'Comment', *The Times*, 7 February.

Coriat, B. (1980) 'The restructuring of the assembly line: a new economy of time and control', *Capital and Class*, 11: 34–43.

Corrigan, P. (1977) 'Feudal relics or capitalist monuments?', *Sociology*, 11(3): 411–63.

Cotgrove, S. (1972) 'Alienation and automation', *British Journal of Sociology*, 23(4): 437–51.

Cowan, R. (1983) *More Work for Mother: The Ironies of Household Technology from the Open Hearth to the Microwave*. New York: Basic Books.

Coyle, A. (1984) *Redundant Women*. London: Women's Press.

Cragg, A. and Dawson, T. (1984) *Unemployed Women: A Study of Attitudes and Experiences, Research Paper No. 47*. London: Department of Employment.

Creighton, C. (1996) 'The rise and fall of the male breadwinner family: a reappraisal', *Comparative Studies in Society and History*, 38: 310–37.

Crocker, B. (2008) 'Women workers: "We brought the Ford Empire to its knees"'. www.workersliberty.org/story/2008/07/14/we-brought-ford-empire-its-knees, pp. 1–4.

Crompton, R. (1990) 'Professions in the current context', *Work, Employment and Society, Special Issue*, May, pp. 147–66.

Crompton, R. (1997) *Women and Work in Modern Britain*. Oxford: Oxford University Press.

Crompton, R. (ed.) (1999) *Restructuring Gender Relations and Employment: The Decline of the Male Breadwinner*. Oxford: Oxford University Press.

Crompton, R. (2002) 'Employment, flexible working and the family', *British Journal of Sociology*, 53(4): 537–58.

Crompton, R., Brockmann, M. and Lyonette, C. (2005) 'Attitudes, women's employment and the domestic division of labour: a cross-national analysis in two waves', *Work, Employment and Society*, 19(2): 213–34.

Crompton, R., Gallie, D. and Purcell, K. (eds) (1996) *Changing Forms of Employment: Organizations, Skills and Gender*. London: Routledge.

Crompton, R. and Harris, F. (1998) 'Explaining women's employment patterns: "orientations to work" revisited', *British Journal of Sociology*, 49(1): 118–36.

Crompton, R. and Harris, F. (1999) 'Attitudes, women's employment, and the changing domestic division of labour: a cross-national analysis', in R. Crompton (ed.), *Restructuring Gender Relations and Employment: The Decline of the Male Breadwinner*. Oxford: Oxford University Press, pp. 105–27.

Crompton, R. and Jones, G. (1984) *White Collar Proletariat: Deskilling and Gender in Clerical Work*. London: Macmillan.

Crompton, R. and Reid, S. (1982) 'The deskilling of clerical work', in S. Wood (ed.), *The Degradation of Work?: Skill, Deskilling and the Labour Process*. London: Hutchinson, pp. 163–78.

Crompton, R. and Sanderson, K. (1990) *Gendered Jobs and Social Change*. London: Unwin Hyman.

Crouch, C. (1999) *Social Change in Western Europe*. Oxford: Oxford University Press.

Curran, J. and Blackburn, R. (1991) 'Changes in the context of enterprise: some socio-economic and environmental factors facing small firms in the 1990s', in J. Curran and R. Blackburn (eds), *Paths of Enterprise: The Future of Small Business*. London: Routledge, pp. 163–92.

Cusumano, M. (1985) *The Japanese Automobile Industry: Technology and Management at Nissan and Toyota*. Cambridge, MA: Harvard University Press.

Cutler, T. (1978) 'The romance of "labour"', *Economy and Society*, 7(1): 74–95.

Dale, A. (1991) 'Self-employment and entrepreneurship: notes on two problematic concepts', in R. Burrows (ed.), *Deciphering the Enterprise Culture: Entrepreneurship, Petty Capitalism and the Restructuring of Britain*. London: Routledge, pp. 35–52.

Daniel, W. (1990) *The Unemployed Flow*. London: Policy Studies Institute.

Dassbach, C. (1991) 'The origins of Fordism: the introduction of mass production and the five-dollar day', *Critical Sociology*, 18(1): 77–90.

Davies, C. (1980) 'Making sense of the Census in Britain and the USA: the changing occupational classification and the position of nurses', *Sociological Review*, 28(3): 581–609.

Davies, C. and Rosser, J. (1986) 'Gendered jobs in the health service: a problem for labour process analysis', in D. Knights and H. Willmott (eds), *Gender and the Labour Process*. Aldershot: Gower, pp. 94–116.

D'Cruz, P. and Noronha, E. (2009) 'Experiencing depersonalized bullying: a study of Indian call centre agents', *Work, Organization, Labour and Globalization*, 3(1): 26–46.

Deakin, S. and Wilkinson, F. (1991) 'Social policy and economic efficiency: the deregulation of the labour market in Britain', *Critical Social Policy*, 11(33): 40–61.

Debrah, Y. and Smith, I. (eds) (2002) *Globalization, Employment and the Workplace: Diverse Impacts*. London: Routledge.

Deery, S. and Kinnie, N. (2004) 'Introduction: the nature and management of call centre work', in S. Deery and N. Kinnie (eds), *Call Centres and Human Resource Management: A Cross-National Perspective*. Basingstoke: Palgrave Macmillan, pp. 1–24.

Delsen, L. (1998) 'Where and why is part-time work growing in Europe?', in J. O'Reilly and C. Fagan (eds), *Part-time Prospects: An International Comparison of Part-time Work in Europe, North America and the Pacific Rim*. London: Routledge, pp. 57–76.

DeWitte, M. and Steijn, B. (2000) 'Automation, job content and underemployment', *Work, Employment and Society*, 14(2): 245–64.

Dex, S. (1985) *The Sexual Division of Work: Conceptual Revolutions in the Social Sciences*. Brighton: Harvester.

Dex, S., Willis, J., Peterson, R. and Sheppard, E. (2000) 'Freelance workers and contract uncertainty: the effects of contractual changes in the television industry', *Work, Employment and Society*, 14(2): 283–305.

Dicken, P. (2011) *Global Shift: Mapping the Changing Contours of the World Economy* (6th edn). London: Sage.

DiPietro, R. and Pizam, A. (2008) 'Employee alienation in the quick service restaurant industry', *Journal of Hospitality and Tourism Research*, 32(1): 22–39.

Doherty, M. (2009) 'When the working day is through: the end of work as identity?', *Work, Employment and Society*, 23(1): 84–101.

Dohse, K., Jürgens, U. and Malsch, T. (1985) 'From "Fordism" to "Toyotism"?: The social organization of the labour process in Japanese automobile industry', *Politics and Society*, 14(2): 115–46.

Doogan, K. (2009) *New Capitalism?: The Transformation of Work*. Cambridge: Polity Press.

Doray, B. (1988) *From Taylorism to Fordism: A Rational Madness*. London: Free Association Books.

Du Gay, P. (1996) *Consumption and Identity at Work*. London: Sage.

Durbin, S. and Tomlinson. J. (2010) 'Female part-time managers: networks and career mobility', *Work Employment and Society*, 24(4): 621–40.

Eardley, T. and Corden, A. (1994) 'Dependency or enterprise?: social security or self-employment', in S. Baldwin and J. Falkingham (eds), *Social Security and Social Change: New Challenges to the Beveridge Model*. Hemel Hempstead: Harvester Wheatsheaf, pp. 116–31.

Ecologist (2010) '"Fat tax" needed to tackle obesity', 4 March. www.theecologist.org/news.

Edgell, S. (1980) *Middle Class Couples: A Study of Segregation, Domination and Inequality in Marriage*. London: Allen and Unwin.

Edgell, S. (1993) *Class*. London: Routledge.

Edgell, S. (2001) *Veblen in Perspective: His Life and Thought*. New York: M.E. Sharpe.

Edgell, S. and Duke, V. (1991) *A Measure of Thatcherism: A Sociology of Britain*. London: HarperCollins.

Edwards, R. (1979) *Contested Terrain: The Transformation of the Workplace in the Twentieth Century*. London: Heinemann.

Ehrenreich, B. (2001) *Nickel and Dimed: On (Not) Getting by in America*. New York: Henry Holt.

Eichengreen, B. (1989) 'Unemployment and underemployment in historical perspective: introduction', *Institute of Industrial Relations, Working Paper Series*. Berkeley CA: University of California. http://respositories.cdlib.org/iirwps-018-89.

Elam, M. (1994) 'Puzzling out the post-Fordist debate: technology, markets and institutions', in A. Amin (ed.), *Post-Fordism: A Reader*. Oxford: Blackwell, pp. 43–70.

Eldridge, J. (1971) *Sociology and Industrial Life*. London: M. Joseph.

Elger, T. (1991) 'Task flexibility and the intensification of labour in UK manufacturing in the 1980s', in A. Pollert (ed.), *Farewell to Flexibility?* Oxford: Blackwell, pp. 46–66.

Elger, T. and Smith, C. (1994) 'Global Japanization? Convergence and competition in the organization of the labour process', in T. Elger and C. Smith (eds), *Global Japanization? The Transnational Transformation of the Labour Process*. London: Routledge, pp. 31–59.

Ellingsaeter, A. (1998) 'Dual breadwinner societies: provider models in Scandinavian welfare states', *Acta Sociologica*, 41(1): 59–73.

Epstein, C., Seron, C., Oglensky, B. and Saute, R. (1999) *The Part-time Paradox: Time Norms, Professional Life, Family and Gender*. New York: Routledge.

Ervasti, H. and Venetoklis, T. (2010) 'Unemployment and subjective well-being: an empirical test of deprivation theory, incentive paradigm and financial strain', *Acta Sociologica*, 53(2): 119–38.

Fagan, C. and O'Reilly, J. (1998) 'Conceptualising part-time work: the value of an integrated comparative perspective', in J. O'Reilly and C. Fagan (eds), *Part-time Prospects: An International Comparison of Part-time Work in Europe, North America and the Pacific Rim*. London: Routledge, pp. 1–31.

Fairbrother, P. and Yates, C. (2003) 'Unions in crisis, unions in renewal?', in P. Fairbrother and C.Yates (eds) *Trade Unions in Renewal*. London: Routledge, pp. 1–31.

Farr, J. (2000) *Artisans in Europe, 1300–1914*. Cambridge: Cambridge University Press.

Feldberg, R. and Glenn, E. (1979) 'Male and female: job versus gender models in the sociology of work', *Social Problems*, 26(5): 524–38.

Felstead, A. (1991) 'Franchising: a testimony to the "enterprise economy" and economic restructuring in the 1980s', in A. Pollert (ed.), *Farewell to Flexibility?* Oxford: Blackwell, pp. 215–38.

Felstead, A., Gallie, D. and Green, F. (2002) *Work Skills in Britain: 1986–2001*. Department of Education and Skills. London: HMSO.

Felstead, A. and Jewson, N. (1996) *Homeworkers in Britain*. London: HMSO.

Felstead, A. and Jewson, N. (1997) 'Researching a problematic concept: homeworkers in Britain', *Work, Employment and Society*, 11(2): 327–46.

Felstead, A. and Jewson, N. (eds) (1999) *Global Trends in Flexible Labour*. London: Macmillan.

Felstead, A. and Jewson, N. (2000) *In Work, At Home: Towards an Understanding of Homeworking*. London: Routledge.

Felstead, A., Jewson, N., Phizacklea, A. and Walters, S. (2001) 'Working at home: statistical evidence for seven key hypotheses', *Work, Employment and Society*, 15(2): 215–31.

Felstead, A., Jewson, N. and Walters, S. (2005) *Changing Places of Work*. Basingstoke: Palgrave Macmillan.

Fernie, S, and Metcalf, D. (1998) '(Not) Hanging on the telephone: payment systems in the new sweatshops', *Centre for Economic Performance, Discussion Paper 390*. London: LSE. www.cep.lse.ac.uk/pubs/download/dp0390.pdf.

Fevre, R. (1987) 'Subcontracting in steel', *Work, Employment and Society*, 1(4): 509–27.

Fevre, R. (1992) *The Sociology of Labour Markets*. London: Harvester Wheatsheaf.

Finch, J. (1983*) Married to the Job: Wives' Incorporation in Men's Work*. London: Allen and Unwin.

Fine, B. (1995) 'From political economy to consumption', in D. Miller (ed.), *Acknowledging Consumption: A Review of New Studies*. London: Routledge, pp. 127–63.

Fineman, S. (1983) *White Collar Unemployment: Impact and Stress*. Chichester: Wiley.

Finifter, A. (ed.) (1972) *Alienation and the Social System*. New York: Wiley.

Ford, H. (2008 [1922]) *My Life and Work*. BN Publishing.

Forde, C. (2001) 'Temporary arrangements: the activities of employment agencies in the UK', *Work, Employment and Society*, 15(3): 631–44.

Fox, A. (1966) *Industrial Sociology and Industrial Relations*. Research Paper 3, Royal Commission on Trade Unions and Employers' Associations. London: HMSO.

Frank, D. (2003) 'Where are the workers in consumer-worker alliances? Class dynamics and the history of consumer-labour campaigns', *Politics and Society*, 31(3): 363–79.

Freathy, P. and Sparks, L. (1992) 'Fordism and retailing: a note on the curious neglect of the Ford commissaries'. www.irs.stir.ac.uk/pdf/Working_papers/9203.pdf.

French, H. (2000) 'Pretending 9–5', *The Guardian*, 20 December.

Frenkel, S., Korczynski, M., Shire, K. and Tam, M. (1999) *On the Front Line: Organization of Work in the Informational Economy*. Ithaca, NY: Cornell University Press.

Friedman, A. (1977) *Industry and Labour: Class Struggle at Work and Monopoly Capitalism*. London: Macmillan.

Friedmann, G. (1955) *Industrial Society: The Emergence of the Human Problems of Automation*. Glencoe, IL: Free Press.

Fröbel, F., Heinrichs, J. and Kreye, O. (1980) *The New International Division of Labour: Structural Unemployment in Industrialized Countries and Industrialization in Developing Countries*. Cambridge: Cambridge University Press.

Fryer, D. and Payne, R. (1984) 'Proactive behaviour in unemployment: findings and implications', *Leisure Studies*, 3(3): 273–95.

Fuller, L. and Smith, V. (1991) 'Consumers' reports: management by customers in a changing economy', *Work, Employment and Society*, 5(1): 1–16.

Gabe, J., Calnan, M. and Bury, M. (eds) (1990) *The Sociology of the Health Service*. London: Routledge.

Galbraith, J. (1979) *Economics and the Public Purpose*. London: Penguin.

Gallie, D. (1978) *In Search of the New Working Class: Automation and Social Integration within the Capitalist Enterprise*. Cambridge: Cambridge University Press.

Gallie, D. (1991) 'Patterns of skill change: upskilling, deskilling or the polarization of skills?', *Work, Employment and Society*, 5(3): 319–51.

Gallie, D. (1994) 'Are the unemployed an underclass?: some evidence from the social change and economic life initiative', *Sociology*, 28(3): 737–58.

Gallie, D. (1996) 'Skill, gender and the quality of employment', in R. Crompton, D. Gallie, and K. Pursell (eds), *Changing Forms of Employment: Organizations, Skills and Gender*. London: Routledge, pp. 133–59.

Gallie, D., Marsh, C. and Vogler, C. (eds) (1994) *Social Change and the Experience of Unemployment*. Oxford: Oxford University Press.

Gallie, D. and Paugam, S. (eds) (2000) *Welfare Regimes and the Experience of Unemployment*. Oxford: Oxford University Press.

Gallie, D. and Vogler, C. (1994) 'Unemployment and attitudes to work', in D. Gallie, C. Marsh and C. Vogler (eds), *Social Change and the Experience of Unemployment*. Oxford: Oxford University Press, pp. 115–53.

Gallie, D., White, M., Cheng, Y. and Tomlinson, M. (1998) *Restructuring the Employment Relationship*. Oxford: Oxford University Press.

Gardner, C. and Sheppard, J. (1989) *Consuming Passions: The Rise of Retail Culture*. London: Unwin Hyman.

Gareis, K. (2010) 'Social impacts of ICT: comparison between Europe and other parts of the world', in Universität Siegen, Fachbereich Wirtschaftsinformatik und Neue Medien (eds), *Study on the Social Impact of ICT, Topic Report 3 (D7.2), Final Version*. Brussels:

European Commission. Downloadable from www.empirica.com/publikationen/publikationen_en.htm.

Garrahan, P. and Stewart, P. (1992) *The Nissan Enigma: Flexibility at Work in a Local Economy*. London: Routledge.

Garson, B. (1988) *The Electronic Sweatshop: How Computers are Transforming the Office of the Future into the Factory of the Past*. New York: Simon and Schuster.

Gartman, D. (1987) *Auto Slavery: The Labour Process in the American Automobile Industry, 1897–1950*. New Brunswick, NJ: Rutgers University Press.

Gatta, M., Boushey, H., and Appelbaum, E. (2009) 'High touch and here-to-stay: future skills demands in US low wage service occupations', *Sociology*, 43(5): 968–89.

Gavron, H. (1968) *The Captive Wife: Conflicts of Housebound Mothers*. London: Penguin.

Gershuny, J. (1994) 'The psychological consequences of unemployment: an assessment of the Jahoda thesis', in D. Gallie, C. Marsh and C. Vogler (eds), *Social Change and the Experience of Unemployment*. Oxford: Oxford University Press, pp. 213–30.

Gershuny, J. (2000) *Changing Times: Work and Leisure in Postindustrial Society*. Oxford: Oxford University Press.

Gershuny, J. (2004) 'Domestic equipment does not increase work: a response to Bittman, Rice and Wajcman', *British Journal of Sociology*, 55(3): 425–31.

Gershuny, J., Goodwin, M. and Jones, S. (1994) 'The domestic labour revolution: a process of lagged adaptation', in M. Anderson, F. Bechhofer and J. Gershuny (eds), *The Social and Political Economy of the Household*. Oxford: Oxford University Press, pp. 151–97.

Giddens, A. (1971) *Capitalism and Modern Social Theory: An Analysis of the Writings of Marx, Durkheim and Max Weber*. Cambridge: Cambridge University Press.

Giddens, A. (1973) *The Class Structure of Advanced Societies*. London: Hutchinson.

Giddens, A. (1997) *Sociology* (3rd edn). Cambridge: Polity.

Ginn, J. and Arber, S. (1998) 'How does part-time work lead to low pension income?', in J. O'Reilly and C. Fagan (eds), *Part-time Prospects: An International Comparison of Part-time Work in Europe, North America and the Pacific Rim*. London: Routledge, pp. 156–74.

Glatzer, W. and Burger, R. (1988) 'Household composition, social networks and household production', in R. Pahl (ed.), *On Work: Historical, Comparative and Theoretical Approaches*. Oxford: Blackwell, pp. 513–26.

Glazer, N. (1993) *Women's Paid and Unpaid Labour: The Work Transfer in Health Care and Retailing*. Philadelphia, PA: Temple University Press.

Glucksmann, M. (1990) *Women Assemble: Women Workers and the New Industries in Inter-War Britain*. London: Routledge.

Goldthorpe, J. (1966) 'Attitudes and behaviour of car assembly workers: a deviant case and a theoretical critique', *British Journal of Sociology*, 17(3): 227–44.

Goldthorpe, J., Lockwood, D., Bechhofer, R. and Platt, J. (1969) *The Affluent Worker and the Class Structure*. Cambridge: Cambridge University Press.

Goode, W. (1970) *World Revolution and Family Patterns*. New York: Free Press.

Gorz, A. (1999) *Reclaiming Work: Beyond the Wage-based Society*. Cambridge: Polity.

Gottfried, H. (1995) 'Developing neo-Fordism: a comparative perspective', *Critical Sociology*, 21(3): 39–70.

Gottfried, H. (2000) 'Compromising positions: emergent neo-Fordisms and embedded gender contracts', *British Journal of Sociology*, 51(2): 235–59.

Gottfried, H. and Graham, L. (1993) 'Constructing difference: the making of gendered subcultures in a Japanese automobile assembly plant', *Sociology*, 27(4): 611–28.

Gould, W. (2010) 'Working at MacDonald's: some redeeming features of McJobs', *Work, Employment and Society*, 24(4): 780–802.

Graham, L. (1995) *On the Line at Subaru-Isuzu: The Japanese Model and the American Worker*. Ithaca, NY: Cornell University Press.

Gramsci, A. (1971) *Selections from the Prison Notebooks of Antonio Gramsci*. Ed. and trans. Q. Hoare and G. Nowell Smith. London: Lawrence and Wishart.

Grandon, M. (2008) 'If you won a million you'd give up work, right? Don't bet on it', *The Guardian*, 3 March.

Granger, B., Stanworth, J. and Stanworth, C. (1995) 'Self-employment career dynamics: the case of "unemployment push" in UK book publishing', *Work, Employment and Society*, 9(3): 499–516.

Granovetter, M. (1985) 'Economic action and social structure: the problem of embeddedness', *American Journal of Sociology*, 91(3): 481–510.

Granter, E. (2009) *Critical Social Theory and the End of Work*, Farnham: Ashgate.

Gray, J. (1998) *False Dawn: The Dimensions of Global Capitalism*. London: Granta.

Greenwood, J. (1977) *Worker Sit-ins and Job Protection*. Farnborough: Gower.

Gregory, A. and Milner, S. (2008) 'Fatherhood regimes and father involvement in France and the UK', *Community, Work and Family*, 11(1): 61–84.

Gregory, A. and Windebank, J. (2000) *Women's Work in Britain and France: Practice, Theory and Policy*. London: Macmillan.

Gregson, N. and Lowe, M. (1994) *Servicing the Middle Classes: Class, Gender and Waged Domestic Labour in Contemporary Britain*. London: Routledge.

Gregson, N. and Lowe, M. (1995) '"Too much work?": Class, gender and the reconstruction of middle-class domestic labour', in T. Butler and M. Savage (eds), *Social Change and the Middle Class*. London: UCL Press, pp. 148–65.

Griffin, R., Hill, C., Perfect, D., Smith, A., Speed, L. and Symmonds, T. (1998) *Social Focus on Women and Men*. London: HMSO.

Grint, K. and Woolgar, S. (1997) *The Machine at Work: Technology, Work, and Organization*. Cambridge: Polity.

Grugulis, I., Bozkurt, O. and Clegg, J. (2010) 'No place to hide? The realities in UK supermarkets', *Skope Research Paper No. 91*. www.skope.ox.ac.uk.

Gruneberg, M. (1979) *Understanding Job Satisfaction*. London: Macmillan.

Guardian (1988) 'Remote control on the High Street', *Guardian*, 2 June.

Guardian (2002) 'Deadline set for cutting working hours', *Guardian*, 6 February.

Guardian (2010) 14 September.

Habermas. J. (1971*) Legitimation Crisis*. London: Heinemann.

Hakim, C. (1980) 'Census reports as documentary evidence: the Census commentaries 1801–1951', *Sociological Review*, 28(3): 551–80.

Hakim, C. (1982) 'The social consequences of high unemployment', *Journal of Social Policy*, 11(4): 433–67.

Hakim, C. (1988) 'Self-employment in Britain: a review of recent trends and current issues', *Work, Employment and Society*, 2(4): 421–50.

Hakim, C. (1991) 'Grateful slaves and self-made women: fact and fantasy in women's work orientations', *European Sociological Review*, 7(2): 101–21.

Hakim, C. (1996) *Key Issues in Women's Work: Female Heterogeneity and the Polarization of Women's Employment*. London: Athlone.

Hakim, C. (2000) *Work–Lifestyle Choices in the 21st Century: Preference Theory*. Oxford: Oxford University Press.

Hakim, C. (2003) 'Public morality versus personal choice: the failure of social attitude surveys', *British Journal of Sociology*, 53(3): 339–45.

Hall, R. (1994) *Sociology of Work: Perspectives, Analyses and Issues*. Thousand Oaks, CA: Pine Forge Press.

Hammersley, B. (2000) 'World's workers united', *The Times*, 7 February.

Handel, M. (2005) 'Trends in perceived job quality, 1989 to 1998', *Work and Occupations*, 32(1): 66–94.

Hardill, I., Green, A., Dudleston, A. and Owen, D. (1997) 'Who decides what?: Decision making in dual-career household', *Work, Employment and Society*, 11(2): 313–26.

Harrison, B. (1997) *Lean and Mean: The Changing Landscape of Corporate Power in the Age of Flexibility*. New York: Guilford Press.

Harrison, R. and Zeitlin, J. (eds) (1985) *Divisions of Labour: Skilled Workers and Technological Change in Nineteenth Century Britain*. Brighton: Harvester.

Harkness, S. (2008) 'The household division of labour: changes in families' allocation of paid and unpaid work', in J. Scott, S. Dex and H. Joshi (eds), *Women and Employment: Changing Lives and New Challenges*. Cheltenham: Edward Elgar, pp. 234–67.

Hartmann, H. (1979) 'The unhappy marriage of Marxism and Feminism: towards a more progressive union', *Capital and Class*, 8: 1–33.

Harvey, D. (1989) *The Condition of Postmodernity*. Oxford: Blackwell.

Harvey, M. (1999) 'Economics of time: a framework for analysing the restructuring of employment relations', in A. Felstead and N. Jewson (eds), *Global Trends in Flexible Labour*. London: Macmillan, pp. 21–41.

Hawarth, J. (1997) *Work, Leisure and Well-being*. London: Routledge.

Head, S. (2005) *The New Ruthless Economy: Work and Power in the Digital Age*. Oxford: Oxford University Press.

Heckley, G. (2005) 'Offshoring and the labour market: the IT and call centre occupations considered', *Labour Market Trends*, September, pp. 373–85. www.statistics.gov.uk/articles/labour_market_trends/offshoring_sept05.

Heckscher, C. (1994) 'Defining the post-bureaucratic type', in C. Heckscher and A. Donnellon (eds) *The Post-Bureaucratic Organization: New Perspectives on Organizational Change*. London: Sage, pp. 14–62.

Heckscher, C and Donnellon, A. (1994) 'Introduction', in C. Heckscher and A. Donnellon (eds), *The Post-Bureaucratic Organization: New Perspectives on Organizational Change*. London: Sage, pp 1–13.

Heery, E. and Salmon, J. (eds) (2000) *The Insecure Workforce*. London: Routledge.

Held, D., McGrew, A., Goldblatt, D. and Perration, J. (1999) *Global Transformations: Politics, Economics and Culture*. Cambridge: Polity.

Hill, C. (1971) *British Economic and Social History 1700–1964* (3rd edn). London: Edward Arnold.

Hill, S. (1981) *Competition and Control at Work*. London: Heinemann.

Hilton, G.W. (1960) *The Truck System, Including a History of the British Truck Acts, 1465–1960*. Westport, CT: Greenwood Press.

Hines, P. (2009) 'Create a winning formula for your organization through lean', *Guardian* (Insert), September, p. 2.

Hirst, P. and Thompson, G. (1996) *Globalization in Question: The International Economy and Possibilities of Governance*. Cambridge: Polity.

Hobsbawm, E. (1969) *Industry and Empire*. London: Penguin.

Hochschild, A. (1990) *The Second Shift: Working Parents and the Revolution in the Home*. London: Piatkus.

Hochschild, A. (2000) 'Global care chains and emotional surplus value', in W. Hutton and A. Giddens (eds) *On the Edge: Living with Global Capitalism*. London: Jonathan Cape, pp. 130–46.

Hochschild, A. (2003 [1983]) *The Managed Heart: Commercialization of Human Feeling*. Berkeley, CA: University of California Press.

Hodson, R. (1996) 'Dignity in the workplace under participative management: alienation and freedom revisited', *American Sociological Review*, 61(5): 719–38.

Horrell, S. (1994) 'Household time allocation and women's labour force participation', in M. Anderson, F. Bechhofer and J. Gershuny (eds), *The Social and Political Economy of the Household*. Oxford: Oxford University Press, pp. 198–224.

Horrell, S., Rubery, J. and Burchell, B. (1994) 'Working-time patterns, constraints and preferences', in M. Anderson, F. Bechhofer and J. Gershuny (eds), *The Social and Political Economy of the Household*. Oxford: Oxford University Press, pp. 100–32.

Houlihan, M. (2004) 'Tensions and variations in call centre management strategies', in S. Deery and N. Kinnie (eds), *Call Centres and Human Resource Management: A Cross-National Perspective*. Basingstoke: Palgrave Macmillan, pp. 75–101.

Hounshell, D. (1984) *The American System of Mass Production 1800–1932: The Development of Manufacturing Technology in the United States*, Baltimore, MD: Johns Hopkins University Press.

Houseman, S. and Osawa, M. (1998) 'What is the nature of part-time work in the United States and Japan?', in J. O'Reilly and C. Fagan (eds), *Part-time Prospects: An International Comparison of Part-time Work in Europe, North America and the Pacific Rim*. London: Routledge, pp. 232–51.

Hudson, P. and Lee, W. (1990) *Women's Work and the Family Economy in Historical Perspective*. Manchester: Manchester University Press.

Hull, F., Friedman, N. and Rogers, T. (1982) 'The effect of technology on alienation from work: testing Blauner's inverted U-curve hypothesis for 110 industrial organizations and 245 retrained printers', *Work and Occupations*, 9(1): 31–57.

Hutson, S. and Jenkins, R. (1989) *Taking the Strain: Families, Unemployment and the Transition to Adulthood*. Milton Keynes: Open University Press.

Huws, U. (2009) 'Working at the interface: call-centre labour in a global economy', *Work, Organization, Labour and Globalization*, 3(1): 1–25.

Hytrek, G. and Zentgraf, K. (2008) *America Transformed: Globalization, Inequality and Power*. Oxford: Oxford University Press.

Ingold, T. (1995) 'Work, time and industry', *Time and Society*, 4(1): 5–28.

Irwin, S. (1995) 'Social reproduction and change in the transition from youth to adulthood', *Sociology*, 29(2): 293–315.

Jacobs, J. (1995) 'Lean production and training: The case of a Japanese supplier firm', in S. Babson (ed.), *Lean Work: Empowerment and Exploitation in the Global Auto Industry*, Detroit: Wayne State University Press, pp. 311–25.

Jahoda, M. (1981) 'Work, employment, and unemployment: values, theories, and approaches in social research', *American Psychologist*, 36(2): 184–91.

Jahoda, M. (1982) *Employment and Unemployment: A Social-Psychological Analysis*. Cambridge: Cambridge University Press.

Jahoda, M. (1984) 'Social institutions and human needs: a comment on Fryer and Payne', *Leisure Studies*, 3(3): 297–99.

Jahoda, M., Lazarsfeld, P.F. and Zeisel, H. (1974 [1933]) *Marienthal: The Sociography of an Unemployed Community*. London: Tavistock.

Janssens, A. (1997) 'The rise and decline of the male breadwinner family? An overview of the debate', *International Review of Social History*, Suppl. 5, 41: 1–23.

Jessop, B. (1994) 'Post-Fordism and the state', in A. Amin (ed.), *Post-Fordism: A Reader*. Oxford: Blackwell, pp. 251–79.

Jones, A. (2004) *Review of Gap Year Provision*. Department of Education and Skills, Research Report 555. London: HMSO.

Jordan, B. (1982) *Mass Unemployment and the Future of Britain*. Oxford: Blackwell.

Joyce, P. (1982) *Work, Society and Politics*. London: Methuen.

Jürgens, U. (1992) 'The transfer of Japanese management concepts in the international automobile industry', in S. Wood (ed.), *The Transformation of Work? Skill, Flexibility and the Labour Process*. London: Routledge, pp. 204–18.

Kalleberg, A.L., Reskin, B.F. and Hudson, K. (2000) 'Bad jobs in America: standard and nonstandard employment relations and job quality in the United States', *American Sociological Review*, 65(2): 256–78.

Kamata, S. (1984) *Japan in the Passing Lane: An Insider's Account of Life in a Japanese Auto Factory*. London: Unwin.

Kan, M. (2007) 'Work orientation and wives' employment careers: an evaluation of Hakim's preference theory', *Work and Occupations*, 34(4): 430–62.

Kan, M. (2008) 'The relationship between work and home: does gender trump money?: Housework hours of husbands and wives in Britain', *Work, Employment and Society*, 22(1): 45–66.

Katz, C. (2001) 'On the grounds of globalization: a topography for feminist political engagement', *Signs*, 26(4): 1213–34.

Keat, R. and Abercrombie, N. (eds) (1991) *Enterprise Culture*. London: Routledge.

Keating, E. (2008) *The Financial Services Call Centre Sector in the North West and an Analysis of the Skills Needs*. Manchester: North West Universities Association. www.nwua.ac.uk/HLSP/docs/Financial_Services_Call_Centre_paper_Jan08.pdf.

Kellner, D. (1999) 'Theorizing/resisting McDonaldization: a multiperspectivist approach', in B. Smart (ed.), *Resisting McDonaldization*. London: Sage, pp. 186–206.

Kelvin, P. and Jarrett, J. (1985) *Unemployment: Its Social and Psychological Effects*. Cambridge: Cambridge University Press.

Kennedy, P. (2010) *Local Lives and Global Transformations: Towards World Society*. Basingstoke: Palgrave Macmillan.

Kenney, M. and Florida, R. (1988) 'Beyond mass production: production and the labour process in Japan', *Politics and Society*, 16(1): 121–58.

Kenney, M. and Florida, R. (1993) *Beyond Mass Production: The Japanese System and Its Transfer to the US*. Oxford: Oxford University Press.

Kiely, R. (2005) *Empire in the Age of Globalization: US Hegemony and Neo-liberal Disorder*. London: Pluto Press

Kilpern, K. (2001) 'A call for change', *The Guardian*, 19 February.

Kirk, N. (1994) *Labour and Society in Britain and the USA, Vol. 1, Capitalism, Custom and Protest, 1780–1850*. Aldershot: Scolar Press.

Klein, N. (2000) *No Logo*. London: Flamingo.

Kodres, L. and Narain, A. (2009) 'What is to be done?', *Finance and Development*, 46(1): 23–6. www.imf.org/fandd.

Korczynski, M. (2009) 'The mystery customer: continuing absences in the sociology of service work', *Sociology*, 43(5): 952–67.

Korczynski, M and Macdonald, C. (eds) (2009) *Service Work: Critical Perspectives*. London: Routledge.

Korczynski, M., Shire, K., Frenkel, S. and Tam, M. (2000) 'Service work in consumer capitalism: customers, control and contradictions', *Work, Employment and Society*, 14(4): 669–87.

Kumar, K. (1978) *Prophecy and Progress: The Sociology of Industrial and Post-Industrial Society*. London: Penguin.

Kumar, K. (1988a) *The Rise of Modern Society: Aspects of the Social and Political Development of the West*. Oxford: Blackwell.

Kumar, K. (1988b) 'From work to employment and unemployment', in R. Pahl (ed.), *On Work: Historical, Comparative and Theoretical Perspectives*. Oxford: Blackwell, pp. 138–64.

Kumar, K. (1995) *From Post-Industrial to Post-Modern Society: New Theories of the Contemporary World*. Oxford: Blackwell.

Kyotani, E. (1999) 'New managerial strategies of Japanese corporations', in A. Felstead and N. Jewson, (eds), *Global Trends in Flexible Labour*. London: Macmillan, pp. 181–97.

Land, H. (1980) 'The family wage', *Feminist Review*, 6: 55–77.

Lash, S. and Urry, J. (1994) *Economies of Signs and Space*. London: Sage.

Layte, R., Levin, H., Hendrickx, J. and Bison, I. (2000) 'Unemployment and cumulative disadvantage in the labour market', in D. Gallie and S. Paugam (eds), *Welfare Regimes and the Experience of Unemployment in Europe*. Oxford: Oxford University Press, pp. 153–74.

Layton, E. (1971) *The Revolt of the Engineers*. Cleveland, OH: The Press of Case Western Reserve University.

Leadbeater, C. (1997) *The Rise of Social Entrepreneurialism*. London: Demos.

Lee, D. (1981) 'Skill, craft and class: a theoretical critique and critical case', *Sociology*, 15 (1): 56–78.

Leidner, R. (1993) *Fast Food, Fast Talk: Service Work and the Routinization of Everyday Life*. Berkeley, CA: University of California Press.

Leidner, R. (1996) 'Rethinking questions of control: lessons from McDonald's', in C.L. MacDonald and C. Sirianni (eds), *Working in the Service Society*. Philadelphia: Temple University Press, pp. 29–49.

Leidner, R. (2002) 'Fast-food work in the United States', in T. Royle and B. Towers (eds), *Labour Relations in the Global Fast-Food Industry*. London: Routledge, pp. 8–29.

Leiter, J. (1985) 'Work alienation in the textile industry: reassessing Blauner', *Work and Occupations*, 12(4): 479–99.

Letkemann, P. (2002) 'Unemployed professionals, stigma management and derived stigmata', *Work, Employment and Society*, 16(3): 511–22.

Levinson, W. (2002) *Henry Ford's Lean Vision: Enduring Principles from the First Ford Motor Plant*. New York: Productivity Press.

Levitt, T. (1972) 'The production-line approach to service', *Harvard Business Review*, 50: 41–52.

Lewchuk, W. (1989) 'Fordist Technology and Britain: The Diffusion of Labour Speed-up', *Warwick Economic Research Papers*, No. 340.

Lewchuk, W. (1995) 'Men and mass production: the role of gender in managerial strategies in the British and American automobile industries', in H. Shiomi and K. Wada (eds), *Fordism Transformed: The Development of Production Methods in the Automobile Industry*. Oxford: Oxford University Press, pp. 219–42.

Lewchuk, W. and Robertson, D. (1997) 'Production without empowerment: work reorganization from the perspective of motor vehicle workers', *Capital and Class*, 63: 37–64.

Lewenhak, S. (1980) *Women and Work*. Glasgow: Fontana.

Lewis, J. (1992) 'Gender and the development of welfare regimes', *Journal of European Social Policy*, 2(3): 159–73.

Lipietz, A. (1992) *Towards a New Economic Order: Postfordism, Ecology, and Democracy*. Cambridge: Polity.

Lipietz, A. (1994) 'Post-Fordism and democracy', in A. Amin (ed.), *Post-Fordism: A Reader*. Oxford: Blackwell, pp. 338–57.

Littler, C. (1982) *The Development of the Labour Process in Capitalist Societies*. Aldershot: Gower.

Littler, C. and Salaman, G, (1982) 'Bravermania and beyond: recent theories of the labour process', *Sociology*, 16(2): 251–69.

Littler, C. and Salaman, G. (1984) *Class at Work: The Design, Allocation and Control of Jobs*. London: Batsford.

Lopata, H. (1972) *Occupation: Housewife*. Oxford: Oxford University Press.

Love, J. (1995) *McDonald's: Behind the Arches* (revised edn). New York: Bantam.

Lown, J. (1990) *Women and Industrialization: Gender and Work in Nineteenth-century England*. Cambridge: Polity.

Luo, T., Mann, A. and Holden, R. (2010) 'The expanding role of temporary help services', *Monthly Review Online*, 133(8): 3–16.

Macdonald, C. (1996) 'Shadow mothers: nannies, au pairs, and invisible work', in C. Macdonald and C. Sirianni (eds) *Working in the Service Society*. New York: Henry Holt, pp. 244–63.

Macdonald, C. and Sirianni, C. (eds) (1996) *Working in the Service Society*. Philadelphia: Temple University Press.

MacDonald, K. (1995) *The Sociology of the Professions*. London: Sage.

MacDonald, R. (1996) 'Welfare dependency, the enterprise culture and self-employed survival', *Work, Employment and Society*, 10(3): 431–47.

MacDuffie, J. (1995) 'Workers' roles in lean production: the implications for worker representation', in S. Babson (ed.), *Lean Work: Empowerment and Exploitation in the Global Auto Industry*. Detroit: Wayne State University Press, pp. 54–69.

MacInnes, J. (1987) *Thatcherism at Work: Industrial Relations and Economic Change*. Milton Keynes: Open University Press.

Macionis, J. (2001) *Sociology* (8th edn). Upper Saddle River, NJ: Prentice-Hall.

MacKenzie, D. and Wajcman, J. (eds) (1999) *The Social Shaping of Technology* (2nd edn). Milton Keynes: Open University Press.

Mackenzie, G. (1977) 'The political economy of the American working class', *British Journal of Sociology*, 28(2): 244–52.

MacRaild, D. and Martin, D. (2000) *Labour in British Society, 1830–1914*. Basingstoke: Macmillan.

Maguire, K. (2003) 'Nissan factory staff ballot strike?', *Guardian*, 18 November.

Mair, A. (1994) *Honda's Global Local Corporation*. London: Macmillan.

Malcolmson, R. (1988) 'Ways of getting a living in eighteenth-century England', in R. Pahl (ed.), *On Work: Historical, Comparative and Theoretical Approaches*. Oxford: Blackwell, pp. 48–60.

Malenfant, R., LaRue, A. and Vezina, M. (2007) 'Intermittent work and well-being: one foot in the door, one foot out', *Work and Occupations*, 55(6): 814–35.

Mann, M. (1986) 'Work and the work ethic', in R. Jowell, S. Witherspoon and L. Brook (eds), *British Social Attitudes: The 1986 Report*. Aldershot: Gower, pp. 17–38.

Marglin, S. (1980) 'The origins and functions of hierarchy in capitalist production', in T. Nichols (ed.), *Capital and Labour: A Marxist Primer*. Glasgow: Fontana, pp. 237–54.

Marr, K. (2009) 'Toyota passes General Motors as world's largest carmaker', *Washington Post*.

Marsden, D. (1982) *Workless: An Exploration of the Social Contract between Society and the Worker* (revised and enlarged edn). London: Croom Helm.

Marshall, G. (1984) 'On the significance of women's unemployment: its neglect and significance', *Sociological Review*, 32(2): 234–59.

Martin, J. and Roberts, C. (1984) *Women and Employment: A Lifetime Perspective*. London: HMSO.

Marx, K. (1970 [1887]) *Capital*, Vol. 1. London: Lawrence and Wishart.

Marx, K. (1970 [1959]) *Economic and Philosophical Manuscripts of 1844*. London: Lawrence and Wishart.

Marx, K. (1973 [1857–58]) *Grundrisse: Foundations of the Critique of Political Economy*. London: Penguin.

Marx, K. and Engels, F. (1962 [1845]) *On Britain* (2nd edn). Moscow: Foreign Languages Publishing House.

Marx, K. and Engels, F. (n.d. [1848]) *Manifesto of the Communist Party*. Moscow: Foreign languages Publishing House.

Matsunaga, L. (2000) *The Changing Face of Japanese Retail: Working in a Chain Store*. London: Routledge.

McGovern, P., Smeaton, D. and Hill, S. (2004) 'Bad jobs in Britain: non-standard employment and job quality', *Work and Occupations*, 31(2): 225–49.

McGrath, D. and Keister, L. (2008) 'The effect of temporary employment on asset accumulation process', *Work and Occupations*, 35(2): 196–222.

McIntosh, I. (1995) '"It was worse than Alcatraz": working for Ford in Trafford Park', *Manchester Regional History Review*, 9: 66–76.

McIvor, A. (2001) *A History of Work in Britain, 1880–1950*. Basingstoke: Palgrave.

McOrmond, T. (2004) 'Changes in working conditions over the past decade', *Labour Market Trends*, 112(1): 25–36.

McRae, S. (1989) *Flexible Working Time and Family Life: A Review of Changes*. London: Policy Studies Institute.

McRae, S. (2003) 'Constraints and choices in mothers' employment careers: a consideration of Hakim's preference theory', *British Journal of Sociology*, 54(3): 317–38.

Mellor, M., Hannah, J. and Stirling, J. (1988) *Worker Co-operatives in Theory and Practice*. Milton Keynes: Open University Press.

Merton, R. (1957) *Social Theory and Social Structure*. New York: Free Press.

Meszaros, I. (1970) *Marx's Theory of Alienation*. London: Merlin.

Meyer, S. (1981) *The Five Dollar Day: Labour Management and Social Control in the Ford Motor Company, 1908–1921*. Albany, NY: State University of New York Press.

Meyer, S. (2004) 'The degradation of work revisited: workers and technology in the American Auto Industry, 1900–2000'. www.autolife.umd.umich.edu.

Milkman, R. and Pullman, C. (1991) 'Technological change in an auto assembly plant: the impact on workers' tasks and skills', *Work and Occupations*, 18(2): 123–47.

Mills, C. (1968 [1951]) *White Collar: The American Middle Classes*. Oxford: Oxford University Press.

Milner, M. (2009) 'BMW accused of "scandalous opportunism" after scrapping 850 jobs at Mini factory', *Guardian*, 17 February.

Mirchandani, K. (2004) 'Practices of global capital: gaps, cracks and ironies in transnational call centres in India', *Global Networks*, 4(4): 355–74.

Mitchell, W. (1970 [1913]) *Business Cycles*. New York: Burt Franklin.

Montgomery, D. (1979) *Workers' Control in America: Studies in the History of Work, Technology and Labour Struggles*. Cambridge: Cambridge University Press.

Montgomery, D. (1987) *The Fall of the House of Labour: The Workplace, the State, and American Labour Activism, 1865–1925*. Cambridge: Cambridge University Press.

Morris, L. (1990) *The Workings of the Household: A US–UK Comparison*. Cambridge: Polity.

Morris, L. (1995) *Social Divisions: Economic Decline and Social Stratification*. London: UCL Press.

Morris, S. (2008) 'When the coal finally ran out', *Guardian*, 28 January.

Muehlberger, U. (2007) *Dependent Self-Employment: Workers on the Border between Employment and Self-Employment*. Basingstoke: Palgrave McMillan.

Mueller, F., Valsecchi, R., Smith, C., Gabe, J. and Elston, M. (2008) '"We are nurses, we are supposed to care for people": professional values among nurses in NHS Direct call centres', *New Technology, Work and Employment*, 23(1): 2–16.

Mulholland, K. (2004) 'Workplace resistance in an Irish call centre: "slammin", "scammin" "smoking" and "leavin"', *Work, Employment and Society*, 18(4): 709–24.

Mumford, L. (1934) *Technics and Civilization*. New York: Harcourt, Brace & World.

Murakami, T. (1997) 'The anatomy of teams in the car industry: a cross national comparison', *Work, Employment and Society*, 11(4): 749–58.

Mythen, G. (2004) *Ulrich Beck: A Critical Introduction to the Risk Society*. London: Pluto.

Nichols, T. and Beynon, H. (1977) *Living with Capitalism: Class Relations and the Modern Factory*. London: Routledge and Kegan Paul.

Nisbet, P. (1997) 'Dualism, flexibility and self-employment in the UK construction industry', *Work, Employment and Society*, 11(3): 459–79.

Nolan, P. and Lenski, G. (1999) *Human Societies: An Introduction to Macrosociology* (8th edn). New York: McGraw-Hill.

Nyman, C. (1999) 'Gender equality in "the most equal country in the world"? Money and marriage in Sweden', *Sociological Review*, 47(4): 766–93.

Oakley, A. (1974) *The Sociology of Housework*. Oxford: Martin Robertson.

Oakley, A. (1976) *Housewife*. London: Penguin.

Oakley, R. (1991) 'Government policy towards high technology: small firms beyond the year 2000', in J. Curran and R. Blackburn (eds), *Paths of Enterprise: The Future of Small Businesses*, London: Routledge, pp. 128–48.

O'Connor, D, (2003) 'Of flying geeks and O-Rings: locating software and IT services in India's economic development', *OECD Working Paper No. 224*. Paris: OECD. www.oecd.org/dataoecd/58/12/20503882.pdf.

OECD (2002) *Employment Outlook*. Paris: OECD.

OECD (2010) *Factbook: Economic, Environmental and Social Statistics*. Paris: OECD.

Oesch, D. (2010) 'What explains high unemployment among low-skilled workers?: Evidence from 21 OECD countries', *European Journal of Industrial Relations*, 18(1): 39–55.

Offe, C. (1985) 'Work: the key sociological category?' in C. Offe, *Disorganized Capitalism*, Cambridge Polity, pp. 129–50.

Ohno, T. (1988) *Toyota Production System: Beyond Large-scale Production*. Cambridge, MA: Productivity Press.

Ollman, B. (1971) *Alienation: Marx's Conception of Man in Capitalist Society*. Cambridge: Cambridge University Press.

O'Reilly, J. and Fagan, C. (eds) (1998) *Part-time Prospects: An International Comparison of Part-time Work in Europe, North America and the Pacific Rim*. London: Routledge.

Osborne, D. and Gaebler, T. (1992) *Reinventing Government: How the Entrepreneurial Spirit is Transforming the Public Sector*. Reading, MA: Addison-Wesley.

Pahl, J. (1989) *Money and Marriage*. London: Macmillan.

Pahl, R. (1984) *Divisions of Labour*. Oxford: Blackwell.

Pardi, T. (2007) 'Redefining the Toyota Production System: the European side of the story', *New Technology, Work & Employment*, 22(1): 2–20.

Parker, M. and Slaughter, J. (1990) 'Management by stress: the team concept in the US auto industry', *Science as Culture*, 8: 27–58.

Parker, M. and Slaughter, J. (1995) 'Unions and management by stress', in S. Babson (ed.), *Lean Work: Empowerment and Exploitation in the Global Auto Industry*. Detroit: Wayne State University Press, pp. 41–53.

Pascall, G. and Lewis, J. (2004) 'Emerging gender regimes and policies for gender equality in a wider Europe', *Journal of Social Policy*, 33(3): 373–94.

Patel, R. (2010) *Working the Night Shift: Women in India's Call Centre Industry*. Stanford, CA: Stanford University Press.

Paugam, S. and Zhou, Y. (2007) 'Job insecurity', in D. Gallie (ed.) *Employment Regimes and the Quality of Work*. Oxford: Oxford University Press, pp. 179–204.

Paul, K. and Batinic, B. (2010) 'The need for work: Jahoda's latent functions of employment in a representative sample of the German population', *Journal of Organizational Behaviour*, 31(1): 45–64.

Peck, J. and Theodore, N. (1998) 'The business of contingent work: growth and restructuring in Chicago's temporary employment industry', *Work, Employment and Society*, 12(4): 655–74.

Peck, J. and Tickell, A. (1994) 'Searching for a new institutional fix: the after-Fordist crisis and the global–local disorder', in A. Amin (ed.), *Post-Fordism: A Reader*. Oxford: Blackwell, pp. 280–315.

Penn, R. (1983) 'Theories of skill and the class structure', *Sociological Review*, 31(1): 22–38.

Penn, R. (1990) *Class, Power and Technology: Skilled Workers in Britain and America*. Cambridge: Polity.

Penn, R., Rose, M. and Rubery, J. (eds) (1994) *Skill and Occupational Change*. Oxford: Oxford University Press.

Pennington, S. and Westover, B. (1989) *A Hidden Workforce: Homeworkers in England, 1850–1985*. London: Macmillan.

Pfau-Effinger, B. (1993) 'Modernization, culture and part-time employment: the example of Finland and West Germany', *Work, Employment and Society*, 7(3): 383–410.

Pfau-Effinger, B. (2004) 'Socio-historical paths to the male breadwinner model – an explanation of cross-national differences', *British Journal of Sociology*, 55(3): 377–99.

Phillips, A. and Taylor, B. (1980) 'Sex and skill: notes towards a feminist economics', *Feminist Review*, 6: 79–88.

Phizacklea, A. and Ram, M. (1996) 'Being your own boss: ethnic entrepreneurs in comparative perspective', *Work, Employment and Society*, 10(2): 319–39.

Picchio, A. (ed.) (2003) *Unpaid Work and the Economy: A Gender Analysis of the Standard of Living*. London: Routledge.

Pinchbeck, I. (1969 [1930]) *Women and the Industrial Revolution, 1750–1880*. London: Frank Cass.

Pine, B. (1993) *Mass Customization: The New Frontier in Business Competition*. Boston: Harvard Business School Press.

Piore, M. and Sabel, C. (1984) *The Second Industrial Divide*. New York: Basic Books.

Piven, F. and Cloward, R. (1974) *Regulating the Poor: The Functions of Public Welfare*. London: Tavistock.

Plantenga, J. (2002) 'Combining work and care in the polder model: an assessment of the Dutch part-time strategy', *Critical Social Policy*, 22(1): 53–71.

Platt, S. (1986) 'Recent trends in parasuicide ("attempted suicide") and unemployment among men in Edinburgh', in S. Allen, A. Waton, K. Purcell and S. Wood (eds), *The Experience of Unemployment*. London: Macmillan, pp. 150–67.

Pollert, A. (1988) 'The "flexible firm": fiction or fact?', *Work, Employment and Society*, 2(3): 281–316.

Price, J. (1995) 'Lean production at Suzuki and Toyota: a historical perspective', in S. Babson (ed.) *Lean Work: Empowerment and Exploitation in the Global Auto Industry*. Detroit: Wayne State University Press, pp. 81–107.

Purcell, K. (2000) 'Gendered employment insecurity?', in E. Heery and J. Salmon (eds), *The Insecure Workforce*. London: Routledge, pp. 112–39.

Pyoria, P. (2003) 'Knowledge work in distributed environments: issues and illusions', *New Technology, Work and Employment*, 18(3): 166–80.

Rainbird, H. (1991) 'Small entrepreneurs or disguised wage labourers?', in A. Pollert (ed.), *Farewell to Flexibility?* Oxford: Blackwell, pp. 200–14.

Ransome, P. (1996) *The Work Paradigm: A Theoretical Investigation of Concepts of Work*. Aldershot: Avebury.

Reed, M. (1996) 'Expert power and control in late modernity: an empirical review and theoretical synthesis', *Organization Studies*, 17(4): 573–97.

Reich, R. (1991) *The Work of Nations: Preparing Ourselves for the 21st Century.* New York: Knopf.

Reid, A. (2005) *United We Stand: A History of Britain's Trade Unions.* London: Penguin.

Reid, D. (1976) 'The decline of Saint Monday 1766–1876', *Past and Present*, 71: 76–101.

Rendall, J. (1990) *Women in an Industrializing Society: England 1750–1880.* Oxford: Blackwell.

Rhode, S. (2002/03) *The History of Credit and Debt.* Myvesta, A Nonprofit Consumer Education Organization. www.dca.org/history_installment.htm.

Richards, E. (1974) 'Women in the British economy since about 1770: an interpretation', *History*, 59: 337–57.

Ridyard, D., Jones, I. and Foster, R. (1989) 'Economic evaluation of the loan guarantee scheme', *Employment Gazette*, August: 417–21.

Rieder, K., Matuschek, I. and Anderson, P. (2002) 'Co-production in call centres: the workers' and customers' contribution', in U. Holtgrewe, C. Kerst and K. Shire (eds), *Re-Organizing Service Work: Call Centres in Germany and Britain.* Aldershot: Ashgate, pp. 204–27.

Rinehart, J., Huxley, C. and Robertson, D. (1995) 'Team concept at CAMI', in S. Babson (ed.), *Lean Work: Empowerment and Exploitation in the Global Auto Industry.* Detroit: Wayne State University Press, pp. 220–34.

Rinehart, J., Huxley, C. and Robertson, D. (1997) *Just Another Factory? Lean Production and Its Discontents.* Ithaca, NY: Cornell University Press.

Rinehart, J., Robertson, D., Huxley, C. and Wareham, J. (1994) 'Reunifying conception and execution of work under Japanese production management? A Canadian case study', in T. Elger and C. Smith (eds), *Global Japanization? The Transformation of the Labour Process.* London: Routledge, pp. 152–74.

Ritzer, G. (1996) *The McDonaldization of Society: An Investigation into the Changing Character of Contemporary Social Life* (revised edn). Thousand Oaks, CA: Pine Forge Press.

Ritzer, G. (1998) *The McDonaldization Thesis: Explorations and Extensions.* London: Sage.

Ritzer, G. and Stillman, T. (2001) 'From person- to system-oriented service', in A. Sturdy, I. Grugulis, and H. Willmott (eds.) *Customer Service: Empowerment and Entrapment.* Basingstoke: Palgrave, pp. 102–16.

Roberts, E. (1995) *Women's Work, 1840–1940.* Cambridge: Cambridge University Press.

Roberts, K. (1984) *School Leavers and their Prospects: Youth and the Labour Market in the 1980s.* Milton Keynes: Open University Press.

Roberts, K., Clark, S. and Wallace, C. (1994) 'Flexibility and individualization: a comparison of transitions into employment in England and Germany', *Sociology*, 28(1): 31–54.

Roberts, K. and Parsell, G. (1988) *Opportunity Structures and Career Trajectories from Age 16–19.* ESRC 16–19 Initiative, Occasional Paper No. 1. London: City University.

Roberts, K. and Parsell, G. (1992) 'Entering the labour market in Britain: the survival of traditional opportunity structures', *Sociological Review*, 46(4): 726–53.

Robertson, B. (1990) 'In bondage: the female farm worker in south-east Scotland', in E. Gordon and E. Breitenbach (eds) *The World is Ill Divided: Women's Work in Scotland in the Nineteenth and Early Twentieth Centuries.* Edinburgh: Edinburgh University Press, pp. 117–35.

Robertson, R. (1992) *Globalization: Social Theory and Global Culture.* London: Sage.

Robins, K. and Webster, F. (1989) *The Technical Fix: Education, Computers and Industry.* London: Macmillan.

Robinson, P. (1999) 'Explaining the relationship between flexible employment and labour market participation', in A. Felstead and N. Jewson (eds), *Global Trends in Flexible Labour*. London: Macmillan, pp. 84–99.

Robinson, R. (2000) 'Insecurity and the flexible workforce: measuring the ill-defined', in E. Heery and J. Salmon (eds), *The Insecure Workforce*. London: Routledge, pp. 25–38.

Rogers, J. (1995) 'Just a temp: experience and structure of alienation in temporary clerical work', *Work and Occupations*, 22(2): 137–66.

Rose, M. (1988) *Industrial Behaviour: Research and Control*. London: Penguin.

Rose, M. (1989) 'Attachment to work and social values', in D. Gallie (ed.), *Employment in Britain*. Oxford: Blackwell, pp. 128–56.

Rosenberg, S. and Lapidus, J. (1999) 'Contingent and non-standard work in the United States: towards a more poorly compensated, insecure workforce', in A. Felstead and N. Jewson (eds), *Global Trends in Flexible Labour*. London: Macmillan, pp. 62–83.

Rothman, R. (1998) *Working: Sociological Perspectives* (2nd edn). Upper Saddle River, NJ: Prentice-Hall.

Royle, T. (2000) *Working for McDonald's: The Unequal Struggle*. London: Routledge.

Royle, T. and Towers, B. (eds) (2002) *Labour Relations in the Fast-Food Industry*. London: Routledge.

Rubery, J. (1980) 'Structured labour markets, worker organization and low pay', in A. Amsden (ed.), *The Economics of Women and Work*. London: Penguin, pp. 242–70.

Rubery, J. and Grimshaw, D. (2003) *The Organization of Employment: An International Perspective*. Basingstoke: Palgrave Macmillan.

Ruiz, Y. and Walling, A. (2005) 'Home-based work using communication technologies', *Labour Market Trends*, 113(10): 405–36. London: Office of National Statistics.

Russell, H. (1999) 'Friends in low places: gender, unemployment and sociability', *Work, Employment and Society*, 13(2): 205–24.

Sabel, C. (1984) *Work and Politics: The Division of Labour in Industry*. Cambridge: Cambridge University Press.

Salaman, G. (1974) *Community and Occupation: An Exploration of Work/Leisure Relationships*. Cambridge: Cambridge University Press.

Salaman, G. (1986) *Working*. London: Tavistock.

Sallaz, J. (2004) 'Manufacturing concessions: attritionary outsourcing at General Motor's Lordstown, USA assembly plant', *Work, Employment and Society*, 18(4): 687–708.

Samuel, R. (1977) 'Workshop of the world: steam power and hand technology in mid-Victorian Britain', *History Workshop Journal*, 3(1): 6–72.

Sarros, J., Tanewski, G., Santora, J. and Densten, I. (2002) 'Work alienation and organizational leadership', *British Journal of Management*, 13(4): 285–304.

Sayer, A. (1989) 'Postfordism in question?', *International Journal of Urban and Regional Research*, 13(4): 666–95.

Sayer, A. and Walker, R. (1992) *The New Social Economy: Reworking the Division of Labour*. Oxford: Blackwell.

Scarpetta, S., Sonnet, A. and Manfreidi, T. (2010) 'Rising youth unemployment during the crisis: how to prevent negative long-term consequences on a generation?', *OECD Social, Employment and Migration Working Papers*, No. 106, Paris: OECD. www. oecd-library.org.

Scase, R. and Goffee, R. (1980) *The Real World of the Small Business Owner*. London: Croom Helm.

Scase, R. and Goffee, R. (1982) *The Entrepreneurial Middle Class*. London: Croom Helm.

Scherer, S. and Steiber, N. (2010) 'Work and family in conflict? The impact of work demands on family life', in D. Gallie (ed.) *Employment Regimes and the Quality of Work*, Oxford: Oxford University Press, pp. 137–78.

Schiller, H. (1996) *Information Inequality: The Deepening Social Crisis in America*. London: Routledge.

Schlosser, E. (2002) *Fast Food Nation: What the All-American Meal Is Doing to the World*. London: Penguin Books.

Scholte, J. (2005) *Globalization: A Critical Introduction* (2nd edn). London: Macmillan.

Scholzman, K. and Verba, S. (1980) *Injury to Insult: Unemployment, Class and Political Response*, Cambridge, MA: Harvard University Press.

Schonberger, R. (1982) *Japanese Manufacturing Techniques: Nine Hidden Lessons in Simplicity*. London: Collier-Macmillan.

Schor, J. (1993) *The Overworked American: The Unexpected Decline of Leisure.* New York: Basic Books.

Scott, J. (1991) *Who Rules Britain?* Cambridge: Polity.

Scott, J. and Tilly, L. (1975) 'Women's work and family in nineteenth-century Europe', *Comparative Studies in Society and History*, 17(1): 36–64.

Seager, A. (2009) 'School leaving age may rise to 18 in effort to tackle unemployment', *The Guardian*, 5 January.

Seeman, M. (1959) 'On the meaning of alienation', *American Sociological Review*, 24(6): 783–91.

Sennett, R. (1998) *The Corrosion of Character: Personal Consequences of Work in the New Capitalism.* New York: W.W. Norton.

Sennett, R. (2006) *The Culture of the New Capitalism.* New Haven, CT: Yale University Press

Sennett, R. (2008) *The Craftsman.* London: Penguin.

Shah, V. and Bandi, R. (2003) 'Capability development in knowledge intensive IT enabled services', *European Journal of Work and Organizational Psychology*, 12(4): 418–27.

Shaw, G. (1992) 'The evolution of large-scale retailing in Britain', in J. Benson and G. Shaw (eds.), *The Evolution of Retail Systems c1800–1914*. Leicester: Leicester University Press, pp. 135–65.

Shepard, J. (1971) *Automation and Alienation: A Study of Office and Factory Workers.* Boston, MA: Colonial Press.

Shiomi, H. (1995) 'Introduction', in H. Shiomi and K. Wada (eds), *Fordism Transformed: The Development of Production Methods in the Automobile Industry*. Oxford: Oxford University Press, pp. 1–7.

Shire, K., Holtgrewe, U. and Kerst, C. (2002) 'Re-organizing customer service work: an introduction', in U. Holtgrewe, C. Kerst, and K. Shire (eds), *Re-Organizing Service Work: Call Centres in Germany and Britain*. Aldershot: Ashgate, pp. 1–16.

Shorter, E. (1976) 'Women's work: what difference did capitalism make?', *Theory and Society*, 3(4): 513–29.

Silverman, D. (1970) *The Theory of Organizations: A Sociological Framework*. London: Heinemann.

Sinfield, A. (1981) *What Unemployment Means*. Oxford: Martin Robertson.

Sjoberg, O. (2000) 'Unemployment and unemployment benefit in the OECD, 1960–1990: an empirical test of neo-classical economic theory', *Work, Employment and Society*, 14(1): 51–76.

Sklair, L. (2002) *Globalization: Capitalism and Its Alternatives*. Oxford: Oxford University Press.

Sloan, A. (1986 [1963]) *My Years with General Motors*. London: Penguin.

Smart, B. (1992) *Modern Conditions, Postmodern Controversies*. London: Routledge.

Smeaton, D. (2003) 'Self-employed workers: calling the shots or hesitant independents?', *Work, Employment and Society*, 17(2): 379–91.

Smelser, N.J. (1972 [1959]) *Social Change in the Industrial Revolution: An Application of Theory to the Lancashire Cotton Industry, 1770–1840*. London: Routledge and Kegan Paul.

Smith, M., Fagan, C. and Rubery, J. (1998) 'Where and why part-time work is growing in Europe', in J. O'Reilly and C. Fagan (eds), *Part-time Prospects: An International Comparison of Part-time Work in Europe, North America and the Pacific Rim*. London: Routledge, pp. 35–56.

Smithers, R. (2008) 'The year of consumer power: new technology enabled media-savvy consumers to change corporate behaviour in 2007', *Guardian*, 2 January.

Solera, C. (2009) *Women in and Out of Paid Work: Changes across generations in Italy and Britain*. Bristol: The Policy Press.

Spencer, D. (2000) 'Braverman and the contribution of labour process analysis to the critique of capitalist production – twenty-five years on', *Work, Employment and Society*, 14(2): 223–43.

Stabile, D. (1984) *Prophets of Order: The Rise of the New Class, Technocracy and Socialism in America*. Boston, MA: South End Press.

Standing, G. (1997) 'Globalization, labour flexibility and insecurity: the era of market regulation', *European Journal of Industrial Relations*, 3(1): 7–37.

Stanworth, J. and Stanworth, C. (1991) 'Enterprise 2000: workbase the electronic cottage?', in J. Curran and R.A. Blackburn (eds), *Paths of Enterprise: The Future of Small Businesses*. London: Routledge, pp. 34–50.

Stark, D. (1980) 'Class struggle and the transformation of the labour process: a relational approach', *Theory and Society*, 9(1): 89–130.

Stedman Jones, G. (1984) *Outcast London: A Study in the Relationships between Classes in Victorian Society*. London: Penguin.

Stewart, P. and Garrahan, P. (1995) 'Employee responses to new management techniques in the auto industry', *Work, Employment and Society*, 9(3): 517–36.

Stewart, P., Richardson, M., Danford, R., Murphy, K., Richardson, T. and Wass, V. (2009) *We Sell Our Time No More: Workers' Struggles Against Lean Production in the British Car Industry*. London: Pluto Press.

Sullivan, O. (2000) 'The division of domestic labour: twenty years of change?', *Sociology*, 34(3): 437–56.

Sussman, W. (1974) 'Comment 1', in J. Laslett and S. Lipset (eds), *Failure of a Dream? Essays in the History of American Socialism*. Garden City, NY: Anchor/Doubleday, pp. 443–55.

Sweet, S. and Meiksins, P. (2008) *Changing Contours of Work: Job Opportunities in the New Economy*. Thousand Oaks, CA: Pine Forge Press.

Swingewood, A. (1975) *Marx and Modern Social Theory*. London: Macmillan.

Taylor, F. (1947 [1903, 1911, 1912]) *Scientific Management*. New York: Harper & Brothers.

Taylor, P. and Bain, P. (1999) '"An assembly line in the head": work and employee relations in the call centre', *Industrial Relations Journal*, 30(2): 111–17.

Taylor, P. and Bain, P. (2001) 'Trade unions, workers' rights and the frontier of control in UK call centres', *Economic and Industrial Democracy*, 22(1): 39–66.

Taylor, P. and Bain, P. (2005) '"India calling to the far away towns": the call centre labour process and globalization', *Work, Employment and Society*, 19(2): 261–82.

Taylor, P., Baldry, C., Bain, P. and Ellis, V. (2003) '"A unique working environment": health sickness and absence management in UK call centres', *Work, Employment and Society*, 17(3): 435–58.

Taylor, P., Mulvey, G., Hyman, J. and Bain, P. (2002) 'Work organization, control and the experience of work in call centres', *Work, Employment and Society*, 16(1): 133–50.

Taylor, R. (2003) 'Managing workplace change', *ESRC Future of Work Programme*. www. esrc.ac.uk.

Taylor, S., Smith, S. and Lyon, P. (1998) 'McDonalization and consumer choice in the future: an illusion or the next marketing revolution?', in M. Alfino, J.S. Caputo and R. Wynyard (eds), *McDonaldization Revisited: Critical Essays on Consumer Culture*. Westport, CT: Praeger, pp. 105–19.

Thomas, G. and Zmroczek, C. (1988) 'Household technology: the "liberation" of women from the home', in P. Close and R. Collins (eds), *Family and Economy in Modern Society*. London: Macmillan, pp. 101–28.

Thomas, J. (1988) 'Women and capitalism: oppression or emancipation? A review article', *Comparative Studies in Society and History*, 30(3): 534–49.

Thompson, E. (1967) 'Time, work-discipline, and industrial capitalism', *Past and Present*, 38: 56–97.

Thompson, E. (1970) *The Making of the English Working Class*. London: Penguin.

Thompson, P. *(1983) The Nature of Work: An Introduction to Debates on the Labour Process*. London: Macmillan.

Thornley, C. (1996) 'Segmentation and inequality in the nursing workforce: re-evaluating the evaluation of skills', in R. Crompton, D. Gallie and K. Purcell (eds), *Changing Forms of Employment: Organizations, Skills and Gender*. London: Macmillan, pp. 160–81.

Tilgher, A. (1977 [1930]) *Work: What It Has Meant to Men through the Ages*. New York: Arno Press.

Tilly, C. (1992) 'Short hours, short shrift: the causes and consequences of part-time employment', in V.L. duRivage (ed.), *New Policies for the Part-time and Contingent Workforce*. New York: M.E. Sharpe, pp. 15–44.

Tomaney, J. (1994) 'A new paradigm of work organization', in A. Amin (ed.), *Post-Fordism: A Reader*. Oxford: Blackwell, pp. 157–94.

Tonkiss, F. (2006) *Contemporary Economic Sociology: Globalization, Production, Inequality*. London: Routledge.

Toynbee, P. (2003) *Hard Work: Life in Low-pay Britain*. London: Bloomsbury.

Upadhya, X. (2009) 'Controlling offshore knowledge workers: power and agency in India's software outsourcing industry', *New Technology, Work and Employment*, 24(1): 2–18.

Urry, J. (1990) 'Work, production and social relations', *Work, Employment and Society*, 4(2): 271–80.

US Bureau of Labor Statistics (2011).

Vallas, S. (1988) 'New technology, job content, and worker alienation: a test of two rival perspectives', *Work and Occupations*, 15(2): 148–78.

Vallas, S. (1990) 'The concept of skill: a critical review', *Work and Occupations*, 17(4): 379–98.

Vallas, S. (1999) 'Rethinking post-Fordism: the meaning of workplace flexibility', *Sociological Theory*, 17(1): 68–101.

Vallas, S. and Yarrow, M. (1987) 'Advanced technology and worker alienation: comments on the Blauner/Marxian debate', *Work and Occupations*, 14(1): 126–42.

van den Broek, D. (2004) 'Call to arms?: Collective and individual responses to call centre labour management', in S. Deery and N. Kinnie (eds), *Call Centres and Human Resource Management: A Cross-National Perspective*. Basingstoke: Palgrave Macmillan, pp. 267–84.

van der Linden, M. (2003) *Transnational Labour History*. Aldershot: Ashgate.

Vanek, J. (1980 [1974]) 'Time spent on housework', in A.H. Amsden (ed.), *The Economics of Women and Work*. London: Penguin, pp. 82–90.

Veblen, T. (1964 [1914]) *The Instinct of Workmanship and the State of the Industrial Arts*. Clifton, NJ: Kelley.

Veblen, T. (1964 [1923]) *Absentee Ownership and Business Enterprise in Recent Times: The Case of America*. Clifton, NJ: Kelley.

Veblen, T. (1970 [1899]) *The Theory of the Leisure Class: An Economic Study of Institutions*. London: Unwin Books.

Veblen, T. (1975 [1904]) *The Theory of the Business Enterprise*. Clifton, NJ: Kelley.

Vickerstaff, S. (2003) 'Apprenticeship in the "golden age": were youth transitions really smooth and unproblematic back then?', *Work, Employment and Society*, 17(2): 269–87.

Vogler, C. (1998) 'Money in the household: some underlying issues of power', *Sociological Review*, 46(4): 687–713.

Vogler, C. and Pahl, J. (1993) 'Social and economic change and the organization of money within marriage', *Work, Employment and Society*, 7(1): 71–96.

Wajcman, J. (1991) 'Patriarchy, technology and conceptions of skill', *Work and Occupations*, 18(1): 29–45.

Wajcman, J. (1995) 'Domestic technology: labour-saving or enslaving?', in S. Jackson and S. Moores (eds), *The Politics of Domestic Consumption*. London: Prentice Hall, pp. 217–30.

Wajcman, J. (1996) 'The domestic basis for the managerial career', *Sociological Review*, 44(4): 609–29.

Walby, S. (1986) *Patriarchy at Work*. Cambridge: Polity.

Walby, S. (1990) *Theorizing Patriarchy*. Oxford: Blackwell.

Warde, A. and Hetherington, K. (1993) 'A changing division of labour? Issues of measurement and interpretation', *Work, Employment and Society*, 7(1): 23–45.

Warhurst, C., Nickson, D., Witz, A. (2000) 'Aesthetic labour in interactive service work: Some case study evidence from the "new" Glasgow', *The Service Industries Journal*, 20(3): 1–18.

Warhurst, C. and Thompson, P. (1998) 'Hands, hearts and minds: changing work and workers at the end of the century', in P. Thompson and C. Warhurst (eds), *Workplaces of the Future*. Basingstoke: Macmillan, pp. 1–24.

Warhurst, C. Thompson, P. and Nickson, D. (2009) 'Labour process theory: putting the materialism back into the meaning of service work' in M. Korczynski and C. Macdonald (eds) *Service Work: Critical Perspectives*. London: Routledge, pp. 91–112.

Warr, P., Jackson, P. and Banks, M. (1988) 'Unemployment and mental health: some British studies', *Journal of Social Issues*, 44(4): 47–68.

Warren, T. (2007) 'Conceptualizing breadwinning work', *Work, Employment and Society*, 21(2): 313–36.

Watson, J. (2006) 'McDonald's as a political target: globalization and anti-globalization in the twenty-first century', in J. Watson (ed.), *Golden Arches East: McDonald's in East Asia* (2nd edn). Stanford, CA: Stanford University Press, pp. 183–97.

Weber, M. (1961 [1948]) *From Max Weber: Essays in Sociology*. Trans. H. Gerth and C. Wright Mills. London: Routledge and Kegan Paul.

Weber, M. (1964 [1947]) *The Theory of Social and Economic Organization*. Trans. A. Henderson and T. Parsons. New York: Free Press.

Weber, M. (1976 [1930]) *The Protestant Ethic and the Spirit of Capitalism*. London: Allen and Unwin.

Weber, M. (2003 [1927]) *General Economic History*. New York: Dover.

Webster, F. (2002) *Theories of the Information Society* (2nd edn). London: Routledge.

Webster, J. (1996) *Shaping Women's Work: Gender, Employment and Information Technology*. London: Longman.

Wedderburn, D. and Crompton, R. (1972) *Workers' Attitudes and Technology*. Cambridge: Cambridge University Press.

Weinkopf, C. (2009) 'Germany: precarious employment and the rise of mini-jobs', in L. Vosko, M. MacDonald and I. Campbell (eds), *Gender and the Contours of Precarious Employment*. London: Routledge, pp. 177–93.

Wells, C. (2007) 'The road to the Model T: culture, road conditions and innovation at the dawn of the American motor age', *Technology and Culture*, 48(3): 497–523.

Westergaard, J., Noble, I. and Walker, A. (1989) *After Redundancy*. Cambridge: Polity.

Whipp, R. (1987) '"A time to every purpose": an essay on time and work', in P. Joyce (ed.), *The Historical Meanings of Work*. Cambridge: Cambridge University Press, pp. 210–36.

Wickens, P. (1987) *The Road to Nissan: Flexibility, Quality, Teamwork*. London: Macmillan.

Wigley, J. and Lipman, C. (1992) *The Enterprise Economy*. London: Macmillan.

Whitmarsh, A. (1995) *Social Focus on Women*. London: HMSO.

Williams, C. (2002) 'A critical evaluation of the commodification thesis', *Sociological Review*, 50(4): 525–42.

Williams, K., Cutler, T., Williams, J. and Haslam, C. (1987) 'The end of mass production', *Economy and Society*, 16(3): 405–39.

Williams, K., Haslam, C. and Williams, J. (1992a) 'Ford versus "Fordism": the beginning of mass production?', *Work, Employment and Society*, 6(4): 517–55.

Williams, K., Haslam, C., Williams, J., and Cutler, T. with Adcroft, A. and Sukhdec, J. (1992b) 'Against lean production', *Economy and Society*, 21(3): 321–54.

Williams, K., Mitsui, H. and Haslam, C. (1994) 'How far from Japan? A case study of Japanese press shop practice and management calculation', in T. Elger and C. Smith (eds), *Global Japanization? The Transformation of the Labour Process*. London: Routledge, pp. 60–90.

Williams, K. and Williams, J. (eds) (1987) *A Beveridge Reader*. London: Allen and Unwin.

Wilson, J. (1995) 'Henry Ford's just-in-time system', *International Journal of Operations and Production Management*, 15(17): 59–75.

Windebank, J. (2001) 'Dual-earner couples in Britain and France: gender divisions of domestic labour and parenting work in different welfare states', *Work, Employment and Society,* 15(2): 269–90.

Witherspoon, S. (1985) 'Sex roles and gender issues', in R. Jowell and S. Witherspoon (eds), *British Social Attitudes: The 1985 Report*. Aldershot: Gower, pp. 55–94.

Womack, J., Jones, D. and Roos, D. (1990) *The Machine that Changed the World*. New York: Rawson Associates.

Wood, S. (ed.) (1982) *The Degradation of Work? Skill, Deskilling and the Labour Process*. London: Hutchinson.

Wood, S. (ed.) (1992) *The Transformation of Work? Skill, Flexibility and the Labour Process*. London: Routledge.

Woodfield, R. (2000) *Women, Work and Computing*. Cambridge: Cambridge University Press.

Wright, E. (1997) *Class Counts: Comparative Studies in Class Analysis*. Cambridge: Cambridge University Press.

Yeandle, S. (1999) 'Women, men and non-standard employment', in R. Crompton (ed.), *Restructuring Gender Relations and Employment: The Decline of the Male Breadwinner*. Oxford: Oxford University Press, pp. 80–104.

Young, M. and Willmott, P. (1973) *The Symmetrical Family: A Study of Work and Leisure in the London Region*. London: Routledge and Kegan Paul.

Zeitlin, J. (1985) 'Engineers and compositors: a comparison', in R. Harrison and J. Zeitlin (eds), *Divisions of Labour: Skilled Workers and Technical Change in Nineteenth Century England*. Brighton: Harvester, pp. 185–250.

Web addresses

www.2warwick.ac.uk/fac/soc/ier
www.aecp.oise.utoronto.ca/main/faculty/mirchandani
www.autolife.umd.umich.edu/
www.bls.gov/news.release/conemp.nr0.htm
www.bls.gov/news.release/ecopro.t06.htm
www.bren.ucsb.edu/academics/courses/289/Readings/Nathan-2007.pdf
www.callcentres.net/
www.consumerreports.org
www.guardian.co.uk/news/datablog/2010/feb/toyota-recalls-full-list
www.ilo.org
www.leeds.ac.uk/futureofwork/
www.msnbc.msn.com/id/35662491
www.oecd.org
www.oecd/dataoecd January 2004
www.statistics.gov.uk
www.statistics.gov.uk/articles/labour_market_trends/offshoring_sept05
www.statistics.gov.uk/pensiontrends
www.statlinks.oecdcode.org
www.strategosinc.com/just_in_time.htm
www.telework.org.uk
www.theworkfoundation.com
www.usdaw.org.uk
www.wcml.org.uk

NAME INDEX

SUBJECT INDEX